Educational Linguistics

Volume 57

Series Editor
Francis M. Hult, Dept. of Education, Sherman Hall A Wing, University of Maryland, Baltimore, MD, USA

Editorial Board Members
Marilda C. Cavalcanti, Universidade Estadual de Campinas, Campinas, Brazil
Jasone Cenoz, University of the Basque Country, Leioa, Spain
Angela Creese, University of Stirling, Stirling, UK
Ingrid Gogolin, University of Hamburg, Hamburg, Germany
Christine Hélot, Université de Strasbourg, Strasbourg, France
Hilary Janks, University of the Witwatersrand, Johannesburg, South Africa
Claire Kramsch, University of California, Berkeley, USA
Constant Leung, King's College London, London, UK
Angel Lin, Simon Fraser University, Burnaby, Canada
Alastair Pennycook, University of Technology, Sydney, Australia

Educational Linguistics is dedicated to innovative studies of language use and language learning. The series is based on the idea that there is a need for studies that break barriers. Accordingly, it provides a space for research that crosses traditional disciplinary, theoretical, and/or methodological boundaries in ways that advance knowledge about language (in) education. The series focuses on critical and contextualized work that offers alternatives to current approaches as well as practical, substantive ways forward. Contributions explore the dynamic and multi-layered nature of theory-practice relationships, creative applications of linguistic and symbolic resources, individual and societal considerations, and diverse social spaces related to language learning.

The series publishes in-depth studies of educational innovation in contexts throughout the world: issues of linguistic equity and diversity; educational language policy; revalorization of indigenous languages; socially responsible (additional) language teaching; language assessment; first- and additional language literacy; language teacher education; language development and socialization in non-traditional settings; the integration of language across academic subjects; language and technology; and other relevant topics.

The *Educational Linguistics* series invites authors to contact the general editor with suggestions and/or proposals for new monographs or edited volumes. For more information, please contact the Editor: Natalie Rieborn, Van Godewijckstraat 30, 3300 AA Dordrecht, The Netherlands.

All proposals and manuscripts submitted to the Series will undergo at least two rounds of external peer review.

This series is indexed in Scopus and the Norwegian Register for Scientific Journals, Series and Publishers (NSD).

Karim Sadeghi • Farah Ghaderi

Editors

Theory and Practice in Second Language Teacher Identity

Researching, Theorising and Enacting

 Springer

Editors
Karim Sadeghi 🆔
English Language Department
Urmia University
Urmia, Iran

Farah Ghaderi 🆔
English Language Department
Urmia University
Urmia, Iran

ISSN 1572-0292   ISSN 2215-1656   (electronic)
Educational Linguistics
ISBN 978-3-031-13163-9   ISBN 978-3-031-13161-5   (eBook)
https://doi.org/10.1007/978-3-031-13161-5

This Springer imprint is published by the registered company Springer Nature Switzerland AG
The registered company address is: Gewerbestrasse 11, 6330 Cham, Switzerland

We dedicate this book to our life teachers (fathers and mothers), school and university teachers, as well as our students and family who have all contributed to the formation of our identities as teachers.
We also dedicate this volume to the souls of language teachers across the globe who lost their lives during the COVID-19 pandemic.

Foreword

The nature of identity has generated an extensive interest and literature in recent years. Identity is now a household term in conferences, graduate curriculum, and seminars as well as the topic of widely read articles and books by leading scholars in the field of applied linguistics. This book therefore provides a welcome opportunity to review how teacher identity is currently conceptualized and researched and what its implications are for applied linguistics and second language teacher education. Two issues form the focus of the chapters in this book: *(1) identity and the language teacher; (2) identity and the novice teacher.*

1. Identity and the language teacher

Teacher identity has been defined as "the beliefs, values, and commitments an individual holds toward being a teacher (as distinct from another professional) and being a particular type of teacher (e.g. an urban teacher, a beginning teacher, a good teacher, an English teacher, etc.)" (Hsieh, 2010, p. 1). During their professional training, the teacher will have acquired a core set of knowledge, principles, beliefs, and practices that will inform the teacher's understanding of language teaching and of his or her identity and role as a language teacher. The teacher's knowledge base may be solidified and maintained throughout a teacher's career, or modified and sometimes replaced by subsequent experiences and professional development opportunities.

For TESOL teachers, English is both the means of teaching as well as the object of learning, and language proficiency has traditionally been viewed as a core element of the teacher's sense of his or her professional identity. However, recognition of the role of English as an international language has led many teachers to question the importance of a native-speaker target for NNESTs (non-native English speaking teacher) and the need for them to position their identities as *multicompetence language users* (Zacharias, 2010) rather than second language learners.

Other identity characteristics are more closely linked to the teacher's sense of him or herself as a teacher and the distinctive attributes that define them as a teacher. These include factors of commitment, self-esteem, agency, and self-efficacy.

Commitment refers to the teacher's personal engagement with teaching, the extent to which he or she has a sense of vocation, identifies with and supports the school's goals and practices and is willing to invest personal resources of time and energy in order to achieve excellence in teaching.

Self-esteem refers to attitudes towards oneself and the extent to which an individual believes themselves to be successful, competent, and of value to others. Positive self-esteem contributes to a teacher's social competence, enabling a teacher to communicate effectively with students and colleagues and to play a part in resolving conflicts and critical incidents in teaching.

Agency refers to the extent to which teachers can actively contribute to and manage change in their own teaching and professional development. Agency is seen in the ability of the teacher to take ownership of their own learning and environment, and to set goals, develop curriculum, initiate change, and make decisions that affect the teacher's work and its conditions.

Self-efficacy refers to the teacher's view of his or her own effectiveness – that is the ability to perform well as a teacher of English, to achieve their goals and potential, to maintain their commitment to teaching in spite of difficulties they may encounter, and to provide support for students' learning (such as having to switch to online teaching during the Covid-19 pandemic).

2. Identity and the novice teacher

The process of becoming a language teacher involves development of a language teacher identity – one that is shaped by experience, course work, readings, and conversations with other student-teachers and instructors, as well as by teaching experiences gained through microteaching, the practicum, and observation of experienced teachers. This developing view of teacher identity may be supported or challenged by the experience of teacher-learning in the teacher education program.

NNESTs: International participants in postgraduate programs in English-speaking countries are often experienced language teachers who may find that their knowledge and experience now have to be put on hold as they assume the status of an NNEST student-teacher, thus framing their professional identity in terms of language proficiency, rather in terms of their professional knowledge and experience. A challenge for a student teacher in this context is either to accept this deficit view of NNESTs or to reject it and transform their identities as language teaching professionals.

Imagined self: An important component of agency, autonomy, and motivation in language learning is the "imagined future self" (Norton, 2000). In teacher education, both pre-service as well as in-service teachers may differ in the extent to which they look forward to their imagined future professional selves as language teachers or as language teaching professionals: how they view their future selves constitutes an important part of their identity as teacher-learners.

Emotions: For novice teachers, the teaching practicum is often an emotionally charged experience, and how emotions are managed can play a role in shaping teacher identity. Emotions teachers experience during their teaching practicum can have a strong influence on their developing teacher identity. Teng (2017) found that

negative emotional experiences resulting from classroom management issues sometimes led student-teachers to question their ability or potential as a teacher.

Conclusions

An important process in teacher education is the opportunity for teachers and
student-teachers to reflect on how they understand their professional identities, the
sources of their identities, if and how they think their identities have changed over
time, and how their identity influences their approach to teaching, professional
development, and interaction with their colleagues. Contributors to this book
describe how narratives, journal writing, and accounts of critical incidents can all
be used to explore aspects of language teacher identity. Acknowledging the role and
power of identity in the contexts in which we work adds a crucial dimension to what
we understand about the nature of language teaching and teacher-learning.

University of Sydney   Jack C. Richards
Sydney, Australia

References

Hsieh, B. Y. (2010). *Exploring the complexity of teacher professional identity*. Ph.D. dissertation:
    University of California, Berkley

Norton, B. (2000). *Identity and language learning: Gender, ethnicity and educational change*.
    Harlow, UK: Pearson Education Limited.

Teng, M. F. (2017). Emotional development and construction of teacher identity: Narrative
    interactions about the pre-service teachers' practicum experiences. *Australian Journal of
    Teacher Education, 42*(11), 117–134.

Zacharias, N. T. (2010). *The evolving teacher identities of 12 South/East Asian Teachers in US
    Graduate Programs*. Ph.D. dissertation. Pennsylvania: Indiana University of Pennsylvania.

Acknowledgments

The essence of this book owes itself to its contributors; without the authors having accepted our invitations to join us in this venture, we wouldn't have even started such a journey. We are very grateful to all scholars who so generously joined hands with us in developing a product which we believe is a timely and significant contribution to the field of second language teacher education and language teacher identity. We are also very thankful to Springer Nature team who welcomed our initial idea and proposal, and supported us in numerous ways to materialize it. We would in particular like to mention the generous support of Natalie Rieborn (the lead editor), Helen van der Stelt (assistant editor), Cynthia Kroonen, Gideon Philip, Joseph Daniel, Aarthi Padmanaban, and their production team for their professional service. We would also like to thank Francis M. Hult, the Educational Linguistics series editor, as well as anonymous reviewers whose constructive feedback helped refine the work. Although as editors we have done our best to ensure a high quality of contributions by inviting some of the renowned researchers and teacher educators to write for this volume, we look forward to readers' feedback to improve future editions.

Christmas Eve 2021

Urmia, Iran   Karim Sadeghi
                                                                                                                          Farah Ghaderi

Contents

About the Editors

Karim Sadeghi has a PhD from the University of East Anglia (UK) and is Professor of TESOL at Urmia University (Iran). He is the founding editor-in-chief of the *Iranian Journal of Language Teaching Research* (the only Iranian journal in humanities with a Scopus-SJR-Q1 Top 15% ranking) and serves on the editorial board of several national and international journals including *RELC Journal* (SAGE), *Research in Post Compulsory Education* (Routledge), *TESOL Journal* (Wiley), *Language Testing in Asia* (Springer), and *Heliyon Education* (Elsevier, as associate editor). He was selected as Iran's top researcher in humanities and social sciences in 2013 and in English language/applied linguistics in 2018. His recent publications have appeared in *RELC Journal*, *System*, *Assessing Writing*, *Journal of Multilingual and Multicultural Development*, and *English for Specific Purposes*. His recent publications include *Assessing Second Language Reading* (Springer, 2021) and *Talking about Second Language Acquisition* (Palgrave, 2022).

Farah Ghaderi holds a PhD from Universiti Putra Malaysia and is Associate Professor of English Literature at Urmia University, Iran. She acts as executive manager of the *Iranian Journal of Language Teaching Research*. Her main research areas include travel and gender studies, otherness, education, and postcolonial studies. Her recent research has focused on gender and intercultural encounters and education, and has appeared in *RELC Journal*, *Interventions*, *Journal of Multicultural Discourses, Gender, Place and Culture*, *Victorian Literature and Culture*, *Iranian Studies*, and *Angelaki*. Her co-translated work (Robert J C Young's *Postcolonialism: A Very Short Introduction*) was published in Iran in 2012.

Chapter 1
Introduction to Research and Practice in Second Language Teacher Identity

Karim Sadeghi ⓘ **and Farah Ghaderi** ⓘ

Abstract Second Language Teacher identity (SLTI) has been a burgeoning area of research over the last decade or so within the field of language teacher education in general and second language education (including TESOL) in particular. Given that overall teaching effectiveness and teachers' classroom practices partially rely on teachers' understanding of who they are, personally and professionally, delving into the construct of teacher identity, how it is constructed, developed and shaped as well as the way it interacts with other teacher characteristics has attracted a good deal of research attention recently. This chapter first situates second language (L2) teacher identity within the broader context of second language teacher education (SLTE) and then reviews a sample of the latest research on the topic. It then briefly introduces the content of the rest of the book and highlights its outstanding features.

Keywords Language teachers · Language teacher identity · Professional development · Teacher education · Teacher identity development

1.1 Introduction

Second Language Teacher Education (SLTE) is a well established discipline within Applied Linguistics and Language Teaching/Teaching English to Speakers of Other Languages (TESOL) (Richards & Burns, 2009). The first book on SLTE (with the same title) was edited by Richards and Nunan (1990) and published by Cambridge University Press some 30 years ago, and since then different books (such as *Cambridge Guide to SLTE,* by Richards & Burns, 2009) and increasingly numerous papers have appeared on various aspects of SLTE in various journals. Given the numeorus branches (like knowledge base of SLTE, standards in SLTE, technology in language teacher education, reflective practice, action research, teacher motivation, teacher cognition, teacher agency, teacher idenity, and the like) covered in

K. Sadeghi (✉) · F. Ghaderi
Urmia University, Urmia, Iran
e-mail: k.sadeghi@urmia.ac.ir

K. Sadeghi, F. Ghaderi (eds.), *Theory and Practice in Second Language Teacher Identity*, Educational Linguistics 57, https://doi.org/10.1007/978-3-031-13161-5_1

SLTE books and due to insufficient tackling of these important issues in the same volume, authored books and edited collections specifically devoted to the mentioned issues are in high demand to examine the intricate and complex nature of these aspects of second language teachers' professional lives. We use the term 'second langauge' or L2 in this volume in the broadest sense possible, and as a cover term, to encompass both English and other foreign or modern languages such as Chinese, Spanish, Portuguese, and so on that are taught and learned in contexts both where the L2 is spoken outside the classroom (such as teaching/learning English as an additional language in a dominantly English speaking country) and where only a limited (or no) use of the language is feasible outside its instructional setting (like learning Persian, Kurdish or Turkish in a UK language centre). Furthermore, 'second language' does not denote second in terms of order; an L2 may be the third, fourth or nth language one is learning/teaching.

One important aspect of second language teachers is their identity (who they are and what they do). Understanding how second language teachers' identities are formed, developed and shaped is key to learning how and why teachers succeed in their profession or burn out. Interest in undersatnding the nature of second langauge teacher identity has been on the rise recently (sepcillay within the last decade or so) and the topic has attracted the attention of a growing number of researchers in the field of SLTE, second language education, and TESOL. Further research on this construct (in English as a Second Language (ESL), English as a Foreign Language (EFL), modern languages and other foreign languages taught in non-English settings) is required since teacher identities can impact teachers' professional lives, including their interaction with students, administrators, and peers, as well as their classroom practices and other aspects of their teaching life. That is why an understanding of these identities and how they are developed and shaped can immensely help L2 teachers become more effective facilitators of language learning which is the ultimate aim of second language teaching enterprise. This edited volume accordingly aims to bring together the current theory/research and practical perspectives in different parts of the world on second language teacher identity in an attempt to better understand what kinds of identities L2 teachers develop, how these are shaped/altered, and the various links between teacher identities and a host of teaching/learning/classroom/educational and societal variables affecting the formation of identities and/or being affected by them.

1.2   Research on Teacher Identity

While research on teachers and teacher education has been in vogue for several decades, research on teacher identity does not have a long history, and only a very limited number of studies attended to issues in teacher identity before 2000. Compared to other SLTE subjects, there has been less attention to identity of of language teachers and even less so as far as second language (L2) teachers are concerned. A simple search in Google Scholar, for example, hits nearly 900 records for 'teacher identity' keyword, but only 6 results for 'language teacher identity' between 1980 and 2000. A similar proportion is found between 2001 and 2010, with 170 documents for 'language teacher identity' and 6630 for 'teacher identity', with documents on the former growing to 2700 and the latter to 22,000+ between 2011 and 2021. These simple figures indicate that the amount of research on teacher identity has been on a steady rise, especially during the last decade, such that in 2021 there were more than 450 works published on 'language teacher identity' and around 4000 works on 'teacher identity'. These figures tell two things: First, interest in research on teacher identity is growingly attracting researchers' attention on a yearly basis; second, comparably more research is being conducted on 'language teacher identity' such that while 3 and 4 decades ago (between 1980 and 2000), research on 'teacher identity' surpassed research on 'language teacher identity' by 150 times, and by less than 40 times between 2001 and 2010, in 2021, research on the latter has taken a great leap reaching almost one tenth of research on the former. Despite this surge of interest in research on language teacher identity, the number of studies devoted to 'second' language teacher identity remains tiny (11 in 2021 and 81 between 2011 and 2021 at the time of drafting this chapter, December 2021). Fairly covering research on L2 teacher identity within the most recent decade will require a full chapter (and the second chapter in this volume does this to some extent); however, in the short space available in an Introduction chapter, we briefly examine a small sample of the seminal works (both books and papers) published after 2010 in a chronological order.

The earliest volume (since 2010) devoted to second language teacher identity is a monograph by Kiernan (2010), where the author interviewed Japanese English teachers to explore the multidimensional nature of L2 teacher identity (narrative identity) through analysing stories told by teachers. In a study of second language teachers' role identities, Farrell (2011) studied three English as a Second Language (ESL) college teachers in Canada and identified 16 main role identities, divided into three major clusters: manager, teacher as professional, and teacher as acculturator, concluding that teacher as acculturator role is unique to ESL teachers. In the second edition of her significant, groundbreaking classic *Identity and Language Learning: Extending the Conversation* (originally published in 2000), and with its focus on L2 learning and learners, Bonny Norton (2013) provided a compelling account that bridged the gap between identity research and practice, considered the relationship between societal structure and human agency, offered insights on the links between Second Language Acquisition (SLA), identity, and social justice, and in short, set the scene for future identity research not only on L2 learning but on L2 teaching and teachers.

Advances and Current Trends in Language Teacher Identity Research by Cheung et al. (2015) is another seminal treatment of key issues in second language teacher identity with topics ranging from the effects of apprenticeship in doctoral training on novice teacher identity to the challenges faced by teachers in the construction of their professional identities, to teacher identity development of beginning and pre-service teachers, to the role of emotions in the professional identities of non-native English speaking teachers, among others. With a focus on gender and identity, Nagatomo

(2016) investigated the development of personal and professional teacher identity among western female teachers (with Japanese spouses) living and teaching in Japan. Kalaja et al.'s (2016) *Beliefs, Agency and Identity in Foreign Language Learning and Teaching* is an insightful exploration of the relationships between the key concepts in the title of the book in the context of teaching and learning second and foreign languages.

A surge on L2 teacher identity research has followed Gary Barkhuizen's (2017) *Reflections on Language Teacher Identity Research*. With its 40+ contributions from some of the most well known scholars in the field, this anthology offers a comprehensive overview of language teacher identity (LTI) from a variety of perspectives in the form of narratives and guided reflections and sets the scene for methodological approaches and future research on LTI. Some of the major topics covered in the book are: teacher autonomy, teacher agency, teacher educator identity, multilingual identity, investment, self disputes, study abroad, researcher identity, ethics, critical teacher identity, race, and gender, among others. The publication of several books on (language) teacher identity in 2018 is a clear indication of a growth in interest in this fledgling field. Yazan and Rudolph's (2018) *Criticality, Teacher Identity, and (In)equity in English Language Teaching,* Schutz et al.'s (2018) *Research on Teacher Identity: Mapping Challenges and Innovations,* and Misfud's (2018) *Professional Identities in Initial Teacher Education: The Narratives and Questions for Teacher Agency* are three prime examples of this expansion in teacher identity research. The first volume offers readers a space to explore critical-practical approaches to identity, (in)equity, and interaction (both within and outside the classroom) envisioned through and beyond binaries like native speaker English teacher (NSET) versus non-native speaker English teacher (NNSET). With its 21 chapters, *Research on Teacher Identity* provides a comprehensive collection of perspectives from international contexts on various aspects of teacher identity such as its social and contextual dimensions, and identifies challenges and innovations of teacher identity research. The research monograph by Misfud draws on narrative data from postgraduate students and explores the perception, construction and performance of professional identities in initial teacher education through school placement, career choice motivations, professional standards, and the like.

Interest in teacher identity research, especially with language teachers (second, foreign, and modern) has grown steadily since 2018. In 2019, for example, Teng (2019) and Gallardo (2019) published *Autonomy, Agency, and Identity in Teaching and Learning English as a Foreign Language* and *Negotiating Identity in Modern Foreign Language Teaching,* respectively. The first book aims at providing English as L2 teachers with frameworks connecting the three key concepts of autonomy, agency and identity to equip them with a deeper appreciation of the challenges in teaching and learning EFL, while the second book (an edited collection) examines modern foreign language teachers' identity construction in the context of UK higher education institutions and offers a range of complex and dynamic views on the contributors' identities, agency, attitudes, relationships and emotions. More recently, two edited volumes by Yazan and Lindahl (2020), and Rudolph et al. (2020) have done due justice to language teacher identity research. In

Language Teacher Identity in TESOL: Teacher Education and Practice as Identity Work, Yazan and Lindahl (through 15 contributions coming from various contexts like Europe, the USA, and Asia) explore the interaction between language teacher identity and professional development in TESOL and elucidate how teacher identity can act as a framework for classroom practice and teachers' professional and personal growth. The focus of *The Complexity of Identity and Interaction in Language Education* by Rudalph et al. is on both learner and teacher identities: the contributors examine such issues as the monolingual bias in English Language Teaching (ELT) in the context of Pakistan, 'other' identities in teaching, French as a second language, translanguaging identities between English and Spanish, intercultural identities in French and German primary teachers, shifting identities, and so on.

In addition to published books on language teacher identity, and as stated above, there are increasingly a growing number of papers published on the topic, the number of which in 2021 amounts to 500 works (according to Google Scholar). Nazari and de Costa (2021), for example, investigate the role of a professional development course based on critical incidents in identity development (and in particular, agency and emotions) of 10 L2 teachers. Transition from an imagined teacher identity to an imposed one by a novice EFL teacher in the context of Turkey is the theme of Goktepe and Kunt's (2021) study. The constructs reported to have shaped this shift include: beliefs about teaching and learning, pre-service education, dynamic relations in communities of practice, and contextual factors. In a Japanese context, Aoyama (2021) studies Japanese English teachers' identity through a multilayered analysis of identity and discourse by analysing their portrayal in national English education policy in Japan as well as their roles as teaching professionals vis-à-vis students and 'nonnative' teachers vis-à-vis imagined 'native' speakers of English. And finally in the context of Korea, Choe and Seo (2021) explore identity negotiation of black teachers of English, examining the intersection of race, ethnicity, and identity and the interplay of sociocultural and political issues in positioning oneself as an authentic teacher. Despite a growing body of research on understanding who second language teachers are, and given a multitude of contexts L2 teachers find themselves working in as well as an array of factors (contextual, internal, and external) shaping their professional and personal development and also due to multiplicity of constructs involved in identity (emotions, agency, investment, etc.), much is still unknown about the process of becoming language teachers; accordingly, further research is still required to help us better understand the nature of L2 teacher identity and ourselves as teachers if we wish to perform our educational duty and deliver to the next generation in the best way possible.

1.3   The Structure of the Book

In addition to this introductory chapter, *Theory and Practice in Second Language Teacher Identity: Researching, Theorising and Enacting* is made up of a Foreword by Jack Richards (University of Sydney and RELC), an Afterword by Peter de Costa

(Michigan State University) and 19 invited chapters by established and active
scholars/teacher educators from reputed universities on various aspects of
in-service and pre-service second language teacher identity development. The
book is made of 3 Parts as follows: Theoretical Stances; Identity Development of
Pre-service L2 Teachers; and Pandemic, Technology, and In-service L2 Teachers'
Identity Development. The first Part is devoted to conceptual and theoretical considerations in research conducted on second language teacher identity, with a
systematic review of second language teacher identity (by Karim Sadeghi and
Akbar Bahari), and chapters on local teacher identities at a time of globalization
(by David Hayes), identity formation (by Ian Thomson), a synthesis of reflections of
applied linguists on teacher identity (by Ng and Cheung), language teacher agency
(by Jenelle Reeves) and teacher identity narrative in the context of intercultural
communication (by Lesley Harbon). Parts II and III are more practical in nature
dealing with reports of studies conducted on L2 teacher identity at various contexts,
with Part II primarily focusing on pre-service teachers and Part III on in-service
teachers as well as the role of technology in shaping L2 teacher identity during the
COVID-19 pandemic.

Chapters in Part II are devoted to a discursive construction of pre-service L2
teachers' identities (by Li Li), co-constructing intercultural identity of pre-service
TESOL teachers (by Ping Yang), teacher students' investment in their professions
(by Anne Pitkänen-Huhta and Maria Ruohotie-Lyhty), the researcher-teacher's
ideologies, tensions and identity negotiations (by Bedrettin Yazan) and identity
construction of a Chinese ESL teacher candidate (by Feifei Fan and Ester de
Jong). The 8 chapters in the final Part of the book (Part III) tackle a range of issues
from pandemic to technology integration to gender and race as well as motivation
and their contributions to L2 teacher identity development. More specifically, Anne
Burns investigates changes in teacher identity at the time of the COVID-19 pandemic; Frank Gong, Andy Gao and Chun Lai look at the link between technology
integration and teacher identity in Chinese as L2; Andwatta Barnes and Donald
Freeman offer insights to teacher identity development from the lives of black
American women working in the UAE; Luke Lawrence and Yuzukio Nagashima
report a similar study within a Japanese context investigating the relationship
between race, gender and second language teacher identity; Matilde Gallardo uses
visual self-representations to explore lifelong journeys of modern language teachers
in the UK context; Anna Sanczyk and Elizabeth Miller consider the interplay
between agency and teacher identity; Kate Shea, Li Shi, and Hayriye Kayi-Aydar
bring into spotlight the role of emotions in teacher identity development; and finally
Karim Sadeghi, Teymour Rahmati and Farah Ghaderi report a study on the role of
vision formation in L2 teachers' identity construction.

This edited volume is both similar to the books already published and different
from them in several respects. The similarity is that the works are all tackling the
central theme of (language) teacher identity. Our volume is however distinct in that,
first, it is one of the few books to concentrate on both theoretical and practical issues
of teacher identity in second language contexts. Most other books focus on either
teacher identity in general (in other fields) or on English as L1 and/or a second

language with little attention paid to other L2s or English in EFL contexts; ours includes second languages (like Chinese) other than English (which is examined at both ESL and EFL contexts) as well as modern and world languages. Second, our book includes both theoretical and pedagogical aspects of L2 teacher identity. While many of the books above look at teacher identity as well as other relevant concepts (like belief, interaction, etc.) in the same volume (and therefore making it difficult to delve properly into teacher identity issues), our book is one of the few devoted exclusively to second language teacher identity. Also, given the current impact of the COVID-19 pandemic on education in general and L2 education in particular, our book has a unique chapter examining how the pandemic has affected L2 teachers' identity development. Furthermore, some of the above books either concentrate on learner identity or consider both teacher and learner identity together while this volume targets L2 teachers only whose identity development is investigated either by teachers themselves through action research or with the assistance of university professors and teacher educators. A systematic review of research on L2 teacher identity is one further unique feature of the book. Although a book of this nature has to be limited in scope and coverage and despite its unique features, we are aware that our book has some shortcomings and there is room for improvements in a future edition. We have, for example, been unable to keep a balance between studies on modern languages and English as an L2. One reason for this imbalanced representation is perhaps that we could not secure studies from all geographical places and especially from the Global South, despite our invitations extended to contributors working in these contexts. These less represented parts of the world offer linguistically rich environments for investigating identity development of teachers of languages such as Spanish and Portuguese, which we call for future researchers to attend to.

References

Aoyama, R. (2021). Language teacher identity and English education policy in Japan: Competing discourses surrounding "non-native" English-speaking teachers. *RELC Journal.* https://doi.org/10.1177/00336882211032999

Barkhuizen, G. (Ed.). (2017). *Reflections on language teacher identity research.* Routledge.

Cheung, Y. L., Ben Said, S., & Park, K. (2015). *Advances and current trends in language teacher identity research.* Routledge.

Choe, H., & Seo, Y. (2021). Negotiating teacher identity: Experiences of black teachers of English in Korean ELT. How race and English language teacher identity intersect in the expanding circle. *English Today, 37*(3), 148–155. https://doi.org/10.1017/S0266078419000531

Farrell, T. S. C. (2011). Exploring the professional role identities of experienced ESL teachers through reflective practice. *System, 39*(1), 54–62. https://doi.org/10.1016/j.system.2011.01.012

Gallardo, M. (2019). *Negotiating identity in modern foreign language teaching.* Springer.

Goktepe, F. T., & Kunt, N. (2021). "I'll do it in my own class": Novice language teacher identity construction in Turkey. *Asia Pacific Journal of Education, 41*(3), 472–487. https://doi.org/10.1080/02188791.2020.1815648

Kalaja, P., Barcelos, A. M. F., Aro, M., & Ruohotie-Lyhty, M. (2016). *Beliefs, agency and identity in foreign language learning and teaching*. Palgrave.

Kiernan, P. (2010). *Narrative identity in English language teaching*. Springer.

Misfud, D. (2018). *Professional identities in initial teacher education: The narratives and questions for teacher agency*. Palgrave.

Nagatomo, D. H. (2016). *Identity, gender and teaching English in*. De Gruyter.

Nazari, M., & de Costa, P. (2021). Contributions of a professional development course to language teacher identity development: Critical incidents in focus. *Journal of Teacher Education*. https://doi.org/10.1177/00224871211059160

Norton, B. (2013). *Identity and language learning: Extending the conversation* (2nd ed.). Multilingual Matters.

Richards, J. C., & Burns, A. (2009). *The Cambridge guide to second language teacher education*. Cambridge University Press.

Richards, J. C., & Nunan, D. (1990). *Second language teacher education*. Cambridge University Press.

Rudolph, N., Selvi, A. F., & Yazan, B. (2020). *The complexity of identity and interaction in language education*. Multilingual Matters.

Schutz, P. A., Hong, J., & Cross Francis, D. (Eds.). (2018). *Research on Teacher Identity: Mapping challenges and innovations*. Springer.

Teng, F. (2019). *Autonomy, agency, and identity in teaching and learning English as a Foreign language*. Springer.

Yazan, B., & Lindahl, K. (Eds.). (2020). *Language teacher identity in TESOL: Teacher education and practice as identity work*. Routledge.

Yazan, B., & Rudolph, N. (Eds.). (2018). *Criticality, teacher identity, and (In)equity in English language teaching*. Springer.

Part I
Theoretical Stances

Chapter 2
Second Language Teacher Identity: A Systematic Review

Karim Sadeghi ⓘ and Akbar Bahari

Abstract Given "the complexities of identities that second/foreign language teachers construct" (Kayi-Aydar, 2019, p. 1) and the role identities play in teachers' professional lives, this chapter systematically reviews studies conducted within the last decade to identify trends in second language (L2) teacher identity research and practice, reflecting on personal and professional identity development issues. The rationale for this review is to shed further light on our understanding of the L2 teacher identity concerns such as professional impact, language ideologies, pedagogical choices and practices, and the like. To this end, sixty one Q1 Scopus and SSCI- indexed journal articles published from 2010 to 2020 that met exclusion-inclusion criteria were systematically reviewed. Pedagogically, the findings of the study inform the practitioners who seek a better understanding of L2 teaching context (e.g. social, political, and cultural) as well as identity types (narrated identities, identities-in-practice, future selves, gendered identities, sociocultural identities) to enhance their professional identity construction during pedagogical interactions. Theoretically, the findings both display the trajectory of studies shifting from a normative paradigm to an interpretative paradigm and introduce mainstream theoretical frameworks (social identity theory, post-structural approaches, critical theory, positioning theory, sociocultural theory, Bakhtinian framework, and communities of practice) adopted in reviewed studies. As TESOL researchers and practitioners, we have limited our review to English as a second or foreign language teacher identity and have excluded studies on modern foreign languages from our definition of L2 in this chapter, although the findings have far-reaching implications for identity development of teachers of other foreign, world or modern languages.

Keywords Second language (L2) teacher identity · Systematic review · Narrative inquiry · Professional development · Identity construction

K. Sadeghi (✉) · A. Bahari
Urmia University, Urmia, Iran
e-mail: k.sadeghi@urmia.ac.ir

2.1   Introduction

Second language (L2) teacher identity refers to L2 teachers' perceptions of their professional role as a language teacher that varies across time and context from one teacher to another. Different scholars have approached L2 teacher identity from different perspectives and have offered different definitions. Miller (2009), for example, emphasized aspects of L2 teacher identity like understanding the working context, perception of teaching, the educational role, personal values, and background experiences as the components that develop identity. Some other scholars have approached L2 teacher identity from the perspective of racial identity (Grant & Lee, 2009; Holliday, 2006). Expanding the same line of research, some other studies have elaborated on White English teacher identity and how it has negatively affected L2 teacher identity of the non-native-speaker teachers' identity (Kim, 2017; Ruecker & Ives, 2015; Yook & Lindemann, 2013). Second language teacher identity is no more limited to English language teacher identity, and with the rapid rise of Chinese learners across the world (25 million; Wang & Zhang, 2021), we should expect new perspectives under the influence of socioeconomic and sociopolitical factors in professional teacher identity construction.

Exploring L2 teacher identity in both face-to-face and e-learning environments has resulted in confirming the significant role of L2 teacher identity in L2 teaching process (Barkhuizen, 2017; Cheung et al., 2015; De Costa & Norton, 2016; Kern, 2015; Thorne et al., 2015). Analyzing research on teacher identity, Kanno and Stuart (2011) prioritized the knowledge about L2 teacher identity over the knowledge about language teaching to emphasize the significance of L2 teacher identity. But the knowledge of L2 teacher identity is a complex issue in teacher training which dynamically evolves under the influence of a variety of factors (e.g. professional qualifications, academic qualifications, etc.) that need to be studied to gain further insights into its nature and construction. The present study aims at systematically reviewing studies on L2 teacher identity between 2010 and 2020 to identify their foci and theoretical frameworks, the employed methodologies as well as the offered implications. In our analysis, we have delimited L2 not to specifically include modern foreign languages (unless this has already been in the definition of L2 in the targeted studies); indeed our focus on English as an L2 or Teaching English to Speakers of Other Languages (TESOL) draws upon our expertise and interest as well as our practitional and research background in this area. Adding studies related to identity construction of teachers of modern, world and other foreign languages would have certainly led to a more representative and comprehensive status quo of L2 teacher identity development, a limitation in our study which we hope future systematic reviews will take into consideration.

2.1.1   Extant Literature

Following postmodern and postcultural movements, L2 teacher identity has witnessed a variety of changes under the influence of universal orientations towards individual professional identity. Ongoing changes have attracted a body of scholarship that devels into transcultural and translinguistic identity-related negotiations and goes beyond simplified views such as native and non-native identity dichotomies. For example, Norton (2000) refers to learner identity formation as an outcome of negotiating discourses of power between the teacher and students. Expanding Norton's study, Goosseff (2014) provides an elaborate overview of identity formation under the influence of power and ideology and how these significant concepts result in professional identity change. Narrative research has enabled L2 teacher identity researchers to gain insights into different aspects of L2 teacher identity including ideological issues (Giri & Foo, 2014), teacher agency and teacher praxis (Chowdhury & Phan, 2014; Toh, 2014).

Exploring teacher identity dynamics, Li (2020) used narrative inquiry to examine the interconnected relationship among emotions, identity, and beliefs in keeping with theorization proposed by Barcelos (2015). The use of an integrated framework enabled Li to address teacher identity from different perspectives and to provide a comprehensive understanding of teacher identity in terms of professional and private factors. The significance of different aspects of language teacher identity (e.g. perception of teaching as a profession, background experiences, personal values and attitudes towards sociocultural role) in developing their individual, educational, and professional identity has been confirmed by previous studies (Benesch, 2017; Burns et al., 2015; Farrell & Ives, 2015; Golombek & Doran, 2014; Kayi-Aydar et al., 2019; Kubanyiova & Feryok, 2015).

Sang (2020) reviewed studies on L2 teacher identity and reported the situated nature of teacher learning as the mainstream trend of research under the influence of the socialization process. Sang emphasized the need to conduct further studies on identity development among pre-service L2 teachers under the socialization process in keeping with previous studies (Freeman, 2016; He & Lin, 2013). The study highlighted the role of the socialization process in identity development by creating opportunities for teachers to negotiate their expectations and perceptions and reconsider their beliefs and identities to be allowed into professional teacher communities.

Taking an integrative perspective, Yang et al. (2021) explored the nexus between EFL teachers' emotions and identity. To provide a nuanced understanding of L2 teacher identity, they explored the relationships between other influential factors (contextual mediation, temporal dimension, and action anchor) as well. Taking an ecological approach to conduct a review with a focus on the impact of action research on L2 teacher identity, Edwards (2021) confirmed the effectiveness of action research on teachers' professional identity development. Barros-del Rio et al. (2021) conducted research to explore the impact of dialogic gatherings on pre-service teacher education and confirmed the effectiveness of dialogic construction of knowledge on the teacher identity development process. During the dialogic gatherings, participants exchanged views concerning academic research findings that were discussed and enhanced their professional knowledge. The researchers argued that these joint activities enhanced the participants' critical assessment of their identity as a teacher.

Language teacher identity has been researched from a variety of perspectives (e.g. sociocultural, sociopolitical, etc.). However, the lack of a systematic review synthesizing the reported findings in a single article remains as a gap in the literature. To bridge this gap, we conducted a systematic review to synthesize and elaborate on the findings of the studies on L2 teacher identity from 2010–2020 to learn about the mainstream research trends and the future direction. Several studies confirm that the development of a solid teacher identity ensures better handling of the identity tensions and a higher emotional involvement with teaching (Hanna et al., 2020; Hong et al., 2017; Pillen et al., 2013). However, there is a gap in the literature concerning the widespread/dominant type of L2 teacher identity.

Under the influence of poststructural and postmodern approaches, L2 teacher identity studies have moved away from oversimplified approaches (e.g. native-speakerism versus non-native-speakerism) towards the appreciation of transcultural and translinguistic identities that are not limited to static categories (Yazan & Rudolph, 2018). Therefore, it is highly critical to trace the current trend of studies in order to find out whether L2 teacher identity research is moving towards a globalized identity discourse or not (Fang, 2018), an identity discourse that is inclusive, non-racist, non-stereotyping, global, and dynamic and one that allows the reconsideration and reconceptualization of the diverse range of L2 teacher identity types in each given time and context (Rudolph et al. 2015).

In addition to the above studies focusing primarily on English as an L2, there have been other works conducted on teacher identity in modern foreign languages. Of particular interest are the following studies: Donato and Davin (2018a) highlighted the role of ontogenetic (i.e. individual's identity development during the life) development as a mediating factor in teacher identity development that can be attributed to a wide range of factors in an individual's past experience. Drawing on practice-based and thought-based data sources, Donato and Davin (2018b) analyzed teachers' discursive practices and reported the significant role of external factors as the nexus in connecting the individual's past experiences and present identity formation. Davin et al. (2018) suggested reflecting on the role models as an effective way of professional identity development towards conceptualization of pedagogical progress in keeping with previous studies (Martel, 2015; Martel & Wang, 2014). Although adding these and other studies related to teacher identity development in modern foreign languages could have enriched this systematic review, we opted out of including such studies in this particular review primarily due to our background in TESOL. We have the least doubt, however, that the findings have far-reaching implications for teacher identity development in modern and other foreign and world languages.

2.1.2   Purpose of the Study

L2 language teacher identity has been researched from a variety of vantage points to find out what factors (e.g. social, cultural, personal) and under what conditions (e.g. professional positions, training facilities) influence L2 teacher development. The main goal of the present study was to put together the findings of earlier studies in a single article to shed light on the achievements made so far and to identify the next critical steps to take.

Given the complexity of L2 teacher identity and the diversity of approaches adopted to analyze it, we reviewed articles with a focus on the research method employed, the aspect of teacher identity analyzed, the theoretical framework adopted, and the theoretical and pedagogical implications reported, to shed light on different aspects of its development in response to the following research questions:

RQ1: What primary aspects of identity were more frequently analyzed in studies on second language teacher identity from 2010–2020?
RQ2: What secondary aspects of identity were more frequently analyzed in studies on second language teacher identity from 2010–2020?
RQ3: What research methods/data elicitation tools were more frequently used in studies on second language teacher identity from 2010–2020?
RQ4: What theoretical frameworks played a more significant role in developing second language teacher identity based on the reviewed studies from 2010–2020?
RQ5: What are the theoretical and pedagogical implications of the studies offered for the status quo?

2.2 Method

To bridge the gap in the literature, different L2 teacher identities reported in earlier research were identified and coded along with their corresponding theoretical frameworks, research methods/data elicitation tools, and reported pedagogical and theoretical implications to provide a detailed picture of the frequently adopted L2 teacher identity types (see Table 2.1).

2.2.1 Data Collection

The data collection procedure as documented below was based on the standard systematic review to facilitate replicating the findings in future studies. Articles on second language teacher identity published in Q1 Scopus and SSCI indexed journals were searched in two electronic academic literature databases of Scopus and Web of Science. Our first keyword was 'language teacher identity' and our second group of keywords covered more specific titles including 'second language teacher identity', 'foreign language teacher identity', 'English as foreign language teacher identity' (EFL), and 'English as a second language teacher identity' (ESL). We wished to limit the scope of our review to English as an L2 (whether as a second or a foreign

Table 2.1 Typlogy of L2 teacher identity, research methods, framewroks and implications

Author	The primary focus of the study	[a]The secondary focus of the study	Adopted research methods/data elicitation tools	Adopted theoretical framework	Theoretical/pedagogical implication (s)
Li (2020)	Plural/multiple identity	Private identity	Narrative inquiry	Integrated perspective	Teachers' beliefs and emotions develop their identity
Macías Villegas et al. (2020)	Identity development	Identity shifts	Narrative inquiry	Sociocultural theory	Identity formation is an ongoing and constantly shifting process
Kim et al. (2020)	Identity development	Digital stories	Mixed methods	Sociocultural theory	Teachers develop professional identity through digital stories
Wolff & De Costa (2017)	Nonnative speaker identity	Emotional demands	Narrative inquiry	Critical theory	Newly-developed pedagogical models can help teachers overcome emotion-related challenges
Tao & Gao (2017)	Professional identity	Agency	Interviews	Sociocultural theory	Identity commitment influences teacher identity
De Costa & Norton (2017)	Professional identity	Transdisciplinarity	Narratives and discourse analysis	Transdisciplinary approach	Linguistic and personal background influences teacher identity formation
Edwards & Burns (2016)	Plural/multiple identity	Teacher-researcher identity Negotiation	Mixed methods	Ecological perspective	Teachers' perceptions influence their identity conceptualization
Kayi-Aydar (2015)	Plural/multiple identity	Agency	Narrative inquiry	Post structural approaches	Complex and mutual relationships exist between teacher identity and agency
Huang & Varghese (2015)	Plural/multiple identity	Personalized and institutionalized identities	Interviews and observations	Identity in discourse and practice	Teachers' perceptions influence their identity conceptualization
Tashma Baum (2014)	Identity development	Self-image	Interviews	Sociocultural theory	Teachers' perceptions influence their identity conceptualization.

Study					
Ruohotie-Lyhty (2013)	Professional identity	Teachers' initial identities	Narrative inquiry	Sociocultural theory	Ideal and forced identities are introduced
Lee (2013)	Identities-in-practice	Identity shifts	Self-report and observations	Identity in discourse and practice	Teacher identity is discursively constructed under the influence of socio-cultural dimensions
Trent (2012)	Professional identity	Teachers' perceptions of teaching	Interviews	Discourse theory	Teachers' perceptions influence their identity conceptualization
Abednia (2012)	Professional identity	Sociocultural identities	Grounded theory approach	Critical theory	Teacher identitie shift over time
Park (2012)	Narrative inquiry	Identity shifts	Narrative inquiry	Identity in discourse and practice	Future pedagogical practices are predictors of L2 teachers' professional identity
Menard-Warwick (2011)	Bilingual identity	Sociocultural identities	Interviews and questionnaires	Bakhtinian theoretical framework	The global imaginary influences teacher identity development
Kanno & Stuart (2011)	Identities-in-practice	Teaching practices	Narrative inquiry	Situated learning perspective	Teaching practices influence identity development
Liu & Xu (2011)	Designated vs. actual identity	Self-image	Narrative inquiry	Game theory	Workplace influences designated and actual identities
Farrell (2011)	Teacher role identity	Self-image	Group discussions	Communities of practice	Teachers from identities such as acculturator (cultural workers), professional, and manager
Ajayi (2011)	Identities-in-practice	Sociocultural identities (race, ethnicity, and culture)	Interviews and questionnaires	Sociocultural theory	Sociocultural identities mediate teachers' teaching practices
Trent (2010)	Identity development	Teachers' perceptions of teaching	Action research	Model of identity formation (Fairclough, 2003)	Teachers' perceptions influence their identity conceptualization

(continued)

Table 2.1 (continued)

Author	The primary focus of the study	[a]The secondary focus of the study	Adopted research methods/data elicitation tools	Adopted theoretical framework	Theoretical/pedagogical implication (s)
Vélcz-Rendón (2010)	Professional identity	Social identity	Observations	Vygotskian sociocultural theory	Native speakerness and male authority influence teachers' professional identity
Ilieva (2010)	Professional identity	Agency	Grounded theory approach	Conceptualization of identity (Varghese et al., 2005)	Future pedagogical practices are predictors of L2 teachers' professional identity

[a](Relevant aspect(s) of L2 teacher identity analyzed in relationship with the primary aspect)

language) and did not include '*modern (foreign) languages teacher identity*' as our search term unless such studies were automatically identified as part of our '*second language teacher identity*' key phrase, such as for example when the located papers had been published in *The Modern Language Journal*. The use of the above key terms/phrases in the search for appropriate articles resulted in 134 articles.

2.2.2 Inclusion/Exclusion Criteria

Peer-reviewed articles published between 2010–2020 reporting results on second language teacher identity were included in the study. The date range was implemented to ensure the sufficiency factor of the included articles and the coverage of the related literature at a time when technology-assisted language learning is being integrated into traditional face-to-face language instruction. Review articles, book reviews, book chapters, conference reports and proceedings, and theses were excluded as they do not undergo a strict review process before publication compared to journal articles reporting research results. Observing inclusion/exclusion criteria resulted in 61 articles which were then systematically reviewed to answer the posed research questions.

2.2.3 Characteristics of Articles

The reviewed articles were published between 2010 and 2020. The most frequently published articles appeared in 2017 (11 articles out of 61 articles (18.03%)) and the least frequently articles appeared in 2019 (2 articles out of 61 articles (3.27%)). Compared to other journals included in the study, *TESOL Quarterly* (16 articles) and *The Modern Language Journal* (14 articles) published more articles on teacher identity from 2010–2010. The rest of the included articles were published in the following journals: *Teaching and Teacher Education* (n = 8), *Language Teaching Research* (n = 7), *System* (n = 5), *Critical Inquiry in Language Studies* (n = 2), *Computers & Education* (n = 1), *Canadian Modern Language Review* (n = 1), *Foreign Language Annals* (n = 1), *Journal of Education for Teaching* (n = 1), *The Urban Review* (n = 1), *International Journal of Bilingual Education and Bilingualism* (n = 1), *Journal of Second Language Writing* (n = 1), *Language and Intercultural Communication* (n = 1), and *International Journal of Educational Research* (n = 1).

2.3 Results

RQ1: The Primary Focus of the Reviewed Studies
Most reviewed studies focused as their prime target on L2 teacher identity construction/development as expected, since this was a key phrase used as a search item. In so doing, many studies concentrated on surrounding concepts like professional/role

Table 2.2 Primary focus of the reviewed articles

Primary focus of the studies

		Frequency	Valid percent	Cumulative percent
Valid	Plural/multiple identities	8	13.1	13.1
	Professional identity	10	16.4	29.5
	Emotional/private identity	3	4.9	34.4
	Identity development/construction	20	32.8	67.2
	Identities-in-practice	7	11.5	78.7
	Teacher role identity	2	3.3	82.0
	Designated vs. actual identity	1	1.6	83.6
	Bilingual identity	1	1.6	85.2
	Multilingual identity	1	1.6	86.9
	Nonnative speaker identity	4	6.6	93.4
	Linguistic identity	1	1.6	95.1
	Gendered identity	1	1.6	96.7
	Future identity	1	1.6	98.4
	Translingual identity	1	1.6	100.0
	Total	61	100.0	

identity, bi/multi/translingual and linguistic identity, as well as non-native speaker along with future, designated, and gendered identities. Table 2.2 displays the findings of the study in response to the first research question with regard to the primary focus of the reviewed studies.

It was revealed that identity development/construction (Frequency = 20, Valid Percent = 32.8%), professional identity (Frequency = 10, Valid Percent = 16.4%), and plural/multiple identities (Frequency = 8, Valid Percent = 13.1%) were the primary focus of the reviewed studies. The next most observed aspects of the reviewed studies were identities in practice (8.1%) and nonnative speaker identity (4.7%).

RQ2: The Secondary Focus of the Reviewed Studies
Anticipatedly, the over-arching and primary focus of almost all studies was L2 teacher identity construction; however, this concept was approached slightly differently in different studies by zooming in on a certain aspect of identity from self-image to agency to race and ethnicity to emotional aspects of identity, among others. Table 2.3 displays the findings of the study in response to the second research question that aimed to address the secondary aspects of L2 teacher identity in the reviewed studies.

It was revealed that self-image (Frequency = 12, Valid Percent = 19.7%), teaching practices and background experiences (Frequency = 8, Valid Percent = 13.1%), and sociocultural identities (race, ethnicity, and culture) (Frequency = 7, Valid Percent = 11.5%) were the most frequent secondary foci of the reviewed studies. The next frequently observed aspects of L2 teacher identity in the

Table 2.3 Secondary focus of the reviewed articles

Secondary focus of the studies

		Frequency	Valid percent	Cumulative percent
Valid	Emotional/private identity	1	1.6	1.6
	Agency	5	8.2	9.8
	Social identity	4	6.6	16.4
	Teachers' perceptions of teaching	4	6.6	23.0
	Sociocultural identities (race, ethnicity, and culture)	7	11.5	34.4
	Self-image	12	19.7	54.1
	Teaching practices and background experiences	8	13.1	67.2
	Identity shifts	3	4.9	72.1
	Teachers' initial identities	3	4.9	77.0
	Emotional demands/negotiations	5	8.2	85.2
	Transdisciplinarity	2	3.3	88.5
	Domestication of dissent	1	1.6	90.2
	Teacher metacognitions	1	1.6	91.8
	Teacher–researcher identity negotiation	1	1.6	93.4
	Digital stories	2	3.3	96.7
	Post-observation feedback	1	1.6	98.4
	Global identity	1	1.6	100.0
	Total	61	100.0	

reviewed studies were agency (Frequency = 5, Valid Percent = 8.2%) and emotional demands/negotiations (Frequency = 5, Valid Percent = 8.2%).

RQ3: Adopted Research Methods/Data Elicitation Tools
There has been some confusion over what reviewed studies have regarded as research methods; for example, while some have referred to interviews are research methods, others have regarded them as data collection tools. Either way, interviews naturally feature prominently in almost all studies and that is why narrative inquiry has been a dominant approach to studying L2 teacher identity in almost a third of the reviewed studies. Obviously, almost all L2 teacher identity research has followed a qualitative paradigm, and not surprisingly a mix of data elicitation techniques such as interviews, observations, and questionaries feature strongly in numerous studies. Table 2.4 displays the findings in response to the third research question. It was revealed that narrative inquiry (Frequency = 20, Valid Percent = 32.8%), mixed methods (Frequency = 13, Valid Percent = 21.3%), and interviews (Frequency = 9, Valid Percent = 14.8%) were the most frequently adopted research methodologies or data collection techniques in the reviewed studies, followed by interviews and questionnaires (Frequency = 4, Valid Percent = 6.6%) and interviews and observations (Frequency = 3, Valid Percent = 4.9%).

Table 2.4 Adopted research methods/data elicitation tools

Adopted research methods/data elicitation tools				
		Frequency	Valid percent	Cumulative percent
Valid	Narrative inquiry	20	32.8	32.8
	Grounded theory approach	2	3.3	36.1
	Observations	3	4.9	41.0
	Action research	2	3.3	44.3
	Interviews and questionnaires	4	6.6	50.8
	Group discussion	1	1.6	52.5
	Case study	1	1.6	54.1
	Interviews	9	14.8	68.9
	Self-report and observations	1	1.6	70.5
	Interviews and observations	3	4.9	75.4
	Narratives and discourse analysis	1	1.6	77.0
	Short story approach	1	1.6	78.7
	Mixed methods (more than two data collection methods)	13	21.3	100.0
	Total	61	100.0	

RQ4: Adopted Theoretical Frameworks

Although an array of methodological frameworks were deployed to situate the reviewed studies ranging from multilingualism to gaming theory to critical discourse analysis, there has been a distinct trend in moving away from primarily cognitive-based models to prioritizing more social frameworks and increasingly drawing on post-structural, social, discoursal and socio-cultural theories. These models collectively signify the fact that L2 teachers are above all human beings whose identities are socially co-constructed within their communities of practice. Table 2.5 displays the findings of the study in response to the fourth research question. It was revealed that socio-cultural theory (Frequency = 18, Valid Percent = 29.5%), identity in discourse and practice (Frequency = 7, Valid Percent = 11.5%), and conceptualization of identity (Frequency = 4, Valid Percent = 6.6%) were the most frequently adopted theoretical frameworks in the reviewed studies. The next frequently observed theoretical frameworks in the reviewed studies were Vygotskian sociocultural theory (Frequency = 4, Valid Percent = 6.6%) and communities of practice (Frequency = 4, Valid Percent = 6.6%).

RQ5: Theoretical/Pedagogical Implications

The themes that emerged from the reviewed studies primarily concentrated on issues such as the link between L2 teacher's identity development and a myriad of individual, professional, and socio-cultural variables shaping and being shaped by the identity construct on the one hand, and the inter-relationships between classroom practices and the identity construction of L2 teachers on the other. The systematic review in particular documented the effect on identity construction and classroom/

Table 2.5 Adopted theoretical framework

Adopted theoretical framework		Frequency	Valid percent	Cumulative percent
Valid	Integrated perspective	3	4.9	4.9
	Conceptualization of identity (Varghese et al., 2005)	4	6.6	11.5
	Vygotskian sociocultural theory	4	6.6	18.0
	Model of identity formation (Fairclough, 2003)	1	1.6	19.7
	Sociocultural theory	18	29.5	49.2
	Communities of practice	4	6.6	55.7
	Situated learning perspective	3	4.9	60.7
	Game theory	1	1.6	62.3
	Bakhtinian theoretical framework	1	1.6	63.9
	Critical discourse theory	3	4.9	68.9
	Identity in discourse and practice	7	11.5	80.3
	Discourse theory	1	1.6	82.0
	Post structural approaches	1	1.6	83.6
	Transdisciplinary approach	1	1.6	85.2
	Poststructural theory	1	1.6	86.9
	Ecological perspective	1	1.6	88.5
	Multilingualism	2	3.3	91.8
	Social identity theory	1	1.6	93.4
	The self and motivation theory	2	3.3	96.7
	Positioning theory	1	1.6	98.4
	Socialization theory	1	1.6	100.0
	Total	61	100.0	

pedagogical practices of L2 teachers' beliefs and emotions, their perceptions, their personal, linguistic, educational, professional, and cultural backgrounds, their commitments, their metacognition, their agency, their native/non-nativeness, their plurilingual competencies, their gender, their workplace, their global imaginaries, and the like. Furthermore, most studies pointed to the direction that identity construction is a multi-layered, complex, ongoing, and constantly shifting process, the proper understanding of which requires further scrutiny.

2.4 Discussion

The findings of the present study revealed that several factors are at work in L2 teacher identity formation, perception, and expression. Several pieces of evidence support this argument; and among them is the diverse range of theoretical frameworks adopted by the reviewed studies that highlight the variety of views concerning the complex concept of teacher identity in general and L2 teacher identity in particular. The next piece of evidence that confirms the complexity of influential factors in L2 teacher identity is the wide range of the foci in studies on L2 teacher identity.

The results also revealed that the primary focus of reviewed articles was not limited to a particular aspect of teacher identity such as academic qualifications. In fact, three primary foci were observed in the studies that elaborated on teacher identity (i.e. identity development/construction, professional identity, and plural/multiple identities). These findings were in keeping with the results reported by Choe and Seo (2021) who argued that influential factors in identity construction go beyond academic skills and linguistic qualifications. They reported that teachers' race and particularly the white skin was a determining factor that prioritized one teacher's identity against other racial groups in the Korean English language teaching environment.

The next finding of the study was the significance of the emotional factors in L2 teacher identity construction. This finding highlights the results of the previous studies investigating teachers' beliefs and emotions (Barcelos, 2017; Zembylas & Schutz, 2009). Among them is the study conducted by Kocabaş-Gedik and Ortaçtepe Hart (2021) that examined the impact of emotional labor on teacher identity formation. They elicited data from two novice native speakers in an EFL context and reported a significant relationship between teacher identity and emotional labor. Emotional factors can influence teachers' decision-making during the teaching process and teachers need to be well-trained about emotional factors prior to taking on teaching responsibilities.

The review of the studies also revealed that socio-cultural factors play a significant role in L2 teacher identity construction (Villegas et al., 2020). Therefore, student teachers need to be trained in handling socio-cultural conflicts. For example, novice teachers need to be exposed to potentially conflicting teaching experiences in order to enhance their adaptation/mediation skills prior to real instructional encounters. Yazan (2017, 2019) argues that language teacher identity formation is not merely influenced by the individual characteristics of the novice teachers, but also by their sociocultural interactions and relationships. He believes that teachers need to develop their emotional competence as a critical aspect of their identity in order to be able to maintain emotional management during instruction.

The most important theme that emerges out of the reviewed studies is that L2 teacher identity is not a straightforward concept in terms of both understanding it and how it is shaped and re-shaped. The multitude of perspectives adopted in tackling this construct as well as the varied observations as to the nature of L2 teacher identity and its course of life is a clear indication that teacher identity is a multi-faceted and complex phenomenon. The reviewed studies also signify that L2 teacher identity development is an ongoing, dynamic process which both affects and is affected by a host of personal, educational, institutional, social, economic, political, and other contextual factors.

This, in essence, signifies that teachers (and the way they develop professionally) like other human beings are difficult-to-understand, since they adapt to, and are influenced by various contextual elements surrounding them. A corollary of such an observation is that L2 teachers with different family backgrounds and those living and working in different educational, economic, social, and political settings will develop different identities as teachers despite similar academic qualifications they may have gained through formal studies. An important consequence of such an understanding is that L2 teachers (with L2 referring to any second, foreign, modern, and world languages) should be scaffolded to develop and retain identities that will enable them to discharge their responsibility (that is, facilitating language learning) in the best way possible. Although the route is person- and context-specific, L2 teacher educators and educational authorities play the most part in facilitating the process on the condition that teachers already have an internal desire to become and remain teachers. This way, they can be helped to co-construct sustainable identities which can prevent them from burnout, the solution to which is, according to Amelia Nagoski, a conductor and author, not self-care but care for each other.

2.4.1 Implications

Pedagogically, the findings of the study inform the practitioners who seek a better understanding of L2 teaching context (e.g. social, political, and cultural) as well as identity types (narrated identities, identities-in-practice, future selves, gendered identities, sociocultural identities) to enhance their professional identity construction during pedagogical interactions. Teacher training courses need to inform novice teachers about the significance of their educational background, competence in the local language if they are to teach in a context where the language they teach is not widely used, and supportive discourse in the professional environment. Teacher training officials should encourage teachers to express their emotional concerns to those outside or inside the teaching profession. Depending on their personality type, teachers need to express their thoughts and feelings and cater to their emotional needs by discussing the emotional problems that they are unable to handle on their own.

Theoretically, the findings both display the trajectory of studies shifting from a normative paradigm to an interpretative paradigm and introduce mainstream theoretical frameworks (socio-cultural theory, identity in discourse and practice, and conceptualization of identity) adopted in reviewed studies. The next theoretical implication of the study is the need to approach L2 teacher identity from a multi-cultural perspective and find out solutions to the racially biased teacher identity that is prevalent in EFL and ESL contexts (Choe & Seo, 2021). Furthermore, there seems to be a gap in research examining factors that influence language teacher identity in English for academic purposes (EAP) programs with content-based instruction. The same is true with other foreign and heritage languages apart from modern languages (whether for general or academic purposes) that require further research attention.

Future studies are accordingly recommended to incorporate metaphorical analysis to analyze teacher identity development in academic contexts (in English and other modern and foreign languages) to overcome dynamic challenges ahead of teacher identity development. Future studies are also needed to approach teacher identity-related issues such as teacher voice, professional discipline, and teachers' dialoguing with others as part of the movement towards subject matter and pedagogy rather than towards the native speaker model of teacher identity. The coming trend of studies on L2 teacher identity seems to be moving away from essentializing binaries (e.g. native/nonnative, monolingual/multilingual, privileged/marginalized, etc.) towards the theoretical frameworks (e.g. dynamic systems theory, complex dynamic systems, etc.) that reflect the complexity, nonlinearity, and dynamicity of L2 teacher identity. Such comprehensive theoretical frameworks make it possible to expand L2 teacher identity studies beyond limited theoretical perspectives such as native speakerism, marginalized identity, and privileged identity.

2.5   Conclusion

The study was an endeavour to shed light on second/foreign language teacher identity research by putting together the findings of the reviewed studies between 2010 and 2020. Based on the reviewed studies the following conclusions can be made: First, identity development/construction, professional identity, and plural/multiple identities have been the primary focus of the reviewed studies so far. Second, self-image, teaching practices and background experiences, and sociocultural identities have been the secondary focus of the reviewed articles. Third, narrative inquiry, mixed methods, and interviews have been the most frequently adopted research methodologies in the reviewed studies. Fourth, socio-cultural theory, identity in discourse and practice, and conceptualization of identity have been the most frequently adopted theoretical framework in the reviewed studies. Fifth, teachers' perceptions of their identity, teachers' sociocultural identities, and teachers' beliefs and emotions have had significant implications for L2 teacher identity development. One limitation of the current review is excluding modern (including world, heritage, and other foreign) languages from the definition of L2 (which we delimited to TESOL due to our background and expertise), which we hope a future systemic review will improve.

References

*Abednia, A. (2012). Teachers' professional identity: Contributions of a critical EFL teacher education course in Iran. Teaching and Teacher Education, 28(5), 706–717. https://doi.org/10.1016/j.tate.2012.02.005.

*Ajayi, L. (2011). How ESL teachers' sociocultural identities mediate their teacher role identities in a diverse urban school setting. The Urban Review, 43(5), 654–680. https://doi.org/10.1007/s11256-010-0161-y.

Barcelos, A. M. F. (2015). Unveiling the relationship between language learning beliefs, emotions, and identities. *Studies in Second Language Learning and Teaching, 5*, 301–325. https://doi.org/10.14746/ssllt.2015.5.2.6

Barcelos, A. M. F. (2017). Identities as emotioning and believing. In G. Barkhuizen (Ed.), *Reflections on language teacher identity research* (pp. 145–150). Routledge.

Barkhuizen, G. (2017). *Reflections on language teacher identity research*. Routledge. https://doi.org/10.4324/9781315643465

Barros-del Rio, M. A., Álvarez, P., & Roldán, S. M. (2021). Implementing dialogic gatherings in TESOL teacher education. *Innovation in Language Learning and Teaching, 15*(2), 169–180. https://doi.org/10.1080/17501229.2020.1737075

Benesch, S. (2017). *Emotions and English language teaching: Exploring teachers' emotion labor.* Routledge.

Burns, A., Freeman, D., & Edwards, E. (2015). Theorizing and studying the language teaching mind: Mapping research on language teacher cognition. *The Modern Language Journal, 99*, 585–601. https://doi.org/10.1111/modl.12245

Cheung, Y. L., Said, S. B., & Park, E. (Eds.). (2015). Advances and current trends in language teacher identity research. *Routledge/Taylor & Francis.* https://doi.org/10.4324/9781315775135

Choe, H., & Seo, Y. (2021). Negotiating teacher identity: Experiences of black teachers of English in Korean ELT: How race and English language teacher identity intersect in the expanding circle. *English Today, 37*(3), 148–155. https://doi.org/10.1017/S0266078419000531

Chowdhury, R., & Phan, L. H. (2014). *Desiring TESOL and international education: Market abuse and exploitation.* Multilingual Matters.

Davin, K. J., Chavoshan, I., & Donato, R. (2018). Images of past teachers: Present when you teach. *System, 72*, 139–150. https://doi.org/10.1016/j.system.2017.12.001

De Costa, P. I., & Norton, B. (2016). Future directions in identity research on language learning and teaching. In S. Preece (Ed.), *The Routledge handbook of language and identity* (pp. 586–601). Routledge/Taylor & Francis.

De Costa, P. I., & Norton, B. (2017). Introduction: Identity, transdisciplinarity, and the good language teacher. Modern Language Journal, 101(s1), 3–14. https://doi.org/10.1111/modl.12368

Donato, R., & Davin, K. J. (2018a). The role of ontogenetic development in teacher education. In J. Lantolf, M. E. Poehner, & M. Swain (Eds.), *Handbook of sociocultural theory and second language learning* (pp. 457–471). Routledge.

Donato, R., & Davin, K. J. (2018b). The genesis of classroom discursive practices as history-in-person processes. *Language Teaching Research, 22*(6), 739–760. https://doi.org/10.1177/1362168817702672

Edwards, E. (2021). The ecological impact of action research on language teacher development: A review of the literature. *Educational Action Research, 29*(3), 396–413. https://doi.org/10.1080/09650792.2020.1718513

Edwards, E., & Burns, A. (2016). Language teacher–researcher identity negotiation: An ecological perspective. *TESOL Quarterly, 50*(1), 735–745. https://doi.org/10.1002/tesq.313

Fairclough, N. (2003). *Analyzing discourse*. Routledge.

Fang, F. (2018). Glocalisation, English as a lingua franca and ELT: Re-conceptualising identity and models for ELT in China. In B. Yazan & N. Rudolph (Eds.), *Criticality, teacher identity, and (in)equity in ELT through and beyond binaries: Issues and implications* (pp. 23–40). Springer. https://doi.org/10.1007/978-3-319-72920-6_2

Farrell, T. S. (2011). Exploring the professional role identities of experienced ESL teachers through reflective practice. System, 39(1), 54–62. https://doi.org/10.1016/j.system.2011.01.012

Farrell, T. S., & Ives, J. (2015). Exploring teacher beliefs and classroom practices through reflective practice: A case study. Language Teaching Research, 19(5), 594–610. https://doi.org/10.1177/1362168814541722

Freeman, D. (2016). *Educating second language teachers.* Oxford University Press.

Giri, R., & Foo, J. (2014). On teaching EIL in a Japanese context: The power within and power without. In R. Marlina & R. Giri (Eds.), *The pedagogy of English as an international language: Perspectives from scholars, teachers and students* (pp. 239–258). Springer.

Golombek, P., & Doran, M. (2014). Unifying cognition, emotion, and activity in language teacher professional development. *Teaching and Teacher Education, 39*, 102–111. https://doi.org/10.1016/j.tate.2014.01.002

Goosseff, K. (2014). Only narratives can reflect the experience of objectivity: Effective persuasion. *Journal of Organization Change Management, 27*(5), 703–709.

Grant, R. A., & Lee, I. (2009). The ideal English speaker: A juxtaposition of globalization and language policy in South Korea and racialized language attitudes in the United States. In R. Kubota & A. Lin (Eds.), *Race, culture, and identities in second language education: Exploring critically engaged practice* (pp. 44–63). Routledge.

Hanna, F., Oostdam, R., Severiens, S. E., & Zijlstra, B. J. S. (2020). Assessing the professional identity of primary student teachers: Design and validation of the teacher identity measurement scale. *Studies in Educational Evaluation, 64*(1), 1–15. https://doi.org/10.1016/j.stueduc.2019.100822

He, P., & Lin, A. M. Y. (2013). Tensions in school-university partnership and EFL pre-service teacher identity formation: A case in mainland China. *The Language Learning Journal, 41*(2), 205–218. https://doi.org/10.1080/09571736.2013.790134

Holliday, A. (2006). Native-speakerism. *ELT Journal, 60*(4), 385–387. https://doi.org/10.1093/elt/ccl030

Hong, J., Greene, B., & Lowery, J. (2017). Multiple dimensions of teacher identity development from pre-service to early years of teaching: A longitudinal study. *Journal of Education for Teaching, 43*, 84–98. https://doi.org/10.1080/02607476.2017

*Huang, I. C., & Varghese, M. M. (2015). Toward a composite, personalized, and institutionalized teacher identity for non-native English speakers in US secondary ESL programs. Critical Inquiry in Language Studies, 12(1), 51–76. https://doi.org/10.1080/15427587.2015.997651

*Ilieva, R. (2010). Non-native English-speaking teachers' negotiations of program discourses in their construction of professional identities within a TESOL program. Canadian Modern Language Review, 66(3), 343–369. https://doi.org/10.3138/cmlr.66.3.343

*Kanno, Y., & Stuart, C. (2011). Learning to become a second language teacher: Identities-in-practice. Modern Language Journal, 95(2), 236–252. https://doi.org/10.1111/j.1540-4781.2011.01178.x

*Kayi-Aydar, H. (2015). Multiple identities, negotiations, and agency across time and space: A narrative inquiry of a foreign language teacher candidate. Critical Inquiry in Language Studies, 12(2), 137–160. https://doi.org/10.1080/15427587.2015.1032076

Kayi-Aydar, H., Gao, X. A., Miller, E. R., Varghese, M., & Vitanova, G. (2019). *Theorizing and analyzing language teacher agency*. Multilingual Matters.

Kern, R. (2015). Language, literacy, and technology. *Cambridge University Press.* https://doi.org/10.1017/CBO9781139567701

Kim, H. A. (2017). Understanding blackness in South Korea: Experiences of one black teacher and one black student. *Global Journal of Human-Social Science (C), 17*(1), 85–93. https://doi.org/10.1017/S0266078419000531

*Kim, D., Long, Y., Zhao, Y., Zhou, S., & Alexander, J. (2020). Teacher professional identity development through digital stories. Computers & Education https://doi.org/10.1016/%20j.compedu.2020.104040

Kocabaş-Gedik, P., & Ortaçtepe Hart, D. (2021). It's not like that at all: A poststructuralist case study on language teacher identity and emotional labor. *Journal of Language, Identity & Education.* https://doi.org/10.1080/15348458.2020.1726756

Kubanyiova, M., & Feryok, A. (2015). Language teacher cognition in applied linguistics research: Revisiting the territory, redrawing the boundaries, reclaiming the relevance. *The Modern Language Journal, 99*, 435–449. https://doi.org/10.1111/modl.12239

*Lee, I. (2013). Becoming a writing teacher: Using 'identity' as an analytic lens to understand EFL writing teachers' development. Journal of Second Language Writing, 22(3), 330–345. https://doi.org/10.1016/j.jslw.2012.07.001

*Li, W. (2020). Unpacking the complexities of teacher identity: Narratives of two Chinese teachers of English in China. Language Teaching Research. https://doi.org/10.1177/1362168820910955

*Liu, Y., & Xu, Y. (2011). Inclusion or exclusion? A narrative inquiry of a language teacher's identity experience in the 'new work order' of competing pedagogies. Teaching and Teacher Education, 27(3), 589–597. https://doi.org/10.1016/j.tate.2010.10.013

*Macías Villegas, D. F., Varona, W. H., & Sanchez A. G. (2020). Student teachers' identity construction: A socially-constructed narrative in a second language teacher education program. Teaching and Teacher Education, 91(1), 1–15. https://doi.org/10.1016/j.tate.2020.103055

Martel, J. (2015). Learning to teach a foreign language: Identity negotiation and conceptualizations of pedagogical progress. Foreign Language Annals, 48(3), 394–412. https://doi.org/10.1111/flan.12144

Martel, J., & Wang, A. (2014). Language teacher identity. In M. Bigelow & J. Ennser-Kananen (Eds.), The Routledge handbook of educational linguistics (pp. 289–300). Routledge.

*Menard-Warwick, J. (2011). Chilean English teacher identity and popular culture: Three generations. International Journal of Bilingual Education and Bilingualism, 14(3), 261–277. https://doi.org/10.1080/13670050031003797466

Miller, J. (2009). Teacher identity. In A. Burns & J. C. Richards (Eds.), The Cambridge guide to second language teacher education. Cambridge University Press.

Norton, B. (2000). Identity and language learning: Gender, ethnicity, and educational change. Pearson Education.

*Park, G. (2012). I am never afraid of being recognized as an NNES: One teacher's journey in claiming and embracing her nonnative-speaker identity. TESOL Quarterly, 46(1), 127–151. https://doi.org/10.1002/tesq.4

Pillen, M. T., den Brok, P. J., & Beijaard, D. (2013). Profiles and change in beginning teachers' professional identity tensions. Teaching and Teacher Education, 34, 86–97. https://doi.org/10.1016/j.tate.2013.04.003

Rudolph, N., Selvi, A. F., & Yazan, B. (2015). Conceptualizing and confronting inequity: Approaches within and new directions for the "NNEST movement". Critical Inquiry in Language Studies, 12(1), 27–50. https://doi.org/10.1080/15427587.2015.997650

Ruecker, T., & Ives, L. (2015). White native English speakers needed: The rhetorical construction of privilege in online teacher recruitment spaces. TESOL Quarterly, 49(4), 733–756. https://doi.org/10.1002/tesq.195

*Ruohotie-Lyhty, M. (2013). Struggling for a professional identity: Two newly qualified language teachers' identity narratives during the first years at work. Teaching and Teacher Education, 30, 120–129. https://doi.org/10.1016/j.tate.2012.11.002

Sang, Y. (2020). Research of language teacher identity: Status quo and future directions. RELC Journal. https://doi.org/10.1177/0033688220961567

*Tao, J., & Gao, X. (2017). Teacher agency and identity commitment in curricular reform. Teaching and Teacher Education, 63, 346–355. https://doi.org/10.1016/j.tate.2017.01.010

*Tashma Baum, M. (2014). 'The aspect of the heart': English and selfidentity in the experience of preservice teachers. Language and Intercultural Communication, 14(4), 407–422. https://doi.org/10.1080/14708477.2014.934379

Thorne, S. L., Sauro, S., & Smith, B. (2015). Technologies, identities, and expressive activity. Annual Review of Applied Linguistics, 35(1), 215–233. https://doi.org/10.1017/S0267190514000257

Toh, G. (2014). English for content instruction in a Japanese higher education setting: Examining challenges, contradictions and anomalies. Language and Education, 28(4), 299–318.

*Trent, J. (2010). Teacher education as identity construction: Insights from action research. Journal of Education for Teaching, 36(2), 153–168. https://doi.org/10.1080/02607471003651672

*Trent, J. (2012). The discursive positioning of teachers: Native-speaking English teachers and educational discourse in Hong Kong. TESOL Quarterly, 46(1), 104–126. https://doi.org/10. 1002/tesq.1

Varghese, M., Morgan, B., Johnston, B., & Johnson, K. (2005). Theorizing language teacher identity: Three perspectives and beyond. Journal of Language, Identity, and Education, 4, 21–44. https://doi.org/10.1207/s15327701jlie0401_2

*Vélez-Rendón, G. (2010). From social identity to professional identity: Issues of language and gender. Foreign Language Annals, 43(4), 635–649. https://doi.org/10.1111/j.1944-9720.2010. 01113.x

Villegas, D. F. M., Varona, W. H., & Sanchez, A. G. (2020). Student teachers' identity construction: A socially-constructed narrative in a second language teacher education program. Teaching and Teacher Education, 91, 103055. https://doi.org/10.1016/j.tate.2020.103055

Wang, D., & Zhang, L. J. (2021). Sustainability as a goal in teaching workforce retention: Exploring the role of teacher identity construction in preservice teachers' job motivation. Sustainability, 13, 2698. https://doi.org/10.3390/su13052698

Wolff, D., & De Costa, P. I. (2017). Expanding the language teacher identity landscape: An investigation of the emotions and strategies of a NNEST. The Modern Language Journal, 101(1), 76–90. https://doi.org/10.1111/modl.12370

Yang, S., Shu, D., & Yin, H. (2021). 'Frustration drives me to grow': Unraveling EFL teachers' emotional trajectory interacting with identity development. Teaching and Teacher Education, 105, 103420. https://doi.org/10.1016/j.tate.2021.103420

Yazan, B. (2017). It just made me look at language in a different way: ESOL teacher candidates' identity negotiation through teacher education coursework. Linguistics and Education, 40, 38–49. https://doi.org/10.1016/j.linged.2017.06.002

Yazan, B. (2019). Toward identity-oriented teacher education: Critical autoethnographic narrative. TESOL Journal, 10(1), 10–388. https://doi.org/10.1002/tesj.388

Yazan, B., & Rudolph, N. (2018). Introduction: Apprehending identity, experience, and (in)equity through and beyond binaries. In B. Yazan & N. Rudolph (Eds.), Criticality, teacher identity, and (in)equity in English language teaching. Educational linguistics (Vol. 35, pp. 67–82). Springer. https://doi.org/10.1007/978-3-319-72920-6_1

Yook, C., & Lindemann, S. (2013). The role of speaker identification in Korean university students' attitudes towards five varieties of English. Journal of Multilingual and Multilingual Development, 34(3), 279–296. https://doi.org/10.1080/01434632.2012.734509

Zembylas, M., & Schutz, P. A. (2009). Research on teachers' emotions in education: Findings, practical implications and future agenda. In P. A. Schutz & M. Zembylas (Eds.), Advances in teacher emotion research (pp. 367–378). Springer.

Chapter 3
Local English Teacher Identities in a Globalized Economy

David Hayes

Abstract In many countries where English is the first foreign language in state educational systems, teachers of English are on the front line as governments attempt to increase language competence amongst school leavers, ostensibly to meet the demands of the global economy. They are subject to multiple pressures and often publicly criticized for 'failing' when targets for improved student outcomes in English are not realized. This occurs despite a lack of adequate preparation and support for teachers and unrealistic curriculum expectations in the context. This chapter explores teachers' perceptions of their roles and their identities as local teachers of a global language in Thailand, a country where teachers are traditionally seen as agents of a national language and culture which is inculcated through formal education. Thai society is acknowledged to be hierarchical and the established role of the teacher is as an unquestioned provider of knowledge. This role is at odds with the expectations of the curriculum for English that the teacher should be a facilitator and scaffolder of students' learning in a collaborative classroom with frequent opportunities for language practice. Themes discussed here are expected to resonate with the experiences of teachers in similar contexts elsewhere in the world.

Keywords English as a foreign language · Globalization and education · 'Non-native' language teacher identity · Teaching and context · Educational inequality

3.1 Influences on Identity Formation: The English Language, Globalization and Education

It is now commonplace for governments around the world to declare that proficiency in English is a necessity for national economic competitiveness in a global market-place of goods, services and intellectual capital and that fluency in the language greatly enhances life chances for its learners. This is true irrespective of the

D. Hayes (✉)
Brock University, St. Catharines, ON, Canada
e-mail: dhayes@brocku.ca

© The Author(s), under exclusive license to Springer Nature Switzerland AG 2022
K. Sadeghi, F. Ghaderi (eds.), *Theory and Practice in Second Language Teacher Identity*, Educational Linguistics 57, https://doi.org/10.1007/978-3-031-13161-5_3

economic level of development of a country. For example, Erling (2017) analyzed the ideological interconnections between English and development in less-developed economies and noted that "English is commonly associated with high social, cultural and economic capital, and English language skills are often positioned in language planning documents in low-income contexts as a means of boosting the economy and increasing opportunities for individuals" (p. 391). Similarly, in the highly developed economy of South Korea, former President Myung-Bak Lee once said bluntly that "English ability is the competitive power of individuals and states" (Lee et al., 2010, p. 337). The consequence of this commitment to English as a language of economic opportunity for millions of students in schools worldwide is that:

> For the first time in foreign language teaching history, national governments and individuals worldwide seem to see teaching a language (English) to all learners in state schools as an important means of increasing the human capital on which future national economic development and political power depends (Wedell, 2013, p. 275).

While it is also clearly regarded by parents of children in school as an aspirational language in many contexts (Enever, 2018), the extent to which fluency in English is a panacea for individual and national economic development remains contested. Labour market evidence indicates that English is an asset for employment when it is linked to high levels of education in a specific, marketable skill such as information technology or engineering, but is not sufficient in itself to guarantee economic advancement (Rassool, 2013). As Ricento (2018, p. 221) concluded, "the role and utility of English worldwide is a vehicle for some people, in some economic sectors, mainly the knowledge economy, but is generally not connected to socioeconomic mobility for the vast majority of the global workforce".

Nonetheless, governments continue to expand the teaching of English across entire education systems though the challenges of doing so in a way that will actually produce the desired levels of proficiency are greatly under-estimated. Most notably, the decision to introduce English into the school curriculum from the earliest grades is often done without first ensuring that there is an adequate supply of teachers who are sufficiently competent in the language and who are appropriately trained in language teaching to be able to provide instruction to all children in the system (Hayes, 2008). As a result, the outcomes from investing significant material and human resources into English teaching are poor in many countries (see, e.g., Ngo, 2021, for information on Viet Nam; Sayer, 2015, on Mexico; Matear, 2008, on Chile). Where there are exceptions to generally low levels of achievement in English in educational systems, these are often to be found amongst children from higher socio-economic groups who attend prestigious well-resourced schools in urban areas where teaching is of higher quality and whose families also have the financial means to access private tuition. In contrast to such prestigious schools, the quality of teaching and provision of resources amongst schools in poorer urban and rural areas in countries such as Thailand, the principal focus of this chapter, is much less favourable – even before the provision of English is taken into account – and results in considerable inequity in learning outcomes. For Thailand, Lathapipat (2018, p. 351) observed that:

In terms of location, the disadvantaged and poorer performing students are clearly concentrated in rural village schools [and] the performance gap between students in village schools and those in large city schools has also expanded over the 2003–2012 period. The difference in the average learning outcome between the two groups in 2012 is estimated to be around 1.8 years of formal schooling.

This 'performance gap' is inevitably replicated in English classes and, increasingly, it seems that English is complicit in exacerbating educational inequality rather than diminishing it (Hayes, 2011).

Nor, with respect to the economic value of English at the national level, does available data support the claims for it as a necessity for continuing development. Arcand and Grin (2013, p. 262) have argued that "widespread competence in a dominant language such as English is in no manner associated with a higher level of economic development, when the latter is measured by its most common incarnation of GDP per capita". This conclusion is reflected in the data from Thailand, which has enjoyed significant rates of economic expansion across recent decades despite its perceived deficiencies in English language proficiency at the national level. GDP growth from 1994–2019 averaged 3.73% (https://tradingeconomics.com/thailand/gdp-growth-annual), a period which includes the major downturns of the 1997 Asian financial crisis and the 2008 global financial crisis, in addition to the negative economic impact of significant political turbulence in 2006, 2010 and 2013–14. It is these financial and political events which can be directly linked to GDP rates rather than the country's English language proficiency levels. For example, in 2013–14 when violent political protests resulted in 28 deaths and more than 800 injuries and gave rise to a military coup, GDP growth declined from 6.5% in 2012 to 0.8% in 2014 before recovering post-coup to 2.9% in 2015 and 4.1% by 2018 (Asian Development Bank, 2019). At the same time, Thailand's performance in the English First (EF) English Proficiency Index (EPI), which is often used by governments as an indicator of a country's success or failure in learning the language which they deem important for economic success, was consistently towards the bottom of the rankings. In 2019, Thailand ranked 74th out of 100 countries in the EPI and 89th in 2020. Regionally, it ranked 20th out of 24 countries in 2020 with a 'very low proficiency' rating which it has held since the inception of the rankings in 2011 except for 2017 and 2018 when it received a 'low proficiency' rating (English First, 2020). Thus, there appears to be an obvious correlation between financial and political crises and a decline in GDP, but no apparent connection between Thailand's GDP rates and its position in the EF EPI rankings.

Thailand's poor showing in the EPI rankings relative to its regional neighbours has been a source of particular concern since the establishment of the ASEAN Economic Community (AEC) in 2015, for which English is the designated working language. Fears that Thai school-leavers and university graduates will be unable to compete for jobs with their peers from ASEAN countries who have higher standards of English are commonplace in the public discourse (Mala, 2016). The tourist industry is thought to provide an exception to this general trend but, though English is used widely in interaction with many tourists, this does not often go far beyond basic proficiency; and, in any case, the largest number of visitors to Thailand has come from China in recent years – 11 million in 2019 (Thaiwebsites.com, 2021) – for whom Mandarin is obviously the preferred language rather than English. The realities of English language use in Thailand, then, do not appear to be consistent with the perceptions about its overwhelming importance to the country. This mismatch has practical consequences for the teaching of English in government schools and for the identities of those teachers required to teach the language.

3.2 Influences on Identity Formation: The English Language and the Thai Education System

In Thailand, English is taught in all government schools from the beginning of primary school through to Grade 12. Until recently, just 1 h a week was allocated to English classes in Grades 1–3 and 2 h a week in Grades 4–6, making a total of 360 h of instruction by the end of primary school. In secondary schools, hours of instruction typically total 90 h per year (Noom-ura, 2013). In October 2020, however, the Office of the Basic Education Commission (OBEC), which oversees education in primary and secondary schools within the Ministry of Education, announced that all students would be required to study the language for 5 h a week "with the objective to increase learners' English proficiency to level B2 [on the CEFR – the Common European Framework of Reference], or upper-intermediate" by the time they left school (Bangkok Post, 2020). It remains to be seen whether this initiative will come to fruition as no information was given about whether the additional hours would be taken from other subjects or whether the school day would be extended to accommodate the extra hours for English. Indeed, this is the second time such an announcement has been made, with the then Deputy Minister of Education making a similar – unfulfilled – statement that instructional hours for English for children in Grades 1–3 would be increased from one to five beginning in November 2016 (Bangkok Post, 2016).

The Basic Education Core Curriculum (Ministry of Education [MOE], 2008) specifies the general content for 'foreign languages', though details are only given for English (content for other foreign languages is left to individual schools to decide, if they are able to offer them). Overall objectives are as follows:

> The learning area for foreign languages is aimed at enabling learners to acquire a favourable attitude towards foreign languages, the ability to use foreign languages for communicating in various situations, seeking knowledge, engaging in a livelihood and pursuing further education at higher levels (MOE, 2008, p. 252).

The prescribed teaching methodology accords with the Communicative Language Teaching (CLT) paradigm, emphasizing meaningful communication in the language, and reflects the stipulations of the National Education Act (NEA) of

B.E. 2542 (1999) concerning learner-centred teaching. The NEA was itself a major reform which attempted to transform the education system, moving it away from being a vehicle for transmission of knowledge and conformity and creating a system which "shall aim at human development with desirable balance regarding knowledge, critical thinking, capability, virtue and social responsibility" (Office of the National Education Commission, 1999, p. 12).

But, irrespective of the reforms encapsulated in the 1999 NEA and the provisions of the 2008 Basic Education Core Curriculum, teaching in general and English language teaching in particular is still said to be dominated by a rote-learning, grammar-translation model as can be seen in the complaint in the Bangkok Post (2016) editorial that the education system should "Rid English of rote-learning". One reason for this reliance on 'traditional' methods is likely to be the language levels of many Thai teachers of English, particularly in primary schools where teachers are predominantly general class teachers who may have little knowledge of the language and received little training in how to teach it, though there are also concerns about teachers' proficiency levels in secondary schools too. Data from a recent large-scale professional development programme involving 8046 primary school and 7126 secondary school teachers revealed that 9.3% were at A1 and 50.6% at A2 level on the CEFR (Hayes, 2018). This "Basic User" level is generally held to be well below the minimum required to function effectively as a teacher of a foreign language, with B1 (Independent User) regarded as the minimum and C1 (Proficient User) the desirable level (Enever, 2011). More than half of these Thai teachers (59.9%) were thus below this minimum, almost a third (32%) were at the minimum level of B1, while just 7.6% were above the minimum with a B2 level, and a mere 0.6% reached the desirable C1 level (Hayes, 2018). Or, put another way, only 7.6% of the teachers had attained the B2 level that OBEC announced in 2020 as the new goal for students exiting school. These levels are confirmed by other research where even secondary school teachers themselves seemed to think that "A2 is normal" for their own English proficiency level (Franz & Teo, 2018). Hence, teachers have little sense of a social identity as proficient speakers of English and are unable to present themselves to their students as models of English language users.

The value of defining teachers' professional identities simply in terms of their proficiency levels on a scale which was not designed for their circumstances is highly questionable, of course; and these proficiency levels are given here not to castigate teachers, whose levels of English are limited by the quality of their own experiences as students in school and as teachers in training in university, but simply to state an important aspect of reality for English language teaching in many classrooms in Thailand. Moreover, given this constraint and that of the surrounding context where English has little use beyond the classroom, it is difficult to envisage how teachers in many schools will be able to use productively the additional hours of instruction the Ministry of Education has asked for: if teachers in primary schools, for example, do not have the skills and resources to teach 1 h of English a week effectively, how can they be expected to teach English for 5 h? This is particularly the case in rural areas where teachers' identities are closely bound up with the

Thai-speaking community surrounding the school. Teachers and students in the largest cities such as Bangkok, which prior to the Covid-19 pandemic, had millions of foreign visitors each year, may have some opportunity, however restricted, to develop social identities as English language speakers but those in rural areas will have no such opportunities for identity development. The policy of providing additional school time for English is, then, unlikely to have any impact other than to exacerbate existing rural-urban divides in levels of achievement.

3.3   Teachers, Schools and 'Thainess' as an Identity Marker

The Ministry of Education operates a top-down, heavily centralized decision-making process. Teachers in government schools in Thailand are civil servants who have to take an examination in order to become certified teachers. The examination does not assess practical teaching skills or subject knowledge, however, but is heavily theoretical with multiple-choice tests on such topics as government regulations and educational ethics (Watson Todd & Darasawang, 2021). The selection system thus promotes a collective teacher identity which is bureaucratic and representative of the state rather than one of autonomous professionalism operating in service of students' needs. This collective identity is enhanced by practices in schools such as the requirement on certain days of the week for teachers, like all other government servants, to wear their official uniforms to work. These uniforms have epaulettes indicating their civil servant grade. In many respects this appears to an outsider to be a quasi-military uniform and is the most obvious manifestation of a graded, hierarchical system which, in a school, has the director at its apex and novice teachers at the base. This hierarchical system reflects Thai society at large and is operationalized in relationships in schools at all levels, as Hallinger (2004, p. 68) explains:

> Principals naturally expect their orders to be followed with relatively little discussion, few questions from staff, and no overt dissent. This would be the same in terms of relationships between principals and their superordinates, as well as between teachers and their students.

The education system thus socializes teachers into a normative Thai identity, one in which the hierarchy is preserved and everyone adopts the identity ascribed to them within the hierarchy.

Reinforcing this socialization, the military government which was in power from 2014–19 (and replaced by a civilian government dominated by former military figures with the coup leader as prime minister) issued twelve 'precepts' which students have to recite at the start of every school day and which, amongst other things, appear designed to reinforce the hierarchical relationships between younger generations and their elders as well as adherence to prescribed notions of 'Thainess' (Watson Todd & Darasawang, 2021). This Thainess reflects acceptable Thai identity and is connected to national values which derive from the 'Twelve Cultural Mandates' originally propounded between 1939 and 1942. Mandate 9, for example, focuses on the centrality of the Thai language to being Thai.

(1) Thai people must extol, honour and respect the Thai language, and must feel honoured to speak it; (2) Thai people must consider it the duty of a good citizen to study the national language, and must at least be able to read and write; Thai people must also consider it their important duty to assist and support citizens who do not speak Thai or cannot read Thai to learn it (Cabinet Secretariat, 1940, p. 78; cited in Draper, 2019, p. 233).

Mandate 9 appears in another form in the Basic Education Core Curriculum which aims to inculcate "Knowledge, skills and culture in [Thai] language application for communication; delight in and appreciation of Thai wisdom; and pride in national language" (MOE, 2008, p. 10). Problems of social identity for both teachers and students are created by the hierarchical nature of Thai society and its emphasis on the centrality of the Thai language and Thai values, particularly respect for elders and those in authority, which conflicts with the espoused national goal of developing citizens who are comfortable with an alternate English-knowing identity, participating in a globalized economy which is dependent for its growth on creativity, critical thinking and problem-solving skills.

3.4 Experiences of English Teachers and Teaching in Thai Schools

Teachers of English in government schools in Thailand are thus at the intersection of the global (the language which their government has deemed is necessary for economic success) and the local (in terms of their place as teachers in schools in Thai society). In the remainder of this chapter, I will discuss teachers' practical responses to this positioning, focusing on the lived experiences of Thai teachers of English in government schools. The data derives from interviews conducted with a selection of teachers who had been participating in a recent, large-scale Continuing Professional Development (CPD) programme across the country and also includes occasional comments from interviews with their students as these pertain to issues of their teachers' classroom behaviours which reflect their identity. All teachers' names have been anonymized and are preceded by 'Ajarn', the honorific for 'teacher' in Thai. The CPD programme in which the teachers were engaged had a dual focus, to enhance the teaching of English in primary and secondary schools and to improve teachers' own language skills. The experiences of these teachers are illustrative of a number of themes which are pertinent to English teaching in Thailand generally. As with all qualitative research, however, there is no claim that these particular teachers' experiences are conclusively generalizable to the wider population of teachers in the country though they are reflected in other published research to which I have referred in this chapter. With respect to wider applicability, readers in other contexts will determine for themselves the extent to which the experiences of these teachers resonate with their own issues and concerns.

Even though the current Thai school curriculum has been in use since 2008 and the NEA first promoted the concept of learner-centred teaching in 1999, the continuing use of 'traditional' teacher-centred teaching styles over the decades since then, and which the Bangkok Post (2016) editorial complained of, is given credence by teachers' own comments on the scale of change that a communicative, student-centred classroom would entail in their current circumstances. Ajarn Malee, from the north-east of Thailand, noted:

> The students, as well, are not used to this educational system or the way to learn. Thai teachers are used to applying a traditional teaching style and if one day it's changed completely, so the students might be shocked. We need to give them some time.

This view is echoed by a teacher from the Bangkok region, Ajarn Wanida, who spoke of the reactions of her students as she tried to implement greater classroom use of English as recommended on her training course:

> When things get changed for the first time, students would feel a little weird about that, but later they get used to it. When I first used English in my class, the students didn't seem to understand much but they changed a bit through time. When I first spoke English in the class, they were like 'What?' and asked me to translate into Thai. Sometimes I translate for them and they get familiar with what I said.

Here we can see an acknowledgement that neither teachers nor students appear to be used to the learner-centred teaching-learning style, alongside the communicative approach entailing use of English for communication, and that the classroom behaviours required do not align with their normative Thai-speaking teacher and student identities. Though Ajarn Wanida indicates that she has begun to use more English in her classes, it is also evident that her students' needs dictate that she does not immediately break with previous methods but continue to translate English into their shared language so as to enhance understanding of the lesson content. Whether this is a transitional phase for her, and for many other teachers, may depend more on what happens in society beyond the classroom than the repeated pronouncements and training courses promoting learner-centred CLT. If society beyond the classroom continues to prioritize the cultivation of 'Thainess', it will be difficult for teachers and their students to cultivate and become comfortable with English-using identities.

The difficulty of realizing an English-knowing identity is evident in other comments from students and teachers. Students, when asked about what happens in English classes, confirm that with their Thai teachers of English the focus is very formal, as we see from these remarks by two Grade 11 students in a secondary school in the northeast of the country.

> [We study] something serious, like grammar and everything in the book.
> Mostly grammar and vocabulary. Mostly from the textbook.

In many classrooms, then, the learner-centred CLT-based curriculum continues to be at odds with prevailing norms of teacher and student behaviour. In part this is because the mandated curriculum requires a degree of English language use which is difficult to achieve in many classrooms. Working in a major city in the north, Ajarn Achara said that using English is:

> not real, because in our society we don't really use English and the students know I can speak Thai. I always try to speak English with my students and they always reply in Thai because they know I can understand Thai. That's the problem for me. [...] All teachers, I think, are willing to speak English but the society doesn't ... like, we use Thai.

In this respect, there is identity conflict amongst both teachers and students as speakers of English which is at odds with Thainess where, as we have noted, the Thai language assumes a central position. Even though the government promotes an international, English-knowing outlook for economic purposes, their emphasis on Thainess inevitably takes precedence for teachers in a society where deference to hierarchy is paramount in school relationships (Hallinger, 2004).

The mismatch between the expectations of the curriculum and its communicative methodology and what can be carried out in the average classroom, is exacerbated by a further mismatch, alluded to above, that is with the actual needs of the students. The curriculum, as in most educational systems, assumes lockstep progress through the years but this does not always equate to actual learning and students may enter a particular grade without the prior knowledge needed. For example, Ajarn Suchada, teaching first year secondary school students in a school in a southern province, noted that *"Many of our M1[1] students cannot read English"*, creating a situation in which additional assistance is required before they can even begin anything approaching grade-level work. As she noted, *"So we do a special camp for them to practice this, including using phonic technique"*, though it must be remembered by this time the students' English levels will be so far below their deemed grade level that the task of catching up is immensely difficult, however much extra support teachers provide.

In another example, Ajarn Kannika, who teaches in a large secondary school in a lower north-eastern province, discussed her classroom reality and alluded to the conflict with students' needs.

> We have big classes, many students. Some of the [communicative] activities cannot be applied in the real [classroom] situation. And they don't serve what our students really want.

Another teacher from the same school, Ajarn Nuntana, clarified students' goals for studying English.

> Their purpose is further study. Not only communication, because in their daily life English communication is not the first factor. We are not in a tourist area and they want to continue their further education.

Thus, in this case, teachers are first of all physically constrained by classroom conditions and then divided between the official prescriptions to focus on communicative methods, reinforced in their recent CPD programme, and their students' avowed needs to pass an exam to enter university. When this happens, the teachers' understanding of their primary duty is that they should do what is necessary to help their students to pass the university entrance exam even if this does not accord with curriculum requirements. Indeed, it is not just the washback from university entrance exam that influences teachers' perceptions of their roles, but from other examinations too, as Ajarn Nuntana made clear:

---

[1] 'M' refers to the secondary level of schooling, 'Mathayom', of which M1 is the first secondary grade.

> I use the [communicative] techniques sometimes, not often. It is because maybe we are
> preparing the students for the tests, such as O-NET,[2] or something like that.

Of course, change is occurring in some areas but this may take place within the
context of more familiar lesson styles. For example, Ajarn Anong, working in an
urban northern school explained the impact that her recent training course had had:

> We used to rely a lot on textbooks. However, after the [training] camp, we look more into
> classroom activities and group work. We play many of the games and students are looking
> forward to it. They are eager to know what game they would play and when, whether it's
> before or during the lesson. In the past, we let students read the textbook followed by doing
> exercises but now we have more participation from the students. We now communicate
> more with students in the classroom when teaching vocabulary.

It appears that teachers like Ajarn Anong may use games and other communicative
activities as an added extra, rather than something which is an integral part of the
lesson. Change is, of course, often slow to be realized and teachers' understandings
develop over time but whether the changes the ministry has been promoting for more
than 20 years will ever take root is difficult to judge. Certainly, teachers' comments
indicate that they see themselves first and foremost as serving the immediate needs
of their students, and this is not displaced by the vision of the Ministry of Education
of them as instruments of change in response to global economic needs, even when
they attend CPD programmes and see the value in theory of the communicative
approach to developing proficiency in English.

Furthermore, connected to their preference to use a shared language, there
remains a perception amongst students that English is something only to be used
with foreign speakers of the language, rather than with their Thai teachers. This
perception is reinforced by the practice in those schools which have the financial
resources to do so to recruit native-speakers of English to take speaking and listening
classes, leaving Thai teachers to focus on grammar, reading and writing. Reflecting a
widespread practice, Ajarn Kannika explained that in her school:

> Foreign teachers only teach listening and speaking, in order to get the students to experience
> the native English-speaking teachers, so the students are not afraid of speaking English.
> That's the whole point. That's what we want.

At issue, then, is the degree to which Thai teachers of English are able to cultivate
identities as English speakers and present themselves as successful role models when
their opportunities to do so are limited by the presence of native speakers in their
schools and by their students' resource to their shared first language in their own
English lessons.

---

[2]O-NET is the Ordinary National Educational Test administered by the National Institute of
Educational Testing Service at the end of Grades 6, 9 and 12.

3.5 Conclusion

Given that a communicative approach to the teaching of English has been recommended since the early 1990s (Hayes, 1995), even prior to the 1999 NEA, it may be thought surprising that grammar-translation style classes with teacher-fronted lessons appear to remain the norm in so many classrooms. However, the continuance of this traditional method is readily understandable if we consider the social context in which English is taught. The government's insistence on students reciting the twelve 'precepts' at the start of every school day prioritizes conformity in a hierarchical society, one which is based on respect for authority. Allied to this is the traditional view of teachers as possessing knowledge which they pass on to their students who honour them by not questioning their knowledge, lest they 'lose face'. The traditional style of teaching allows teachers to avoid the potential for unpredictable language use which may put them in situations where the focus of classroom instruction is beyond their control. Hence, for many Thai teachers of English there is a conflict between the identity which the curriculum and the mandates of a centralized educational bureaucracy attempt to impose on them as proficient speakers of English who use the language in classroom communicative activities with their students and the identity that accords with the reality of their teaching circumstances as teachers whose main function is to help their students to pass examinations which are crucial to their future prospects. They are also first and foremost government servants and, as such, models of Thainess rather than models of successful speakers of an international language.

Government mandates position teachers of English as agents of change for society at large. They are expected to assume identities as speakers of an international language, teaching in a learner-centred communicative way, facilitating societal engagement in a globalized economy. This is at odds with norms of behaviour in schools and does not reflect lived reality in a hierarchical society beyond schools where powerful conservative forces militate against teacher and student agencies as active participants in a changing society. Rather, then, than castigating teachers for being obstacles to educational progress, governments and the wider society, as represented by national media, would do well to listen to teachers' voices about the realities of their schools and classrooms. It is difficult to expect teachers of English to be in the vanguard of change when the government promotes conformity and idealized notions of Thainess in schools as a bulwark against change in society more widely, thus severely restricting the range of possible identities open to them. In these circumstances, local teacher identities are always likely to take precedence over chimerical English-speaking global identities.

References

Arcand, J.-L., & Grin, F. (2013). Language in economic development: Is English special and is linguistic fragmentation bad? In E. J. Erling & P. Sergeant (Eds.), *English and development: Policy, pedagogy and globalization* (pp. 243–266). Multilingual Matters.

Asian Development Bank. (2019). *Asian development outlook 2019*. Strengthening disaster resil-ience. https://www.adb.org/sites/default/files/publication/492711/ado2019.pdf

Bangkok Post. (2016, June 8). *Rid English of rote-learning*. Bangkok Post. https://www.bangkokpost.com/opinion/opinion/1004593/rid-english-of-rote-learning.

Bangkok Post. (2020, October 15). *Intensive push to lift English proficiency*. Bangkok Post. https://www.bangkokpost.com/thailand/general/2002315/intensive-push-to-lift-english-proficiency.

Draper, J. (2019). Language education policy in Thailand. In R. Kirkpatrick & A. J. Liddicoat (Eds.), *The Routledge international handbook of language education policy in Asia* (pp. 229–242). Routledge.

Enever, J. (2011). Policy. In J. Enever (Ed.), *ELLiE, early language learning in Europe* (pp. 23–42). British Council.

Enever, J. (2018). *Policy and politics in global primary English*. Oxford University Press.

English First. (2020). *EF English proficiency index*. A ranking of 100 countries and regions by English skills. https://www.ef.com/assetscdn/WIBIwq6RdJvcD9bc8RMd/legacy/__/~/media/centralefcom/epi/downloads/full-reports/v10/ef-epi-2020-english.pdf

Erling, E. J. (2017). Language planning, English language education and development aid in Bangladesh. *Current Issues in Language Planning, 18*(4), 388–406. https://doi.org/10.1080/14664208.2017.1331496

Franz, J., & Teo, A. (2018). 'A2 is normal' = Thai secondary school English teachers' encounter with the CEFR. *RELC Journal, 49*(3), 322–338. https://doi.org/10.1177/0033688217738816

Hallinger, P. (2004). Meeting the challenges of cultural leadership: The changing roles of principals in Thailand. *Discourse: Studies in the Cultural Politics of Education, 25*(1), 61–73. https://doi.org/10.1080/0159630042000178482

Hayes, D. (1995). In-service teacher development: Some basic principles. *ELT Journal, 49*(3), 252–261. https://doi.org/10.1093/elt/49.3.252

Hayes, D. (2008). *Primary English language teaching in Vietnam*. A research study.

Hayes, D. (2011). Primary English language teaching: Another obstacle to achievement for the world's poor?/ La enseñanza del inglés en la Educación Primaria: ¿otro obstáculo Para el logro educativo de los más desfavorecidos? In P. Powell-Davies (Ed.), *Word for word: The social, economic and political impact of Spanish and English/palabra por palabra: El impactico social, económico y político del Español y del Inglés* (pp. 329–344). British Council.

Hayes, D. (2018). *Regional English training Centre project final evaluation for the Office of the Basic Education Commission, Ministry of Education, & British Council*. Unpublished report.

Lathapipat, D. (2018). Inequalities in educational attainment. In G. W. Fry (Ed.), *Education in Thailand: An old elephant in search of a new mahout* (pp. 345–372). Springer.

Lee, J.-H., Han, M. W., & McKerrow, R. E. (2010). English or perish: How contemporary South Korea received, accommodated, and internalized English and American modernity. *Language and Intercultural Communication, 10*(4), 337–357. https://doi.org/10.1080/14708477.2010.497555

Mala, D. (2016, January 2). *Thais fear AC English barrier*. Bangkok Post. https://www.bangkokpost.com/thailand/general/813756/thais-fear-ac-english-barrier. Accessed September 2, 2021.

Matear, A. (2008). English language learning and education policy in Chile: Can English really open doors for all? *Asia Pacific Journal of Education, 28*(2), 131–147. https://doi.org/10.1080/02188790802036679

Ministry of Education. (2008). *The basic education core curriculum B.E* (Vol. 2551/A.D, p. 2008). Ministry of Education.

Ngo, X. (2021). Vietnam's trillion-dong attempt to reform English education: A laudable reform or a costly failure? *English Today, 37*(2), 115–119. https://doi.org/10.1017/S0266078419000440

Noom-ura, S. (2013). English teaching problems in Thailand and Thai teachers' professional development needs. *English Language Teaching, 6*(11), 139–147. https://doi.org/10.5539/elt.v6n11p139

Office of the National Education Commission. (1999). *National education act of B.E. 2542 (1999).* *Office of the Prime Minister.* Bangkok.

Rassool, N. (2013). *Global issues in language, education and development: Perspectives from postcolonial countries.* Multilingual Matters.

Ricento, T. (2018). Globalization, language policy and the role of English. In J. W. Tollefson & M. Pérez-Milans (Eds.), *The Oxford handbook of language policy and planning* (pp. 221–235). Oxford University Press.

Sayer, P. (2015). Expanding global language education in public primary schools: The national English programme in Mexico. *Language, Culture and Curriculum, 28*(3), 257–275. https://doi.org/10.1080/07908318.2015.1102926

Tourist arrivals to Thailand by nationality in 2019. (2021). Thaiwebsites.com. Retrieved September 3, 2021, from https://www.thaiwebsites.com/tourists-nationalities-Thailand.asp

Watson Todd, R., & Darasawang, P. (2021). English language teacher education in Thailand: A mixture of global and local. In A. B. M. Tsui (Ed.), *English language teaching and teacher education in East Asia* (pp. 195–215). Cambridge University Press.

Wedell, M. (2013). More than just 'technology': English language teaching initiatives as complex educational changes. In H. Coleman (Ed.), *Dreams and realities: Developing countries and the English language* (pp. 275–296). British Council.

Chapter 4
Identity Formation in Beginning English Teachers

Ian Thompson

Abstract Developing the pedagogy necessary to teach a disciplinary subject to a variety of young people, alongside the ability to use formative and summative assessment to help their students to progress, are complex developmental processes for beginning teachers. Yet just as language and thought have potential developmental functions, so context has a formative role in identity formation. Beginning English teachers face at least two contexts that impact on their social situations of development: their position as learners, within the academic environment of a university; and within the specific professional contexts of their placement schools. These social situations intersect in a complex and dialectical interplay between theory and practice. The focus on the complexity of identity development in this chapter develops a view of teaching and learning as a process through which beginning teachers as learners take on what is valued in a culture and, in turn, develop the agency that allows them to begin to contribute to that culture. The chapter will use the example of beginning teachers' learning to teach English within a school and university partnership.

Keywords Identity development · Beginning teachers · Social situation of development · Teaching and learning · English school subject

4.1 Introduction

English as a school subject has historically suffered from a crisis of identify. Whilst English is regarded as a 'world language' or international lingua franca, spoken by around a billion as a second language, it is also the first language of some 400 million people. What constitutes the subject of 'English' and related questions of what content English teachers should be teaching, have long been contested areas of school curricula. These questions engender further questions into the complex and

I. Thompson (✉)
University of Oxford, Oxford, UK
e-mail: ian.thompson@education.ox.ac.uk

multiple identities of the English teacher. In English speaking countries, learning the pedagogy of English involves both teaching English as a language and the literature written in the English language. Beginning English teachers are both subject specialists with strong academic credentials in specific areas of English (most frequently an aspect of literature) and subject learners within the sociocultural and multicultural settings of schools and classrooms. This chapter is concerned with identity formation in beginning teachers of English. Developing the pedagogy necessary to teach a disciplinary subject to a variety of young people, alongside the ability to use formative and summative assessment to help their students to progress, are complex developmental processes for beginning teachers. This chapter argues that in ways analogous to the potential developmental functions of language and thought, context has a formative role in identity formation within specific social situations of development. The analysis of beginning teachers' social situations of development presented in this chapter explores the complex relationship between English subject student teachers' individual learning and the social situations in which that learning occurs.

4.2   The English Teacher in English Schools

The state school education system in England, in contrast to some degree to the other jurisdictions of the UK, is highly performative with published league tables and punitive accountability systems (Ball, 2018; Thompson, 2020). Within this competitive system, English as a discipline in English schools is both a high status and a high stakes subject. It is the subject that perhaps produces the most controversy and argument in terms of curriculum design and delivery at both primary and secondary school level. It is a 'core' or compulsory subject in secondary schools (in primary schools, students have lessons called 'literacy'). English as a subject has been subject to continual change since the introduction of the National Curriculum in 1988. The high stakes status of the subject has increased with the use of English alongside Mathematics as indicators of success in subject specific General Certificates of Secondary Education (GCSE) both in the reporting of post 16 examination results as well as the English Baccalaureate (a school accountability measure based on the proportion of children who secure a good pass in English, Maths, Science, a humanity subject and a modern language GCSE).

English departments teach at least two GCSEs for most students: English Language and English Literature. Media Studies and Film Studies are also often taught by the English department. Until 2014–15 it was English Language that counted in the reported school overall success data but now schools can count either Language or literature. The majority of qualified English teachers are English Literature graduates and often feel uncomfortable teaching linguistics and grammar. Indeed, Ellis (2007) has argued that the very notion of what constitutes subject knowledge is both contested and complex and that English as a subject in schools requires different forms of knowledge from the requirements of English Language and English Literature courses at university degree levels.

> Subject knowledge is communal, a form of collective knowledge. The 'subject', specifically, is the school subject – which has an important relationship with, but is not identical to, the university subject, or governed by it. Those who teach the subject in schools (just as those who teach the university subject) – collectively – are the principal sources of authority over the production of the subject in schools. In this task, they can be supported by teacher educators and educational researchers, advisers and inspectors, and many others. And with this authority comes responsibility for development and for continually examining the boundaries of 'what counts' as subject knowledge (Ellis, 2007, pp. 458–459).

This conception of the teachers of subject knowledge in schools raises a key point when considering the developing identities of beginning English teachers. McIntyre and Hobson (2016) argue that 'an important aspect of a teacher's identity formation involves their identification with the subject they teach' (p. 143). In the case of English, historically, English as a subject in English schools has seen political debates about whether literacy should be viewed as a skills-based activity and literacy as a tool for making meaning and sense in both oral and written modes of communication.

Beginning English teachers, in common with all those learning to teach, face the challenge of learning to understand and use the knowledge that matters in the school context and to pitch their teaching at the appropriate level for their learners to develop. They also have to understand the challenges that their particular students face in the literacy curricula of schools. For example, official government statistics (DfE, 2021) show that there are around 1.6 million students in state maintained schools in England that have a first language other than English. This figure represents 19.2% of the school population. Of course, those students who use English as an Additional Language (EAL) are not a homogenous group but one with a diverse range of prior school experience, exposure to English, and cultural and social backgrounds. English classrooms, particularly in the cities, are also increasingly multicultural and multilingual at a time when the restoration of the literary canon in English literature reflects monocultural or white, predominantly male, and middle-class perspectives of texts (Nelson-Addy et al., 2019).

English teachers need to avoid excluding the interests and experiences of a diversity of learners and to understand the diverse cultural worlds of their students. They also need to understand what Schwab (1978) describes as substantive knowledge (key concepts) and syntactic knowledge (ways of knowing and representing) of the subject. Indeed, there are many 'subjects' of English study including using and understanding: a variety of literary forms and narrative structures; aspects of linguistics; and issues related to media, film, and cultural studies. This involves planning lessons that draw on both 'students' current and developing understandings of everyday concepts such as love and loss and also introduces new concepts such as literary criticism or linguistic analysis' (Thompson, 2015a). This ability to think like a teacher of English is closely linked to professional identity development.

4.3   Identity and the Beginning English Teacher

Research in the sociocultural and cultural historical traditions (e.g. Cole & Engeström, 1993; Edwards, 2017; Holland et al., 1998; Penuel & Wertsch, 1995; Tatto et al., 2019) highlights the critical role of mediation in identity formation, particularly in periods of crisis in development. Erikson's (e.g. Erikson, 1968) theory of psycho-social stages of crisis has been particularly influential in analyses of crises in psychological development particularly in identity formation in adolescence. However, researchers in the sociocultural tradition (e.g. Holland & Lachicotte, 2007; Penuel & Wertsch, 1995) point to the fundamental role of mediation for the study of identity formation. Holland and Lachicotte (2007) point out that Erikson viewed identity formation as individuals' attempts to answer the overarching question of who they are and what their place is in society than on the ways that identities are constructed in interaction with others. Penuel and Wertsch (1995) argue that whilst both Erikson and Vygotsky 'asserted the importance of cultural and historical resources in individual functioning' (p.91) they place different emphases on the unit of analysis: for Erikson the choices individuals make from these cultural tools to establish their identity and for Vygotsky 'the social origins of mental functioning and the role of signs and tools in mediating action' (p. 89).

The identity formation of beginning English teachers reflects the multiple and at times contradictory social and cultural demands involved in becoming a professional. Identity is a slippery term with many conflicting definitions. McIntyre and Hobson (2016), from the context of initial teacher education (ITE) (one year post graduate or three or four year teacher training programmes involving university and school partnerships), argue that identifies need to be viewed as 'multilayered, multifaceted, dynamic and constantly evolving or in continual flow' (p. 136). Hochstetler (2011) makes the case for an early focus on English teachers' developing identities in ITE courses and defines this work as 'thinking critically about what it means to be a teacher' (p. 256). This is a conception of identity within the professional contexts of schools and schooling and suggests that context is central to professional identity formation. Côté (2005) developed the concept of 'identity capital' involving young people's identity negotiation within specific social environments). Dreier (1999, 2009) has argued that we must conceptualise identity formation within the contexts of local social practices.

Identity formation is therefore both relational in terms of being formed in social practices and situated in particular places and cultures. Holland and Lachicotte (2007) define identity as 'a self-understanding to which one is emotionally attached and that informs one's behaviour and interpretations' (p. 104). Holland and Lachicotte's (2007) concept of the figured world refers to the way that individuals position themselves in relation to the 'socially and culturally constructed realms of interpretation and performance' (p.115). Identities that develop in activities in action emerge as a 'heuristic means to guide, authorize, legitimate, and encourage their own and others' behaviour' (Holland et al., 1998, p.18) and involve both the appropriation of professional knowledge and improvisation.

4.4   Transitions Through Social Situations of Development

Beginning teachers are in a process of complex transition in their identity as they move from learner to practitioner. This involves trying to translate their own subject domain expertise to the pedagogy required to teach young people. Holland and Lachicotte (2007) argue that the identities that individuals develop are products of both social and cultural encounters, mediated through social and professional experience and through interactions with others. From a sociocultural perspective, learning and identity formation are viewed as relational involving both social and situated cultural activity (Edwards, 2009, 2017; Moll & Arnot-Hopffer, 2005).

In English classes, the activities of writing, reading, speaking and listening in English subject classrooms are both distributed in the sense of the multiple actors who contribute to these acts of literacy and situated within the specific context of the classroom and school environment (Thompson & Wittek, 2016). Vygotsky (1987) argued that learning involves mediated activity through psychological tool usage and in particular the culturally acquired conceptual tool of language. Sociocultural theory also highlights the importance of social interaction and cultural contexts in the development of individual consciousness. Learning for the beginning teacher, in this sense is, rooted in the society and culture in which they develop. Edwards (2010) has argued that examining 'learning in practice' requires 'a focus on the changing relationship between learner and social situation of development' (p. 65). The development of beginning teachers is particularly complex as their experience is refracted through the multiple lenses that they encounter within schools and academia. Edwards (2010) argues that 'relationships change as learners take in what is culturally valued, consequently interpret their social worlds differently and therefore act in and on them in newly informed ways, which in turn impact on the social situations' (p. 64). In this sense, learners are active participants in their own learning. They are both changed by the social situations they encounter and actively renegotiate their social relations within them.

Vygotsky's (1997, 1998) concept of the social situation of development for children is characterised by developmental changes that arise from critical periods as the child or young person encounters contradictions between their own psychological development and the demands of the learning situation. Vygotsky's argument was that there are critical periods for development when the learner encounters contradictions between their own psychological development and the demands of the learning situation. These critical periods are both personal to the particular needs and history of the individual but they are also socially experienced and mediated by interaction with others. The key to development lies in the ability of individuals to perceive the limitations of the situation they are in and to imagine a different role for themselves (Holland et al., 1998).

Edwards (2009), Tatto et al. (2019) and others have applied the concept of the social situation to adults' learning in social settings. Tatto et al. (2019) argue that an analysis of beginning teachers' social situations of development requires a close focus on the complex relationship between individual learning and the social situations in which that learning occurs. As Edwards (2017) has argued, 'in con-trived and time-limited learning situations, such as schools and teacher education programmes, mediation from a more expert other is also needed' (p. 9). Mediation in the context of learning to teach involves a dynamic negotiation between the social situations they encounter and the beginning teachers' own experiences and under-standings that they bring to their learning. At times these preconceptions are based on deficit ideologies that pathologise learning difficulties in ways that are difficult to challenge over the course of their studies (Thompson et al., 2016). Beginning teachers enrolled in traditional university/school partnership courses also need to negotiate the practices and understandings involved in both the university and school settings that at times give out contradictory messages. In these situations, beginning teachers may experience transitions as challenging (Beach, 1999, 2003) as they involve crossing boundaries. Akkerman and Bakker (2011) define boundaries as 'sociocultural differences leading to discontinuity in action or interaction' (p. 133). From sociocultural and activity theory perspectives, whilst discontinuity might be challenging, this rupture also creates opportunities for negotiating a social situation of development through new understandings or changes in practice (Engeström, 2010; Engeström & Sannino, 2010; Tatto et al., 2019).

Beginning teachers then face at least two important educational contexts that impact on their social situation of development: their position as learners, within the academic environment of a university; and their position as learners within the specific professional contexts of their placement schools. Their experience is also mediated by both university tutors and school mentors. At times, these social situations intersect in a complex and dialectical interplay between theory and practice (McIntyre, 1993). At other times, the immediacy of the school or university setting may dominate the student teachers' time and thoughts. Crafter and Maunder (2012) argue that understanding this process involves a close focus on learning transitions. As Tatto et al. (2019) point out:

> An understanding of learning to teach needs to go beyond the concept of the transferable acquisition of pedagogical knowledge in different settings towards a more complex under-standing of the transitions involved. These transitions, between school and university and between school placements present both pedagogical challenges and opportunities (p. 51).

Dreier (2009) argues for the need for research to focus on the learning trajectories of individuals over time and across the different social practices that they encounter. However, beginning teachers' learning trajectories are complex and not necessarily linear (Burn et al., 2003). Zittoun (2006) has portrayed transitions as symbolic transitions that involve identity rupture through changes in cultural contexts, rela-tionships or interaction. In a study on youth development, she found that transitions involve processes of social relocation, knowledge construction and meaning-making (Zittoun, 2007). These categories have relevance for the transitions and potential moments of crisis encountered by beginning teachers.

4.5 The Mediation of Learning in ITE

Vygotsky (1987) argued that individual human development is mediated through interactions with others and through the use of mediational tools, especially psychological tools or signs (Daniels, 2014; Thompson, 2015b). Wertsch (1993) has advanced the view that mediated actions has to be the starting point for any analysis of development and should precede analysis at the individual level. The cultural tools involved in mediated action also reflect the cultural, historical and institutional dimensions in which they have developed and are subsequently enacted. This has important implications for the study of identity formation. Wertsch (2007) has also made a distinction between explicit and implicit mediation within a social situation of development. In the case of beginning teachers, they are not only acquiring the psychological tools for effective pedagogy but also engaging with the cultural assumptions that govern what are deemed to be appropriate ways of being a teacher in a particular school and in society as a whole.

In ITE programmes, the explicit mediation of university settings and mentor meetings is balanced and sometimes countered by the implicit mediation of the culture of personal experience or the cultural norms and expectations of the staff or subject room setting. Beginning teachers' ideas are formed and developed through this dialectical interplay between the explicit mediation of teacher education and the implicit mediation of learning to teach in the classroom.

A common curriculum task set by a university tutor or school mentor may be the deliberate introduction of a stimulus designed to mediate the experience for the beginning teacher of teaching a particular concept in a subject within a classroom setting. An example of this explicit mediation in the early stages of teaching practice is where the student teacher might be asked to plan a lesson which is actually taught by the mentor. The experience of planning for learning here is mediated both through observing the success of the lesson and through the subsequent discussion of the learning observed.

More implicit mediation might come from the experience of the student teacher planning and delivering a lesson that goes wrong. Task design in the English classroom involves teachers translating the curriculum into the tasks and activities designed to engage both the cognitive and affective processes involved in learners' development (Thompson, 2015a). However, the teaching of these tasks is mediated by the particular social interactions involved in classroom activities that may change the focus of the activity in ways not envisaged by the lesson planner. Doyle (1977) has previously described ways in which classroom tasks are negotiated between the students and the teacher, both anxious to avoid a breakdown in the social order. In this context, attempts to reflect on the process of classroom interaction for the beginning teacher can result in discussions around behaviour management strategies rather than the pedagogic appropriateness of the task for the students' learning. The mediation of the beginning teacher's learning may be implicit and difficult to understand.

To illustrate this, I will refer to a case of a beginning English teacher drawn from our previous study of the development of beginning teachers in England and the USA (Tatto et al., 2019). Megan was a beginning English teacher entering the second term of her year long ITE programme in a well established school/university partnership. She was a mature student in her late twenties who had extensive prior experience working with young people both as a classroom assistant and through research activities. She was exceptionally well qualified having obtained a first class degree in English and Modern Languages from an elite university as well as a Master's and a doctorate in Applied Linguistics from the same institution. Her language and linguistics background, alongside her advanced research interests in English as an Additional Language, marked her out from the majority of her beginning English teacher cohort who were English Literature specialists.

From the beginning of the course Megan was extremely sensitive to the language needs of the learners in her classroom. In her English subject knowledge audit at the start of the year Megan had identified teaching English grammar and sentence structure to mixed linguistic ability classes as a key target. These concerns reflected her identity as an applied linguist encapsulated in her belief in the central importance of semiotic mediation in the English classroom as well as the importance of understanding and using practical pedagogic tools. However, Megan's experience at school was heavily influenced by the dominant discourse and culture of the school which at the time of her placement focussed on behaviour management and social control in the classroom. Although the English department in her school placement were aware of her academic credentials and interests, she was viewed as a novice in the context of the classroom. Her mentor (school teacher responsible for assessing her progress as a beginning teacher) and other English teachers reported that she was making good progress as an English teacher in terms of lesson planning, but her targets were based on classroom management.

As part of the research project, a researcher observed Megan teach a mixed ability Year 7 (aged 11–12) English lesson. Megan's school mentor also observed the lesson. The lesson and the feedback session immediately after the lesson were video recorded and subsequently analysed. The lesson was from a sequence of lessons on a novel aimed at adolescents. The lesson was about control: both of atmosphere (behaviour) and learning. The first 22 of the 50 minutes available were given over to silent reading and procedural tasks with very little pedagogic purpose. When the main task was introduced, there was very little time given over to classroom talk aside from teacher direction and explanation as well as some clarification in response to students' questions. The task outlined an individual response to text using a highly structured scaffold that gave students very little opportunity for creative responses to the text. Students were actively dissuaded from talking about the task or discussing ideas. Megan's reflections after the lesson were interesting as they suggest an unease with mixed-ability teaching. Indeed, she seemed to equate low ability labels with disruptive behaviour:

> The students' level of maturity was not really reflected in this lesson. There are a few quite immature students in this class who can be disruptive. This is a mixed-ability classroom, with the full range of abilities. Megan, Beginning English teacher.

Megan felt that her modelling of the central task had been particularly effective, her instructions were generally clear, and that she had moved well around the room engaging with students. The discussion with her mentor after the lesson focussed on the transitions between parts of the lesson. The school mentor remarked that she felt that Megan had taught a very good lesson for that stage of the course. Megan felt that not all students understood at all times what they were supposed to do. She had set herself the target of rewording instructions to provide differentiated support. At the end of the visit Megan was set the following targets by her mentor:

- Give opportunities for learners to evaluate and improve their performance.
- Make accurate and productive use of assessment and feedback.
- Continue work on being aware of low level poor behaviour/ disengagement and using appropriate behaviour management strategies to address this.

None of these targets were subject specific. Although there was a potential peda-gogical focus in the first two targets, institutional priorities (assessment/behaviour/ school policy) were central.

Megan's mentor was a school Head of Year (a leader of a team of form tutors who are responsible for the academic progress and pastoral care of the students in their form group). The year team leadership was reactive to issues of behaviour manage-ment in the school, which often involved her intervening in other lessons, and this both took up a considerable proportion of her time but also framed her object motives for what she deemed to be important in the pastoral welfare of students. As a consequence of this time pressure the mentor frequently missed planned meetings with Megan. The discussion between the mentor and Megan focussed on questions of behaviour management which perhaps reflects the mentor's and the school's priorities. Indeed, much of the pedagogic discourse in the school centred on issues of behaviour management and reward structures.

In Megan's case, the school culture was not at this stage conducive to her development as an English teacher even though she was seen as succeeding by her mentor because she could control the behaviour of a class. It was only when Megan moved to a second school placement, with a school culture more focussed on subject learning, that she was able to recognise the complexity of her social situation of development as a teacher of English. A school culture that was both supportive and open to challenge meant that Megan was able to move beyond her preconceptions of what it meant to be an English teacher to become a teacher who focused on the social environment of the English classroom as necessary precursor to learning. Megan's previous experience as a researcher of English as an Additional Language (EAL) led to her involvement in a school research project in this second placement that looked at the experiences of EAL learners who had arrived in the school with relatively low levels of learning about English literature in an English classroom setting. In this project Megan developed through using both her previous expertise as a researcher of second language acquisition with her newly acquired knowledge of essential concepts such as genre and culture from her teaching of English literature.

There is a moral argument here about school cultures and the placements within which beginning teachers develop their identities. Inevitably, school cultures vary with some placing more emphasis on instructional discourse than regulative discourse (Bernstein, 2000) and not all beginning teachers will find themselves in placements that might be seen as conducive to their development. Yet, as we have previously argued (Tatto et al., 2019), challenging school placements can bring about opportunities for development and change in certain circumstances. In terms of identity development this means that ITE courses need to be explicit about the role of school culture and ways that the beginning teacher can avoid simply being apprenticed into that culture. As Mockler (2011) and Hochstetler (2011) argue, this means ITE programmes taking the concept of teacher identity seriously as a practical and political tool. For, as del Rio and Alvarez (1995) state, identity formation is an integral part of any cultural system:

> Morality and directivity cannot be constructed by processing a set of knowledge and rules, by the management of propositions. Identity, directivity, the construction of self, emotion, and the mythologies we produce and that produce us are indispensable requirements in any cultural system that is strong in the human sense (pp. 505–406).

Within the cultural systems of schools, this means that beginning teachers should understand this culture, and enact the systems and rules whilst learning within the placement, but not become encultured by their environment.

4.6   Conclusion

Secondary level beginning student teachers are both subject specialists with strong academic credentials and subject learners within the sociocultural settings of schools and classrooms. The dialectical tensions involved in learning to teach involves a complex renegotiation of identities as the beginning teacher develops their understanding and use of subject pedagogy within school settings and an awareness from their academic setting of what it means to engage critically with theories of teaching and learning.

   This chapter has argued that context plays an important role in the identity formation of beginning teachers. This requires ITE programmes to place greater emphasis on the academic and school contexts that influence beginning teachers' social situation of development. The focus on the complexity of identity development for beginning English teachers in this chapter has developed a view of learning to become a teacher as being a challenging but developmental process. This process involves beginning teachers being both supported and challenged by the culture of the social environment of particular schools and departments of English. Claxton (2007) has described the importance of 'potentiating environments' that 'stretch learners' (p.125). Although Claxton was referring to school students' learning, the same can be applied to the development of beginning teachers' identities. As Derry (2013) points out, 'the learning environment must be designed and cannot rely on the spontaneous response to an environment which is not constructed according to, or involves, some clearly worked out conceptual framework' (p.61). In the case of the design of courses for beginning teachers this conceptual framework should involve an explicit focus on identity formation. This suggests the need to create learning environments for beginning teachers within initial teacher education that allow risk and experimentation, mediated by interaction with university tutors, school mentors, other professionals and the students that they encounter.

References

Akkerman, S. F., & Bakker, A. (2011). Boundary crossing and boundary objects. *Review of Educational Research, 81*, 132–169. https://doi.org/10.3102/0034654311404435

Ball, S. J. (2018). Commercialising education: Profiting from reform! *Journal of Education Policy, 33*(5), 587–589. https://doi.org/10.1080/02680939.2018.1467599

Beach, K. (1999). Consequential transitions: A sociocultural expedition beyond transfer in education. *Review of Research in Education, 24*, 101–139. https://doi.org/10.3102/0091732X024001101

Beach, K. (2003). Consequential transitions: A developmental view of knowledge propagation through social organizations. In T. Tuomi-Gröhn & Y. Engeström (Eds.), *Between school and work. New perspectives on transfer and boundary-crossing* (pp. 29–61). Pergamon.

Bernstein, B. (2000). *Pedagogy, symbolic control and identity theory: Research and critique* (2nd ed.). Rowan & Littlefield Publishers.

Burn, K., Hagger, H., Mutton, T., & Everton, T. (2003). The complex development of student teachers' thinking. *Teachers and Teaching: Theory and Practice, 9*(4), 309–331. https://doi.org/10.1080/1354060032000097235

Claxton, G. (2007). Expanding young people's capacity to learn. *British Journal of Educational Studies, 55*(2), 115–134. https://doi.org/10.1111/j.1467-8527.2007.00369.x

Cole, M., & Engeström, Y. (1993). A cultural-historical approach to distributed cognition. In G. Salomon (Ed.), *Distributed cognitions: Psychological and educational considerations* (pp. 1–46). Cambridge University Press.

Côté, J. (2005). Identity capital, social capital and the wider benefits of learning: Generating resources facilitative of social cohesion. *London Review of Education, 3*(3), 237.

Crafter, S., & Maunder, R. (2012). Understanding transitions using a sociocultural framework. *Educational and Child Psychology., 29*(1), 10–18.

Daniels, H. (2014). Vygotsky and dialogic pedagogy. *Cultural-historical Psychology, 10*(3), 19–29.

del Rio, P., & Alvarez, A. (1995). Directivity: The cultural and educational construction of morality and agency. Some questions arising from the legacy of Vygotsky. *Anthropology and Education Quarterly, 26*(4), 384–409. https://doi.org/10.1525/aeq.1995.26.4.05x1060t

Department for Education. (2021). *Schools, pupils and their characteristics: Academic year 2020–21*. Department for Education.

Derry, J. (2013). *Vygotsky: Philosophy and education*. Wiley Blackwell.

Doyle, W. (1977). Learning the classroom environment: An ecological analysis. *Journal of Teacher Education, 28*(6), 51–5.10.1177/002248717702800616.

Dreier, O. (1999). Personal trajectories of participation across contexts of social practice. *Outlines, 1*(1), 5–32.

Dreier, O. (2009). Persons in structures of social practice. *Theory and Psychology, 19*(2), 193–212. https://doi.org/10.1177/0959354309103539

Edwards, A. (2009). From the systemic to the relational: Relational agency and activity theory. In A. Sannino, H. Daniels, & K. Gutierrez (Eds.), *Learning and expanding with activity theory* (pp. 197–211). Cambridge University Press.

Edwards, A. (2010). How can Vygotsky and his legacy help us to understand and develop teacher education? In V. Ellis, A. Edwards, & P. Smagorinsky (Eds.), *Cultural-historical perspectives on teacher education and development* (pp. 63–77). Routledge.

Edwards, A. (2017). The dialectic of person and practice: How cultural-historical accounts of agency can inform teacher education. In J. Clandinin & J. Husu (Eds.), *International handbook on research on teacher education* (pp. 269–285). Sage.

Ellis, V. (2007). Taking subject knowledge seriously: From professional knowledge recipes to complex conceptualizations of teacher development. *Curriculum Journal, 18*(4), 458–459. https://doi.org/10.1080/09585170701687902

Engeström, Y. (2010). Activity theory as a framework for analyzing and redesigning work. *Ergonomics, 43*(7), 960–974. https://doi.org/10.1080/001401300409143

Engeström, Y., & Sannino, A. (2010). Studies of expansive learning: Foundations, findings and future challenges. *Educational Research Review, 5*(1), 1–24. https://doi.org/10.1016/j.edurev.2009.12.002

Erikson, E. H. (1968). *Identity: Youth and crisis.* Norton.

Hochstetler, S. (2011). Focus on identity development: A proposal for addressing English teacher attrition. *The Clearing House: A Journal of Educational Strategies, Issues and Ideas, 84*(6), 256–259. https://doi.org/10.1080/00098655.2011.590552

Holland, D., & Lachicotte, W. (2007). Vygotsky, Mead and the new sociocultural studies of identity. In H. Daniels, M. Cole, & J. Wertsch (Eds.), *The Cambridge companion to Vygotsky* (pp. 101–135).

Holland, D., Lachicotte, W., Skinner, D., & Cain, C. (1998). *Identity and agency in cultural worlds.* Harvard University Press.

McIntyre, D. (1993). Theory, theorizing and reflection in initial teacher education. In J. Calderhead & P. Gates (Eds.), *Conceptualizing reflection in teacher development* (pp. 97–114). Falmer Press.

McIntyre, J., & Hobson, A. J. (2016). Supporting beginner teacher identity development: External mentors and the third space. *Research Papers in Education, 31*(2), 133–158. https://doi.org/10.1080/02671522.2015.1015438

Mockler, N. (2011). Beyond 'what works': Understanding teacher identity as a practical and political tool. *Teachers and Teaching, 17*(5), 517–528. https://doi.org/10.1080/13540602.2011.602059

Moll, L. C., & Arnot-Hopffer, E. (2005). Sociocultural competence in teacher education. *Journal of Teacher Education, 56*(3), 242–247. https://doi.org/10.1177/0022487105275919

Nelson-Addy, L., Dingwall, N., Elliott, V., & Thompson, I. (2019). Back to the future: the restoration of canon and the backlash against multiculturalism in secondary English curricula. In A. Goodwyn, C. Durrant, A. H. Sawyer, D. Zancanella, & L. Scherff (Eds.), *The future of English teaching worldwide: Celebrating 50 years from the Dartmouth conference* (pp. 191–202). Routledge.

Penuel, W. R., & Wertsch, V. J. (1995). Vygotsky and identity formation: A sociocultural approach. *Educational Psychologist, 30*(2), 83–92. https://doi.org/10.1207/s15326985ep3002_5

Schwab, J. J. (1978). In I. Westbury & N. Wilkof (Eds.), *Science, curriculum and Liberal education: Selected essays.* University of Chicago Press.

Tatto, M., Burn, K., Menter, I., Mutton, T., & Thompson, I. (2019). *Learning to teach in England and the United States: The evolution of policy and practice.* Routledge.

Thompson, I. (2015a). Communication, culture and conceptual learning: Task design in the English classroom. In I. Thompson (Ed.), *Designing tasks in secondary education: Enhancing subject understanding and student engagement* (pp. 86–106). Routledge.

Thompson, I. (2015b). Researching contradictions: Cultural historical activity theory research (CHAT) in the English classroom. *English in Australia., 50*(3), 21–26.

Thompson, I. (2020). Poverty and education in England: A school system in crisis. In I. Thompson & G. Ivinson (Eds.), *Poverty in education across the UK: A comparative analysis of policy and place* (pp. 115–140). Policy Press.

Thompson, I., & Wittek, A. L. (2016). Writing as a mediational tool for learning in the collaborative composition of texts. *Learning, Culture and Social Interaction, 11*, 85–96. https://doi.org/10.1016/j.lcsi.2016.05.004

Thompson, I., McNicholl, J., & Menter, I. (2016). Student teachers' perceptions of poverty and educational achievement. *Oxford Review of Education, 42*(2), 214–229. https://doi.org/10.1080/03054985.2016.1164130

Vygotsky, L. S. (1987). Thinking and speech. In R. W. Rieber & A. S. Carton (Eds.), *The collected works of L.S. Vygotsky* (Vol. 1, pp. 37–285). Plenum Press.

Vygotsky, L. S. (1997). The history of the development of higher mental functions. In R. W. Rieber (Ed.), *The collected works of L.S. Vygotsky* (Vol. 4, pp. 1–254). Plenum Press.

Vygotsky, L. S. (1998). Problems of *child psychology*. In R. W. Rieber (Ed.), *The collected works of L.S. Vygotsky* (Vol. 5, pp. 185–296). Plenum Press.

Wertsch, J. V. (1993). Commentary. *Human Development, 36*, 168–171.

Wertsch, J. V. (2007). Mediation. In H. Daniels, M. Cole, & J. Wertsch (Eds.), *The Cambridge companion to Vygotsky* (pp. 178–192). Cambridge University Press.

Zittoun, T. (2006). *Transitions: Development through symbolic resources*. Information Age Publishing.

Zittoun, T. (2007). Symbolic resources and responsibility in transitions. *Young: Nordic Journal of Youth Research., 15*(2), 193–211. https://doi.org/10.1177/110330880701500205

Chapter 5
Second Language Teacher Identity: A Synthesis of Reflections from Applied Linguists

Chiew Hong Ng and Yin Ling Cheung

Abstract This chapter synthesizes eighteen reflections on language teacher identity research through the analytic framework of pragmatistic, critical, hermeneutic and phenomenological approaches and perspectives. These eighteen applied linguistics scholars from Spain, Pakistan, Sri Lanka, South Africa, Austria, Slovakia, New Zealand, Brazil, Columbia, Iceland, Finland, South Korea, Japan, China and Singapore examine the substance of second language teacher identity research on a topic that has witnessed an exponential growth of interest among ELT / TESOL researchers from the applied linguists' perspective. In reflecting on one's identity as a language teacher/applied linguist through the framework of four approaches and perspectives, the chapter covers the following areas: definition of language teacher identity, the impact of social, cultural, and political factors in influencing the construction of teacher identity, the relevance of second language teacher identity in one's specialized field, and future directions for teacher identity research in various specializations in applied linguistics. This chapter will inform second language teachers, teacher educators and researchers not only in Asia, but also globally, of second language teacher identity as a dynamic concept that can be changed and developed, subject to cultural, social, contextual, and political situations.

Keywords Second language teacher identity · Personal reflections · Applied linguists · Definition · Dynamic concept

5.1 Introduction

Many theoretical and empirical/data-driven research papers have addressed the issue of Language Teacher Identity (LTI) (Varghese et al., 2005). Qualitative reviews that focus on cognitive aspects, such as reflexivity and self-introspection, have remained relatively unexplored. To fill this gap, this chapter uses reflections as a prism through

C. H. Ng · Y. L. Cheung (✉)
Nanyang Technological University, Singapore, Singapore
e-mail: yinling.cheung@nie.edu.sg

© The Author(s), under exclusive license to Springer Nature Switzerland AG 2022
K. Sadeghi, F. Ghaderi (eds.), *Theory and Practice in Second Language Teacher Identity*, Educational Linguistics 57, https://doi.org/10.1007/978-3-031-13161-5_5

which LTI is explored. We focus on reflections because the process of identity development is a non-linear one and involves reflexivity and self-introspection and we do this through an analytical framework of pragmatistic, critical, hermeneutic and phenomenological approaches and perspectives to synthesize reflections by applied linguists. Eighteen book chapters on LTI were selected. These applied linguistics scholars are from Spain, Pakistan, Sri Lanka, South Africa, Austria, Slovakia, New Zealand, Brazil, Columbia, Iceland, Finland, South Korea, Japan, China and Singapore. To offer insights to deepen the field's understanding of how applied linguists develop and negotiate their identities as educators and researchers, we describe the research methodology for qualitative review/qualitative evidence synthesis using four approaches and perspectives of reflections adopted for the study: pragmatistic, critical, hermeneutic and phenomenological. We then present the findings and discussion in terms of the four approaches and perspectives for these areas: definition of language teacher identity, the impact of social, cultural, and political factors in influencing the construction of identity for applied linguists, the relevance of second language teacher identity in one's specialized field, and future directions for teacher identity research in various specializations in applied linguistics.

5.2 Literature Review

5.2.1 Definition of Language Teacher Identity

Researchers have agreed that language teacher identity is multi-faceted and dynamic (Beijaard et al., 2004) and a complex and ongoing process (Barcelos, 2017). Identity development is both an individual and a social process (Rodgers & Scott, 2008). Miller (2009) analyzed definitions of seven researchers working in a second language field to conclude identity as relational, "negotiated, constructed, enacted, transforming, and transitional" (p. 174). To Varghese et al. (2005), "theories of language teacher identity explain and account for power and agency" (p. 38).

5.2.2 Social, Cultural, and Political Factors Influencing the Construction of Teacher Identity

Teacher identity is affected by internal (organisational) factors defined by personal and social histories, current roles, beliefs and the kind of teacher they aspire to be through personal biographies to reveal their values, beliefs, ideologies (Day et al., 2006). It is also influenced by external (policy) factors – political, social, institutional or "the social/cultural/organisational formations of schools and teacher education" (Day et al., 2006, p. 611).

For language teacher identity from a sociocultural perspective, Varghese et al. (2005) consider both specific contextual influences of the teacher and external contextual influences from the environment. They define EFL teacher identity as "multiple, shifting, and in conflict. . . [which] is crucially related to social, cultural, and political context" (p.35). Kocabaş-Gedik and Hart (2021) looked at language teacher identity in terms of teacher investment within imagined communities of practice and the social-constructivist notion of the interplay between unequal power relations and emotional labor. In sociocultural theory on identity, the construction and reconstruction of self is through participating in social and political interactions (Meihami et al., 2019). However, new experiences which originate from the widening of social networks may cause identity reconstruction, modification, and reconstruction (Lave & Wenger, 1991; Wenger, 1998).

To Chen and Lin (2016), "cultural identity has been employed as an umbrella construct to encompass, or subsume, related group identities such as nationality, race, ethnicity, age, gender, socioeconomic status, regional identity, ethnolinguistic identity, political affiliation, and (dis)ability" (p. 2). Lawrence and Nagashima (2020), through duoethnography, found the intersection of gender, sexuality, race, and native-speaker status affecting their professional identities as language teachers and teaching practices.

Political changes are macro contextual factors and according to Menter (2010) "teacher identity [is] very directly [related] to questions of policy, politics and governance" (p. 35). For instance, Phyak and Baral (2019) analyzed the experiences of six university lecturers to find existing political hierarchy in university affecting the professional identity of the lecturers.

5.2.3 Second Language Teacher Identity in One's Specialized Field in Applied Linguistics

Applied linguists specializing in teacher education in teaching English as additional language or TESOL can experience identity issues. For instance, Lee (2010) engaged in a critical reflection in terms of her identity positioning as a nonnative English-speaking (NNES) teacher educator working with native English-speaking (NES) pre- and in-service teachers in the field of literacy education at an American university. Many beginning teacher educators draw on their classroom teacher identities to guide their teaching initially (Boyd & Harris, 2010; Carrillo & Baguley, 2011; McKeon & Harrison, 2010; Wood & Borg, 2010). For instance, Skerrett (2008) narrated how her identity as a schoolteacher impacted her beliefs about teaching and teacher education and helped her address social and racial divides. Still Boyd and Harris (2010) highlighted the risk of conservatism in teacher education when new lecturers "hold on to their identity as schoolteachers rather than develop a new professional identity as academics" (p. 21). Through a literature search, Swennen et al. (2010) identified these four sub-identities of teacher educators: "schoolteacher, teacher in Higher Education, teacher of teachers (or second order teacher) and researcher" (p. 131) in facing pressing need to transform their identity to become "teachers of teachers in Higher Education [and] researchers of teaching and teacher education" (p. 131).

Applied linguists can specialize in specific fields such as writing and L2 writing specialists' identities are discursively constructed (Kubota, 2017; McGriff, 2015). According to Wilson (2018) there are few empirical studies using identity as a theoretical lens to analyze how writing specialists' pedagogical practices have been influenced by L2 writing teachers' disciplinary and intellectual backgrounds. Kim (2017) has highlighted difficulties in choosing terms to describe her training in a Second Language Studies program – "linguist," "L2 writing scholar," or "English teacher-trainer" – for her transdisciplinary identity as an L2 writing specialist. Racelis and Matsuda (2015) have differentiated language teacher identity, writing teacher identity, and L2 writing teacher identity to reflect the need for assumption of multiple professional roles across disciplines, the field of L2 writing being dynamic and cross-disciplinary. Besides, in applied linguistics, L2 writing specialists, are not just teachers or instructors, but researchers in writing pedagogical practices in an internationally recognized field – highlighting complexities in second language teacher educator identity in various specializations in applied linguistics.

5.3   Methodology

Three databases (i.e., EBSCO, ProQuest, and Google Scholar) were searched for publications that included qualitative data on reflections by applied linguists on LTI. The following key terms were used: "language teacher", "teacher identity", "applied linguists" and "reflections". The search results were examined and these inclusion criteria were applied to select relevant papers: (1) the paper was published in a peer reviewed journal or in edited book collections; (2) the paper was published between 2011 to 2022; (3) the paper was written by researchers in the fields of applied linguistics and TESOL, with applied linguists defined as experts in their chosen field of specialization (e.g., linguistics, second language acquisition or classroom research, English as a lingua franca) who address language pedagogy (e.g., language teaching, academic writing, and teacher education) (Ellis, 2016); and (4) the author of the paper makes reflective comments to reveal the author's personalized take on the definition of LTI and the methodological approaches used to investigate LTI; or the author weaves narration, recounts or biographical accounts of professional lives and research work about LTI throughout the paper. Besides rejecting papers with no relevance to LTI, the following exclusion criteria were applied: (1) master's or doctoral dissertations were not included; (2) papers focusing on research methodologies for LTI such as life histories approach or narrative inquiry were not included; (3) papers which were reviews of empirical studies on reflection were not included; (4) papers which were research reports about findings from a collection of reflections or reflections through interview data were not included; and (5) papers focusing on the nature of reflections of students, preservice teachers or school teachers were not included.

Using the university's online library database, EBSCO search hit 15 results which did not meet the inclusion criteria (for example, a research article that focused on reflections of Vietnamese English language educators on their writer identities was excluded because it was a research report on interview results). ProQuest search resulted in 200 results. There were 106 dissertations (which were excluded based on exclusion criterion 1), 21 books (which were excluded since they were published before 2011 or had no relation to LTI). *Becoming and being an applied linguist: The life histories of some applied linguists* (2016) seemed relevant but the book was excluded since it uses the life histories approach to talk about the professional lives of applied linguists. Of the 73 journal articles, 39 were published before 2011, 28 were published between 2011 and 2022 but they were not about LTI and six were published after 2011 which were shortlisted for an in depth study but they were found to deal with writer identity construction, identity of students, systematic review of researcher identity, description of research tasks on identity in language learning and teaching. Google Scholar found 100 search results. 32 articles/book chapters/books were excluded because they were written before 2011. One thesis was excluded (exclusion criterion 1). Chapters from 'reflections' on language teacher identity research edited by Barkhuizen (2017) figured strongly (i.e., 27 occurrences) because the book deals specifically with the reflections of experienced researchers in the fields of applied linguistics and Teaching English to Speakers of Other Languages (TESOL). Forty journal articles/book chapters/books not from Barkhuizen (2017) were carefully checked through for reflections on LTI as the key criterion. Journal articles from the Google Scholar search were excluded because they were not reflections, though they were reviewing research on LTI, theorizing about LTI concepts or LTI research methodology, advocating teaching approaches or programmes.

As a result, 18 chapters from five books (i.e., 14 selected from Barkhuizen (2017) and four chapters – Choi (2014), Dávila (2018), De Costa (2015), and Ingvarsdóttir (2014) – from four other books) were found to meet the criteria focusing on "applied linguists" and "teacher identity" written from a reflective stance. The authors reflected on LTI by drawing on their personal experiences within their areas of expertise and research activity to present their conceptual understanding or definition of LTI and the methodological approaches used to investigate LTI. These reflective chapters are viewed as qualitative data given the narrative nature of the chapters with "the authors embedding their discussions within biographical accounts of their professional lives and research work" (Barkhuizen, 2017, p. 2). The 18 chapters from five books written by different authors represent data in terms of narratives for qualitative review/qualitative evidence synthesis. This is "a method for integrating or comparing the findings from qualitative studies ... [to develop] ... an overarching 'narrative', a wider generalization or an 'interpretative translation' " (Grant & Booth, 2009, p. 99). It involves looking for themes or constructs across individual qualitative studies and is interpretative in seeking "a holistic interpretation of a phenomenon" (Grant & Booth, 2009, p. 100) which is reflecting on LTI for the present study. This is because "a more selective search approach may be acceptable as long as the method of sampling papers for inclusion is appropriate" (Grant & Booth, 2009, p. 100).

Complex and multi-faceted reflections on language teacher identity can be viewed as reflection- in-action and reflection-on-action (Schön, 1983). Mortari (2015) has offered four philosophical perspectives and approaches to look at types of reflection in terms of pragmatistic (Dewey, 1933), critical (Foucault, 1985), hermeneutic (Van Manen, 1977, 1991), and phenomenological (Husserl, 1982).

The pragmatist approach to reflection conceives experience as action oriented – turning "impulsive action into intelligent action" (Dewey, 1933, p. 17). Reflection increases power of control over experience and enables intelligent methods of inquiry into effectiveness of action (Mortari, 2015). The critical perspective in reflection involves unveiling prejudices and assumptions about class, race, and gender produced through language (Giroux & McLaren, 1989; Mortari, 2015). To Foucault (1985) a critical thinker explores how language and discourse reproduces relations of power, exercises critical appraisal to reject predefined authority and adopts an ethical stance as a way of life.

The hermeneutic perspective involves these types of reflection: technical reflection on the efficiency and effectiveness of the means (Van Manen, 1977); practical reflection on the means and ends of one's actions (Van Manen, 1977); critical reflection on questions of justice in one's professional field within wider social, economic, and political contexts (Van Manen, 1977); anticipatory reflection about possible future alternatives (Van Manen, 1991); active reflection - Schönian concept of reflection-in-action (Van Manen, 1991); recollective reflection to make sense of past experiences (Van Manen, 1991); and the mindfulness posture in terms of a practitioner maintaining a certain distance from the actions taken.

The phenomenological perspective looks at the processes that take place in the mind, as cognitive phenomena "can become the object of investigation in introspection" (Arendt, 1958, p. 280). The cognitive act that characterizes the phenomenological reflection is "reflective turning of regard" (Husserl, 1982, p. 78) with reflection on the thinking acts themselves as their object to realize reflection of "a higher level" (Husserl, 1982, p. 177) or a "meta reflection" (Mortari, 2015, p. 6).

To synthesize reflections on identities for applied linguists, Mortari's (2015) perspectives and approaches are adopted. The 18 articles were read in detail for content analysis and coded in terms of the four perspectives and approaches. Three have been classified as pragmatist in approach: Choi (2014), Gao (2017) and Oda (2017). Seven studies pertain to the critical perspective: Toohey (2017), Mahboob (2017), Block (2017), Dávila (2018), Norton (2017), Kubota (2017) and de Oliveira e Paiva (2017). There are five studies under the hermeneutic perspective: Ingvarsdóttir (2014), De Costa (2015), Canagarajah (2017), White (2017) and Kalaja (2017) while three studies are from the phenomenological perspective: Kubanyiova (2017), Mercer (2017) and Barcelos (2017).

5.4 Findings

The findings on various aspects of language teacher identity from the four approaches and perspectives will be synthesized in terms of themes. These themes pertain to definition of language teacher identity; the impact of social, cultural, and political factors in influencing the construction of teacher identity; the relevance of second language teacher identity in one's specialized field and future directions for teacher identity research in various specializations in applied linguistics.

5.4.1 Definition of Language Teacher Identity in Terms of the Four Approaches and Perspectives

The three applied linguists under the pragmatist approach define language teacher identity in relation to the effectiveness of teaching and research experiences. Choi (2014) highlights the complexity of her LTI: English for Speakers of Other Languages (ESOL) and Korean language teacher and a beginning linguistics professor. Gao (2017) defines language teacher educator professional identity as foundational upon projection of a particular professional self, associated with professional communities and mediated or constrained by cultural traditions and dominant societal discourses such as government policies and educational curricula documents. To Oda (2017) language teacher identity is a teacher's perception and understanding of accumulated resources from past experiences inside and outside of the classroom translated into teaching actions which corresponds with reflection-on-action.

In terms of the critical perspective, Block (2017) has defined language teacher identity as how individuals, who both self-position and are positioned by others as teachers, affiliate to different aspects of teaching in their lives . . . related to factors such as one's ongoing contacts with fellow teachers and students as well as the tasks that one engages in, which can be said to constitute teaching. (p. 13).

Toohey (2017) argues that with translanguaging, language teacher identities will be tied to new conceptions of language where traditional distinctness and boundaries are unclear and identities have to do with multilinguals drawing on many linguistic resources. Mahboob (2017) looks at at non-native English speaking teacher (NNEST) identity as a combination of three aspects: Teachers' use of language where language teacher identity is negotiated through the linguistic choices made; Teachers' classroom practices impacted by different stakeholders (e.g., students, colleagues, parents, administration); and Teachers' presentation of curriculum through language (as used in textbooks and other curricular material) and teachers' interpretations and teaching practices.

Kubota (2017) talks about critical language teacher identity as characterized by a firm commitment to social justice, underpinned by critical approaches to language pedagogy, which range from Freirean critical pedagogy to a poststructuralist orientation and ethical commitment. Dávila (2018) problematizes LTI in Teacher

Educators (TEs) using an epistemological perspective – mainly power relations and practices of resistance from Focault's perspective. de Oliveira e Paiva (2017) uses chaos and complexity theories to view LTI as fractual – a complex interactive system where teachers must cope with several identities: Brazilian identity, cultural identity, political identity (involving conflicts in teaching a language associated with the idea of imperialism), professional identity, bilingual identity, researcher identity, and identity in relation to gender, social class and religions.

For the five studies related to the hermeneutic perspective, in defining the identity of a teacher of multilingual writing, Canagarajah (2017) talks about teacher identity as central to pedagogy where one's identity is part and parcel of one's teaching practice and expertise. White (2017) sees distance language teacher identity and self in e-language teaching as "multiple, dynamic, and conflictual, closely related to sociocultural contexts, and is constructed, enacted, and negotiated largely through discourse and intention"(pp. 335–336). For Kalaja (2017), teachers construct their identities either as professionals who are sensitive and willing to adapt to the needs of their pupils (after a critical incident), or as professionals who resist changes. To Ingvarsdóttir (2014), LTI is revealed through reflection on the interplay between a teacher's life story and subjective theories involving Schönian concept of reflection-in-action. De Costa (2015) sees the need to shift and combine multiple identities in practiced identity when enacting pedagogical practices as NNESTs.

For the three studies from the phenomenological perspective in terms of processes in the mind, Mercer (2017) conceptualizes language teacher identity as language teacher selves. From language teacher cognition perspective, Kubanyiova (2017) identifies these possible language teacher selves: ideal language teacher selves, future-oriented identity-relevant investment or ought-to language teacher selves, and feared language teacher selves. To Barcelos (2017), LTI is a complex, multiple, fragmented, dynamic and ongoing process formed by beliefs (or tacit theories, lay observations), emotions, and experiences (personal, work related, cultural, professional, among others) and shaped and reshaped by interactions with others – social, and cultural experiences, and the institutional environment.

5.4.2 The Impact of Social, Cultural, and Political Factors in Influencing the Construction of Teacher Identity

Under the pragmatist approach, Gao (2017) believes professional identity is mediated or constrained by cultural traditions and dominant societal discourses. Choi (2014) discusses how her cultural, linguistic, and teaching identities were challenged and transformed while learning English and completing PhD studies in the United States.

From the critical perspective, social factors are highlighted by these applied linguists: Toohey (2017) sees language boundaries (identification) as a social process benefitting some speakers over others. Block (2017) defines identities as socially constructed where individuals are shaped by their socio-histories but also shape their socio-histories in the face of unequal power relations around the different capitals – economic, cultural, and social – in communities of practice and are related to categories such as ethnicity, race, nationality, migration, gender, social class, and language.

As for social and political factors, Kubota (2017) suggests how critical language teacher identity indexes both social structure and human agency, which shift over historical time and social context. Critical language teachers may have an identity of being politically radical and ethically committed to social justice, which influences pedagogical orientation. Dávila (2018) talks about the need to include the social, political and cultural aspects in teacher education and not just teach pedagogy. To Mahboob (2017), NNEST language variation is political and historical. de Oliveira e Paiva (2017)) highlights how cultural identity and social class identity influence both teacher formation and student motivation while political identity arises from conflicts in teaching a language associated with the idea of imperialism.

Social factors are also highlighted from the hermeneutic perspective. Canagarajah (2017) believes multilingual teacher identity involves drawing from the diverse social identities, institutional policies, and dominant social ideologies regarding monolingualism and multilingualism. To White (2017), teacher identity is "closely related to sociocultural contexts, and is constructed, enacted, and negotiated largely through discourse and intention''(pp. 335–336). Kalaja (2017) talks about novice teachers emphasizing the social nature of learning English. De Costa (2015) shows how LTI is shaped by the social context of the classroom in practiced identity. Ingvarsdóttir (2014) demonstrates how the LTI (in terms of teachers' beliefs and pedagogical practices) of two Icelandic teachers was influenced by a culture of reflective collaboration and collegial support.

From the phenomenological perspective, Mercer (2017) believes language teacher selves can be mapped to a range of psychological and social constructivist perspectives. To understand possible language teacher selves, Kubanyiova (2017) used an overarching metaphor for selves that are socially constructed and personally meaningful. To Barcelos (2017), language teacher identity is tied to the personal, social class, cultural experiences, the institutional environment and the political context and to the sorts of ideologies and beliefs about English language teaching in different parts of the world.

5.4.3 The Relevance of Second Language Teacher Identity in One's Specialized Field

The 18 applied linguists have linked the relevance of second language identity to their specialized fields: research, teacher education and writing specialists. From the hermeneutic perspective, Mahboob (2017) is a researcher of NNEST language variation, critical applied linguistics and World Englishes. From the phenomenological perspective Kubanyiova (2017) researches language teacher cognition and possible language teacher selves.

In the field of teacher education, from the pragmatist approach, Gao's (2017) concern was improving his professional standing in teaching pre-service teacher as he had no teaching experiences to draw upon. As a beginner professor coordinating an online ESOL/Reading program, Choi (2014) believes ESOL teachers need to adopt an international perspective as part of their teacher identity to better serve English Language Learners (ELLs). In contrast, Oda (2017) believes in drawing on her past teaching experiences as resources for further developments having moved from English language teacher, to teacher trainer, and then to administrator. From the hermeneutic perspective, Kalaja (2017) examines the development of the identities of novice teachers and teachers of English in Finland and De Costa (2015) investigates the language identity of a non-native South Korean teacher. Ingvarsdóttir (2014) believes using one's life stories will enhance language teacher identity formation in teacher training through revealing subjective theories. White (2017), as a lecturer in linguistics and methodology, talks about distance language teacher identity and self in e-language teaching.

For teacher educators who are also researchers from the critical perspective, Block (2017) defines identities as socially constructed in TESOL teacher education and development. To Dávila (2018), it is important to understand the epistemological aspects of Columbian English language teacher educator's identity in terms of policies, relations of power and resistance practices. Kubota (2017) connects research concerns of two domains of applied linguistics – second language acquisition (SLA) and language teacher cognition through critical language teacher identity. de Oliveira e Paiva (2017) researches and reflects on second language acquisition and teacher identity development in light of chaos and complexity. Having taught and researched in apartheid South Africa – Uganda – and multilingual Canada, Norton (2017) proposes transdisciplinary and a model of investment locating investment at the intersection of identity, capital, and ideology (Darvin & Norton, 2015). Having taught Chilean refugees, English-as-an-additional-language teachers in university and indigenous and heritage language teachers, Toohey (2017) proposes translanguaging. From the phenomenological perspective, Mercer (2017) looks at language teacher selves in EFL teacher training and academic research on SLA. Barcelos (2017) is a teacher educator researching and writing extensively on teachers' and learners' beliefs about language learning and their relation to other constructs such as identities and emotions.

As for applied linguists specializing in writing, from the hermeneutic perspective, Canagarajah (2017), as a teacher of multilingual writing, proposes teacher identity as pedagogy in translanguaging or the merging of competing rhetorical traditions possessed by a multilingual to create a new discourse or text.

5.4.4 Future Directions for Teacher Identity Research in Various Specializations in Applied Linguistics

In terms of proposed theories and methods for future research, for applied linguists focusing on the hermeneutic perspective, Mahboob (2017) proposes tracing NNEST teachers' negotiation of their identity through detailed linguistic analysis of teacher talk – both in and out of the classroom. From the phenomenological perspective, Kubanyiova (2017) proposes discourse-analytic, narrative, and ethnographic approaches in the development of learners' multilingual repertoires and intercultural competences, while taking account of wider sociopolitical and educational structures for images of teachers' future selves.

In terms of the field of teacher educators, from the pragmatist approach, Gao (2017) offers a conceptual framework for future research to look at self, agency/power, situated activity (e.g., interactions with colleagues and departmental policies), institutional setting and macro contexts (sociocultural discourses, ideology), economic and political conditions and cultural traditions using ethnographic case studies and narrative methods. To Choi (2014), a teacher can also be a researcher and scholar by engaging in experimentation with new methodologies and theories in teaching as research. Oda (2017) advocates reflection for critical incidents for identity formation through longitudinal studies. From the hermeneutic perspective, Kalaja (2017) suggests looking at teacher identities in relation to teachers' sense of agency, regulation of emotions, or beliefs in the learning and teaching of English. White (2017) recommends mentoring to engage and shape distance language teacher identity to develop more situated perspectives on how agency, emotion, and identity are interrelated at particular moments in specific settings. Ingvarsdóttir (2014) advocates reflecting on one's own subjective theories in developing pedagogy in practice as part of LTI in teacher education. De Costa (2015) shows how the development of an NNEST's practiced identity can be tracked through reflective practices. From the critical perspective, Dávila (2018) is interested in how English language teacher educators' identity is constructed and the influence of internal and external forces on identity formation.

For research concerning the dual identity of teacher educator and researcher, from the critical perspective, Block (2017) advocates these LTI research methods: narrative-based research, linguistic ethnography to analyze interactions in language teaching, critical discourse analytic processes and procedures and incorporation of a political economy perspective. Kubota (2017) suggests individual and collective critical language teacher identities. For teacher identity in terms of chaos and complexity, de Oliveira e Paiva (2017) suggests surveys, action research to change teaching practices and identities, narrative research through autobiographies or interviews and tracking changes in environments influencing the emergence of new identities or identities impacting environments. Norton (2017) advocates using the model of investment (Darvin & Norton, 2015) as an analytical tool for language teacher identity. Toohey (2017) suggests examining language teacher identities creation in various milieux – classroom resources, school and government policies. Mercer (2017) proposes theoretical and methodological plurality complexity theories to understand "how the self is related to other facets of situated psychology such as belief systems, emotions, attributions, motivations, goals, resilience, flow experiences" (p. 97). Barcelos (2017) suggests auto-ethnographies to study identities of language teacher educators and student-teachers.

As for research for applied linguists specializing in writing, from the hermeneutic perspective, Canagarajah (2017) proposes autoethnographies of multilingual teachers on their identity development and challenges in multilingual writing from the perspective of a community of practice.

5.5   Discussion

All four approaches and perspectives talk about the impact of social factors in influencing the construction of teacher identity with the critical perspective emphasizing unequal power relations around the different capitals – economic, cultural, and social - in communities of practice (e.g., Block, 2017). In terms of cultural factors, Gao (2017) believes professional identity is mediated or constrained by cultural traditions. The applied linguists in the 18 studies discuss the teacher identity construction being impacted by social, cultural, and political factors. From the critical perspective, NNEST language variation is political and historical (Mahboob, 2017); critical language identity involves social and political factors (Kubota, 2017) besides cultural identity, social class identity and political identity (Dávila, 2018; de Oliveira e Paiva, 2017). From the phenomenological perspective, language teacher identity is constant negotiation within certain social, cultural, historical, and political contexts (Kocabaş-Gedik & Hart, 2021), and tied to the personal, social class, cultural experiences, the institutional environment and the political context (Barcelos, 2017; Lawrence & Nagashima, 2020). However, the categories for the four approaches and perspectives are overlapping at times. For instance, Mahboob (2017) could be categorized under hermeneutic perspective in terms of critical reflection on questions of justice in one's professional field within wider social, economic, and political contexts (Van Manen, 1977).

All 18 applied linguists have drawn on their specialized fields in delineating second language teacher identity and projecting future directions in LTI as researchers, teacher educators and writing specialists. Most of the applied linguists who are teacher educators draw on their classroom teacher identities to guide their teaching as reflected in the literature review (see Boyd & Harris, 2010; Carrillo & Baguley, 2011; McKeon & Harrison, 2010; Wood & Borg, 2010). There are also applied linguists reflecting on identity positioning as a nonnative English-speaking (NNES) teacher educator (Canagarajah, 2017; Mahboob, 2017). Writing specialists have used identity as a theoretical lens to analyze how writing specialists' pedagogical practices have been influenced by L2 writing teachers' disciplinary and intellectual backgrounds (Wilson, 2018) – language teacher identity, writing teacher identity, and L2 writing teacher identity (Racelis & Matsuda, 2015).

5.6 Conclusion

The chapter contributes to second language teacher identity research by explicating how the four approaches and perspectives – pragmatistic, critical, hermeneutic and phenomenological – can offer a means to synthesize widely diverse reflections in terms of definitions from the four perspectives for multifaceted and dynamic second language teacher identity. They also offer valuable insights into cultural, social, contextual, and political factors affecting identity formation. The perspectives and approaches show that these scholars from Spain, Pakistan, Sri Lanka, South Africa, Austria, Slovakia, New Zealand, Brazil, Columbia, Iceland, Finland, South Korea, Japan, China and Singapore situate second language teacher identity in their specialized fields in applied linguistics. How second language teachers, teacher educators and researchers globally can engage in future research on language teacher identity has also been synthesized in terms of the four perspectives in this study. Though the study can be deemed limiting in looking at only 18 book chapters from five books, they represent reflective narratives as data for qualitative review and synthesis.

When considering the four perspectives for multifaceted and dynamic second language teacher identity mentioned above, we must caution readers about one limitation of this study: although Scopus and Web of Science databases could have resulted in more papers relevant to the current study, we did not conduct more searches using these databases due to insufficient manpower. Future reviews should consider addressing this limitation in order to provide a fuller picture of second language teacher identity research.

References

Arendt, H. (1958). *The human condition*. The University of Chicago.

Barcelos, A. M. F. (2017). Identities as emotioning and believing. In G. Barkhuizen (Ed.), *Reflections on language teacher identity research* (pp. 145–150). Routledge.

Barkhuizen, G. (2017). *Reflections on language teacher identity research*. Routledge.

Beijaard, D., Meijer, P., & Verloop, N. (2004). Reconsidering research on teachers' professional identity. *Teaching and Teacher Education, 20*, 107–128. https://doi.org/10.1016/j.tate.2003.07.001

Block, D. (2017). Journey to the center of language teacher identity. In G. Barkhuizen (Ed.), *Reflections on language teacher identity research* (pp. 31–36). Routledge.

Boyd, P., & Harris, K. (2010). Becoming a university lecturer in teacher education: Expert school teachers reconstructing their pedagogy and identity. *Professional Development in Education, 36*(1–2), 9–24. https://doi.org/10.1080/19415250903454767

Canagarajah, S. (2017). Multilingual identity in teaching multilingual writing. In G. Barkhuizen (Ed.), *Reflections on language teacher identity research* (pp. 67–73). Routledge.

Carrillo, C., & Baguley, M. (2011). From school teacher to university lecturer: Illuminating the journey from the classroom to the university for two arts educators. *Teaching and Teacher Education, 27*(1), 62–72. https://doi.org/10.1016/j.tate.2010.07.003

Chen, Y., & Lin, H. (2016). Cultural identities. *Oxford Research Encyclopedia of Communication*. Retrieved from http://communication.oxfordre.com/view/10.1093/acrefore/978019022 8613.001.0001/acrefore-9780190228613-e-20

Choi, J. (2014). A beginning professor's linguistic and teaching identity. In G. T. Sachs & G. Verma (Eds.), *Critical mass in the teacher education academy: Symbiosis and diversity* (pp. 87–97). Common Ground Publishing.

Darvin, R., & Norton, B. (2015). Identity and a model of investment in applied linguistics. *Annual Review of Applied Linguistics, 35*, 36–56. https://doi.org/10.1017/S0267190514000191

Dávila, A. (2018). Who teaches the teachers? Analyzing identities of English language teacher educators at English language teaching education programs. In H. Castañeda Peña, C. Helena Guerrero, P. Méndez Rivera, A. Castañeda Londoño, A. M. Dávila Rubio, C. A. Arias Cepeda, E. Y. Lucero Babativa, J. E. Castañeda Trujillo, J. Z. Posada Ortiz, & Y. S. Samacá Bohórquez (Eds.), *ELT local research agendas I* (pp. 221–243). Universidad Distrital Francisco José de Caldas.

Day, C., Kingtona, C., Stobartb, G., & Sammons, P. (2006). The personal and professional selves of teachers: Stable and unstable identities. *British Educational Research Journal, 32*(4), 601–616. https://doi.org/10.1080/01411920600775316

De Costa, P. (2015). Tracing reflexivity through a narrative and identity lens. In Y. L. Cheung, S. Ben Said, & K. Park (Eds.), *Advances and current trends in language teacher identity research* (pp. 135–147). Routledge.

de Oliveira e Paiva, V. L. M. (2017). Language teaching identity: A fractal system. In G. Barkhuizen (Ed.), *Reflections on language teacher identity research* (pp. 258–263). Routledge.

Dewey, J. (1933). *How we think*. Heat.

Ellis, R. J. (2016). *Becoming and being an applied linguist: The life histories of some applied linguists*. Benjamins Publishing Company.

Foucault, M. (1985). *Discourse and truth: The problematization of Parrhesia*. Northwestern University Press.

Gao, X. (2017). Questioning the identity turn in language teacher (educator) research. In G. Barkhuizen (Ed.), *Reflections on language teacher identity research* (pp. 189–195). Routledge.

Giroux, H., & Mclaren, P. (1989). *Critical pedagogy, the state, and cultural struggle*. State University of New York Press.

Grant, M. J., & Booth, A. (2009). A typology of reviews: An analysis of 14 review types and associated methodologies. *Health Information Library Journal, 26*(2), 91–108. https://doi.org/10.1111/j.1471-1842.2009.00848.x

Husserl, E. (1982). *Ideas pertaining to a pure phenomenology and to phenomenological philosophy*. (F. Kersten, trans.). Martinus Nijhoff.

Ingvarsdóttir, H. (2014). Reflection and work context in teacher learning: Two case studies from Iceland. In C. J. Craig, L. Orland-Barak, & S. Pinnegar (Eds.), *International teacher education: Promising pedagogies (Part A)* (pp. 91–112). Emerald Publishing Limited.

Kalaja, P. (2017). "English is a way of travelling, Finnish the station from which you set out": Reflections on the identities of L2 teachers in the context of Finland. In G. Barkhuizen (Ed.), *Reflections on language teacher identity research* (pp. 196–202). Routledge.

Kim, S. H. (2017). Emergent professional identities of an early career L2 writing scholar. In P. K. Matsuda, S. Snyder, & K. D. O'Meara (Eds.), *Professionalizing second language writing* (pp. 54–65). Parlor Press.

Kocabaş-Gedik, P., & Hart, D. O. (2021). "It's not like that at all": A poststructuralist case study on language teacher identity and emotional labor. *Journal of Language, Identity, & Education, 20*(2), 103–117. https://doi.org/10.1080/15348458.2020.1726756

Kubanyiova, M. (2017). Understanding language teachers' sense-making in action through the prism of future self guides. In G. Barkhuizen (Ed.), *Reflections on language teacher identity research* (pp. 100–106). Routledge.

Kubota, R. (2017). Critical language teacher identity. In G. Barkhuizen (Ed.), *Reflections on language teacher identity research* (pp. 210–214). Routledge.

Lave, J., & Wenger, E. (1991). *Situated learning: Legitimate peripheral participation.* Cambridge University Press.

Lawrence, L., & Nagashima, Y. (2020). The intersectionality of gender, sexuality, race, and native-speakerness: Investigating ELT teacher identity through duoethnography. *Journal of Language, Identity, & Education, 19*(1), 42–55. https://doi.org/10.1080/15348458.2019.1672173

Lee, C. J. (2010). Native versus nonnative: A literacy teacher educator's story. *Language and Literacy, 12*(1), 46–56. https://doi.org/10.20360/G2VC7P

Mahboob, A. (2017). Recognizing the local in language teacher identity. In G. Barkhuizen (Ed.), *Reflections on language teacher identity research* (pp. 49–53). Routledge.

Mcgriff, M. (2015). Teacher identity and EL-focused professional learning in a suburban middle school. *Action in Teacher Education, 37*(1), 82–98. https://doi.org/10.1080/01626620.2014.970675

McKeon, F., & Harrison, J. (2010). Developing pedagogical practice and professional identities of beginning teacher educators. *Professional Development in Education, 36*(1–2), 25–44. https://doi.org/10.1080/19415250903454783

Meihami, H., Rashidi, S. R., & Razmjoo, S. A. (2019). A review of language teachers' identity development: A focus on cultural identity theories. *Journal of Language Teaching, Literature & Linguistics, 2*(2), 49–75. https://doi.org/10.22034/JLTLL.V2I2.52

Menter, I. (2010). *Teachers – Formation, training and identity: A literature review.* Great North House.

Mercer, S. (2017). Boundary disputes in self. In G. Barkhuizen (Ed.), *Reflections on language teacher identity research* (pp. 93–99). Routledge.

Miller, J. (2009). Teacher identity. In A. Burns & J. C. Richards (Eds.), *The Cambridge guide to second language teacher education* (pp. 172–181). Cambridge University Press.

Mortari. (2015). Reflectivity in research practice: An overview of different perspectives. *The International Journal of Qualitative Methods, 14*(5), 1–9. https://doi.org/10.1177/1609406915618045

Norton, B. (2017). Learner investment and language teacher identity. In G. Barkhuizen (Ed.), *Reflections on language teacher identity research* (pp. 80–86). Routledge.

Oda, M. (2017). Reflecting on my flight path. In G. Barkhuizen (Ed.), *Reflections on language teacher identity research* (pp. 222–227). Routledge.

Phyak, P., & Baral, R. K. (2019). Teacher identity in higher education: A phenomenological inquiry. *The Batuk: A Peer Reviewed Journal of Interdisciplinary Studies, 5*(2), 74–86.

Racelis, J. V., & Matsuda, P. K. (2015). Multiple identities of L2 writing teachers. In Y. L. Cheung, S. Ben Said, & K. Park (Eds.), *Advances and current trends in language teacher identity research* (pp. 203–216). Routledge.

Rodgers, C. R., & Scott, K. H. (2008). The development of the personal self and professional identity in learning to teach. In M. Cochran-Smith, S. Feiman-Nemser, D. J. McIntyre, & K. E. Demers (Eds.), *Handbook of research on teacher education* (pp. 732–755). Routledge.

Schön, D. A. (1983). *The reflective practitioner.* Temple Smith.

Skerrett, A. (2008). Biography, identity, and inquiry: The making of teacher, teacher educator, and researcher. *Studying Teacher Education, 4*(2), 143–156.

Swennen, A., Jones, K., & Volman, M. (2010). Teacher educators: Their identities, sub-identities and implications for professional development. *Professional Development in Education, 36*(1), 131–148. https://doi.org/10.1080/19415250903457893

Toohey, K. (2017). Tangled up with everything else: Toward new conceptions of language, teachers, and identities. In G. Barkhuizen (Ed.), *Reflections on language teacher identity research* (pp. 12–17). Routledge.

Van Manen, M. (1977). Linking ways of knowing with ways of being practical. *Curriculum Inquiry, 6*, 205–228.

Van Manen, M. (1991). *The tact of teaching.* The Althouse Press.

Varghese, M., Morgan, B., Johnston, B., & Johnson, K. (2005). Theorizing language teacher identity: Three perspectives and beyond. *Journal of Language, Identity, and Education, 4*(1), 21–44. https://doi.org/10.1207/s15327701jlie0401_2

Wenger, E. (1998). *Communities of practice: Learning, meaning, and identity*. Cambridge University Press.

White, C. J. (2017). Searching for identity in distance language teaching. In G. Barkhuizen (Ed.), *Reflections on language teacher identity research* (pp. 107–113). Routledge.

Wilson, J. A. (2018). *Identity and transdisciplinarity: A study of L2 WA study of L2 writing specialist identity across contexts*. University of Tennessee, Knoxville.

Wood, D., & Borg, T. (2010). The rocky road: The journey from classroom teacher to teacher educator. *Studying Teacher Education, 6*(1), 17–28. https://doi.org/10.1080/17425961003668914

Chapter 6
Understanding Language Teacher Agency

Jenelle Reeves

Abstract The concept of language teacher agency (LTA) has experienced a recent surge of research interest, particularly within scholarship on language teacher identity. Yet, what language teacher agency is (and is not) remains elusive. Variously, language teacher agency is *exercised*, *achieved*, or *generated*, and with each new iteration of agency within language teacher identity studies, our understanding of the concept becomes increasingly opaque. This chapter will first explore the multiple conceptualizations of agency and, specifically, language teacher agency in language teacher research today with a brief review of how the concept is being operationalized in scholarship. Then, a revised conception of language teacher agency utilizing sociocultural theory and identity scholarship from various fields (e.g. sociology, psychology and applied linguistics), including Darvin and Norton's (Ann Rev Appl Linguisti 35:36–56, 2015) model of investment, is offered. This revised conceptualization explores agency as meaningful, temporal engagement that leaves open the possibility that such engagement may reach beyond action or enactment. A profile of Sarah, a secondary English as a second language teacher, provides an example case for analysis through the revised concept of LTA.

Keywords Language teacher agency · Language teacher identity · Agency · Language teacher development

6.1 Background

When we talk about language teacher agency (LTA), what are we talking about exactly? Variously, language teacher agency has been described in recent scholarship as something that is *deployed, achieved, generated, realized*, or *exercised*, which may leave readers wondering just what LTA is. Is it a personality trait? A skill to be developed? A synonym for teacher choices or decision-making? Such

J. Reeves (✉)
University of Nebraska-Lincoln, Lincoln, NE, USA
e-mail: jreeves2@unl.edu

© The Author(s), under exclusive license to Springer Nature Switzerland AG 2022   75
K. Sadeghi, F. Ghaderi (eds.), *Theory and Practice in Second Language Teacher Identity*, Educational Linguistics 57, https://doi.org/10.1007/978-3-031-13161-5_6

confusion is not limited to language teachers or even to educators in general. Several fields of study lay claim to agency: psychology, philosophy, and sociology among them. And, as sociologists, Hitlin and Elder (2007) observe, the term agency remains "slippery" and "curiously abstract" (p. 170). Pantić (2015) also found current conceptualizations of agency to suffer from a "lack of conceptual clarity" (p. 760) despite decades of attention by scholars across several disciplines. Therefore, in this chapter, I will explore how agency has been defined, particularly in terms of language teacher agency, and seek to clarify key aspects of language teacher agency which have been under-theorized to date, including action, time, and investment. I will draw upon extant scholarship on agency, within and outside of LTA. I will also draw upon the profile of one language teacher, Sarah, from my own past research to explicate elements of LTA.

This chapter will investigate meaningfulness and engagement as aspects of language teacher agency in depth. This is not to say these are the only aspects of language teacher agency that exist or are worthy of study. Rather, these concepts may provide a useful path forward as applied linguists and language teaching professionals continue to theorize language teacher agency and language teacher identity.

6.2   The Slippery Concept of Agency

The work of Emirbayer and Mische (1998), two scholars within sociology, has had a deep impact on current conceptualizations of agency within LTA research and theorizing. Emirbayer and Mische define agency as

> the temporally constructed engagement by actors of different structural environments—the temporal-relational contexts of action—which, through the interplay of habit, imagination and judgement, both reproduces and transforms those structures in interactive response to the problems posed by changing historical situations. (p. 970)

This definition centers an individual's engagement with people and social structures as elemental to agency and refrains from restricting or limiting agency to a simple personality trait or easily-bounded, static cognitive entity. Yanchar (2011) echoes Emirbayer and Mische, and identifies agency as "meaningful engagement in the world" (p. 285).

Expanding on the work of Emirbayer and Mische (1998), sociologists Hitlin and Elder (2007) propose that there are actually four types of agency: existential, pragmatic, identity, and life course. Existential agency refers to humans' capacity to act in self-directed ways but also recognizes that such capacity is shaped by both social structures and perceptions of self-efficacy (which are, themselves, shaped by social engagements). Pragmatic agency is concerned with in-the-moment agentive engagement with novel circumstances. "Pragmatic agency is expressed in the types of activities that are chosen when habitual responses to patterned social actions break down" (p. 178). Identity agency stands in contrast to pragmatic agency in that identity agency explicates habitual agentic engagements.

> Because such interactions involve a great deal of the taken-for-granted, our attentional focus becomes less concerned with the problematic now and more with goal attainment or enjoying successful interactions. While novel situations require estimates about one's ability to act successfully, over time one no longer needs to reappraise the fit between abilities and the task at hand. (p. 179)

Finally, Hitlin and Elder add life course agency to their four-element model. Life course agency is designed to capture how one "exerts influence to shape one's life trajectory," (p. 182), which adds a more expansive time dimension (and commitment) to agency. Life course agency "complicates the nature of agency, as our reflexive capacities extend to incorporate distal goals and our beliefs about our ability to reach such goals gets folded into such agentic action" (p. 182). Hitlin and Elder's theorization provides nuance to the temporal nature of agency.

6.2.1 The Self and Agency

Assumed within nearly all definitions of agency is the existence of the self—or selfhood. A *self* that is to some degree self-determining is taken-for-granted in identity and agency research. The self deserves a lengthy exploration on its own, yet, this is not the work of this chapter. For the sake of expediency and the need to get into discussion of language teacher agency, I adopt Owens' (2003) definition of self as "an organized and interactive system of thoughts, feelings, identities, and motives that (1) is born of self-reflexivity and language, (2) people attribute to themselves and (3) characterize specific human beings" (p. 206). This definition, like most recent conceptualizations of self, highlights the reflexive nature of selfhood, wherein agency is an assumed and necessary component of the development of self. Further, I posit the self as inescapably (immutably) situated and the work of selfhood is, in no small part, the distinguishing of self from and in relation to other (humans, social structures).

Until the 1990s and 2000s, agency was largely defined as an individual's enacted will. That is, agency was the expression, typically viewed only in terms of actions, of an autonomous self acting in their world. However, as sociocultural theory gained new traction around the turn of the century, so-called independent and autonomous behavior was recast as socially mediated and not simply individually or internally directed. Such definitions of agency as an "actor-situation transaction" (Biesta et al., 2015, p. 626) have become well accepted in research and theory on agency.

A common thread in most origin stories of agency, however, remains an individual's values and beliefs/aspirations. Emirbayer and Mische (1998), for example, assert that agency is "the imaginative generation by actors of possible future trajectories of action, in which received structures of thought and action may be creatively reconfigured in relation to actors' hopes, fears, and desires for the future" (p. 971). Within the field of LTA, Haneda and Sherman (2016) similarly observed, "For teachers, exercising agency involves choosing actions that align with their commitments and values and with their sense of who they are as professionals, and continuously evaluating the effectiveness of their actions" (p. 745). Increasingly, values and beliefs are understood as socially mediated, as individual variables that are informed and shaped by lived experiences. Utilizing an expanded understanding of values, beliefs and aspiration as individual yet socially mediated, rich theorizing continues around the role of values, beliefs and aspiration in human agency (Biesta et al., 2015; Leal & Crookes, 2018; Pantić, 2015; Venegas-Weber, 2019; Yanchar, 2011).

6.2.2   Agency as a Social Construction

Recent conceptualizations of agency, particularly those stemming from sociocultural theory, challenged the overly individualistic understanding of agency as simple self-determination with too little consideration of social factors and contextual influences. Toward a more expansive, social understanding of agency, Bucholtz and Hall (2005) observed that "the role of agency becomes problematic only when it is conceptualized as located within an individual rational subject who consciously authors his identity without structural constraints" (p. 606). Hall (2019) further clarified, "individuals are not agents of free will, independent decision makers, with unrestricted power and authority to use their resources to carry out any kind of action they want. . . . Rather, individual agency is a social construction" (p. 89). Flores and Rosa (2019) noted the accreted, socially-mediated nature of agency, describing it as "sedimented social knowledge" (p. 148). Agency, then, in much current scholarship assumes interplay between individual will and external constraints, but also recognizes that one's agency transforms and morphs according to perceptions of how efficacious one's agentic engagement is, what is perceived to be possible, and the strength and durability of social structures.

6.2.3   Time and Attention

Two additional elements that figure into many contemporary conceptualizations of agency are time and attention. Agency has a temporal nature, and many definitions of agency include reference to past, present and future dimensions of time. Emirbayer and Mische (1998), for example, conceptualize agency as a

> temporally embedded process of social engagement, informed by the past (in its habitual aspect), but also oriented toward the future (as a capacity to imagine alternative possibilities) and toward the present (as a capacity to contextualize past habits and future projects within the contingencies of the moment). (p. 963)

Beyond noting past, present and future orientations within agency, Hitlin and Elder (2007) note that perceptions of compressed or expanded time are *time horizons*. These time horizons are one explanation for the waxing and waning of individual's agentive engagement.

> Actors' temporal orientations are shaped by situational exigencies, with some situations calling for extensive focus on the present and others requiring an extended temporal orientation. Agentic behavior is influenced by the requirements of the interaction; as actors become more or less concerned with the immediate moment versus long-term life goals, they employ different social psychological processes and exhibit different forms of agency. (p. 171)

Therefore, to understand in-the-moment as well as long-term agentive engagement, it is necessary to unpack the time horizons that overlap, and sometimes compete with one another.

Three time horizons for agentive engagement are routine engagement, agency in novel situations, and life-course agency. Routine engagement is individuals' habitual actions and thinking around tasks that occur regularly or are familiar. This kind of engagement in the quotidian shortcuts the attention one needs to devote to recurring situations. Novel situations, those that are unexpected or challenge routine engagement in some way, require individuals to think again or make a quick decision. "[A] novel or ruptured situation drastically focuses one's attention" (Hitlin & Elder, 2007, p. 186). Finally, life-course agency, a concept introduced by Hitlin and Elder, describes the long-term agentive engagement individuals may have, for example, to achieving a career goal. These three time horizons, and perhaps additional ones, overlap in individuals' lives, yet, particularly within the field of LTA, the temporal nature of agency has not received much research or theorization.

Attention, as noted above, is closely related to time horizons, and the term attention refers to which priority within a person's values, beliefs, and aspirations takes precedence at any particular moment.

> Circumstances may require heightened attention and thus extensive conscious control. Other situations involve monitoring one's role enactment and do not necessitate the same heightened focus on one's own behavior; but, role internalization leads to some automaticity in habits and routines. (Hitlin & Elder, 2007; p. 175)

Darvin and Norton's theory of investment, discussed at greater length below, seems to also speak to attention as their work re-envisions how individuals' (understood in their work as language learners') values, beliefs and aspirations exert themselves through agentive engagement that is understood to be socially mediated (and not merely as internal to the individual). As Kramsch, in Darvin and Norton (2015) observed, "Norton's notion of investment … accentuates the role of human agency and identity in engaging with the task at hand, in accumulating economic and symbolic capital, in having stakes in the endeavor and in persevering in that endeavor" (p. 37). This recasts attention slightly to include the power of real and symbolic power to shape one's agentive engagement.

6.3   Language Teacher Agency

Definitions of language teacher agency (LTA), a concept relatively new to the teacher agency literature (Kayi-Aydar, 2019b), share a view on agency as socially situated. The situated nature of LTA is highlighted in much recent scholarship (e.g. Kayi-Aydar, 2019a, b; Kasun et al., 2019; Leal & Crookes, 2018; Peña-Pincheira & De Costa, 2021). Pantić (2015) described this situatedness:

> [T]eachers' exercise of their agency is highly relational and context-contingent rather than a matter of 'application' of the knowledge generated by research. The way teachers act in a particular environment is likely to result from complexly interdependent relations of their personal and professional beliefs and dispositions, degrees of autonomy and power, and interactions with other actors within the social contexts in which they work. (p. 760)

Peña-Pincheira and De Costa (2021) further explicate the situated nature of agency by enfolding the Douglas Fir group's micro, meso, and macro levels of engagement into Pantić's (2015) model of teacher agency for social justice: "we posit that teacher agency is a complex combination of teacher purpose, competence, autonomy and reflexivity, and is influenced by micro-, meso-, and macro-level factors" (p. 4).

Agency within applied linguistics and education is sometimes framed as a skill one can build or strengthen, such as in conceptualizations of *generating* (Kasun et al., 2019) or *achieving* agency (Biesta et al., 2015; Biesta & Tedder, 2007).

> Agency, in other words, is not something that people can have – as a property, capacity or competence – but is something that people do. More specifically, agency denotes a quality of the engagement of actors with temporal–relational contexts-for-action, not a quality of the actors themselves. (Biesta et al., 2015, p. 626)

Other conceptualizations frame teacher agency as a construct that exists but may need to be first uncovered or recognized before it can be *exercised* (Edwards, 2019; Kayi-Aydar, 2019b). This conceptualization is slightly different from agency as *generated* or *achieved* in that there is no assumption that agency needs to be built up or created. Yet, both conceptualizations assume or account for an element of efficacy in agentive engagement; that teachers may gain in their agentive abilities through either practice, confidence, experience, cooperation, or strategy. Teachers will be effective in shaping their social environments to varying degrees (Kasun et al., 2019; Miller & Gkonou, 2018; Warren, 2019), and such effectiveness has the potential to strengthen agentive behavior or engender more powerful agentive engagement.

Pantić's (2015) model of teacher professional agency also links agency to the effectiveness of agentive engagement, which relies on competence in her model. By competence, Pantić means, one's knowledge of the agentive "act" (p. 762). "Competent agents will usually be able to describe what they do, elaborate on the reasons for their behaviour, rationalise and motivate their own and others' actions" (p. 762). This kind of competence describes the individual's view of their effectiveness in agentive engagement. However, this is not necessarily the same as achieving change in other people or change in social structures.

Perhaps the most comprehensive conceptualization of LTA to date is Kayi-Aydar's (2019b), which is offered in the edited book, *Theorizing and Analyzing Language Teacher Agency* (Kayi-Aydar et al., 2019). LTA, Kayi-Aydar argues, is "a language teacher's intentional authority to make choices and act accordingly in his or her local context" (2019b, p. 15). This definition is accompanied by five considerations, drawn from social cognitive theory, the ecological approach (closely aligned with the agency conceptualizations within sociology, such as Emirbayer and Mische (1998) discussed above), and positioning theory. The five considerations are:

1. LTA is individual and collective.
2. LTA is highly context dependent.
3. Teachers' perceptions of their competence/efficacy affects agency.
4. LTA has temporal dimensions (past, present and future).
5. LTA is exercised through acts (including discourse) but also possibly through non-acts such as emotions.

This model, like Pantić's, captures the socially situated nature of LTA and that LTA has an efficacious element. Kayi-Aydar's conceptualization also argues that LTA can be collective (in addition to being individual), that LTA is temporal in nature, and that action is one way, but perhaps not the only way, LTA exists (or is perceived to exist). It is in these latter elements, in particular, that more research is needed to better understand how both time and action/non-action play a role in language teachers' agentive engagement.

The various elements of LTA, I argue, can be sorted into two general categories: meaningfulness and engagement. Without losing the nuanced definition of LTA that has already begun to take shape in scholarship, I propose these two categories as an avenue for understanding how elements of LTA, such as the five components outlined by Kayi-Aydar (2019b) above, may interact. LTA, in this conceptualization, is *meaningful engagement* (Yanchar, 2011) with the world, and the next sections address meaningfulness and engagement in turn by asking: (1) how do language teachers give and prioritize meaning in their teacher agency; and (2) what is the nature of language teachers' agentive engagement.

6.4 Meaningfulness and LTA

One question that endures throughout the last decade or so of scholarship on language teacher agency is *why* does teachers' agency seem to wax and wane? In other words, what accounts for teachers' decisions to engage or "step back" (Miller & Gkonou, 2018); to focus their attention deeply or superficially on aspects of their teaching; to act or not to act? Meaningfulness, how language teachers attach meaning to life, work, and those around them, may speak to this seeming inconsistency in LTA. Further, meaningfulness, I posit, is closely related to Darvin and Norton's (2015) conceptualization of investment, and theorization of investment as related to meaningful, agentive engagement remains under-theorized.

6.4.1 Darvin and Norton's Model of Investment

Three elements comprise Darvin and Norton's (2015) model of investment: ideology, capital, and identity. Ideology is a "normative set of ideas" (p. 43) infused throughout our personal, social, and professional worlds. Language learners (and teachers) may be largely unaware or simply entirely accustomed to the ideologies in which they are embedded. Making those ideologies visible and open to analysis is key. "[T]he construct of ideology in this model of investment allows us to analyze the relation between communicative practices and systemic patterns of control at both micro and macro levels" (p. 43). Similarly, exploration of ideologies within teaching contexts may open insight not only onto LTA but also opportunities for challenging inequitable power structures.

Capital, in Darvin and Norton's (2015) model, is power. Drawing on Bourdieu, the model assumes that power is not only economic but also social and cultural. Symbolic capital is that which shifts from context to context as ideologies shift and the value of capital gets renegotiated. Perceptions of the value and strength of one's capital, then, will figure into one's agentic engagement.

Identity is the multiple selves held within each individual, selves which are socially situated and mutable. Darvin and Norton define identity as

> multiple, a site of struggle, and continually changing over time and space. What this model seeks to do is to elucidate further that identity is a struggle of habitus and desire, of competing ideologies and imagined identities. Governed by different ideologies and possessing varying levels of capital, learners position themselves and are positioned by others in different contexts. (p. 45)

An individual's identity investments are indexes of meaningfulness. As a person perceives what is possible within ideological affordances and constraints of their setting, negotiates their own capital and its value within particular contexts, and claims identity positions, they are expressing (and enacting) investments. In light of their investments, in other words, teachers prioritize meaningful agentive engagements.

6.4.2 Meaningfulness in the Case of Sarah

Darvin and Norton's (2015) model of investment furthers our understanding of agency as socially situated and mediated, and through the model's three elements (ideology, capital, and identity) we gain insight into how language teachers may assign meaningfulness within their work. Let us explore meaningfulness through the example of Sarah, a secondary (grades 9–12) English as a second language (ESL) teacher whom I have profiled in previous work (Reeves, 2010, 2018). Sarah a white woman in her early 30's teaching ESL to mostly Latinx high school students in a rural school in the American Midwest. What primarily gave meaning to Sarah within her identity as a teacher was her care for her students, and this focus on care stemmed from her childhood. The child of a funeral home director, she was familiar with and keenly sensitive to others' feelings. She was also an empathic teacher, continually checking in on her students' emotional and physical well-being (Reeves, 2018). Prepared through her teacher education program to teach mathematics rather than language, Sarah lacked confidence in her ability to teach English, even though she was a six-year veteran ESL teacher at the time of the study. "I just feel like I've been lacking the skills to get that to my kids in an efficient manner to help them move up the ranks as fast as possible" (Reeves, 2018, p. 102). As a result of lack of confidence in her ability to teach English and pressure from her school administration to raise her multilingual learners' standardized test scores (in tests given only in English), Sarah chose to teach with a scripted curriculum program. Scripted curricula provide a script for teachers, and highly scripted programs like Sarah's provide the exact words teacher should say and actions they should take. Initially she was quite satisfied with the program; however, after about 18 months of following the program's guidelines closely (in which Sarah's instruction was prescribed in minute detail), Sarah saw that her students were bored and listless in class. Sarah became increasingly disenchanted with the program because it impeded her from enacting a major element of her identity: her deep care for her students. When Sarah began to see how the scripted program required her to teach in ways that she felt were uncaring, she slowly began to go off script in order to better express her care for her students. For example, she let student errors pass when the script directed her to immediately address them, and she stopped enforcing the program's strict choral response regiment.

Sarah's meaningful engagement around the curriculum of her classrooms was influenced by the deep care and responsibility she felt for her students; she was invested in her identity as a caring teacher. Her choice to adopt the scripted program was, initially, an expression of that identity. Prior to adopting the program, the curriculum consultant told Sarah her students could gain full or nearly full English proficiency in 24 months, maybe less. "I'm like, wow, you know, if that kind of progress can be made in that amount of time, we'd be doing a disservice to our kids if we didn't offer more of it [scripted curriculum program]" (Reeves, 2018, p. 102). Care for her students meant, at least in part, raising their test scores. Ideological dimensions of her investment included her school's neoliberal valuing of standardized test scores above all else and the way that the school (and Sarah herself, initially) linked her success as a teacher to good test scores. In terms of capital, Sarah understood she had the power to choose curriculum for her class, though that power was premised on her making a good choice and raising test scores. In a way,

Sarah surrendered power to the curriculum, speaking and acting as she was directed because she had little faith in her own ability. Ultimately, however, Sarah took power back from the script after she began to recognize that her investment in her identity as a caring teacher conflicted with her investment in raising students' test scores. Finally, in terms of identity, Sarah was easily persuaded that she was not a successful teacher because her students' test scores were low. Importantly, though, her identity position as a caring teacher, one who watched out not just for her learners' test scores but also their overall well-being, compelled her to take back some control of her curriculum. In Sarah's example, we see how she attributed and attached meaningfulness in her teaching, and the concept of investment further explicates how local ideologies, capital, and Sarah's identity positions afforded and restricted Sarah's agentive engagement.

A second element of meaningfulness that has yet to receive a thorough exploration within LTA scholarship is time. Meaningfulness can wax and wane according to investment, but also temporally. "[A]gency should be understood as a configuration of influences from the past, orientations towards the future and engagement with the present" (Biesta et al., 2015, p. 626). In addition to understanding agency as oriented in the past, present, and future, there are also overlapping time horizons within individuals and contexts. These can include long-term and short-term aspirations, commitments, and investments, each competing for prioritized meaning. Further, novel situations, as described by Hitlin and Elder (2007) arise and require one's immediate attention. For Sarah, a novel situation interrupted her routine engagement with the scripted curriculum, focusing her attention on a conflict between her identity position and her chosen curriculum. When Sarah shared her newcomer student's writing with the consultant for her scripted curriculum program, Sarah was surprised to be admonished by the consultant. Sarah was full of pride that her newcomer student had written multiple lines of prose after having been silent and withdrawn since her arrival in Sarah's classroom several weeks prior. Praising the student and encouraging her to continue writing, Sarah was enacting her care for the student. The consultant, however, pointed out that *all* errors—and the student's writing sample had several, including a run-on sentence—must be corrected immediately if the curriculum were to be effective. Sarah balked and began to question the curriculum program's fit for her classroom, even if students test scores were improved. This incident focused Sarah's attention on what was most meaningful to her, in which identity positions she was most invested.

6.5 Engagement and LTA

Agency in most conceptualizations, as noted above, assumes action, and in some cases agency requires action that must result in *change* in others (Stewart, 2019). Optimal agency is often framed as transformative action (Pantić, 2015) that dramatically alters social structures or cultural mores. But, is there agency without action? Without delving too deeply into the meaning of *action,* some attention should be paid to how agency may be too simplistically understood only as observed behavior. To act or to *enact*, which is a common phraseology in LTA scholarship, particularly within the ecological perspective on agency (Biesta & Tedder, 2007; Kayi-Aydar, 2019a), is assumed in much representation of agentive engagement. The teacher in Kasun et al. (2019) embedded narratives (sharing her own oral narrative and requiring students to write narratives) in her teaching; this is an example of a teacher acting agentively. But, is agency always and only expressed through action? The teacher in Kasun, et al. could have thought about embedding narratives in her teaching; perhaps she might only have made a mental note to consider doing so in the future. Is making a mental note but exhibiting no visible behavior an example of agency? Currently, few research examples in LTA scholarship take up this notion of agentive engagement as non-action. Consideration of agency, however, ought to explore not just what is visible but what teachers are thinking and how and why they may be refraining from action (or are actually engaging by not acting).

Further, interpreting agentive engagement out of teaching behavior and/or (non)-action is fraught. In light of both overlapping, even competing time horizons and variously prioritized investments, fully understanding any single action in its entirety would require exhaustive exploration not only of the action but of the actors' intentions and understandings as well as contextual factors. Bucholtz and Hall (2005) warn against interpreting intentionality through action alone. "[A]gency does not require that social action be intentional, but it allows for that possibility; habitual actions accomplished below the level of conscious awareness act upon the world no less than those carried out deliberately" (p. 607). Recent scholarship on language teachers' emotions and emotions' relationship to agency also suggests that action-based analyses may be insufficient to understand LTA (Miller & Gkonou, 2018).

There is promising work suggesting a need to more fully explore teachers' emotions within conceptualizations of language teacher agency. "[T]eacher emotions provide necessary 'signals' for language teachers to initiate reflection on how particular discourses of teaching intersect with their emotion experiences and choices to exercise agency through emotion labor" (Miller & Gkonou, 2018, p. 57). Reflection not only on action but also on teacher emotions and emotional responses are elements of agentive engagement in need of additional theorization.

6.5.1   Engagement in the Case of Sarah

In the case of Sarah, her agentive engagement with and around the curriculum in her classes was marked by emotion, conflict, and varying degrees of attention. Early after the adoption of the curriculum, Sarah was satisfied with the curriculum as she saw her learners initially respond positively and attentively to the strict protocols of the program. When her students were compliant and learning, Sarah too was satisfied and felt her teaching aligned with her care for her students. She began to sense discontentment in her students (through their boredom and lack of enthusiasm) when the critical incident around her newcomer student's error-laden writing caused a rupture. The incident brought Sarah up short in terms of what she should do to best care for her student; Sarah feared causing her newcomer to feel either embarrassed or discouraged, which was something Sarah, as a caring teacher, was loathe to do. At the same time, Sarah wanted her students to improve their test scores to have better access to educational opportunities. In the end, Sarah's dismay at seeing her students bored and/or discouraged caused Sarah to step back from the scripted program.

Sarah's actions did not always align with her intentions. For example, Sarah's teaching behavior while on script initially aligned with her investment in her identity as a caring teacher. And, even as that alignment began to slip, Sarah's actions, for a time, remained the same; she performed the script as directed. But, her actions did not capture her intentions and her feelings of discontent, indicating that action and engagement are not the same. It is in Sarah's actions and her inactions, but also in her levels of attention and investment, that we can best understand her LTA.

Expanding our understanding of agentive engagement to include, but to not be limited by, behavior or physical action seems critical to understanding LTA. If educational researchers and teacher educators are to gather and apply research on LTA, the full scope of engagement must be allowed for—even if we cannot yet account for all aspects at present.

6.6   Conclusion

Understanding language teacher agency requires us to further investigate just what language teacher agency is. Viewing LTA as meaningful engagement may provide new theoretical avenues for continuing this investigation. In particular, at least these four aspects of LTA need more research attention: investment, time, (non)action, and emotions.

The implications of a better understanding of LTA include the potential for teacher educators and teachers themselves to design and carry out meaningful, useful teacher preparation and professional development. Teachers' own explorations of their investments could lead to more meaningful engagement as teachers come to understanding the affordances and constraints of their context. Teacher preparation and development programs ought to include attention to what LTA is and how it can function, including exploration of the temporal and emotional dimensions of teachers' agency. Such insight could assist teachers in understanding their own identities and the ways they are constrained, by self, by others, and through their contexts. And, most importantly, understanding language teacher agency may give teachers the tools to be more in control of their own teaching lives, to fight against inequities, and to work effectively toward positive change.

References

Biesta, G., & Tedder, M. (2007). Agency and learning in the lifecourse: Towards an ecological perspective. *Studies in the Education of Adults, 39*, 132–149. https://doi.org/10.1080/02660830.2007.11661545

Biesta, G., Priestley, M., & Robinson, S. (2015). The role of beliefs in teacher agency. *Teachers and Teaching, 21*, 624–640. https://doi.org/10.1080/13540602.2015.1044325

Bucholtz, M., & Hall, K. (2005). Identity and interaction: A sociocultural linguistic approach. *Discourse Studies, 7*, 585–614. https://doi.org/10.1177/1461445605054407

Darvin, R., & Norton, B. (2015). Identity and a model of investment in applied linguistics. *Annual Review of Applied Linguistics, 35*, 36–56. https://doi.org/10.1017/S0267190514000191

Edwards, E. (2019). English language teachers' agency and identity mediation through action research: A Vygotskian sociocultural analysis. In H. Kayi-Aydar, X. Gao, E. R. Miller, M. Varghese, & G. Vitanova (Eds.), *Theorizing and analyzing language teacher agency* (pp. 141–159). Multilingual Matters.

Emirbayer, M., & Mische, A. (1998). What is agency? *American Journal of Sociology, 103*, 962–1023. https://doi.org/10.1086/231294

Flores, N., & Rosa, J. (2019). Bringing race into second language acquisition. *The Modern Language Journal, 103*, 145–151. https://doi.org/10.1111/modl.12523

Hall, J. K. (2019). The contributions of conversation analysis and interactional linguistics to a usage-based understanding of language: Expanding the transdisciplinary framework. *The Modern Language Journal, 103*, 80–94. https://doi.org/10.1111/modl.12535

Haneda, M., & Sherman, B. (2016). A job-crafting perspective on teacher agentive action. *TESOL Quarterly, 50*(3), 745–754. http://www.jstor.org/stable/44984711

Hitlin, S., & Elder, G. H. (2007). Time, self, and the curiously abstract concept of agency. *Sociological Theory, 25*(2), 170–191. https://doi.org/10.1111/j.1467-9558.2007.00303.x

Kasun, G. S., Spencer Clark, J., Jyoti Kaneria, A., & Staker, E. (2019). 'What if you don't' have boots', let alone bootstraps? An ELL teacher's use of narrative to achieve and generate agency in the face of contextual constraints. In H. Kayi-Aydar, X. Gao, E. R. Miller, M. Varghese, & G. Vitanova (Eds.), *Theorizing and analyzing language teacher agency* (pp. 44–62). Multilingual Matters.

Kayi-Aydar, H. (2019a). A language teacher's agency in the development of her professional identities: A narrative case study. *Journal of Latinos and Education, 18*, 4–18. https://doi.org/10.1080/15348431.2017.1406360

Kayi-Aydar, H. (2019b). Teacher agency: Major theoretical considerations, conceptualizations and methodological choices. In H. Kayi-Aydar, X. Gao, E. R. Miller, M. Varghese, & G. Vitanova (Eds.), *Theorizing and analyzing language teacher agency* (pp. 10–23). Multilingual Matters.

Kayi-Aydar, H., Gao, X., Miller, E. R., Varghese, M., & Vitanova, G. (Eds.). (2019). *Theorizing and analyzing language teacher agency*. Multilingual Matters.

Leal, P., & Crookes, G. V. (2018). "Most of my students kept saying, 'I never met a gay person'": A queer English language teacher's agency for social justice. *System, 79*, 38–48. https://doi.org/10.1016/j.system.2018.06.005

Miller, E. R., & Gkonou, C. (2018). Language teacher agency, emotion labor and emotional rewards in tertiary-level English language programs. *System, 79*, 49–59. https://doi.org/10.1016/j.system.2018.03.002

Owens, T. J. (2003). Self and identity. In J. De Lamater (Ed.), *Handbook of social psychology* (pp. 205–232). Kluwer.

Pantić, N. (2015). A model for study of teacher agency for social justice. *Teachers and Teaching, 21*, 759–778. https://doi.org/10.1080/13540602.2015.1044332

Peña-Pincheira, R. S., & De Costa, P. I. (2021). Language teacher agency for educational justice–oriented work: An ecological model. *TESOL Journal, 12*, e561. https://doi.org/10.1002/tesj.561

Reeves, J. (2010). Teacher learning by script. *Language Teaching Research, 14*, 241–258. https://doi.org/10.1177/1362168810365252

Reeves, J. (2018). Teacher identity work in neoliberal schooling spaces. *Teaching and Teacher Education, 72*, 98–106. https://doi.org/10.1016/j.tate.2018.03.002

Stewart, A. (2019). Using actor-network theory to problematize agency and identity formation of Filipino teachers in Japan. In H. Kayi-Aydar, X. Gao, E. R. Miller, M. Varghese, & G. Vitanova (Eds.), *Theorizing and analyzing language teacher agency* (pp. 82–100). Multilingual Matters.

Venegas-Weber, P. (2019). Bi/multilingual teachers' professional holistic lives: Agency to enact inquiry-based and equity-oriented identities across school contexts. In H. Kayi-Aydar, X. Gao, E. R. Miller, M. Varghese, & G. Vitanova (Eds.), *Theorizing and analyzing language teacher agency* (pp. 121–140). Multilingual Matters.

Warren, A. N. (2019). Language teacher agency and high-stakes teacher evaluation: A positioning analysis. In H. Kayi-Aydar, X. Gao, E. R. Miller, M. Varghese, & G. Vitanova (Eds.), *Theorizing and analyzing language teacher agency* (pp. 63–81). Multilingual Matters.

Yanchar, S. C. (2011). Participational agency. *Review of General Psychology, 15*, 277–287. https://doi.org/10.1037/a0024872

Chapter 7
An Arts-Informed Teacher Identity for Intercultural Language Teaching

Lesley Harbon

Abstract This chapter argues that a language teacher's identity develops in a particular way when the teacher embeds an intercultural orientation and an arts-informed pedagogical approach in their teaching of languages and cultures. An intercultural language education curriculum enhanced by an arts-informed pedagogy (Forehand, J Philos Hist Educ 58:77–82, 2008; Piazzoli, Embodying language in action: the artistry of process drama in second language education. Palgrave Macmillan, London, 2018; Shier, Foreign Lang Ann 23:301–314, 1990) can allow language teachers to prepare their learners to mediate meaning and 'absorb' perspectives (Bresler, The Routledge international handbook of intercultural arts research. Routledge, London, 2016). As the idea of 'intercultural', or the "language-culture nexus" (Risager, Language and culture: global flows and local complexity. Multilingual Matters, Clevedon, 2006, p. 185), is a dynamic notion, presumably a creative dynamism resulting from arts integrated with languages will result in richer teaching and learning. The claim "who I am is how I teach" (Farrell, Reflections on language teacher identity research. Routledge, New York and London, 2017, p. 183) refers to the close relationship between teacher identities and their personal and professional lives (Barkhuizen, Reflections on language teacher identity research. Routledge, New York and London, 2017). If the language teacher's identity is shaped by artistic and creative ways of knowing, then intercultural teaching and learning of languages may be oriented in that way. This chapter proposes that understanding teachers' arts-oriented identities can result in both teachers and learners acting as intercultural mediators (Witte, Blending spaces: mediating and assessing intercultural competence in the L2 classroom. De Gruyter Mouton, Boston/Berlin, 2014) in the 'interpretive zones' (Bresler, The Routledge international handbook of intercultural arts research. Routledge, London, 2016) between the two (or more) languages and cultures in teachers' and learners' repertoires.

L. Harbon (✉)
University of Technology Sydney, Sydney, NSW, Australia
e-mail: Lesley.Harbon@uts.edu.au

© The Author(s), under exclusive license to Springer Nature Switzerland AG 2022   89
K. Sadeghi, F. Ghaderi (eds.), *Theory and Practice in Second Language Teacher Identity*, Educational Linguistics 57, https://doi.org/10.1007/978-3-031-13161-5_7

Keywords Identity · Language teacher · The arts · Intercultural language teaching · Intercultural pedagogy

7.1   Introduction

In a recent volume, alluding to the difficulty in finding a comprehensive definition of, or theory for, language teacher identity, Barkhuizen (2017, p. 2) devised an "unplugged" method to explore those problems further. The unplugged nature of his comment referred to how he asked numerous scholars to reflect on the definition and theorising of language teacher identity in a grounded way, and through a narrative-oriented methodology. The resulting proposition discussed language teacher identities not purely as who the teacher is, rather how the language teacher identity is shaped by myriad factors. According to Barkhuizen (2017, p. 4),

> Language teacher identities (LTIs) are cognitive, social, emotional, ideological, and historical … being and doing, feeling and imagining, and storying… They are core and peripheral, personal and professional, they are dynamic, multiple, and hybrid, and they are foregrounded and … change, short-term and over time—discursively in social interaction with teacher educators, learners, teachers, administrators, and the wider community, and in material interaction with spaces, places and objects in classrooms, institutions, and online.

The layering and complexity of the myriad facets of language teacher identity presented in Barkhuizen's (2017) volume challenge researchers to continue examining language teacher identity as a key impacting factor in accomplished (Australian Federation of Modern Language Teachers Associations [AFMLTA], 2021) teaching and learning of languages and cultures. As one such further examination of how the whole of a teachers' personal and professional life can impact their identity, this chapter will explore language and meaning-making, culture-learning, and how the arts are seen to employ a way of investigating experience, similar to what the language teacher does when teaching interculturally. Should a language teacher build on the 'sensemaking' aspect of what is embedded in 'art-making', then the language teacher's arts-informed identity can enrich the type of learning outcomes possible for students learning languages.

7.2   Planning for Accomplished Teachers to Teach Interculturally and Communicatively

Language is "a system of symbols with agreed-upon meanings" enabling us to think about things present and not present, "to think abstractly, to have ideas and share them" (Eubanks, 2003, p. 13). Scholars maintain that learning and language are closely connected and that learning "develops from social interactions between language users" (Farenga & Ness, 2005, p. 688), a proposition emerging from the work of Vygotsky (1978) and notions of social constructivism. Swain (2006, p. 98) described this notion as "languaging", an activity involving a "process of making meaning and shaping knowledge and experience through language". Swain and Watanabe (2013) later conceptualised this activity of 'learning through language' as collaborative dialogue.

Scholars have long linked language and culture. Linked to anthropological definitions of language and culture, Geertz (1973, p. 89, cited in Marczak, 2013, p. 2) claimed that culture is "a historically transmitted pattern of meanings embodied in symbols, a system of inherited conceptions, expressed in symbolic form by means of which men communicate, perpetuate and develop their knowledge about, and attitudes towards life." Hartle and Jaruszewicz (2009, p. 187) contend that "learning, making, and using symbols are at the essence of being human". Both language and culture, then, are embedded with symbols and signs. The field of scholarship focusing on systems of symbols and signs is semiotics, and "how these are used to communicate, provides a framework for understanding the processes [we] use in making meaning" (Hartle & Jaruszewicz, 2009, p. 187).

Language teachers must develop the ability to teach learners to make meaning and use those symbolic systems. The development of an intercultural competence is an intended language learning outcome (Kramsch, 1993), with language teachers encouraging learners to move between first and second (or third or more) languages and cultures to mediate meaning. Planning and policy-making can assist language teachers to develop this competence. Language education sits in national educational policies (Wiley et al., 2014) and at the core of language policy and planning are the languages themselves. Language planning focuses on how governments structure and offer languages in education, specifically (Tollefson, 2008, p. 3) ". . . statements of goals and means for achieving them that constitute guidelines or rules shaping language structure, language use, and language acquisition".

Embedded in a nation's language planning and policy is a belief that within a well-rounded education, language learning can deliver many outcomes. In the United States, for example, a government report (United States Department of Education [USDE], 2012) linked foreign language acquisition and skills to global competence, citing the power of language learning to improve communication, working relationships, and cross-cultural understanding. Other intended outcomes of language education include notions such as ". . . cultural understanding, cognitive development, globalization, economic opportunity" (Hellmich, 2018, p. 320). Indicating similar learning outcomes in an Australian context, the Australian government (Australian Curriculum and Assessment Reporting Authority [ACARA], 2020, p. 1) claims that "learning languages also contributes to strengthening the community's social, economic and international development capabilities." Further assertions are that language education offers the learner a general language awareness: "... a person's sensitivity to, and conscious awareness of, the nature of language and its role in human life" (James & Garrett, 1992, p. 8, cited in Van Essen, 1997, p. 1). In Australia, the professional language teacher association aspires to achieve policy aims via the aforementioned accomplished teaching of languages and cultures (AFMLTA, 2021, p. 1).

Accomplished language teaching can skill language learners to 'communicate' with those who speak a different language. Savignon (2006, p. 673) describes the process of teaching languages communicatively as the development of a communicative competence: the term 'communicative' referring to "both the process and goals of learning". Language curricula are structured to allow language teachers and learners to demonstrate learners' communicative learning outcomes. Lillis (2006, p. 667) defines communicative competence in terms of the "language capabilities of the individual that include both knowledge and use". Such goals link this communicative competence to a teacher's ability to prepare learners to communicate with speakers of the target language, and while traveling to, and through, the places where the target language is spoken. Much emphasis has been placed on the notion that language teaching can be considered to be culture learning (Moran, 2001), referring to the language teacher emphasising an intercultural competence.

7.3   Culture and an Intercultural Competence

Moran (2001, p. 121) proposes that the process of language learning is, in fact, "learning culture", and that "we use language to learn culture" (2001, p. 39). Researching this phenomenon in the Australian context, Scarino (2008, p. 5.8) noted a "direction towards teaching language *as* culture in languages education". Langacker (1999, p. 16) also refers to the nexus between language and culture, stating that language is "an essential instrument and component of culture, whose reflection in linguistic structure is pervasive and quite significant". We may understand that language is "a cultural activity and, at the same time, an instrument for organizing other cultural domains" (Palmer & Sharifian, 2007, p. 1). The outcome of language teaching referred to here is the way language knowledge may therefore be the conduit which provides learners with insights into another culture.

Many terms exist which describe teaching and learning between languages and cultures. Teaching languages with an intercultural orientation can contribute to a process known as 'internationalisation'. Arasaratnam-Smith (2017) traces the notion of intercultural competence back to the middle of the twentieth century when statements were being made about intercultural education more generally. Arasaratnam-Smith (2017, p. 7) cites research which alludes to the notion of "cross-cultural effectiveness" in education "also labelled intercultural competence, or intercultural adaptation".

According to Moran (2001, p. 47), "members of the culture use their language to portray their culture, to put their cultural perspectives into practice, to carry out their way of life." Such an examination of cultural perspectives allowed Hull and Hellmich (2018, p. 2) to refer to an "international mindedness" which results from language teachers providing an international stance on the curriculum. According to Moran (2001, p. 38) "language is the central means of learning culture in the language classroom" and intercultural competence is a highly valued outcome of the educational process.

In essence, a language teacher who prioritises an intercultural approach can equip learners for an enriched life experience. Language teachers explore language and culture with their students, showing how to use language for specific functions: for interpersonal communication, for informational communication, and also to be creative (for aesthetic use) (Vale et al., 1991). These notions are related to the "affective aspect of learning an additional language and culture" (Harbon, 2014, p. 17). Language teachers can emphasise how we 'transact' with our language, how we can 'express our thoughts and feelings' through our language, and interestingly, how we can also 'create' through our artistic abilities and the language we use to be creative and respond to the arts. Language teachers can learn to emphasise this pedagogical strategy for learners to be creative and use language in their responses to music, dance, visual arts, or dramatic performance. It is as if 'the arts' could be best defined as 'another language' through which we can deliver and receive meaning, a concept explored as the 'languages/arts nexus'. Language teachers can realise and develop these understandings in their own identity, and can also aim to realise and develop the same in their learners.

7.4   Languages and the Arts: Interpretive Zones

As described above, language is a symbolic system for meaning-making and communicating, and scholars argue that it is a similar case for 'the arts' (Black, 2011; Hartle & Jaruszewicz, 2009). Research has variously explored what can occur at the juncture between language and the arts. In an empirical study, Spina (2006, p. 99) found that "an arts-based curriculum provides significant cognitive advantage to ESL students by building on the cognitive strengths inherent in bilingualism". We can choose any one, or a combination of, art forms and methods – dance, drama, music, visual arts – for our meaning-making; we do not have to rely solely on language to communicate meaning. The semiotic system of the arts allows learners/users of more than one language to "approach symbolisation in a creative, nuanced way" (Spina, 2006, p. 100).

The arts enrich our personal and professional lives, and as Black (2011, p. 68) maintains, "as well as encouraging a creative inquiry process, arts-based methods can reveal tacit knowledge and make knowledge and meaning construction visible". Schooling has experimented intermittently with integrating 'the arts' across the curriculum (Meyer, 2005). We only need look at the impact of Gardner's multiple intelligences theory (Gardner, 1983) to know how broadly educationalists have long believed in, acknowledged, and catered to learners' artistic and creative learning preferences (Groff, 2013). Learners, according to Whitfield (2009, p. 153) ". . . come to know in a multitude of ways and those whose roots lie in oral, visual, or kinaesthetic cultures are placed at a disadvantage when their first experiences with schooling are bereft of joy and individual expression related to their cultural roots". This line of thought refers to the fact that in different cultures, and through different languages, there are many symbolic systems allowing individuals to experience life within the boundaries of their communities. The strands of 'the arts' – music, visual arts, dance, drama – provide us with symbolic systems, as do languages. The arts also provide us with the creative processes and procedural methods through which we can communicate and make meaning. Language teachers can bring together these strands of knowing and understanding, of languaging and the arts, in their planning for student learning.

Wang and Kokotsaki (2018) explore the notion of "creativity" and refer to Piaget's premise that creativity is a major goal of education. Ewing (2010, p. 8) cites Perkins (1981), and notes that "people with creative dispositions or habits of mind are able to probe ideas more deeply, ask open-ended questions, seek multiple responses and listen to their inner voice; critiquing, reflecting and persisting." The arts allow us to become more aware of the human experience (Ewing, 2010), and the technology which helps us think this through is human language. There is more than one way to view the world of human experience (Ingold, 2014). If creative experience can be achieved through different cultural lenses, through our 'own' and 'other' languages, then a richer creativity may result – there is not just one creativity through one language. Again, the language teacher's own identity can be shaped by these understandings, impacting the kind of teaching planned.

Scholars and teacher-practitioners have traced schooling programs where the arts and language learning enjoy an equal place in the curriculum. The early childhood schooling experience in northern Italy, known as Reggio Emilia (Millikan, 2010; Vecchi, 2010), is centred on creativity, arts and languages. According to Millikan (2010, p. 14), it was the founder of this schooling experience for very young children who prioritised imagination and creativity, with the Reggio Emilia schooling system extending the definition of language "beyond the verbal". Vecchi (2010, p. xviii) also commenting on the Reggio Emilia schooling system, noted the different ways that "children (and human beings) represent, communicate, and express their thinking in different media and symbolic systems."

The arts allow individuals and groups in our communities to become more aware of, and make meaning from, the human experience (Ewing, 2010). All teachers can enrich curriculum and pedagogies by opting to integrate the arts with other subject areas. Sulentic Dowell and Goering (2018, p. 87) define arts integration as "a pedagogical approach combining a core curricular concept with an art form (or art forms) such as visual art, music, theatre, or dance". In fact Gallas (1994, p. 116, cited in Whitfield, 2009, p. 156) emphasises why the arts should be centrally integrated in school curricula, maintaining that an art experience,

fills a number of roles: (1) the arts as representing a methodology for acquiring knowledge; (2) the arts as subject matter for study, in and of themselves; and (3) the arts as an array of expressive opportunities for communicating with others.

Piazzoli (2018, p. 4) encourages teachers to work in an "in-between space" where meaning-making is a dynamic process of negotiation: negotiation of signs, symbols, and therefore language, and the 'language' of the arts, and their meanings. Piazzoli's focus on the dramatic arts in particular, emphasises a process strategy, suggesting that the drama classroom community (Piazzoli, 2018, p. 8) is like a:

classroom ecology, thriving on a pattern of exchanges, creates various forms of learner engagement ... the teacher/artist engages students as co-artists in a process involving not only cognition, but also affect, imagery, sensation, different forms of memory, emotion and embodiment. This dynamic relation between teacher and students' artistry and engagement is the work of art.

Crutchfield and Schewe (2017, p. xiv, cited in Piazzoli, 2018, p. 28) describe performative language teaching as "an approach to language teaching and learning that emphasises embodied action and that makes use of techniques, forms and aesthetic processes adapted from the performing arts". In such a "performative approach" – or process – to teaching languages (Piazzoli, 2018), the language teacher 'performs' as an artist would. In other words, in an integrated arts/drama language classroom, language users mediate meaning in differing, creative ways.

Expanding this idea, Piazzoli (2018, p. 39) claims that "a 'performative' approach to language is an embodied approach, with particular attention to the aesthetic domain." Piazzoli (2018, p. 29) claims "embodiment is also tightly interconnected with intercultural education". Commenting specifically on dramatic arts, Fleming's (2002, p. 88) view is that all drama education can be seen as a form of intercultural education, allowing students to "learn about other cultures which is at least the beginning of a form of intercultural education", and providing opportunities "... to create, observe and practise forms of social behaviour with the safety of the fictitious context" (Fleming, 2002, p. 99).

The 'language education' and 'arts' interpretive zones, and the cultural symbols we utilise within them, as we live out our lives and as we 'travel' in and between our communities, are dynamic. According to Bresler (2016, p. 325), "navigating cultural zones suggests dynamic processes – exchange, transaction, intensity and absorption". This idea of navigating cultural zones establishing that some aspects of our lives are familiar, and some are "strange" (Bresler, 2016, p. 325), indicates that communications and meanings within the space are continually in a dynamic state of fluidity. A "dialectical tension" between familiar and strange, between self and other, between one way of making meaning and another (Bresler, 2016, p. 325) can maintain the dynamism of meaning-making in the life-worlds we establish.

Also located in this language-and-the-arts informed space are 'travels' or 'journeys'. The language teacher's 'journey' teaching a second or foreign language involves the development of intercultural competencies. Bresler (2016, p. 321) discusses what occurs in "interdisciplinary and intercultural travels", especially if there is "sustained exchange of perspectives" (p. 324). What Bresler (2016) calls the "absorption of perspectives [in] an interpretive zone" (p. 324) may equate to individuals bringing together "their various areas of knowledge, cultural background and beliefs, to forge new meanings through the process of joint inquiry in which they are engaged" (p. 324). Teaching in these interpretive zones may also result in teachers' and learners' constructive responses to 'otherness' (Calcutt et al., 2009), and perhaps greater understandings of self.

Moran's statements (2001, p. 40) about the link between 'the arts' and 'intercultural language learning' relate to "cultural practices, where people need to express themselves, communicate, and carry out the affairs of their shared way of life." A language teacher's identity shapes this type of language learning. According to Moran (2001, p. 45),

> language functions ... serve to help learners express their responses to the cultural phenomenon at hand ... Learners' responses include feelings, opinions, values, beliefs, questions, concerns or awarenesses, as well as intentions, strategies, decisions... Essentially these functions entail learners' self-expression. The focus is knowing oneself, self-awareness.

Hoecherl-Alden and Fegely (2019, p. 57) assert that "learning a second language (L2) through art ... appeals to emotions and engages the senses", because of its "intercultural and interdisciplinary nature" (p. 58). In their book titled "*Creative multilingualism: a manifesto*", Kohl et al., (2020, p. 1) highlight how language plays "a creative force in our thought and emotions, our expression and social interaction, and our activity in the world". There is, they posit, an intricate relationship between (Kohl et al., 2020, p. 29):

- our cognition, including our emotions and imagination,
- our bodies in their spatial environment,
- our cultural heritage and cultural context,
- our language(s) in its/their oral and written manifestations,
- our linguistic and situational context.

For decades, scholars have suggested that teaching languages can be enhanced by a pedagogy informed by 'the arts' (Forehand, 2008; Piazzoli, 2018; Shier, 1990), as 'the arts' through language can allow teachers and learners to mediate meaning and 'absorb' perspectives (Bresler, 2016), one of the definitions of an intercultural orientation to teaching languages. Language teachers who plan teaching and learning through the riches of language, cultures and the arts can plan that learners experience an energy lived through, and mediated in, the zones of languages, cultures and the arts.

7.5 Artmaking and 'Languaging' as Sensemaking for Mediating Meaning

In the same way that windows and bridges span the gaps in between two places, Forehand (2008, p. 78) suggests that 'the arts' are contributors to a feeling of 'other culture' belonging – she used metaphors to label the arts as "walls, windows or bridges across cultures". Bower (2004, p. 23, cited in Gibson & Anderson, 2008, p. 104) claims that teaching the arts to students "has been linked to better visual thinking, problem solving, language and creativity ... by learning and practising art, the human brain actually wires itself to make stronger connections". Gibson and Anderson (2008) state that the arts are at the heart of cultural expression, and it is cultural expression which is at the heartbeat of our societies. The "in-betweenness" (Ortega, 2009, p. 1) of the intercultural space is bridged by languages – in their widest definition to include the meaning-making of the arts – for community to build its solid foundations.

Creating through the arts, or 'artmaking', can be considered as a form of 'sensemaking' (Boske, 2020). An intercultural orientation to teaching languages has also been considered as form of 'sensemaking', or 'culture-knowing' (Moran, 2001). Making sense of the learning about language, the notion of "languaging" described by Swain (2006, p. 98) involves the "process of making meaning and shaping knowledge and experience through language". The "language to learn culture", says Moran (2001, p. 39), occurs via the sensemaking possible through 'language' itself, and 'the arts'.

According to Boske (2020), artmaking is sensemaking – language teaching and learning is all about the embodied pedagogy using mind, senses, imagination, reality, while artmaking too, involves the tools and processes for constructing meaning through the senses. An intercultural orientation to learning a culture through another language (Moran, 2001) is based on this sensemaking, or 'knowings'. Both 'language' and 'the arts', essentially another language, provides us with an intercultural competence, giving us frames to mediate and negotiate third spaces (Kramsch, 1993), allowing us to access other 'knowings' (Moran, 2001). Once we interpret, we can make some sense of our life-worlds. In this way, meaning-making is a 'literacy'.

7.6 Languages, the Arts and an Arts-Informed Language Teacher Identity

According to Switzer (2009, p. 135), "the broader view of literate activities as forms of communicative practice would also include drawing, singing songs, dancing, or even creating musical sounds to convey and/or evoke feeling or emotional response." If artmaking, in and of itself, requires the audience to relate, engage, and make sense of meaning, then such meanings will be made differently by different people coming from different cultural communities, who live by means of the tools and technologies of their different languages.

Artmakers cannot ever know the meaning that their audiences will take away from their work. Even though two people speak the same language, intended meanings of a message are not always the received meanings. Scarino (2008, p. 5.8) discusses what an interculturally competent language learner can presume: "they cannot fully anticipate what others will bring, but coming to know and understand means hearing what others bring, observing, noticing, responding, comparing, elaborating, adjusting, reflecting and, through these processes, developing understanding." Artmakers too can expect their audiences to engage with what is created by observing, noticing, responding, comparing, elaborating, reflecting, and hopefully taking away an understanding which suits their purposes.

Lilliedahl (2018) examines the notion of language as a mode of conveying information, similar to the thinking of Halliday and Hasan (1989), including: "art forms such as painting, sculpture, music, the dance . . . modes of exchange, modes of dress, structures of the family, and so forth. These are all bearers of meaning in the culture" (Halliday & Hasan, 1989, p. 4). The intercultural, "in-betweenness" (Ortega, 2009, p. 1) aspects of 'knowing' (Moran, 2001), are located in the modes of expression located in the interpretive zones of the arts and languages.

In teaching and learning languages, when living, 'languaging' and making meaning, we access the 'signs' and 'symbols' – through languages and the arts – which allow us to experience 'travels' in 'intercultural zones'. As noted by Bresler (2016, p. 325) "navigating cultural zones suggests dynamic processes— exchange, transaction, intensity, and absorption." Teachers whose personal, professional identity is informed by the arts, play a role in such navigational, investigative meaning-making.

Barkhuizen's (2017) volume discussed in the opening lines of this chapter highlights the many facets and the many factors impacting – the complexity of – the development of language teacher identity. The notion of "who I am is how I teach" (Farrell, 2017, p. 183; Harbon, 2017) suggests language teachers' identities cannot be separated from the wholistic view of a language teacher and we would find it impossible to conceive of understanding language teachers' identities as disembodied aspects of teachers' whole beings. With language teachers' identities encased in the activities of teachers' daily lives, including the social and emotional aspects, in dynamic spaces and places, it is likely that many language teachers' identities are influenced by the creative facets encountered in their life-worlds: the arts in one form or another.

Following Piazzoli's (2018, p. 25) "simplex" perspective – 'simplex' referring to a mix of the 'simple' and the 'complex' – both arts education and language education can be based on 'embodied' pedagogies, a notion which at one level appears simply to be individuals enacting the pedagogy, but at another level a more complex reference to what the pedagogy actually involves. Embodied pedagogies in artmaking and teaching 'living' languages relate to how teachers work with the mind, senses, reality, ideas, and imagination to enable learning to take place. Language teaching with an "intercultural stance" (Scarino, 2008, p. 5.2) and artmaking involving the tools and processes for constructing meaning through the senses, can utilise an embodied pedagogy using mind, senses, and imagination.

7.7   Conclusion

'Languages', 'the arts' and how those components shape a teacher's professional identity are at the heart of this chapter. Knowing that in formal and informal educational settings, an 'intercultural' stance can be taken to teach and learn languages and cultures, it can be the case that an experiential, exploratory and investigative pedagogy may work well. The interpretive zones through which this occurs can be either, or both, 'language education' and 'the arts', firmly embedded in the "language-culture nexus" (Risager, 2006, p. 185) in the teacher's own repertoire. An arts-informed curriculum allows the 'performative', 'experiential/sensory' and 'embodied' pedagogies to drive teaching and learning, with the development of learners' intercultural competence. With wider, interpretive, mediating zone-definitions of 'language education' and 'the arts', individuals learning in our educational systems have more opportunities to explore, create and make meaning. Individuals can grow and develop as they experience these language 'travels', through different languages, exploring different cultures. We can understand, therefore, how a language teacher's identity is sometimes developed through the interplay of language and meaning-making, culture-learning, and arts-informed experience. Should a language teacher build on the 'sensemaking' aspect of what is embedded in 'art-making', then the language teacher's arts-informed identity can enrich the type of learning outcomes possible for students learning languages.

The interpretive zones for 'meaning-making' and 'sensemaking', the intercultural mediating (Witte 2014), moving between languages and cultures, or the investigating involved in an arts experience, are the zones where teachers of languages and cultures work. An arts-informed pedagogy for language teachers' intercultural orientation is significant as a tool for teachers to enable student understanding and communication across and beyond cultures. Teachers whose identity is shaped in an arts-informed way, can act as an intercultural mediators in their teaching of students in today's complex world.

References

Arasaratnam-Smith, L. A. (2017). Intercultural competence: An overview. In D. K. Deardorff & L. A. Arasaratnam-Smith (Eds.), *Intercultural competence in higher education: International approaches, assessment and application* (pp. 7–18). Routledge.

Australian Curriculum and Assessment Reporting Authority. (2020). *Australian curriculum: Languages, rationale*. Retrieved from https://www.australiancurriculum.edu.au/f-10-curriculum/languages/rationale/

Australian Federation of Modern Languages Teachers Associations. (2021). *Professional standards for accomplished teaching of languages*. Retrieved 22 August 2021, from: https://afmlta.asn.au/wp-content/uploads/2021/05/AFMLTA-Professional-Standards-2020-FINAL2.pdf

Barkhuizen, G. (Ed.). (2017). *Reflections on language teacher identity research*. Routledge.

Black, A. (2011). Making meaning with narrative shapes: What arts-based research methods offer educational practitioners and researchers. *Studies in Learning Evaluation, Innovation and Development, 8*(2), 67–82.

Boske, C. (2020). Artmaking as sensemaking: A conceptual model to promote social justice and change. In R. Papa (Ed.), *Handbook in promoting social justice in education* (pp. 1–18). Springer. https://doi.org/10.1007/978-3-319-74078-2_71-1

Bresler, L. (2016). Interdisciplinary, intercultural travels. In P. Burnard, E. Mackinlay, & K. Powell (Eds.), *The Routledge international handbook of intercultural arts research* (pp. 321–332). Routledge. https://www.routledgehandbooks.com/doi/10.4324/9781315693699.ch29

Calcutt, L., Woodward, I., & Skrbis, Z. (2009). Conceptualising otherness: An explanation of the cosmopolitan schema. *Journal of Sociology, 45*(2), 169–186. https://doi.org/10.1177/1440783309103344

Eubanks, P. (2003). Codeswitching: Using language as a tool for clearer meaning in art. *Art Education, 56*(6), 13–18.

Ewing, R. (2010). *Australian education review, the arts and Australian education: Realising Potential*. Australian Council for Educational Research. ISBN: 9780864318077.

Farenga, S. J., & Ness, D. (2005). *Encyclopedia of education and human development* (1st ed.). Routledge. E-ISBN: 9781315704760.

Farrell, T. S. C. (2017). Who I am is how I teach: Reflecting on language teacher professional role identity. In G. Barkhuizen (Ed.), *Reflections on language teacher identity research* (pp. 183–188). Routledge.

Fleming, M. (2002). Intercultural experience and drama. In G. Alred, M. Byram, & M. Fleming (Eds.), *Intercultural experience and education* (pp. 87–100). Multilingual Matters. https://doi.org/10.21832/9781853596087

Forehand, C. (2008). Beijing to Broadway: A conversation of the possible relationships at work among cultural transmission, language acquisition and the arts. *Journal of Philosophy and History of Education, 58*, 77–82.

Gardner, H. (1983). *Frames of mind: The theory of multiple intelligences*. Basic Books.

Gibson, R., & Anderson, M. (2008). Touching the void: Arts education research in Australia. *Asia Pacific Journal of Education, 28*(1), 103–112. https://doi.org/10.1080/02188790701849818

Groff, J. S. (2013). Expanding our "frames" of mind for education and the arts. *Harvard Educational Review, 83*(1), 15–39.

Halliday, M. A. K., & Hasan, R. (1989). *Language, context, and text: Aspects of language in a social-semiotic perspective*. Oxford University Press.

Harbon, L. (2014). AFMLTA 19th biennial conference Horwood address: Accomplished teaching of languages and cultures doesn't happen by chance: Reflective journal entries of a 'returnee' to the learner seat. *Babel, 49*(1), 4–16.

Harbon, L. (2017). Acknowledging the generational and affective aspects of language teacher identity. In G. Barkhuizen (Ed.), *Reflections on language teacher identity research* (pp. 176–182). Routledge.

Hartle, L., & Jaruszewicz, C. (2009). Rewiring and networking language, literacy and learning through the arts: Developing fluency through technology. In M. Narey (Ed.), *Making meaning: Constructing multimodal perspectives of language, literacy and learning through arts-based early childhood education* (pp. 187–205). Springer. https://doi-org.ezproxy2.library.usyd.edu.au/10.1007/978-0-387-87539-2

Hellmich, E. A. (2018). Language in a global world: A case study of foreign languages in U.S. K-8 education. *Foreign Language Annals, 51*, 313–330.

Hoecherl-Alden, G., & Fegely, K. (2019). Picturing another culture: Developing language proficiency, empathy, and visual literacy through art. *North East Conference on the Teaching of Foreign Languages (NECTFL) Review, 83*, 57–58.

Hull, G., & Hellmich, E. A. (2018). Locating the global: Schooling in an interconnected world. *Teachers College Record, 120*, 1–36.

Ingold, T. (2014). *Making: Anthropology, archaeology, art and architecture*. Routledge.

Kohl, K., Dudrah, R., Gosler, A., Graham, S., Maiden, M., Ouyang, W., & Reynolds, M. (Eds.). (2020). *Creative multilingualism: A manifesto*. Open Book Publishers. https://doi.org/10.11647/OBP.0206

Kramsch, C. (1993). *Context and culture in language teaching*. Oxford University Press.

Langacker, R. (1999). Assessing the cognitive linguistic enterprise. In T. Janssen & G. Redeker (Eds.), *Cognitive linguistics: Foundations, scope and methodology* (pp. 13–59). Mouton de Gruyter.

Lilliedahl, J. (2018). Building knowledge through arts integration. *Pedagogies: An International Journal, 13*(2), 133–145. https://doi.org/10.1080/1554480X.2018.1454320

Lillis, T. M. (2006). Communicative competence. In K. Brown (Ed.), *Encyclopedia of language and linguistics* (2nd ed., pp. 666–673). Elsevier Science and Technology Books. ISBN 978-0-08-044854-1.

Marczak, M. (2013). *Communication and information technology in (intercultural) language teaching*. Cambridge Scholars Publishing.

Meyer, L. (2005). The complete curriculum: Ensuring a place for the arts in America's schools. *Arts Education Policy Review, 106*(3), 35–39.

Millikan, J. (2010). The hundred languages of children and a hundred more: A symbiotic relationship between the visual arts and learning in Reggio Emilia. *Australian Art Education, 33*(2), 12–25.

Moran, P. (2001). *Teaching culture: Perspectives in practice*. Heinle & Heinle.

Ortega, L. (2009, December 2). *Participation, acquisition, and in-betweenness as metaphors for L2 learning*. Plenary address delivered at the 1st combined ALANZ-ALAA conference (Applied Linguistics association of New Zealand & Applied Linguistics Association of Australia), Auckland.

Palmer, G. B., & Sharifian, F. (2007). Applied cultural linguistics: An emerging paradigm. In F. Sharifian & G. B. Palmer (Eds.), *Applied cultural linguistics*. John Benjamins.

Piazzoli, E. (2018). Embodying language in action: The artistry of process drama in second language education. *Palgrave Macmillan*. https://doi.org/10.1007/978-3-319-77962-1

Risager, K. (2006). *Language and culture: Global flows and local complexity*. Multilingual Matters.

Savignon, S. J. (2006). Communicative language teaching. In K. Brown (Ed.), *Encyclopedia of language and linguistics* (2nd ed., pp. 673–679). Elsevier Science and Technology Books. ISBN 978-0-08-044854-1.

Scarino, A. (2008). Community and culture in intercultural language learning. *Australian Review of Applied Linguistics, 31*(1), 5.1–5.15. https://doi.org/10.2104/aral0805

Shier, J. H. (1990). Integrating the arts in the foreign/second language curriculum: Fusing the affective and the cognitive. *Foreign Language Annals, 23*(4), 301–314.

Spina, S. O. (2006). Worlds together . . . words apart: An assessment of the effectiveness of arts-based curriculum for second language learners. *Journal of Latinos and Education, 5*(2), 99–122.

Sulentic Dowell, M., & Goering, C. (2018). Editors' introduction: On the promise and possibilities of arts integration in education. *Pedagogies: An International Journal, 13*(2), 85–91.

Swain, M. (2006). Languaging, agency and collaboration in advanced second language learning. In H. Byrnes (Ed.), *Advanced language learning: The contributions of Halliday and Vygotsky* (pp. 95–108). Continuum.

Swain, M., & Watanabe, Y. (2013). Languaging: Collaborative dialogue as a source of second language learning. In C. A. Chapelle (Ed.), *The encyclopedia of applied linguistics* (pp. 1–8). Blackwell. https://doi.org/10.1002/9781405198431.wbeal0664

Switzer, S. C. (2009). Multiple modes of communication of young Brazilian children: Singing, drawing and English language learning. In M. Narey (Ed.), *Making meaning: Constructing multimodal perspectives of language, literacy and learning through arts-based early childhood education* (pp. 133–152). Springer.

Tollefson, J. W. (2008). Language planning in education. In S. May & N. H. Hornberger (Eds.), *Encyclopedia of language and education* (2nd ed., pp. 3–14). Springer. Online ISBN: 978-0-387-30424-3.

United States Department of Education. (2012). *United States Department of Education international strategy 2012–16: Succeeding globally through international education and engagement*. Retrieved from http://www2.ed.gov/about/inits/ed/internationaled/international-strategy-2012-16.pdf

Vale, D., Scarino, A., & Mackay, P. (1991). *Pocket ALL*. Curriculum Corporation.

Van Essen, A. (1997). Language awareness and knowledge about language: An overview. In L. Van Lier & D. Corson (Eds.), *Encyclopedia of language and education* (Vol. 6). Springer.

Vecchi, V. (2010). *Art and creativity in Reggio Emilia: Exploring the role and potential of ateliers in early childhood education*. Routledge.

Vygotsky, L. S. (1978). *Mind in society: The development of higher psychological processes*. Harvard University Press.

Wang, L., & Kokotsaki, D. (2018). Primary school teachers' conceptions of creativity in teaching English as a foreign language (EFL) in China. *Thinking Skills and Creativity, 29*, 115–130.

Whitfield, P. T. (2009). The heart of the arts: Fostering young children's ways of knowing. In M. Narey (Ed.), *Making meaning: Constructing multimodal perspectives of language, literacy and learning through arts-based early childhood education* (pp. 153–165). Springer.

Wiley, T. G., Garcia, D. R., Danzig, A. B., & Stigler, M. L. (2014). Language policy, politics and diversity in education. *Review of Research in Education, 38*(1), vii–xxiii. https://doi.org/10.3102/0091732X13512984

Witte, A. (2014). *Blending spaces: Mediating and assessing intercultural competence in the L2 classroom*. De Gruyter Mouton.

Chapter 8
Learning to Teach: A Discursive Construction of Pre-service EFL Teachers' Identities

Li Li

Abstract Language teacher identity has received considerable attention in the past decade for its crucial roles in improving effective pedagogy and enhancing teacher learning. The literature suggests that teacher identity is displayed and constructed in social interactions when teachers engage with teacher educators, learners, other teachers, administrators, and the broader community. While a large number of studies have been conducted to investigate the multidimensional nature and complexities of in-service teacher professional identity, there is still insufficient knowledge regarding pre-service teachers. In particular, very little is known about how teacher-learners construct and negotiate identities in the process of learning to teach. This chapter addresses this gap by drawing on 'applied' conversation analysis to explore the experience of two Chinese student teachers who lived and studied away from home in a socially, culturally and educationally different context. The findings revealed how pre-service teachers negotiate and construct professional identities, including building pedagogical knowledge, exercising agencies and developing confidence and authority. The research contributes to the emerging literature on language teacher identity and has implications for teacher learning and development and effective pedagogy.

Keywords Professorial identity · Pre-service teachers · Classroom discourse · Conversation analysis · Pedagogical knowledge

8.1 Introduction

In the last decade, teacher identity has become an important agenda for teacher education. In second language teacher education, the development of language teacher identity is viewed as an essential process in L2 teachers' growth (Freeman, 2020; Gray & Morton, 2019; Johnson & Golombek, 2020; Li, 2020a, b). Globally,

L. Li (✉)
University of Exeter, Exeter, UK
e-mail: Li.Li@exeter.ac.uk

K. Sadeghi, F. Ghaderi (eds.), *Theory and Practice in Second Language Teacher Identity*, Educational Linguistics 57, https://doi.org/10.1007/978-3-031-13161-5_8

much attention has been given to the identity development of pre-service teachers (Cobb et al., 2018; Chu, 2021), as the process of developing an identity is considered a learning tool for teachers (Ruohotie-Lyhty & Moate, 2016; Yuan & Mak, 2018). However, in the field of language teacher education, as noted by various scholars, insufficient research has been carried out to understand the process of identity construction within the context of language teaching and teachers (Barkhuizen, 2017; Trent, 2015; Vallente, 2020). Indeed, very little is known about how teacher-learners construct and negotiate identities in the process of learning to teach when they study in a socially, educationally and culturally different learning environment.

The current literature on teacher education directs attention to the importance of identity in teacher development (Beauchamp & Thomas, 2009; Kanno & Stuart, 2011). In that respect, Li (2020b) argues that there is an intricate relationship between teacher identity construction and teacher learning. Teachers are not neutral players in the classroom because how teachers position themselves in relation to the learners and the broader context is critical in teaching and learning (Varghese et al., 2005). Researching teacher identity, thus, can be utilised as an analytic frame to highlight the holistic, dynamic and situated nature of teacher development (Cheung et al., 2015; Li, 2020a; Olsen, 2008; Tsui, 2007).

Against this background, this chapter explores how pre-service teachers make sense of themselves and their practice through identity construction. I adopt a sociocultural approach in this study to understand identity that recognises the influence of socially situated experiences on identity construction. The significance of this research lies in two aspects. Firstly, this study focuses on the insights of identity construction work that pre-service teachers do in their professional contexts and illuminate their multiple fluid identities. Secondly, the majority of research into professional identity has taken up a narrative approach or ethnography; this research will add to the body of the research to advance the social and dialogic nature of teacher identity (e.g., Gray & Morton, 2019; Li, 2020a, b). To this end, the chapter examines the moment-by-moment positioning of pre-service teachers in their professional encounters and seeks to illuminate how they use interactional resources and strategies to construct professional and social images. In particular, I examine how pre-service teachers position themselves in the moment-by-moment talk with significant others. In so doing, I look at the multiple and fluid identities that teachers construct in professional learning through the lens of conversation analysis. The research contributes to the emerging literature on the discursive-oriented perspective of language teacher identity and has implications for teacher learning and development.

8.2 Language Teacher Identity

Identity is a "resource that people use to explain, justify, and make sense of themselves in relation to others, and to the world at large" (MacLure, 1993, p. 311). Teacher identity, or 'teacher-self' or subjectivity and individuality, can be defined as "how a person understands his or her relationship to the world, how that relationship is structured across time and space, and how the person understands possibilities for the future" (Norton, 2013, p. 45). The concept has been theorised as multiple, shifting and conflicted, and it has been widely recognised that identity is closely related to the social, cultural and political context (Varghese et al., 2005).

Researchers have approached the concept from different theoretical positions, and as a result, the concept has been defined differently. Barkhuizen (2017) cautions that "producing any single definition of LTI [language teacher identity] is improbable, exclusionary, and possibly counterproductive" (p. 3). Based on this, he further proposes that we need to develop a comprehensive understanding of the concept of identity. Varghese (2017) proposes a working definition, which views language teacher identity as "an interaction of how we see ourselves as language teachers ... and how others see us – a claimed and an assigned identity" (p. 45). Elsewhere, Block (2015, p. 13) takes a similar position, suggesting an teacher has "an occupational identity, and specifically a language teaching identity". He further argues,

> Such an identity may be defined in terms of how individuals, who both self-position and are positioned by others as teachers, affiliate to different aspects of teaching in their lives. Thus, identity is related to factors such as one's ongoing contacts with fellow teachers and students as well as the tasks that one engages in, which can be said to constitute teaching. (Block, 2015, p. 13)

8.2.1 Pre-service Teacher Identity

Arguably, teacher education is about preparation for a specific professional role and understanding the becoming and being a teacher, which involves a transformation from student to teacher. Therefore, learning to teach is consequently a process of understanding of 'who I am' and identity development, rather than just the learning of subject and pedagogical knowledge (Clarke, 2008). Essentially, identity can be viewed as a dual process that participants engage in during the identification and negotiation of meaning (Wenger, 1998).

There is great value to study pre-service teachers' identities. For one thing, pre-service teachers with a strong sense of teacher identity are found to be more active in their learning about teaching and more reflective in their teaching practices. As such, if the focus of teacher education is to empower student teachers to engage with future learning, then it is vitally important for these programmes to focus on teacher identity and how it can impact on teacher learning. For another, there is a strong link between teacher cognition and teacher identity (Gray & Morton, 2019;

Li, 2017, 2020a). To facilitate teacher knowing and developing cognitively, we need to turn our attention to see how 'becoming', 'being' and 'doing' teacher manifests in student teachers' practical work. There is a great deal of literature to suggest the significance of teaching practice on teacher learning (Farrell, 2011; Li, 2017), especially the negative experience. For example, Li (2017) reports how the negative experiences of the two trainee teachers influenced their conception of English and their image. Of course, as Li (2017) argues, the negative experiences can be utilised as a tool for teacher learning if they can be treated as critical incidents to address teachers' cognitive and emotional understanding of being a teacher. Again, the emotional dimension of language teacher identity can be untangled by a focus on social interaction and discursive construction.

8.2.2   The Discursive Construction of Teacher Identity

There is a growing interest in exploring the dynamic nature of identity construction and its relationship to discourse in professional contexts where teachers carry out their work, notably the classroom as a community. Barkhuizen (2017) highlighted the identity is 'enacted, dynamic and multifaceted' because teachers are "in social interaction with teacher educators, learners, other teachers, administrators, and the broader community, and material interaction with spaces, places, and objects in classrooms and institutions" (p. 659). Gray and Morton (2019) echoed this view by claiming that teacher identity, especially for novice teachers, is ascribed, rejected, negotiated, claimed and inhabited, and that this is displayed in teaching. To argue the close connection between discourse and teacher identity, Li (2020a) writes, "the language they (the teachers) use and how it is used in instruction could be a window into their professional identities and possible selves" (p. 248).

Benwell and Stokoe (2006) define a discursive perspective on identity as entailing "who people are to each other, and how different kinds of identities are produced in spoken interaction and written texts" (p. 6). More specifically, Tracy and Robles (2013) describe the close link between discursive practices and identity, claiming that "[T]he identities a person brings to an interaction influence how that person communicates. At the same time, the specific discursive practices a person chooses will shape who he or she is taken to be and who the partner is taken to be" (pp. 25–26). In an educational setting, the professional identities are situated identities that participants display naturally and unconsciously, although other types of identities might tag along, such as transportable identities (Zimmerman, 1998). Gray and Morton (2019) argue that discourse enables the articulation of situated identities through the moment-by-moment organisation of interaction or production of discourse identities. It is through the discourse lens that we can see how participants project and display their situated identities.

All this work signifies the role of 'interaction' in teachers' identity work. Teacher identity is displayed and constructed in social interactions when teachers engage with teacher educators, learners, other teachers, administrators, and the broader community (Barkhuizen, 2017; Li, 2020a). As such, it is important to investigate the 'becoming' and 'being' a teacher through the lens of social interaction given that "what teachers know and do is part of their identity work, which is continuously performed and transformed through interaction in classroom" (Miller, 2009, p.175). As such, the interactional work that teachers engage in their professional practice displays their thinking, their positioning, and their individual and collective images of being teachers. Teachers then construct and negotiate identities in and through interaction, participation and action. Hence, they display "situated identity" (Gee, 2005). Of course, this process is influenced by the broader political, social, educational and cultural context.

8.3 The Study

8.3.1 The Context

The data reported in this paper is derived from a large study of teacher learning, including both pre-service and in-service teachers. The original project was designed to investigate how teachers developed their beliefs, understanding and knowledge in their professional (learning) context. These teachers were recruited through a combination of convenience and snowball sampling strategies. Information about the project was offered to the teachers, and consent was sought from all participants. They were specifically reminded of the right to withdraw from the study and how their data would be stored, used and destroyed. Participants were named under pseudonyms of their choice.

This study reports two Chinese students who enrolled in a MA TESOL programme in the UK. One of the core modules they had to undertake was teaching methodology. During this module, the student teachers were provided theoretical input and practical guidance. In addition, students had lesson planning sessions with the tutor, practice teaching and video-based reflections. The purpose of these activities was to offer students opportunities to make a connection to the professional community they will become a member of in the future.

Georgina had some teaching internships before she started the master's course. Her spoken English was much better than her written English, and she was very lively in class, participating in all the activities and raising interesting questions. She wanted to become a teacher because her university major was in English language teaching. Georgina graduated as one of the best students in her cohort.

Simon was relatively quiet in class. He didn't have any formal teaching experience but worked as a private tutor before he came to the UK. He took some pre-sessional English courses because he was not confident about his English proficiency. His choice of becoming an English teacher was much influenced by his family, as both his parents were teachers. Simon studied communication in one of the elite universities in China but he described himself as a 'less competitive' student in the class.

8.3.2   Data and Analysis

During the course, students engaged in group lesson-planning sessions, discussing their lesson plan with the tutor and peers. In addition, they also needed to teach the session based on the lesson plans, and then reflected on the miro-teaching by watching back their teaching with the tutor. These activities were video recorded. The dataset include 182 minutes of lesson-planning discussion, 120 minutes of teaching, and 203 minutes of video-based reflection in total. The recordings were watched several times before they were transcribed. Detailed transcriptions of verbal and non-verbal behaviours were made and subjected to fine-grained analysis, following the conversation analysis (CA) convention developed by Jefferson (see Appendix for transcription conventions). The pauses, gestures and intonation revealed in the transcripts were subjected to detailed micro-analysis. In this way, the focus was placed on how the teachers position themselves in doing interactional work with the others and their stance-taking of the moment. It should be noted that CA principles are adopted in uncovering teacher identity, more precisely "applied" CA, which uses "CA concepts and methods for accomplishing a particular agenda" (ten Have, 2007, p. 56). CA concerns how sequences of action are generated and how participants' turns display their interpretation of each other's utterances and the social actions they represent (Hutchby & Wooffitt, 2008). In principle, CA considers talk as an action rather than a channel to action. Thus, in conversation, participants do and perform identities and their being is constituted in talk-in-interaction. In this sense, the conversation also "performs a social display of the interactants' cognitive, emotional and attitudinal states" (Li, 2017, p. 57). It is useful to note that the main differences between 'pure' and 'applied' CA is that the former "concerns naturally occurring interactional data to uncover the organisation of the talk, whereas 'applied CA' in institutional talk focuses more on politically or socially relevant themes or materials" (Li, 2020a, p. 66).

8.4   Findings

For novice teachers, developing pedagogical knowledge and establishing professional images are important aspects of becoming a teacher (Farrell, 2003; Li, 2012, 2020a; Ruohotie-Lyhty, 2013; Sabar, 2004). On the one hand, pre-service teachers are using their pre-existing beliefs and knowledge to filter the input from the course to develop their personal theories. On the other hand, they also bring knowledge to the learning community, and they engage in re-negotiation between their prior learning experience, input from the course and the knowledge that is recognised in the immediate context. This re-negotiation will further contribute to the development of the collective beliefs, values and identity as pre-service teachers.

8.4.1 Developing Pedagogical Knowledge

Morton and Gray (2010) argue knowledge can be seen as largely a matter of identity in the context of learning to teach when student teachers go through "a process of practical knowledge-building characterized by an ongoing integration of what is individually and collectively seen as relevant to teaching" (p. 123). In their work, they described how the concepts of knowledge and identity had been conflated. Similarly, Li (2017) claims that developing pedagogical knowledge is "very personal and contextualised and closely related to the teachers' learning and teaching experience" (p. 109). Li (2020a) further argues that when student teachers "gain new insights into teaching and learning, or realise new pedagogical ideas, they explore ways to re-imagine or reconstruct their pedagogy" (p. 223).

Extract 1

```
 1   I   right so overall what what's your thinking what
 2       what's your thought about this teaching?

 3   G   (2.0)
 4       well I guess I didn't prepare (1.0) very WELL
 5       (.) because uh that thing I can if like (.)
 6       actually (.) I can um do something (.)
 7       before the accident happen but I didn't think
 8       (0.8)much so (.) it's like hmmm=

 9   I   =an-that's experience isn't it? so cos
10       you are new and so you don't really
11       realise that things can go wrong=
12   G   =yeah I didn't realise (.)
13   I   hmmm=
14   G   =and um (0.8) I don't know that I was (0.5)
15       too↓ focused on the   technical(.)
16       I think hmmm maybe I can do this an- maybe
17       I can do that but actually (.)I didn't (.)
18       like managed it very well=
19   I   =uh huh
```

Extract 1 is taken from Georgina's post-reflection, where she discussed her teaching performance. As shown in the data, the teacher trainer directs the reflection by asking the first pair part exchange (line 1–2), offering an opportunity for Georgina to deliver self-evaluation. After a longish pause (line 3), Georgina takes the turn and offers an evaluation, noting that her preparation was not good (line 4). Here, it is interesting to see Georgina's positioning – she starts with, I guess, to indicate that her evaluation might not be accurate as she is the novice one who receives the assessment from the expert, the teacher trainer. This is further revealed when she modifies the degree of her preparation after a 1.0 second pause. Here, Georgina claims insufficient knowledge of engaging in self-evaluation (Koshik, 2002). One could argue that this is to do with confidence or power issue in this talk, as the teacher trainer's default position is the expert, whereas Georgina's situated identity is a trainee teacher. The following lines (line 5–8) display the process of Georgina developing reflective knowledge of her teaching. Again, the pause in line 8 helps her to gain a space to articulate how well she responded to the unexpected event in teaching. The assistance provided by the teacher trainer for the student to develop the understanding of her pedagogical practice is also evidenced in the teacher trainer's action of taking the turn in line 9 when a hesitation from the student teacher is observed. This helps both parties to collaboratively construct the common knowledge of the student being a 'trainee teacher' as the teacher trainer refers to the student teacher as 'new' and associates pedagogical knowledge and expertise with 'experience' (line 9–10). Here, the student teacher is also assigned with the status of lacking realisation or awareness (line 10–11). We can clearly see the student teacher is labelled with a situated identity, an inexperienced student teacher who lacks expertise in an unexpected event. The student teacher also assumes such an identity (line 12), which is followed by a claim of insufficient knowledge (line 14). In what follows, Georgina explains her pedagogical decision prior to teaching and it is at this moment that we can see Georgina starts to develop pedagogical knowledge through reflecting on her teaching experience. It is important to note that by accepting the situated identity as a 'novice' teacher, who 'lacks experience' and shows 'insufficient knowledge', she could develop her pedagogical knowledge and build expertise in making interactive decisions.

Extract 2

```
1    G    so I think maybe um I can use a clip of video↑=
2    I    =uh huh=
3    G    =so it may VARIED the material I use
4         in the classroom=
5    I    =ok (.) so um you use material sorry (.)
6         you use the video to vary the materials
7         you used=
8    G    =uh huh ((nodding her head))=
9    I    =Is that the only purpose?=
10   G    =not really (.) it's also very interesting to
11        see something and listen to others (.) not
12        just the teacher=
13   I    =yeah (.)
14   G    It's motivating
```

Extract 2 again is taken from Georgina's teaching planning session where she discussed her plan of integrating a new technological tool in teaching. As can be seen in this conversation, Georgina takes the lead to articulate the idea of how she would like to teach the vocabulary lesson (line 1). This idea is hedged as she again positions herself as a novice who seeks approval from the expert, the teacher trainer. In this statement, Georgina conceptualises her pedagogical knowledge by having a try-out attempt to describe the way she wants to use technology, a video clip in this case. The teacher educator's acknowledgement token (line 2) is interpreted by Georgina as encouragement to justify the idea (lines 3–4), noting that she is using emphatic pitch when elaborating the purpose of the video clip (line 3). Here, it is clear that Georgina is visualising the function of the technology by talking about the presentational feature (Li, 2014). This is then being followed up by the tutor who first acknowledges the idea and after a brief pause, echoes Georgina's pedagogical idea as a confirmation request. Georgina's immediate confirmation and gesture suggest that she is now certain about the role of technology in her teaching (line 8). At this point, the tutor follows up with a first pair part, requesting her to reflect on her pedagogical decision (line 9). Obviously, the tutor is trying to do some collaborative work with Georgina to help her to be clear about her pedagogical decision when it comes to the use of technology. This facilitation positions Georgina as a novice who needs to learn to do reflective and critical thinking about her decisions. The request is immediately taken up by Georgina in line 10, who first of all denies the sole purpose of the video clip and then provides a further elaboration (lines 10–12). Several ideas are put forward here; first of all, the technology can engage students because the digital material is interesting; and secondly, it potentially addresses the audio visual needs of learners. Now, we can see in this dialogue, Georgina is showing a clear development of her pedagogical decision regarding the use of technology, scaffolded by the interactive work from the tutor. This conversation shows how Georgina displays a novice identity in this task, but also gradually co-constructs the idea with the teacher educator.

8.4.2 Establishing Authority Through Exercising Agency

Developing and managing a classroom dynamic is an important aspect of teacher learning. For student teachers, establishing close relationships and maintaining their authority is an important agenda. Hargreaves (2000, 2005) warns that a failure to establish such relationships may make teachers prone to experiencing emotional misunderstandings. In that respect, Li (2012) demonstrates two non-native English-speaking pre-service teachers' authority moves in attempting to manage the classroom. Li (2017) suggests that newly trained teachers tend to establish authority through demonstrating subject knowledge, class control and reinforcement of the gap between the teacher and learners. In the following extract, Simon establishes his authority by controlling the activity and managing students' behaviour.

Extract 3

```
1    S    class (.)
2         now I'd like you to work in groups
3         to discuss how we deal with one of the issues=
4    L1   =°wha::t? °
5    LL   ((laughing))
6    S    ((going back to the PowerPoint slide)) ok (.)
7         here (.) take one of the issues (.) for example
8         pollution (.) you can discuss how we deal with
9         it (0.2) or you can talk about other aspects
10        (.)now (.) please discuss
11   LL   ((8 mins students are chatting))
12   S    I will ask you to come to the front to present
13        so maybe you want to write notes?
14        ((checking time)) are you done?
15   LL   no:::
16   S    Ok (.) two more minutes (.) you have to decide
17        what you are going to say
```

In Extract 3, Simon is delivering a micro-teaching session, organising a group activity. Simon first addresses the class by using authoritative discourse (line 1), which indicates the different identities are assigned and assumed in this setting. This can also be treated as 'pre-announcement' to draw students' attention (Terasaki, 2005). Then he gives instruction to the class (line 2–3), which is immediately followed by a question from a student (line 4). The low voice suggests that it is not a genuine question from the student; rather, it displays confusion on the student's part. Here, we can see this is perceived by the class as a distraction, hence, the laughter (line 5). Then Simon moves the PowerPoint slide backwards to make a further explanation on the task he set, with an example (line 7–9). In line 10, Simon gives an instruction once again, this time requesting students to discuss the issues that he pre-selects. It seems that students are fully engaged in the conversation in line 11. To reinforce his authority, Simon follows up with further instruction, this time telling students how they will be checked (line 12–13). Again, here we can see Simon display 'deontic' authority, which means that he holds the authority to set the rules and norms (Stevanovic & Peräkylä, 2012).

Conscious about the time issue, Simon checks with students to see how they have progressed (line 14). Upon receiving 'dispreferred' response from the students (line 15), Simon makes an interactive decision to allow more time for students, emphasising the students need to agree on what to report (Pomerantz, 1984). The rule-setting is one key element of classroom management. Here Simon manages the class to show that he has the absolute authority of directing the class and the right to speak. Even though students are allowed more time, Simon's instruction here entails 'telling', suggesting his dissatisfaction with students' learning behaviour (Li, 2020b).

Extract 4

```
 1   I    so how did you feel about that lesson?
 2        (2.5)
 3   S    £terrible?£ (.) no (.) it's ok (.) not the best
 4        I think um::(2.0)I think I spent too much time
 5        on that group task=
 6   I    =Yeah [((nodding))
 7   S          [but uh tasks worked (.) well (.)
 8        but then I didn't finish the next part=
 9   I    =yeah (.) um (.) then maybe you need to drop
10        (.) one of the tasks=
11   S    =hmmm (.) I could have managed it if I
12        planned the student bit (.) but we didn't
13        know (.) I think that's good as we now learn
14        to plan students' response time=
15   I    =that's [right
16   S            [so those two activities are linked
17        very well (.) so I don't want to drop one of
18        them (.)BUT I could have given clearer guidance
```

Extract 4 is Simon's reflection with the tutor after the session. In this conversation, Simon displays agency to exercise power when he develops a set of useful 'organising principles' in his professional life.

By asking a question to request Simon to engage in self-evaluation in line 1, the tutor directs the learning event for Simon. In a reflective session, the tutor usually takes the situated position of 'expert' who offers advice and guides the structure of the 'learning event', whereas the students are generally positioned as the novice. However, in this extract, Simon, the situated novice, switches his positioning to control the focus of the learning event. This repositioning is unpacked in the moment-by-moment interactive work he does with the tutor. After a long pause, he jokes about his teaching, assessing it as being terrible through a counter-question technique in a smiley voice. Humour and hedging are used as an interactional resource/strategy to maintain politeness while critiquing others, but here, this strategy is used to bring about a subtle shift in identity positioning. Following self-criticism, Simon reverts to offer a proper evaluation of his lesson it's ok (.) not the best. At this point, Simon provides further elaboration on why it is not the best (line 4–5), suggesting a time management issue. Clearly, Simon has identified a learning point for himself. The issue is acknowledged by the tutor briefly (line 6), as Simon unpacks his evaluation further to suggest that the tasks went well despite the time issue. Here, we can see the tutor now assumes the authority position, offering advice to Simon (line 9–10). Again, the power/authority displayed here is that of 'deontic' authority, which indicates the tutor bears the right to set rules and norms about what should be done. Rather than accepting the advice, Simon subtly disagrees with the tutor (line 11–14). For Simon, it is not about dropping a task; instead, it is about developing awareness of planning students and their responses to tasks. It is interesting here that when offering his position, Simon uses 'we' (line 12–13). The use of 'we' and 'us' is person deixis that usually indicates inclusion in the group (Holmes & Marra, 2002). Here, Simon uses 'we' to refer to the common practice among student teachers and identifies the learning point for the group. Here, Simon moves his position from being an individual student to representing a group, thereby displaying a collective identity. Here, the tutor offers agreement (line 15), which overlaps with Simon's reflective account. In line 16–18, he orients to a situated identity of a novice, developing principles through practical work and reflective practice.

8.5   Conclusions and Implications

The findings of this study reveal two major themes of teacher identity regarding pre-service teachers: developing practical pedagogical knowledge and establishing authority through exercising agency. Of course, pre-service teachers can display multiple 'situated identities' in their professional contexts (see Li, 2020a), but these two distinct themes emerged from the conversations in their professional contexts.

Research in novice teachers' identity suggests that constructing professional identity can be interpreted as a journey of developing pedagogical knowledge in their contexts (Beijaard et al., 2004; Li, 2020b). The findings of this study strongly resonate earlier research on novice teachers, highlighting the significance of personal practical pedagogical knowledge negotiation and development in novice teachers' identity work. Indeed, identity formation is "a process of practical knowledge-building characterized by an ongoing integration of what is individually and collectively seen as relevant to teaching" (Beijaard et al., 2004, p. 123).

Akkerman and Meijer (2011) conceptualise teacher identity as "an ongoing process of negotiating and interrelating multiple I-positions in such a way that a more or less coherent and consistent sense of self is maintained throughout various participations and self-investments in ones' life" (p. 315). As such, teachers must have a core identity, *the self,* according to the authors, which is rather stable and is released through different I-positions according to circumstances they are in. So, for student teachers, their core position remains as a student/novice who is developing pedagogical knowledge through negotiation and re-negotiation. They also display membership of imagined community in the interaction with the significant others or exercise agency in the process of developing the overarching principles (Li, 2020a). Given the intertwined relationship between practical pedagogical knowledge and identity construction, it is vital for teacher educators to be aware of the ongoing identity construction in the process of developing pedagogical knowledge and vice versa. So, teacher education programmes should incorporate raising student teachers' awareness of identity construction into the pedagogy module.

The second area of work that is worth further pursuing is student teachers' desire to establish authority and its significance in developing professional identity. Li (2017) observes that novice teachers prioritise a desire to establish authority in classrooms, which might be because newly qualified teachers or student teachers feel less confident and flexible in their job because they are still at the 'launching phase' and lack experience (Gatbonton, 2008), or do not have alignment with the imagined community.

As data suggest, reflection plays a significant role in teacher learning, as it allows teachers to see objectively what beliefs, value and identity they are developing, and potentially enable them to move from actual identity to an ideal identity (Danielewicz, 2014). In that sense, CA is a useful methodology to gain insights into the situated identity through moment-by-moment interactive work that individuals do with others, including (guided) reflections. Teachers, including trainee teachers, need to learn how to uncover and understand their identities through the lens of discourse. Therefore, teacher education and development should empower individuals to be able to engage in this line of work.

As a final word, this chapter demonstrates how identity is studied and approached through conversation analysis and what insights can be gained regarding how the subtleties of identity work and pedagogical knowledge are displayed and mediated. Although the data used in this chapter come from a specific cohort of students in a specific language teacher education setting, the analyses show the complex and subtle shifts in positioning. In this line of inquiry, Li (2020a) proposes CA-for-TC (conversation analysis for teacher cognition), highlighting the importance of social interaction and contexts in the development of intersubjectivity. As we see, a great deal of what teachers do in their professional context is to perform social actions through talk, meaning that they demonstrate knowing, believing, conceptualising, stance-taking, being and feeling in a specific context through the interactive work. I argue that there is a strong link between discourse, identity, positioning, knowledge and socially distributed cognition. As such, the identity-related topics need to take into account the dynamic and co-constructed nature of the interactional settings in which identity-relevant language and discourses are produced (Gray & Morton, 2019).

Appendix Transcription Conventions

Adapted from Hutchby and Wooffitt (2008)

(1.8)	Numbers enclosed in parentheses indicate a pause. The number represents the number of seconds of duration of the pause, to one decimal place.
(.)	A pause of less than 0.2 seconds.
=	An equal sign is used to show that there is no time lapse between the portions connected by the equal signs. This is used where a second speaker begins their utterance just at the moment when the first speaker finishes.
[ ]	Brackets around portions of utterances show that those portions overlap with a portion of another speaker's utterance.
((looking))	a description enclosed in a double bracket indicates a non-verbal activity.
an=	A dash indicates an abrupt cut off, where the speaker stopped speaking suddenly.
sou::nd	A colon after a vowel or a word is used to show that the sound is extended. The number of colons shows the length of the extension.

?	A question mark indicates a rising intonation.
CAPS	Capital letters indicate that the speaker spoke the capitalised portion of the utterance at ta higher volume than the speakers's normal volume.
°would°	This indicates an utterance that is much softer than the normal speech of the speaker. This symbol will appear at the beginning and at the end of the utterance in question.
£C'mon£	Sterling signs are used to indicate a smiley or jokey voice.
↑↓	Up or down arrows are used to indicate that there is sharply rising or falling intonation. The arrow is placed just before the syllable in which the change in intonation occurs.

References

Akkerman, S. F., & Meijer, P. C. (2011). A dialogical approach to conceptualizing teacher identity. *Teaching and Teacher Education, 27*(2), 308–319. https://doi.org/10.1016/j.tate.2010.08.013

Barkhuizen, G. (Ed.). (2017). *Reflections on language teacher identity research*. Routledge.

Beauchamp, C., & Thomas, L. (2009). Understanding teacher identity: An overview of issues in the literature and implications for teacher education. *Cambridge Journal of Education, 39*, 175–189. https://doi.org/10.1080/03057640902902252

Beijaard, D., Meijer, P. C., & Verloop, N. (2004). Reconsidering research on teachers' professional identity. *Teaching and Teacher Education, 20*(2), 107–128. https://doi.org/10.1016/j.tate.2003.07.001

Benwell, B., & Stokoe, E. (2006). *Discourse and identity*. Edinburgh University Press.

Block, D. (2015). Becoming a language teacher: Constraints and negotiation in the emergence of new identities. *Bellaterra Journal of Teaching & Learning Language & Literature, 8*(3), 9–26. https://doi.org/10.5565/rev/jtl3.648

Cheung, Y.-L., Said, S. B., & Park, K. (2015). *Advances and current trends in language teacher identity research*. Routledge.

Chu, Y. (2021). Preservice teachers learning to teach and developing teacher identity in a teacher residency. *Teaching Education, 32*(3), 269–285. https://doi.org/10.1080/10476210.2020.1724934

Clarke, M. (2008). *Language teacher identities: Co-constructing discourse and community*. Multilingual Matters.

Cobb, D. J., Harlow, A., & Clark, L. (2018). Examining the teacher identity-agency relationship through legitimate peripheral participation: A longitudinal investigation. *Asia-Pacific Journal of Teacher Education, 46*(5), 495–510. https://doi.org/10.1080/1359866X.2018.1480010

Danielewicz, J. (2014). *Teaching selves: Identity, pedagogy and teacher education*. SUNY Press.

Farrell, T. S. (2003). Learning to teach English language during the first years: Personal influences and challenges. *Teaching and Teacher Education, 19*(1), 95–111. https://doi.org/10.1016/S0742-051X(02)00088-4

Farrell, T. S. (2011). Exploring the professional role identities of experienced ESL teachers through reflective practice. *System, 39*, 54–62. https://doi.org/10.1016/j.system.2011.01.012

Freeman, D. (2020). Arguing for a knowledge-base in language teacher education, then (1998) and now (2018). *Language Teaching Research, 24*(1), 5–16. https://doi.org/10.1177/1362168818777534

Gatbonton, E. (2008). Looking beyond teachers' classroom behaviour: Novice and experienced ESL teachers' pedagogical knowledge. *Language Teaching Research, 12*(2), 161–182. https://doi.org/10.1177/1362168807086286

Gee, J. P. (2005). *An introduction to discourse analysis theory and method* (2nd ed.). Routledge.

Gray, J., & Morton, T. (2019). *Social interaction and teacher identity*. Edinburgh University Press.

Hargreaves, A. (2000). Four ages of professionalism and professional learning. *Teachers and Teaching Theory and Practice, 6*(2), 151–182. https://doi.org/10.1080/713698714

Hargreaves, A. (2005). Educational change takes ages: Life, career and generational factors in teachers' emotional responses to educational change. *Teaching and Teacher Education, 21*, 967–983. https://doi.org/10.1016/j.tate.2005.06.007

Holmes, J., & Marra, M. (2002). Over the edge? Subversive humor between colleagues and friends. *Humor, 15*(1), 65–87. https://doi.org/10.1515/humr.2002.006

Hutchby, I., & Wooffitt, R. (2008). *Conversation analysis* (2nd ed.). Polity Press.

Johnson, K. E., & Golombek, P. R. (2020). Informing and transforming language teacher education pedagogy. *Language Teaching Research, 24*(1), 116–127. https://doi.org/10.1177/1362168818777539

Kanno, Y., & Stuart, C. (2011). Learning to become a second language teacher: Identities-in-practice. *The Modern Language Journal, 95*(2), 236–252. https://doi.org/10.1111/j.1540-4781.2011.01178.x

Koshik, I. (2002). Designedly incomplete utterances: A pedagogical practice for eliciting knowledge displays in error correction sequences. *Research on Language and Social Interaction, 35*, 277–309. https://doi.org/10.1207/S15327973RLSI3503_2

Li, L. (2012). Belief construction and development: Two tales of non-native English speaking student teachers in a TESOL programme. *Novitas-ROYAL (Research on Youth and Language), 6*(1), 33–58.

Li, L. (2014). Understanding language teachers' practice with educational technology: A case from China. *System, 46*, 105–119. https://doi.org/10.1016/j.system.2014.07.016

Li, L. (2017). *Social interaction and teacher cognition*. Edinburgh University Press.

Li, L. (2020a). *Language teacher cognition: A sociocultural perspective*. Palgrave Macmillan.

Li, L. (2020b). Novice teachers' discursive construction of their identity: Insights from foreign language classrooms. *Iranian Journal of Language Teaching Research, 8*(3), 57–76. https://doi.org/10.30466/IJLTR.2020.120934

MacLure, M. (1993). Arguing for your self: Identity as an organising principle in teachers' jobs and lives. *British Educational Research Journal, 19*, 311–323. https://doi.org/10.1080/0141192930190401

Miller, J. (2009). Teacher identity. In A. Burns & J. C. Richards (Eds.), *The Cambridge guide to second language teacher education* (pp. 172–181). Cambridge University Press.

Morton, T., & Gray, J. (2010). Personal practical knowledge and identity in lesson planning conferences on a pre-service TESOL course. *Language Teaching Research, 14*(3), 1–21. https://doi.org/10.1177/1362168810365243

Norton, B. (2013). *Identity and language learning: Extending the conversation* (2nd ed.). Multilingual Matters.

Olsen, B. (2008). *Teaching what they learn, learning what they live*. Paradigm Publishers.

Pomerantz, A. M. (1984). Agreeing and disagreeing with assessment: Some features of preferred/dispreferred turn shapes. In M. Atkinson & J. Heritage (Eds.), *Structures of social action: Studies in conversation analysis* (pp. 57–101). Cambridge University Press.

Ruohotie-Lyhty, M. (2013). Struggling for a professional identity: Two newly qualified language teachers' identity narratives during the first years at work. *Teaching and Teacher Education, 30*, 120–129. https://doi.org/10.1016/j.tate.2012.11.002

Ruohotie-Lyhty, M., & Moate, J. (2016). Who and how? Preservice teachers as active agents developing professional identities. *Teaching and Teacher Education, 55*, 318–327. https://doi.org/10.1016/j.tate.2016.01.022

Sabar, N. (2004). From heaven to reality through crisis: Novice teachers as migrants. *Teaching and Teacher Education, 20*(2), 145–161. https://doi.org/10.1016/j.tate.2003.09.007

Stevanovic, M., & Peräkylä, A. (2012). Deontic authority in interaction: The right to announce, propose, and decide. *Research on Language and Social Interaction, 45*(3), 297–321. https://doi.org/10.1080/08351813.2012.699260

ten Have, P. (2007). *Doing conversation analysis* (2nd ed.). Sage.

Terasaki, A. (2005). Pre-announcement sequences in conversation. In G. Lerner (Ed.), *Conversation analysis: Studies from the first generation* (pp. 171–224). John Benjamins.

Tracy, K., & Robles, J. S. (2013). *Everyday talk: Building and reflecting identities* (2nd ed.). Guilford.

Trent, L. (2015). "Inclusive and different?" Discourse, conflict, and the identity construction experiences of preservice teachers of English language learners in Australia. *Australian Journal of Teacher Education, 40*(10), 106–124. https://doi.org/10.14221/ajte.2015v40n10.7

Tsui, A. B. M. (2007). Complexities of identity formation: A narrative inquiry of an EFL teacher. *TESOL Quarterly, 41*, 657–680. https://doi.org/10.1002/j.1545-7249.2007.tb00098.x

Vallente, J. P. C. (2020). Framing pre-service English language teachers' identity formation within the theory of alignment as mode of belonging in community of practice. *Teaching and Teacher Education, 96.* https://doi.org/10.1016/j.tate.2020.103177

Varghese, M. M. (2017). Language teacher educator identity and language teacher identity: Towards a social justice perspective. In G. Barkhuizen (Ed.), *Reflections on language teacher identity research* (pp. 51–56). Routledge.

Varghese, M., Morgan, B., Johnson, B., & Johnson, K. A. (2005). Theorizing language teacher identity: Three perspectives and beyond. *Journal of Language, Identity, and Education, 4*(1), 21–44. https://doi.org/10.1207/s15327701jlie0401_2

Wenger, E. (1998). *Communities of practice: Learning, meaning, and identity.* Cambridge University Press.

Yuan, R., & Mak, P. (2018). Reflective learning and identity construction in practice, discourse and activity: Experiences of pre-service language teachers in Hong Kong. *Teaching and Teacher Education, 74*, 205–214. https://doi.org/10.1016/j.tate.2018.05.009

Zimmerman, D. H. (1998). Identity, context and interaction. In C. Antaki & S. Widdicombe (Eds.), *Identities in talk* (pp. 87–106). Sage.

Chapter 9
Co-constructing Intercultural Identity in the Work-Integrated Learning: Pre-service TESOL Teachers' Professional Development

Ping Yang

Abstract This chapter focuses on how pre-service novice TESOL teachers developed their intercultural identity while assisting their students of different language and cultural backgrounds in learning ESL and engaging in work-integrated learning in Australia. Based on the theoretical framework of intercultural communication competence, this project used a qualitative method and collected data from ten pre-service novice TESOL teachers who took work placements at English language colleges in Sydney. Data included two types of written documents, including TESOL internship/placement reports each pre-service novice teacher completed and TESOL teacher mentor reports provided by their mentors. Data were coded and analyzed to identify emerging themes. The results showed that the pre-service TESOL teachers constructed their intercultural identity through working collaboratively with their mentors and students, valued online work-integrated learning experience, demonstrated intercultural empathy, and developed their verbal and nonverbal communication skills. The research implications were discussed to inform the current TESOL theories and practices as well as the future research directions.

Keywords Intercultural identity · Pre-service TESOL teacher education · Work-integrated learning (WIL) · Intercultural communication · Professional development

9.1 Introduction

One of the most important parts of TESOL teacher education in Australia is placement experience that pre-service TESOL teachers can gain through work-integrated learning (WIL). WIL is defined as follows.

> Work-integrated learning…refers to a range of practical experiences designed to give students valuable exposure to work-related activities relevant to their course of study. To

P. Yang (✉)
Western Sydney University, Sydney, NSW, Australia
e-mail: P.Yang@westernsydney.edu.au

© The Author(s), under exclusive license to Springer Nature Switzerland AG 2022
K. Sadeghi, F. Ghaderi (eds.), *Theory and Practice in Second Language Teacher Identity*, Educational Linguistics 57, https://doi.org/10.1007/978-3-031-13161-5_9

produce the highly skilled workforce that the community and industry needs, universities and employers partner to offer students internships, projects, simulations, fieldwork and other activities. (Universities Australia, 2019, p. 4)

The WIL experience can provide them with in-context knowledge about the teaching syllabi in the workplace, develop practical skills to deliver ESL programs there, and increase their employability (Carter et al., 2017). In the multicultural workplace, as pre-service teachers work with their colleagues and students from diverse language and cultural backgrounds their intercultural communication competence plays a key role in their everyday interaction in and outside of the classroom, thus helping them to develop intercultural verbal and nonverbal communication skills and construct intercultural identity (Yang, 2018). Although students' intercultural identity has been extensively studied and reported (Hu & Dai, 2021; Kislev, 2012; Shardakova, 2013; Tian & Lowe, 2014; Ye, 2018) and that of language teachers has been published (Moloney et al., 2016; Tajeddin & Ghaffaryan, 2020), TESOL teacher intercultural identity development is a less-researched area.

This chapter focuses on how pre-service TESOL teachers develop their intercultural identity while undertaking WIL experience in various English language colleges in Australia. I will first review relevant literature and the theoretical framework of intercultural communication competence, then I will describe the methodology used, analyze the major themes, and discuss the pedagogical implications.

9.2   Literature Review

9.2.1   Intercultural Identity

I start from the concept of cultural identity and then proceed to that of intercultural identity. Cultural identity refers to "collective identifications with specific cultural contents that characterize given values, habits, territories and peoples, homogeneously shared, and effectively fashioned on the model of the nation" (Sassatelli, 2009, p. 29). For example, the cultural values include social norms, religious rituals, and moral standards, and the cultural habits may be represented by the food tradition and communication (verbal and nonverbal) styles, and so on. All these specific cultural identity features are shared by peoples in a country where some cultural differences exist between the sub-cultural groups or ethnicities. Many countries are characterized by their cultural diversity.

Intercultural identity is formed when cultural identity is becoming intercultural. "Just as cultural identity serves as a linkage between a person and a specific cultural group, the emerging identity links a person to more than one cultural group" (Kim, 2001, p. 65). When speakers from one language and cultural background interact with those of other languages and cultural backgrounds regularly, they cross the language and cultural boundaries and develop the languages and cultural identities of the others. The construction of a new identity is seen as some changes to one's verbal and nonverbal behaviours. This would include intercultural attitudes towards other languages and cultures. This intercultural identity is developed through constant negotiation between different cultural identities and management of potential issues.

9.2.2 Work-Integrated Learning

WIL is meaningful to pre-service teachers as the work experience enables them to observe mentors teaching and practice supervised teaching in the classroom and or online. Walkington (2010, p. 177) states that "professional experience offers opportunities for pre-service teachers to explore theories, ideas and strategies in various contexts, assisting them to formulate their own philosophy and practice". The pre-service teachers can reflect on teaching theories and apply them to a learner group at a particular class level. They learn and practice on the ground concerning the programs and syllabi, learner needs and backgrounds, learner ability and their learning styles, teaching methods and techniques, assessment types, and learner feedback. Although facing challenges in terms of learners' mixed abilities, individual learning needs, and assessment tasks, it is through WIL that they immerse themselves working with the culturally diverse students, scaffolding their learning needs, group or individual, and helping develop language skills and communicative competence. In return, they gain experience testing out teaching techniques, growing confident interacting with students in the classroom and online, and preparing themselves for future employment.

WIL in student internship is meaningful under the collaborative university-industry partnership. Carter et al. (2017) describe how the internship is designed as an academic unit for business and economics students, linking their university coursework with the practical skills learning and building in the workplace, for example, "business etiquette, making good first impressions, networking skills, ethics, and reflective practices" (p. 206). They also describe how the students develop practical business communication and management skills in the real world under the mentorship of experienced business mentors in the Australian workplace. Similarly, teacher education students at Australian universities participate in WIL-related academic units that have school placements. Through these placements they learn WIL knowledge and skills and become ready for teaching at schools upon graduation as part of university-school collaboration and partnership (Manton et al., 2021).

9.2.3 Teacher Professional Development

Teachers can undertake professional development in various ways. Online teaching space has recently emerged as a dominant platform where teachers interact with their students for language teaching experiences and take it as professional development. Although online communication is not new, they do find it somewhat challenging to fully use its resources for effective teaching and learning. While the technical puzzles can be worked out with more practice and technical support, it needs more work to understand the "social, linguistic and cultural complexity" embedded in online teaching and learning practices (Meskill, 2013).

Teacher professional development is ongoing as teaching contributes to the acquisition of new knowledge, development of new skills in addition to consolidating the existing ones. Teaching as socialization helps acquire new knowledge and develop new skills. While classroom socialization is common in the normal time, online socilization meets the needs of social distancing during the COVID-19 pandemic and has been used on a compulsory basis because university campuses were locked down for health reasons. Teachers realize the true value of computer-mediated communication and socialization as professional development (Meskill, 2009). Not only do language teachers need to work out effective online instructional strategies but also become aware of student perception and what strategies they use to respond to their learning needs (Ceglie & Black, 2020). Online teaching and learning centres around authentic language and communication activities supplemented with many culturally appropriate materials and resources. In online social interaction with their students, TESOL teachers understand how culturally diverse the learning environment and the participants are and that they need to develop intercultural communication competence to meet the needs of cultural diversity (Selvi & Peercy, 2016). Through online interaction, teachers and students engage in language activities as intercultural communication and work collaboratively to achieve expected teaching and learning outcomes (Othman & Ruslan, 2020).

9.3 Methodology

9.3.1 Participants

A qualitative method was used in this project. The participants were 20 pre-service TESOL teachers (hereafter mentee(s), 15 females and 5 males ranging from 20 to 50 years old) and as many mentors (15 females and 5 males ranging from 30 to 55 years old) working at MTC (Marrickville Community Training Centre) Australia. The mentees came from diverse language and cultural backgrounds, such as Australian, Arabic, Chinese, Spanish, Korean, and Vietnamese. They were enrolled in a postgraduate TESOL course at an Australian university. They have studied the course for 1 or 2 years. The TESOL Internship unit informed them of the background information about the TESOL industry in Australia and our partnership with the major TESOL employers in Sydney. As they have completed a few other TESOL units, such as English Linguistics for TESOL, TESOL Methodology and Curricula, and Second Language Assessment and Testing, these units provided them with essential knowledge and skills they needed for effective work-integrated learning and for teaching adult speakers of other languages.

9.3.2 Data Collection

Data were collected from written work by the above 40 participants in Autumn and Spring 2020. Two written documents included Internship Report and Teacher Mentor Report. The former was the assessment in which pre-service TESOL teachers reported their critical reflections on three placement activities, including 20 hours of service learning, 10 hours of supervised teaching, and 10 hours of voluntary tutoring (Yang, 2015). The latter had three features: (1) assessing lesson contents, presentation skills, teaching activities, student learning activities, class management, and use of equipment; (2) assessing teaching methods, classroom interaction, lesson planning and preparation, and communication skills; (3) multiple assessment reports. The mentor reports for each mentee could vary in numbers ranging from three to six or more. When a mentee received 5 mentor reports for teaching 10 hours, an average counted towards their placement marks. Each report had 200 words on average. Each mentor assessed the mentee's teaching according to the university assessment standards and criteria. The advantage of using these documents as a resource of data was that they provided formal information about the placement progress of the mentees. Both Internship Reports and Mentor Reports were carefully prepared before being finalized and submitted. Eventually, 120 copies of documents with roughly 80,000 words were collected (See Table 9.1).

9.3.3 Data Analysis

All the data collected were studied and analyzed through Nvivo (Jackson, 2019). This research tool allowed the researcher to import all documents into the system, build free nodes to develop potential key points based on a high frequency of relevant words and phrases leading to sub-themes, and conduct constant comparative analysis. Eventually, major themes emerged from the sub-themes. The following major points were identified for detailed analysis and discussion and presented to support how the mentees worked with their students and co-constructed their

Table 9.1 Quantified data information

Document name	Copy	Words
TESOL Internship Reports (TIR)	20	20×3000 words $= 60,000$
TESOL Mentor Reports (TMR)	$20 \times 5 = 100$	100×200 each $= 20,000$
Total	120	80,000

intercultural identity through the work-integrated learning leading to transformative education and learning experience through the work placements.

9.4 Constructing Intercultural Identity Through WIL

The mentees engaged in WIL through work placement with English language centres in more than 10 of its 20 locations of MTC Australia in Great Western Sydney. MTC provides work-related education (e.g., literacy and numeracy) and nationally accredited training courses to adult learners in Australia. These courses help many community members to update their skills needed for the jobs and return to the workforce. One of these courses is the Skills for Education and Employment (SEE) program. SEE is funded by the Australian Government and is delivered by MTC to assist adult learners in learning ESL. "It provides eligible job seekers with language, literacy, numeracy, job-search and computer literacy training, to help improve their skills in English for use at work or in their studies" (Skills for Education and Employment, 2021). Although SEE is designed for ESL learners, some native Australian English speakers too take this course to improve their literacy (readings and writing) and numeracy needed for employment.

In the Autumn and Spring semesters of 2020 when the COVID-19 pandemic hit, MTC had to switch from face-to-face to online teaching. It was in this challenging context that the mentees undertook their WIL. The online teaching created challenges and opportunities for them to work their way through, developing new skills and co-constructing intercultural identity which was approached through the following three perspectives.

9.4.1 Meeting the Online Teaching and Learning Challenges

Because of the COVID-19 pandemic, the quick switch from face-to-face to an online mode was challenging to the mentees and even more to the MTC SEE senior-age students who had to learn at home and were generally unfamiliar with online learning environment. However, each mentee worked with an MTC teacher mentor who started training their students how to use a Microsoft Team app for online learning. This app was new to the mentees, but their experience using Zoom and the online learning space at the university gave them much confidence in learning the new app. Supervised by the mentor, they took the opportunity to take on challenges and immersed in the WIL experience. Before teaching online each time, they practised many times and worked out technical issues so that they could scaffold their student learning skills. However, student issues arose, with some students using mobile phones with a small screen. A lot of noise (the shouting and crying of the kids, the siren, etc.) came through. But the mentees understood that their students put so much effort into their learning despite many setbacks from the pandemic and low technical skills.

Online language learning could be flexible with the home environment. Many students were mature learners with families and children and they were looking after kids learning English with MTC. Before the COVID-19 pandemic, they attended classes at an SEE centre and their kids were usually supervised by the childcare staff therein. Now, when these mums and dads learn at home, their kids were playing around by themselves. As their phone microphone was on, the kid's shouting and crying came through. Similar issues were raised in the mentor report. It stated that as the students were attending lessons from home there were instances where family members might distract the students from the lesson. They appreciated that the mentee demonstrated tolerance and understanding as the student was making great efforts in learning English despite challenges arising from family commitments and online environment constraints. Another mentor report stated that the distraction did not only come from the family members in the household, but also the family pets. The added distraction occurred when animals suddenly appeared during the online lesson. While this could be reasonably considered if it did cause a big issue or occur at a critical moment, as a distractor by some persons, their (cat and dog) appearance could help online students become less anxious and more relaxed, and reduce the potential monotony of online learning. Using a flexible approach to engage students in the online learning environment, the mentee was quick-minded and kind-hearted and used this opportunity to ask the student to introduce the pets. As seen from the facial expressions of those that used video, most of them seemed to be light-hearted as this fun moment did give everybody something different for a change.

Despite various challenges to meet in online learning environment, the mentees used many useful resources to increase student learning interest and develop their student capacity to explore on their own. Being aware that the students might have a short span of attention in the online learning space (Zeng et al., 2020), the mentees prepared authentic online materials, such as images and photos. One mentee reported how she googled the image of the Opera House and how students learned the proper nouns associated with the image. Here, the visual potential of multiple intelligence theory (Gardner, 2011) was used to achieve the learning of the specialized word group through establishing an association between images and words. Furthermore, the use of the Opera House was an affect display of the user's cultural identity indicating the country location the mentee was sharing with their students. Another mentee reported how she encouraged students to find an image of the great wonders of other countries than their own. Shortly, one student requested to share his screen with an image of the Great Pyramid in Egypt, another student with an image of the Great Wall in China, and still another student with the image of the Colosseum in Rome. When the mentees reflected on the student feedback on teaching, they understood how effectively the use of visual learning resources could engage students in online learning and how well it could help develop student intercultural identity.

9.4.2   Demonstrating Intercultural Empathy

Empathy means that one can think and feel what another person thinks and feels in the same or similar fashions while engaged in interaction (Segal, 2018) or that one can walk in a student's shoes (Debbie & Roberta, 2016), or that it is the ability to place oneself in another person's position (Maibom, 2020). To build on this, intercultural empathy means that one can think and feel what another person of a different language and cultural background thinks and feels in the same or similar manners. This concept is typical of those that have intercultural identity displayed in intercultural interaction in the classroom setting or in online learning space. When developing intercultural empathy, a person has an appropriate attitude towards different languages and cultures. This is found in a mentee's report. She appreciated her students (some were above 50 years old) using their first language (L1) in learning ESL and saw this in perspectives. On the one hand, the flexible use of L1 can help students learn the second language, for example, when both languages have similar metaphorical expressions (Türker, 2016), thus providing a sense of confidence and security for the learners. The second language learners would automatically use L1 in online processing of the second language idioms (Carrol et al., 2016). Furthermore, it helped save a great deal of time and could quickly clarify difficult words and abstract concepts.

On the other hand, it could be a double-edged sword if L1 dominated the class because its frequent use could limit students' second language exposure and hinder their second language development. The mentees suggested that for nonnative English learners, the limited and judicious use of translation and mother tongue improves the teaching and learning processes, and increases language acquisition. They continued that the best way to go about using it was through making the learners aware of the translation equivalence issues and helping them distinguish the differences between the two languages and understand that what works grammatically in their native language may not work with English. The students appreciated their teachers' advice on how to best use L1 in learning ESL for a clear purpose and they took care to make rational decisions. Such mutual intercultural empathy helped the mentees and students construct their mutual intercultural identity showing respect and understanding to one another and building collaborative student-teacher rapport.

Their intercultural identity demonstrated in the language attitude laid a base on which their intercultural attitude towards other cultures was emerging. One mentee reported that his learning of different cultural contents from the students changed an online learning space into a welcoming platform where the students shared their cultural festivals (e.g., Chinese Moon Festival and Indian Diwali Festival), cultural handicrafts, and cultural calligraphies (e.g., Arabic and Chinese styles). They came to understand one another better and better through interaction and negotiation. This process led to learners' willingness to communicate, use their personal autonomy, and participate in various task-based learning activities designed to increase their employment opportunities (Al-Murtadha, 2019). In addition, one female mentor reported that the mentee she supervised used the teaching materials in a respectful manner as the students were all adult students from a variety of different backgrounds and cultures. The mentee demonstrated her ability to feel and think what her students who were older than herself felt and thought about appropriate intercultural communication (DeVito, 2016; Lankiewicz, 2014) and the students felt at home in the online learning space.

Effective teachers were able to use learning resources relevant to their students' everyday life experiences so that they were motivated to participate in learning activities (Díaz, 2016; Harmer, 2015). Another male mentor reported that the female mentee he supervised asked the students to name a few cultural and traditional foods that would normally be prepared for the most important festivals in their home culture after she talked about an article on different English foods, such as turkeys, ham, and salad, which are prepared for the Christmas Eve in Australia. Then, a few students either put up their hands or used a raise-hand symbol on their screen. They took turns talking about their unique cultural foods as a special festive celebration in different countries, for example, dumplings as a family get-together for the Chinese Spring Festival. As the foods are available in the shops and restaurants in Sydney, many students had experience with them and felt the beauty and power of these cultural foods that made their everyday life good. They became excited and talkative when foods were used as a topic. Indeed, cultural foods are commonly used as a meaningful communication of folk tales and cultural representation in many cultures (Reinhard et al., 2021) with some of them highlighting food and language communication (e.g., stories and jokes) (Karatsu, 2014; Riley & Paugh, 2019) and others focusing on foods and nonverbal communication and behaviour (e.g., manners of eating foods) (Szatrowski, 2014).

The mentees were also playing the role of an educator with a purpose to build their students' confidence in learning English for employment and socialization. For example, a female mentee learned that some students in their 40s and 50s felt ashamed of speaking English in front of others because their children often mocked them for poor speaking skills. This affected their self-confidence in speaking English. The mentee convinced their students that they were already capable and successful L1 speakers and had thinking and analytical skills that could be deployed in learning English as a second language. As discussed above, the mentees did not completely ban their students from using L1 but encouraged them to use it thoughtfully and flexibly for specific purposes. One pedagogical purpose was to help grow students' confidence and remove their fear of being unable to speak in online space and public. Other measures they took included minimization of correcting students' speaking errors, focusing on speaking fluency, and moving from pair to individual presentation step by step.

One mentee reported how he used the tutoring opportunity to share his own learning experience as part of TESOL teacher education and explained the pedagogies used in Australia. One day soon after the tutoring started, the mentee learned from the female student that she did not want to go to the English college anymore and that she did not like the teacher's methods. When asked why, she complained that the teacher was not teaching English in a formal and structured lesson as in the textbook but took the students to the bus and train stations and showed them how to buy tickets on a student trip. On another student trip, the teacher took them to the beach and showed them how to book a tour or a canoe. After listening to her complaints, the mentee explained that the teaching approach her teacher used was functional and situational use of English to meet the daily communication needs of the learners (Kakarla, 2019). English in real use can help language learners develop relevant communication skills and survive their everyday life, and effective teachers would use different teaching resources and learning materials, including print textbooks and teacher-developed handouts (Brown, 2015), selectively and for a definite purpose. After this dialogue, the student was happily continuing her English college course. It is evident that the mentee's teaching experience and the student's learning experience were mutually meaningful and educational, and both gained insight into the teaching and learning philosophies through individual reflections and informal conversation.

9.4.3   Collaborative Teaching as Professional Development

The mentees and their mentors worked together to aim at making sense of online interaction, using many handy resources, such as breakout rooms, peer learning groups, and nonverbal communication cues, to achieve online collaborative teaching and learning. This collaboration includes teamwork before, during, and after each teaching session. The mentees consulted their mentors throughout their placement and they worked closely during the supervised teaching. Similar to collaborative teaching of the development process of a research proposal (Khabiri & Marashi, 2016), they had completed some project-based and essay assignments in their TESOL coursework through researching resources, brainstorming, group discussions, drafting and re-drafting, getting feedback, and revising before submission. All these coursework assessments concentrated on the understanding and context-free study of relevant TESOL subjects without combining with practice in a specific teaching setting or student group. As it was the first time for these mentees to teach online, they took it as a form of in-context professional development.

Before teaching each session, the mentees prepared teaching plans in consultation with their mentors, such as studying the course syllabus, meeting with their mentors, getting to know student profiles, and preparing lesson plans. The plans include teaching aims and objectives, learning materials, teaching techniques (e.g., role plays and game-based learning activities), online assessments (e.g., oral and written), and time allocation, etc. (Brown, 2015; Harmer, 2015). Mentors made critical and constructive comments on the lesson plans and the mentees clarified for additional information, researched further resources, and revised their plans before teaching online. One of them wrote that the mentor was always willing to give advice or share their own experience in teaching practice. Another recalled in her report that when she was observing her mentor teaching online she could see that the mentor was very passionate about helping her students learn English and other matters as well. The mentor inspired the mentee who wanted to follow her as a model person.

While the mentee herself was teaching online, she was also collaborating with her mentor who was observing and assisting her as a team member when needed. For example, she used breakout rooms to facilitate student group discussion so that each group could participate and practise their communication skills. Breakout rooms create space to increase student learning engagement and peer collaboration (Paterson & Maxfield, 2016). She was able to have a special breakout room in which to help individual students who needed additional assistance. Meanwhile, her mentor was working with another group of students in a different breakout room. Sometimes, before the mentee chose to take care of a few different breakout rooms one after another, she first gave clear instructions that each breakout room would be headed by one student as a team leader who managed student peer learning and reported the group discussion to the class later. Then, the mentee was visiting each breakout room and assisted the student learning. Saltz and Heckman (2020) think that such online learning can accommodate structured pair activities so that peer learning is possible to support each other. It also has a flexible combination of student-teacher and student-student interactive collaboration in purpose-designed breakout rooms which students find accommodating and scaffolding.

The mentees met with the mentors for after-teaching feedback as part of the interactive collaboration to gain feedback. They wanted to hear some advice on what to improve for professional development. Research shows that pre-service teachers can get helpful feedback from an experienced mentor no matter whether it is provided through implicit hints or explicit prompts (Nassaji, 2017; Nassaji & Kartchava, 2020). When the mentees had inquires about the feedback, they would have a collaborative talk with their mentors, discussing it and asking for more information. For example, after receiving the feedback one mentee sought further advice on how to slow down his pace. The mentor explained that he could try repeating words and phrases while observing students' nonverbal response, such as facial expressions. Another two mentees also had to manage their speech pace as they were advised to speak multiple times and at a slower pace sometimes due to poor audio or unstable Internet connection. One mentor noted that it made sense for mentees to use non-verbal resources such as eye contact for attention, appropriate facial expression (smiling) for positive emotions, posture to project confidence, appropriate movement to show enthusiasm to project energy, and culture-appropriate gestures to enhance verbal communication effect. TESOL teachers can deploy intercultural nonverbal communication resources and cues to demonstrate their intercultural literacy and facilitate their teaching and achieving collaborative learning and interaction with their culture-diverse students (Yang, 2020). It is through collaborative teamwork in teaching that they experience professional development in terms of effective combination of TESOL theories and practices, and co-construct intercultural identity.

9.5 Conclusion

This chapter has focused on how pre-service TESOL teachers developed their intercultural identity through online WIL in the Australian context. The discussion has highlighted three key themes, including how the mentees, mentors, and students worked together to meet the challenges of online teaching and learning environment, how they demonstrated intercultural empathy and understanding of one another, appreciated different languages and cultures, and achieved successful intercultural communication in online interaction, and how they collaborated with one another for effective teaching and learning as a team.

This discussion has two implications for pre-service TESOL teacher professional development through co-constructing intercultural identity with online WIL experience. First, the WIL-based reflective practice has the potential to prompt TESOL practitioners to reflect on teaching philosophy and principles, thus bridging the gaps between practice and theory about TESOL teacher intercultural identity. Further reflection is needed on two key factors, including interactional teaching and learning as intercultural verbal communication and intercultural nonverbal communication need (Yang, 2018), and intercultural interaction in online space. Second, the mentees' online WIL experience helps make job-ready graduates. The online mode of WIL has validated their willingness and success in learning new apps and emerging technologies and techniques, and has increased their confidence in online collaboration with mentors and students (Nami et al., 2018).

As the discussion in this chapter focuses on qualitative data only, future research can employ a quantitative method or mixed methods. They provide opportunities for researchers and readers to understand the complexities of intercultural identity construction of pre-service TESOL teachers and to what extent the collaboration of each major stakeholder, the use of various resources, and different delivery modes (online and face-to-face) could contribute to the further success of WIL.

References

Al-Murtadha, M. (2019). Enhancing EFL learners' willingness to communicate with visualization and goal-setting activities. *TESOL Quarterly, 53*(1), 133–157. https://doi.org/10.1002/tesq.474

Brown, H. D. (2015). *Teaching by principles: An interactive approach to language pedagogy* (4th ed.). Pearson Education.

Carrol, G., Conklin, K., & Gyllstad, H. (2016). Found in translation: The influence of the L1 on the reading of idioms in an L2. *Studies in Second Language Acquisition, 38*(3), 403–443. https://doi.org/10.1017/S0272263115000492

Carter, L., Ruskin, J., & Cassilles, A. (2017). Three modes of work-integrated learning: Stories of success. In L. N. Wood & Y. A. Breyer (Eds.), *Success in higher education: Transitions to, within and from university* (pp. 203–215). Springer. https://doi.org/10.1007/978-981-10-2791-8_12

Ceglie, R. J., & Black, G., C. (2020). Lessons from the other side of the computer: Student perceptions of effective online instruction. In A. W. Thornburg, D. F. Abernathy, & R. J.

Ceglie, (Eds.), *Handbook of research on developing engaging online courses* (pp. 72–92). IGI Global. https://doi.org/10.4018/978-1-7998-2132-8.ch005

Debbie, P., & Roberta, J. A. (2016). Walking in English learners' shoes: Preservice teacher struggles result in empathy. In D. M. Velliaris & D. Coleman-George (Eds.), *Handbook of research on study abroad programs and outbound mobility* (pp. 621–650). IGI Global. https://doi.org/10.4018/978-1-5225-0169-5.ch025

DeVito, J. A. (2016). *The interpersonal communication book* (14th ed.). Pearson.

Díaz, A. R. (2016). Developing interculturally-oriented teaching resources in CFL: Meeting the challenge. In R. Moloney & H. L. Xu (Eds.), *Exploring innovative pedagogy in the teaching and learning of Chinese as a foreign language* (pp. 115–135). Springer. https://doi.org/10.1007/978-981-287-772-7_7

Gardner, H. (2011). *Frames of mind the theory of multiple intelligences* (3rd ed.). Basic Books.

Harmer, J. (2015). *The practice of English language teaching* (5th ed.). Pearson Education.

Hu, Y., & Dai, K. (2021, January 1). Foreign-born Chinese students learning in China: (re)shaping intercultural identity in higher education institution. *International Journal of Intercultural Relations, 80*, 89–98. https://doi.org/10.1016/j.ijintrel.2020.11.010

Jackson, K. (2019). *Qualitative data analysis with NVivo* (3rd ed.). SAGE Publications.

Kakarla, U. (2019). *Functional English for communication.* SAGE Publications.

Karatsu, M. (2014). Repetition of words and phrases from the punch lines of Japanese stories about food and restaurants: A group bonding exercise. In P. E. Szatrowski (Ed.), *Language and food: Verbal and nonverbal experiences* (pp. 185–207). John Benjamins Publishing Company.

Khabiri, M., & Marashi, H. (2016). Collaborative teaching: How does it work in a graduate TEFL class? *TESOL Journal, 7*(1), 179–202. https://doi.org/10.1002/tesj.196

Kim, Y. Y. (2001). *Becoming intercultural an integrative theory of communication and cross-cultural adaptation.* SAGE Publications.

Kislev, E. (2012). Components of intercultural identity: Towards an effective integration policy. *Intercultural Education, 23*(3), 221–235. https://doi.org/10.1080/14675986.2012.699373

Lankiewicz, H. (2014). Teacher interpersonal communication abilities in the classroom with regard to perceived classroom justice and teacher credibility. In M. Pawlak, J. Bielak, & A. Mystkowska-Wiertelak (Eds.), *Classroom-oriented research: Achievements and challenges* (pp. 101–120). Springer. https://doi.org/10.1007/978-3-319-00188-3_7

Maibom, H. L. (2020). *Empathy.* Routledge.

Manton, C., Heffernan, T., Kostogriz, A., & Seddon, T. (2021). Australian school–university partnerships: The (dis)integrated work of teacher educators. *Asia-Pacific Journal of Teacher Education, 49*(3), 334–346. https://doi.org/10.1080/1359866X.2020.1780563

Meskill, C. (2009). CMC in language teacher education: Learning with and through instructional conversations. *Innovation in Language Learning & Teaching, 3*(1), 51–63. https://doi.org/10.1080/17501220802655474

Meskill, C. (Ed.). (2013). *Online teaching and learning: Sociocultural perspectives.* Bloomsbury.

Moloney, R., Harbon, L., & Fielding, R. (2016). An interactive, co-constructed approach to the development of intercultural understanding in pre-service language teachers. In F. Dervin & Z. Gross (Eds.), *Intercultural competence in education: Alternative approaches for different times* (pp. 185–213). Palgrave Macmillan. https://doi.org/10.1057/978-1-137-58733-6_10

Nami, F., Marandi, S. S., & Sotoudehnama, E. (2018). Interaction in a discussion list: An exploration of cognitive, social, and teaching presence in teachers' online collaborations. *ReCALL, 30*(3), 375–398. https://doi.org/10.1017/S0958344017000349

Nassaji, H. (2017). Negotiated oral feedback in response to written errors. In H. Nassaji & E. Kartchava (Eds.), *Corrective feedback in second language teaching and learning: Research, theory, applications, implications* (pp. 114–128). Routledge.

Nassaji, H., & Kartchava, E. (2020). Corrective feedback and good language teachers. In C. Griffiths & Z. Tajeddin (Eds.), *Lessons from good language teachers* (pp. 151–163). Cambridge University Press. https://doi.org/10.1017/9781108774390.015

Othman, A., & Ruslan, N. (2020). Intercultural communication experiences among students and teachers: Implication to in-service teacher professional development. *Journal for Multicultural Education, 14*(3/4), 223–238. https://doi.org/10.1108/JME-04-2020-0024

Paterson, T., & Maxfield, J. (2016). *Breakout the breakout rooms: Increasing online student engagement and collaboration.* Innovate and educate: Teaching and learning conference by blackboard, 28–31 August 2016, Sydney, NSW, Australia.

Reinhard, C. D., Largent, J. E., & Chin, B. (2021). *Eating fandom: Intersections between fans and food cultures.* Routledge.

Riley, K., & Paugh, A. (2019). *Food and language: Discourses and foodways across cultures.* Routledge.

Saltz, J., & Heckman, R. (2020). Using structured pair activities in a distributed online breakout room. *Online Learning, 24*(1), 227–244. https://doi.org/10.24059/olj.v24i1.1632

Sassatelli, M. (2009). *Becoming Europeans: Cultural identity and cultural policies.* Palgrave Macmillan. https://doi.org/10.1057/9780230250437

Segal, E. (2018). *Social empathy: The art of understanding others.* Columbia University Press.

Selvi, A. F., & Peercy, M. M. (2016). Diversity within TESOL teacher education programs. In J. Crandall & M. Christison (Eds.), *Teacher education and professional development in TESOL: Global perspectives* (pp. 86–98). Routledge.

Shardakova, M. (2013). "I joke you don't": Second language humor and intercultural identity construction. In C. Kinginger (Ed.), *Social and cultural aspects of language learning in study abroad* (pp. 207–237). John Benjamins Publishing Company.

Skills for Education and Employment. (2021). Program (SEE/Learn English). https://www.mtcaustralia.com.au/education-training/see/

Szatrowski, P. E. (2014). Introduction to language and food: Verbal and nonverbal experiences. In P. E. Szatrowski (Ed.), *Language and food: Verbal and nonverbal experiences* (pp. 3–28). John Benjamins Publishing Company.

Tajeddin, Z., & Ghaffaryan, S. (2020). Language teachers' intercultural identity in the critical context of cultural globalization and its metaphoric realization. *Journal of Intercultural Communication Research*, 1–19. https://doi.org/10.1080/17475759.2020.1754884

Tian, M., & Lowe, J. A. (2014). Intercultural identity and intercultural experiences of American students in China. *Journal of Studies in International Education, 18*(3), 281–297. https://doi.org/10.1177/1028315313496582

Türker, E. (2016). The role of L1 conceptual and linguistic knowledge and frequency in the acquisition of L2 metaphorical expressions. *Second Language Research, 32*(1), 25–48. https://doi.org/10.1177/0267658315593336

Universities Australia. (2019). *Work-integrated learning in universities: The final report.* Universities Australia, Issue. https://apo.org.au/sites/default/files/resource-files/2019-04/apo-nid242371.pdf

Walkington, J. (2010). Teacher educators: The leaders in work-integrated learning. *Asia-Pacific Journal of Teacher Education, 38*(3), 177–180. https://doi.org/10.1080/1359866x.2010.493580

Yang, P. (2015). Developing intercultural competence in TESOL service-learning: Volunteer tutoring for recently-arrived adult refugees in learning English as a second language. In J. M. Perren & A. J. Wurr (Eds.), *Learning the language of global citizenship: Strengthening service-learning in TESOL* (pp. 328–351). Common Ground Publishing. https://doi.org/10.18848/978-1-61229-815-3/CGP

Yang, P. (2018). Developing TESOL teacher intercultural identity: An intercultural communication competence approach. *TESOL Journal, 9*(3), 525–541. https://onlinelibrary.wiley.com/doi/full/10.1002/tesj.356

Yang, P. (2020). Towards intercultural literacy of language teacher education in the 21st century. In G. Neokleous, A. Krulatz, & R. Farrelly (Eds.), *Handbook of research on cultivating literacy in diverse and multilingual classrooms* (pp. 22–40). IGI Global. https://doi.org/10.4018/978-1-7998-2722-1.ch002

Ye, L. L. (2018). *Intercultural experience and identity: Narratives of Chinese doctoral students in the UK*. Springer. https://doi.org/10.1007/978-3-319-91373-5

Zeng, S., Zhang, J., Gao, M., Xu, K. M., & Zhang, J. (2020). Using learning analytics to understand collective attention in language MOOCs. *Computer Assisted Language Learning*, 1–26. https://doi.org/10.1080/09588221.2020.1825094

Chapter 10
Teacher Identity and Investment: First Year Language Teacher Students Investing in Their Future Profession

Anne Pitkänen-Huhta, Maria Ruohotie-Lyhty, and Päivikki Jääskelä

Abstract Professional identity is central in understanding the socially embedded and personally experienced character of teachers' professional development. Particularly in the early stages of identity construction, we need to focus not only on the past and present but also on the images of the future in order to support identity construction during education. This study investigates how student teachers approach their future work as language teachers and how they perceive the ways in which they can invest in their futures. As part of a broader project, data were collected from 61 student teachers during the first semester in the language teacher education programme and it comprised visualizations of student teachers' future work and verbal descriptions of factors facilitating or hindering the dream of their future profession. The focus here is on the verbal descriptions. Becoming aware of student teachers' future goals and the ways in which they are planning to reach their dream provides valuable insights into the processes needed to support student teacher development.

Keywords Teacher identity · Investment · Envisioning · Language teachers · Teacher education

10.1 Introduction

Professional identity is central in understanding the socially embedded yet personally experienced character of teachers' professional development and engagement in professional practices (e.g., Barkhuizen, 2016; Kanno & Stuart, 2011; Ruohotie-Lyhty, 2013). The centrality of identity has also turned the interest of teacher education institutes to questions of identity construction during pre-service training. Teacher education programmes are recognized as places for reflecting on and challenging established ideas of the teaching profession. Furthermore, students are

A. Pitkänen-Huhta (✉) · M. Ruohotie-Lyhty · P. Jääskelä
University of Jyväskylä, Jyväskylä, Finland
e-mail: anne.pitkanen-huhta@jyu.fi

expected to become aware of the need of identity construction and receive tools for the analysis and development of their identities when they start working as teachers.

Reflection on the past and present has been used as a medium of affecting the identity construction of pre-service and in-service teachers. However, focusing on the narratives of the future and the students' imagined identities is also important for identity construction (Kanno & Norton, 2003). Examining how student teachers imagine their future reveals how they are willing to invest in their professional development (Barkhuizen, 2016) and how realistic their ideas of investment are. Becoming aware of students' future goals and the means of reaching them can provide valuable insights into the processes needed to support student teacher development.

The importance of future goals has been studied in connection to language learner identities. Learners' commitment to language learning is mediated by their ideal L2 (second language) selves (Dörnyei, 2005). The ideal L2 self projects into the future, to how learners see themselves as language users in future imagined communities (Norton, 2001; Xu, 2012). The concept of investment (Darvin & Norton, 2015; De Costa & Norton, 2017; Norton, 2000) has been used to concretize a person's possibilities and willingness to put effort into their own development in the circumstances constrained by social, cultural and historical factors (Darvin & Norton, 2015; Kim, 2014). Fewer studies have, however, addressed the question of investment related to future language teacher profession.

This study thus aims to fill this gap by investigating how student teachers approach their future work through expressions of investment in their futures as language teachers. Theoretically the study is anchored in the intertwined concepts of teacher identity, envisioning as an aspect of identity construction, and investment. This study extends the previous analyses for the data collected during language teacher education on 61 first-year student teachers' visualizations of their future work (Ruohotie-Lyhty & Pitkänen-Huhta, 2020) with analyzing the student teachers' verbal descriptions related to the visualizations. These descriptions reveal the student-perceived factors facilitating or hindering their dream of their future profession, thus indirectly indicating their willingness and ability to invest in their futures. We provide answers to the following research questions: (1) In which ways do student teachers perceive they can invest in their professional future? and (2) How are the student-described forms of investment related to their visions of the professional future?

10.2   Identity and Investment

Since 1990's, the concept of teacher identity has received growing attention in research (Block, 2007; Duff, 2013). This is connected to the interactional nature of teaching and learning, in which both teacher and learner identities are central (Varghese et al., 2005). In the same vein, the practices of language teacher education have been examined from the perspective of identity construction (Barcelos, 2016; Barkhuizen, 2009; Kalaja, 2016; Trent, 2013).

Although there are several approaches to identity (e.g., narrative theory, Barkhuizen, 2016; Ruohotie-Lyhty, 2013; poststructuralist perspectives, Varghese et al., 2005), recent approaches agree on some characteristics concerning the concept of teacher identity. First, identity is seen as particular ways of looking at the world, i.e., "how a person understands his or her relationship to the world" (Norton, 2013, p. 45) or more specifically, as a means of making sense of one's professional practices (Barkhuizen, 2016). The concept of identity is also perceived to have process-like characteristics, related to how the relationship to the world is expressed in terms of identity being "structured across time and space, and how the person understands possibilities for the future" (Norton, 2013, p. 45). Accordingly, identity is simultaneously in the state of "being" and "becoming", constantly affecting the teachers' actions and views of the profession and shaped by the flux of professional practices. Second, identity is seen as the relation between personal and social aspects (Duff, 2013). However, individuals are not mere products of their environment, but agentic participants in their identity development (Sade, 2009).

The concept of investment ties teacher identities to the future possibilities (Darvin & Norton, 2015; Norton, 2013). Investment as a construct was originally used in relation to language learning and language learners by Norton (2001, 2013) to highlight "the socially and historically constructed relationship between language learner identity and learning commitment" (Darvin & Norton, 2015, p. 37). Investment also means acquiring a range of symbolic and material resources that increase the learner's cultural capital and social power (Darvin & Norton, 2015; Bourdieu, 1991). Investment is thus inherently tied to the post-structuralist understandings of teacher identity construction: identities and investment are dynamic, fluid, and in a constant state of change.

There have been a fairly large number of previous studies on teacher identities using the concept of investment (e.g., Barkhuizen, 2016; Dunn & Downey, 2018) but few on student teacher's identity construction and investment. However, Mora et al. (2016) examined the learning trajectories of Mexican novice language teachers drawing on the concept of investment. Comparison of teachers born and educated in Mexico and those who had returned to Mexico for their studies after spending their childhood in the US revealed a difference in investment which was related to the teachers' personal life-histories.

10.3   Envisioning as an Aspect in Identity Construction

As pointed out above, orienting towards the future is an important component of identity (Barkhuizen, 2016; Norton, 2013). This is especially relevant during teacher education, as students are reaching towards an anticipated future. A key character of their development is the way in which they imagine their future tasks and roles as language teachers. People orient to the future with hopes and desires (e.g., Kanno & Norton, 2003) but also with fears (e.g., Barkhuizen, 2016).

There is a growing body of research on teacher and student teacher identity construction (e.g., Barkhuizen, 2016; Kalaja & Melo-Pfeifer, 2019; Kalaja & Ruohotie-Lyhty, 2019; Ruohotie-Lyhty, 2013), also those focusing on student teachers' visions of their future. Recent examples relevant to the present study include Barcelos (2016), Kalaja and Mäntylä (2018), Brandão (2019) and Pinho (2019). Barcelos (2016) examined narratives of language teacher students longitudinally. She found that negative features relating to teacher profession hindered teachers' identity construction and made them question their future profession. Kalaja and Mäntylä (2018) examined student teachers' expectations of the future by asking them to envision a classroom of their dreams. The authors found great variation among the students and concluded that the variation is due to both the stage of their studies and their experience of teaching English. Brandão (2019) examined how student teachers imagined their future in teaching EFL in Brazil and found that how the student teachers make sense of their past experiences as pupils and their present status as student teachers is strongly shaped by their idea of the professional future. Pinho's (2019) study on one student teacher's self-image as an EFL teacher revealed that experiences are strongly context bound.

The present study complements earlier studies with its focus on investment in relation to envisioning the future profession. We draw on, firstly, the concept of identity as socially and personally constructed and connected to future desires and fears and secondly, on the concept of investment, as connecting to future visions and allowing us to extend our focus beyond the individual to the contextual and social elements of teacher identity construction. The study seeks answers to the following research questions: (1) In which ways do student teachers perceive they can invest in their professional future? and (2) How are the student-described forms of investment related to their visions of the professional future?

10.4   Method

10.4.1   Context and Participants

The participants were 61 Finnish foreign language teacher students (ca. 20 years old), who had just started their studies at the University of Jyväskylä in a language teacher education programme. In contrast to many other teacher education programmes in Finland, the courses of this programme specialize in language teaching from the very beginning of studies. These practices are introduced to accompany the professional identity construction of student teachers throughout their studies. Data consist of students' responses to a course assignment in "Becoming a language teacher" course in their teacher education programme. A written consent was obtained for the use of their responses as research data. The present study connects to a larger project examining agency in the professional identity construction of language teacher students (Jääskelä et al., 2021; Ruohotie-Lyhty & Pitkänen-Huhta, 2020).

10.4.2   Data Collection

In the course assignment, the student teachers were asked to envision their professional future in 10 years' time. To better understand the key elements connected to language teachers' work, we drew on the Method of Empathy Based Stories (MEBS) (Wallin et al., 2018) and asked the student teachers to visually produce two alternative images of their future: their desired job and its antithesis. In the original form of the method, the participants produce two alternative storylines altering only one central feature of the story, often either success or failure connected to the phenomenon in focus (Wallin et al., 2018, p. 4). We asked the student teachers to contrast the desired and feared professional future and write a description of the image as well as a reflection on how realistic the two futures were and what might facilitate or hinder their dream. In terms of investment, we examined student-reported ways of influencing one's future, i.e., what facilitates and/or hinders the dream. The instruction for the task was as follows (translated from Finnish):

> Visualize yourself at work ten years from now in two images. In one image you are in your dream job, in the other you are at work that is not your dream.

> Write a short text in which you describe what your images portray, how realistic the two futures are, and *what facilitates or hinders your dream.*

We have previously analyzed the visual data and the first part of the student teachers' verbal description, i.e., what their image portrays (Ruohotie-Lyhty & Pitkänen-Huhta, 2020; Ruohotie-Lyhty et al., 2021). In this chapter, the previous results serve as a point of reference for further analyses. Here we focus on the latter part of the verbal descriptions, i.e., how investment was expressed in student teachers' reactions to the part "*what facilitates or hinders your dream*". We explore, first, in which ways the student teachers believe they are able and willing to invest in their professional dream and second, which other factors student teachers bring out in the realization of their dream.

10.4.3   Orientations to Future Profession as a Point of Reference for the Present Study

In our previous study (Ruohotie-Lyhty & Pitkänen-Huhta, 2020) focusing on the visual data, we discerned two different orientations to the future profession: *nature of work oriented* view and *status oriented* view to language teacher profession. Majority of the participants (45 out of 61) represented the *nature of work orientation*, where the content, relationships and conditions of teachers' work constructed the main tension between desired and feared professional futures. Typical of these envisioned futures was a rather detailed description of the places, emotions and artefacts that were connected to desired and feared futures. In the pictures and accompanying texts, the student teachers described their future work in terms of progressive pedagogy, extended collaboration with colleagues and agreeable physical environment.

A minority of 16 participants envisioned their desired and feared professional futures in terms of the *status* of the profession. In the visualizations and verbal descriptions of the images of this group, the teacher profession was presented as providing a certain status in society. The tension created between the desired and feared professional futures was built between appreciated and less-appreciated social positioning. Typically, the content of work was not clearly described. In contrast, the main themes were linked to stereotypical descriptions of teaching and the envisioned professional future was very briefly described. Some of the participants only mentioned their willingness "to become a teacher". Some of them, however, provided some additional explanation, such as comparing teachers' work with the feared professional status.

After analyzing the visualizations, we wanted to understand more thoroughly the ways in which these student teachers believed they could reach and how they invested in reaching their dreams. This became the research task for the present study.

10.4.4 Data Analysis

To answer our first research question, we analyzed the verbal descriptions by following the basic principles of content analysis (Patton, 2015). The categorization was inductive, i.e., we formed the categories based on what we saw in the explanations. The categorization was refined through several readings of the data as well as cross-coding by two of the researchers.

For our second research question, we analyzed these results against the findings of our previous study (Ruohotie-Lyhty & Pitkänen-Huhta, 2020). The categories of investment established by the content analysis were cross-tabulated with the two orientations to work revealed in our previous analyses of the visual data, i.e., *the nature of work* and *the status* orientation to the future profession. To learn if there are any statistical associations between investment and the categorization of the participants in *nature-of-work-oriented* and *status-oriented* future visions, the number of respondents for each classified category was first calculated using cross-tabulation. After that the chi-square tests and the values of the adjusted residuals were used to examine associations between the factors of investment and the groups of orientations to work.

10.5 Findings

10.5.1 Factors Facilitating and Hindering the Envisioned Professional Futures: Different Types of Investment

Different types of investment could be detected when the student teachers reflected on the factors facilitating or hindering their desired or feared professions and the probability of the two alternative futures. Five types of investment were detected in the analysis: (1) student teachers' own volition, (2) motivation and personal characteristics, (3) hard work, (4) getting a degree, and (5) external conditions. A student teacher's description could include any number of these categories, ranging from one to five categories. There were also two student teachers who had not included any description or did not mention anything that could be seen as investment. The following two descriptions (translated from Finnish by the authors) are examples of a short description where only one factor came out.

> I can facilitate my dreams coming true by studying and concentrating on studies properly. If I give up, it's very likely that I end up in a job that does not correspond to my dreams.
>
> I myself influence my dreams coming true.

The first one was categorized as "getting a degree" and the second one as "student teacher's own volition".

In the following example, the student teacher has written a lengthy description, which includes all five detected factors facilitating and/or hindering the dream:

> Finishing my degree can facilitate my wishes coming true. Being self-directed at school but also at work can help in getting a job. If one wishes to gain qualifications, one has to work for it. Having a good combination of subjects [in your degree] can be useful in finding work. Energetic, positive and diligent attitude take you far in life! I believe firmly in my qualifications in the future and in finding a job. Of course, if there is a serious shortage of money and I have to find a job, it may be that I end up in my detested job, because one has to work in life. I'm not picky either.

This student teacher mentions the MA degree as a facilitating factor as well as one's own self-initiation, hard work, and a positive attitude. The student teacher also mentions an external condition, i.e., lack of money that might push one to a feared job.

Table 10.1 presents the overall distribution of the descriptions across the five categories. Four of the categories were fairly equal in size and only one (hard work) was clearly smaller than the others.

Table 10.1 The overall distribution of the categories of investment

Category	N
Student teachers' own volition	27
Motivation and personal characteristics	25
Hard work	10
Getting a degree	31
External conditions	26

Student Teachers' Own Volition

In this category, the participants of the study described the ways in which their own volition could support them in reaching their professional dreams. In these descriptions, the student teachers referred to their own will as well as their current choices and their future activity as members of the work community. They also often perceived their own activity as potentially reversing the negative influence of the environment. The words *I*, *me*, and *myself* appear often in these examples.

> The future of my dreams is not fully in my own hands, but I can myself influence the variability in my work. I can facilitate the plan by examining/asking about/discussing new possibilities and ideas. It is also important that I take the students and their opinions into account.

> I believe that my dream job can be reached, if I myself take part in developing the future and reach for my dreams boldly and not giving up when facing small setbacks.

In these examples, the participants describe some of the ways in which being an active member of the working community can help them in reaching the cooperative learning culture at work. They also refer to teacher autonomy in being able to decide themselves the working methods and practices in the class and believe this could support the fulfilment of their dream.

Motivation and Personal Characteristics

In this category, the student teachers highlighted the significance of their own motivation and attitude in reaching their dream job in the future. They described possessing the necessary characteristics that are needed to reach their dream. The following example illustrates the type of answers in this category:

> Skills and knowledge are of course needed, but the most important thing is motivation and attitude, with which one can have results.

In this example, the type of motivation and attitude are not directly expressed, whereas some participants were more explicit about the type of characteristics that they possessed. One of the student teachers refers to their own work experiences as something that will help them in finding a dream job:

> My wishes coming true can be facilitated by my experiences as a teacher [in a specific school for the Deaf], my work experiences in development co-operation.

For this student teacher, the previous experiences as a teacher in certain schools as well as experiences of working in developing countries increase the probability to do the kind of work the student teacher wants in the future.

Hard Work

In this category, the participants named hard work as something that is needed to reach the dream. Hard work could be related to studies or to finding a job or to just being hard-working. Being lazy was associated with negative future expectations. Differently from the volition group, the actions that hard work entailed were not described in detail. The following two examples illustrate this category:

> I know, however, that with hard work and diligence I can reach my dream, up to a point.

> If you wish to gain qualifications, you have to work for it.

In this example, the student teacher sees that the dream can be reached if one just works hard for it and is diligent.

Getting a Degree
The student teachers in this category identified getting a degree as the necessary precondition for success in finding their dream job. Their investment was straight-forwardly connected to their studies, whereas failure was a consequence of dropping out of studies. The following two excerpts provide typical examples of this category:

> My teacher-future is hindered by quitting studies and facilitated by continuing my studies.

> My dream coming true is facilitated by completing my degree.

In these examples, the quality of the studies was not opened up, as the main thing appeared to be just to complete studies to get a degree. In some examples, however, student teachers linked some qualities to the ways in which they wanted to conduct their studies, as in the following example:

> I can facilitate my dream coming true by studying my Finnish-as-a-second-language studies well.

In the examples in this category, the quality of investment was mostly described in very general terms and very briefly.

External Conditions
In the final category, the investment was not dependent on the student teachers themselves but on some external conditions, which appeared to be beyond one's own volition or activities. Many of these concerned the future job situation or various societal or political changes.

> In addition, funding for schools as well as structural and political changes influence the future of work.

> It is difficult to estimate the likelihood for these options to come true, as political decisions, one's own choices as well as the general atmosphere in the area where one ends up working influence these.

In the above examples, the student teachers see that their future is dependent on the funding for schools, on political changes and decisions or the general atmosphere in the future location of work. Some of the examples were indirectly related to one's own activities as well, as in the next example:

> If I stayed in a place where there's not much work for language teachers that could prevent my dream from coming true. A facilitating factor could be the fact that I would be open to different options and would be ready to live in a place where I could find work.

In this example, the student teacher sees that their future is dependent on the job situation in the area where they live, but this was also related to their own activities in that they should be open to moving to another location. The following example is also related to external conditions but now they are related to health or skills. The student teacher in this example feels that the dream may not come true if a serious illness hinders them from working as a teacher:

> If there were something that would prevent my dream from coming true that would probably be lack of jobs matching my profession or lack of professional skills or something related to health. For example, if I would get a serious illness which would prevent me from working as a teacher.

Through the qualitative analysis of the student teachers' descriptions of the factors facilitating and hindering their desired or feared future profession, we learned that the student teachers saw both internal and external influences on their future. They saw that they could invest in their future by their own persistent actions and with the right attitude and motivation. If they just want something and are active in pursuing the dream, they can reach it. They also saw that merely getting the appropriate degree would guarantee the desired future as a teacher. Many also saw that some influences are beyond their own hands in external conditions, such as funding for education, job situation or personal health.

10.5.2 Investment in Relation to the Orientation to Work

To answer our second research question, we present the results of the statistical analysis of the associations between the factors of student teachers' investment described and categorized above and their two orientations to the future profession. We wished to see if the student teachers' investment was related to how they saw their professional future. The analysis was done by cross-tabulating the categories of investment and the categories of the two orientations to work. The five factors, i.e., (1) student teachers' own volition, (2) motivation and personal characteristics, (3) hard work, (4) getting a degree, and (5) external conditions, were cross-tabulated with the two categories of orientations to work (*nature of work* and *status of work*).

In the analysis, all the categories of investment were cross-tabulated with the two orientations to work, but only one factor (category of investment) showed a statistically significant difference between the two orientations to work. This was the "getting a degree" category. A chi-square test of independence was performed to examine the association between "getting a degree" and the orientation to work. The association between these variables was significant $c^2 (1, N = 61) = 11.68, p = .001$. Those who had a status orientation to future work were more likely to say that getting a degree facilitates their dream rather than those who had a nature of work orientation to work. The results are presented in Table 10.2.

None of the other factors (categories of investment) showed any statistically significant differences between the two orientations to work. It was also examined whether there was a difference in the number of factors in any one description and the orientation to work, but none was detected. We can thus conclude that there is an association between the student teachers' investment in terms of *getting a degree* and their orientation to future work. In other words, those student teachers who orient to their future work mainly to gain the status of a teacher are more inclined to invest into their future through getting a degree than those who orient to their future work in terms of its nature. Getting a degree leading to the teacher profession is

Table 10.2 Cross-tabulation of "getting a degree" and orientation to future work

Orientation to work		Getting a degree		
		Not mentioned	Mentioned	Total
Nature of work	Count	28	17	45
	Expected count	22.1	22.9	45
	Standardized residual	1.2	−1.2	
Status of work	Count	2	14	16
	Expected count	7.9	8.1	16.0
	Standardized residual	−2.1	2.1	
Total	Count	30	31	61
	Expected count	30.0	31.0	61.0

logical of course and this kind of "technical" investment is in line with the orientation to the future in terms of gaining a specific social status in society. For the nature-oriented group the other factors – both internal and external – seemed to be more important investments in reaching their desired professional future.

10.6   Discussion

This study examined how student teachers approach their future work as language teachers, how they perceive the ways in which they can invest in their futures and if there are associations between their orientation to future work and their investment. This study adds to the body of research on teacher identity development (Barkhuizen, 2016; Dunn & Downey, 2018) and investment (Darvin & Norton, 2015) by focusing on student teachers and their visions of the future profession.

Our analyses showed that student teachers see both internal and external influences on their professional futures with the internal ones gaining more prominence. We identified five factors in student teachers' description of aspects that can facilitate or hinder their desired futures. These were (1) student teachers' own volition, (2) motivation and personal characteristics, (3) hard work, (4) getting a degree, and (5) external conditions. Four of these categories can be seen as internal factors and only one comprised of external factors. The student teachers thus have differing ideas about how they can influence their own future and these findings are in line with earlier studies examining student teachers envisioning their futures (Barcelos, 2016; Brandão, 2019; Kalaja & Mäntylä, 2018; Pinho, 2019). In line with Barkhuizen (2016) and Dunn and Downey (2018), some student teachers' accounts point towards investing in their future profession by their own actions and strong will. However, some participants in our study felt that getting the degree is enough or that there are external conditions which are beyond their control and they cannot influence their future. Sometimes the student teachers seemed quite firm that one's own volition is central but this was then mitigated by saying that the job situation or personal health can hinder the dream coming true. These different forms of investment are related to different perceptions of identity construction: identity construction is either strongly in the possession of the individual or it is a by-product of their studies or constrained by external conditions (Sade, 2009).

The results further indicated that there was not much difference in student teachers' investment when contrasted with their orientation to the future profession either in terms of the nature or status of work. Only one factor – getting a degree – was associated with the orientation in that those orienting to the status of a teacher thought more often that getting the degree was important (and often enough) in reaching their dream. This might be related to the fact that these student teachers were first year students just beginning their studies and their professional future might not have been very clear yet. But is may also be that not all student teachers are able to reflect on the nature of their future work, especially at the beginning of their studies.

As to the theoretical implications, we found the combination of identity, investment and envisioning useful in shedding light on the beginning student teachers' identity construction, and thus our study complements the findings of earlier studies both in terms of investment (Mora et al., 2016) and envisioning (Kalaja & Mäntylä, 2018). The concept of investment helps in understanding how future visions mediate professional identity construction and how it is related to acquiring "a wider range of symbolic and material resources, which will in turn increase the value of their cultural capital and social power" (Darvin & Norton, 2015, p. 37). Student teachers invest in their professional futures differently, anticipate gaining different kinds of symbolic and material resources (degree, knowledge, resilience) and thereby gain different kinds of cultural capital. However, even though student teachers might vision their futures in very different terms, their ideas and willingness to invest does not necessarily depend on their vision of the future profession. This has important implications for teacher education.

10.7   Conclusion

This study was conducted with 61 students in a specific context of teacher education in one university in one country. Despite the limited context, the study offers implications for teacher education and teacher identity research more broadly. The process of envisioning can potentially reveal the varying starting points student teachers have when entering teacher education programmes and can thus offer support to different kinds of students. Envisioning can also reveal how differently student teachers see their possibilities and volition to invest in their future profession. As Brandão (2019, p. 210) notes: "It is important for us, language teacher educators, to be aware of how student teachers imagine the profession, together with the experiences, expectations and anxieties that go with it." A nuanced idea of the teaching profession may not necessarily connect to richer investment. It is crucial to take this into account in teacher education, as teacher educators can then support students' conscious development beyond success in studies, which may lead to the development of a rich and nuanced understanding of the future profession. Further studies are needed to get a deeper understanding of the process of envisioning and investment and development of teacher identity longitudinally in teacher education and in different socio-political contexts of teacher education.

References

Barcelos, A. (2016). Student teachers' beliefs and motivation, and the shaping of their professional identities. In P. Kalaja, A. Barcelos, M. Aro, & M. Ruohotie-Lyhty (Eds.), *Beliefs, agency and identity in foreign language learning and teaching* (pp. 71–98). Palgrave Macmillan.

Barkhuizen, G. (2009). An extended positioning analysis of a pre-service teacher's better life small story. *Applied Linguistics, 31*(2), 282–300. https://doi.org/10.1093/applin/amp027

Barkhuizen, G. (2016). Narrative approaches to exploring language, identity and power in language teacher education. *RELC Journal, 47*(1), 25–42.

Block, D. (2007). The rise of identity in SLA research, post Firth and Wagner (1997). *Modern Language Journal, 91*, 863–876. https://doi.org/10.1111/j.1540-4781.2007.00674.x

Bourdieu, P. (1991). *Language and symbolic power*. Polity.

Brandão, A. (2019). Imagining second language teaching in Brazil: What stories do student teachers draw? In P. Kalaja & S. Melo-Pfeifer (Eds.), *Visualising multilingual lives. More than words* (pp. 197–213). Multilingual Matters.

Darvin, R., & Norton, B. (2015). Identity and a model of investment in applied linguistics. *Annual Review of Applied Linguistics, 35*, 36–56. https://doi.org/10.1017/S0267190514000191

De Costa, P., & Norton, B. (2017). Introduction: Identity, transdisciplinarity, and the good language teacher. *The Modern Language Journal, 101*, 3–14.

Dörnyei, Z. (2005). *The psychology of the language learner: Individual differences in second language acquisition*. Lawrence Erlbaum.

Duff, P. (2013). Identity, agency, and second language acquisition. In S. Gass & A. Mackey (Eds.), *The Routledge handbook of second language acquisition* (pp. 428–444). Routledge.

Dunn, A., & Downey, C. (2018). Betting the house: Teacher investment, identity, and attrition in urban schools. *Education and Urban Society, 50*(3), 207–229.

Jääskelä, P., Alanen, R., Ruohotie-Lyhty, M., & Pitkänen-Huhta, A. (2021). Pre-service language teachers' agency experiences – Constructing professional identities through agentive participation in university courses. In P. Jenlink (Ed.), *Understanding teacher identity: The complexities of forming an identity as professional teacher* (pp. 141–162). Rowman & Littlefield Publishers.

Kalaja, P. (2016). 'Dreaming is believing': The teaching of foreign languages as envisioned by student teachers. In P. Kalaja, A. Barcelos, M. Aro, & M. Ruohotie-Lyhty (Eds.), *Beliefs, agency and identity in foreign language learning and teaching* (pp. 124–146). Palgrave Macmillan.

Kalaja, P., & Mäntylä, K. (2018). "The English class of my dreams!": Envisioning teaching a foreign language. In S. Mercer & A. Kostoulas (Eds.), *Language teacher psychology* (pp. 34–52). Multilingual Matters.

Kalaja, P., & Melo-Pfeifer, S. (Eds.). (2019). *Visualising multilingual lives. More than words*. Multilingual Matters.

Kalaja, P., & Ruohotie-Lyhty, M. (2019). Narratives in L2 learner identity development. *Learner Development Journal, 1*(3), 79–95.

Kanno, Y., & Norton, B. (2003). *Imagined communities and educational possibilities: A special issue of the Journal of Language, Identity, and Education*. Routledge.

Kanno, Y., & Stuart, C. (2011). Learning to become a second language teacher: Identities-in-practice. *The Modern Language Journal, 95*(2), 236–252.

Kim, H. (2014). Learner investment, identity, and resistance to second language pragmatic norms. *System, 45*, 92–102. https://doi.org/10.1016/j.system.2014.05.002

Mora, A., Trejo, P., & Roux, R. (2016). The complexities of being and becoming language teachers: Issues of identity and investment. *Language and Intercultural Communication, 16*(2), 182–198. https://doi.org/10.1080/14708477.2015.1136318

Norton, B. (2000). *Identity and language learning: Gender, ethnicity and educational change.* Longman/Pearson Education.

Norton, B. (2001). Non-participation, imagined communities, and the language classroom. In M. Breen (Ed.), *Learner contributions to language learning: New directions in research* (pp. 159–171). Pearson Education.

Norton, B. (2013). *Identity and language learning: Extending the conversation.* Multilingual Matters.

Patton, M. (2015). *Qualitative research and evaluation methods: Integrating theory and practice.* SAGE.

Pinho, A. (2019). Plurilingual education and the identity development of pre-service English language teachers: An illustrative example. In P. Kalaja & S. Melo-Pfeifer (Eds.), *Visualising multilingual lives. More than words* (pp. 214–231). Multilingual Matters.

Ruohotie-Lyhty, M. (2013). Struggling for a professional identity: Two newly qualified language teachers' identity narratives during the first years at work. *Teaching and Teacher Education, 30*, 120–129. https://doi.org/10.1016/j.tate.2012.11.002

Ruohotie-Lyhty, M., & Pitkänen-Huhta, A. (2020). Status, self-fulfillment and well-being: First year language teacher students envisioning their future work. *European Journal of Teacher Education*, published online: https://doi.org/10.1080/02619768.2020.1788535.

Ruohotie-Lyhty, M., Aragão, R., & Pitkänen-Huhta, A. (2021). Envisioning language teacher identities in two different contexts: Finnish and Brazilian student teachers' desired and dreaded futures. *Teaching and Teacher Education, 100*. https://doi.org/10.1016/j.tate.2020.103270

Sade, L. (2009). Complexity and identity reconstruction in second language acquisition. *Revista Brasileira de Linguística Aplicada, 9*(2), 515–537. https://doi.org/10.1590/S1984-63982009000200008

Trent, J. (2013). From learner to teacher: Practice, language, and identity in a teaching practicum. *Asia-Pacific Journal of Teacher Education, 41*(4), 426–440. https://doi.org/10.1080/1359866X.2013.838621

Varghese, M., Morgan, B., Johnston, B., & Johnson, K. (2005). Theorizing language teacher identity: Three perspectives and beyond. *Language, Identity and Education, 4*, 21–44.

Wallin, A., Koro-Ljungberg, M., & Eskola, J. (2018). The method of empathy-based stories. *International Journal of Research and Method in Education, 42*, 1–11.

Xu, H. (2012). Imagined community falling apart: A case study on the transformation of professional identities of novice ESOL teachers in China. *TESOL Quarterly, 46*(3), 568–578.

Chapter 11
Language Teacher Educator's Identity Work in Using Critical Autoethnography as a Teacher-Learning Activity

Bedrettin Yazan

Abstract In this chapter, I engage in an analysis of my "ethical self-formation" (Clarke, Educ Philos Theory 41:185–200, 2009) as a language teacher educator, particularly when I designed critical autoethnographic narrative (CAN) as a teacher learning activity in my teacher education classes. This writing here will include my voice analyzing my identity work as a teacher educator, and at the same time, my writing itself is a form of investment in my identity work. Methodologically, I follow the principles of self-study which aims to improve practices of teacher education by conducting a systematic investigation of the relationship between my ongoing professional learning, practices, agency, emotions, and identity. My chapter will make a contribution to this collection at two levels. On one level, it will describe the use of an identity-oriented teacher learning activity, i.e., CAN, in language teacher education. On another, it will discuss my experiences designing and implementing that activity as a language teacher educator by particularly focusing on my identity as a teacher educator.

Keywords Language teacher educator identity · Self-study · Ethical self-formation · Critical autoethnographic narrative · Language teacher identity

11.1 Introduction

> I make my offerings of incense and cracked corn, light my candle. In my head I sometimes will say a prayer – an affirmation and a voicing of intent. Then I run water, wash the dishes or my underthings, take a bath, or mop the kitchen floor. This "induction" period sometimes takes a few minutes, sometimes hours. But always I go against a resistance. Something in me does not want to do this writing. Yet once I'm immersed in it, I can go fifteen to seventeen hours in one sitting and I don't want to leave it. (Anzaldúa, 1987, p. 67)

B. Yazan (✉)
The University of Texas at San Antonio, San Antonio, TX, USA
e-mail: bedrettin.yazan@utsa.edu

© The Author(s), under exclusive license to Springer Nature Switzerland AG 2022   151
K. Sadeghi, F. Ghaderi (eds.), *Theory and Practice in Second Language Teacher Identity*, Educational Linguistics 57, https://doi.org/10.1007/978-3-031-13161-5_11

As soon as I read the above paragraph from Anzaldúa's (1987) book *Borderlands/La frontera: The new mestiza*, I knew it should be at the top of this chapter which I took so long to start writing. I was definitely "go[ing] against a resistance" (p. 67), which I am attributing to the fact that this chapter will unpack my identity as a language teacher educator when using critical autoethnography with my teacher candidates. Before beginning that analysis, I would like to share how I bumped into Anzaldúa's description of and thoughts about "induction" into her writing. I see that sharing as part of my efforts to become more self-reflexive in my own writing.

Earlier today, I remembered that I needed to respond to an email from Rashi and Suresh. We are planning our next project in which we would like to experiment with unusual genres of research writing collaboratively. Rashi had shared a tentative outline and Suresh had emailed us a link to an open-access book *Race, rhetoric, and research methods* by Alexandria Lockett and colleagues with University Press of Colorado. After sending my email, I started reading the book further and exploring the webpage where there are additional resources. I noticed the authors posted a YouTube playlist of the resources they are referring to throughout their book. I clicked on the link and began checking out the titles of the videos. As I scrolled down, I noticed there were two videos about Anzaldúa whose work I am interested in already, so I played the one "Anzaldua, Rhetoric, Hybridity, and Exclusionary Identity" by Dr. Ellwanger who seems to have recorded it for his graduate class. At around minute 5, he started reading aloud from *Borderlands/La frontera* and I carefully listened until he said "full of variations and seeming contradictions" (p. 66). I paused and decided to read that section from the book. Seeming contradiction was something that my doctoral student and I discussed in relation to identity 1 days ago. She was concerned that her parental identity contradicted her bilingual teacher identity in terms of translanguaging and she said she was afraid of acting like a hypocrite. I asked why she does what she does at school and at home and our question-and-answer session included some analysis of her identity. That is why hearing "seeming contradictions" in the video piqued my interest and I was interested in learning what exactly Anzaldúa said about it. I opened the book and found the part which was about "Invoking Art" on the second page of Chap. 6.

Fascinated by Anzaldúa's reflexivity on her writing through metaphors "a mosaic pattern (Aztec-like) emerging, a weaving pattern, thin here, thick there" (p. 66), I kept reading and the next paragraph felt like it was describing what I have been struggling with for a while. I read it again and again. Eerie enough, I did almost everything (e.g., lighting my candle, mopping my kitchen floor) she talks about as part of her "induction" into starting her writing. It took me some time to describe what I felt when I saw my day being reflected in Anzaldua's words. Earlier today, I talked to my parents from Turkey on the phone before it was too late in their time zone. Was it the part of "say a prayer – an affirmation and a voicing of intent" (p. 67)? I had just talked to my dad who taught me my first prayer which I tend to say before starting to write. I think, affinity is what I felt; an affinity with the writer who I admire: having almost exactly the same pre-writing experiences, albeit ordinary. I carried on reading that page where she discusses what story means to her, which reminded me that I needed to start telling my story in this chapter which is due to the editors in a few days.

In the space I was offered in this volume, I engage in an analysis of my "ethical self-formation" (Clarke, 2009) as a language teacher educator, particularly when I designed critical autoethnographic narrative (CAN) as a teacher learning activity in my teacher education classes (Yazan, 2019a, b). I wanted to keep the focus on my identity work during the CAN experience to ensure that my analysis is manageable and realistic to discuss within the confines of a traditional book chapter length. This writing here will include my voice analyzing my identity work as a teacher educator, and at the same time, my writing itself is a form of investment in my identity work. Methodologically, I follow the principles of self-study which aims to improve practices of teacher education by conducting a systematic investigation of the relationship between my ongoing professional learning, practices, agency, emotions, and identity (Peercy & Sharkey, 2020).

My chapter will make a contribution to this collection at two levels. On one level, it will describe the use of an identity-oriented teacher learning activity, i.e., CAN, in language teacher education. On another, it will discuss my experiences designing and implementing that activity as a language teacher educator by particularly focusing on my identity as a teacher educator. I have engaged in similar self-exploration in my earlier work (Yazan, 2018a, 2022a, b), but in the present chapter, I am going to use an entirely new theoretical framework, i.e., "ethical self-formation" (Clarke, 2009), which I have not used before in my research. Utilizing a new lens, I believe I will be able to open up and examine new dimensions of my identity as a teacher educator to myself, fellow teacher educators, and those researchers of teacher (educator) identity. Just to briefly share my reasoning here, I decided to write this chapter to externalize a learning process or experience that usually happens implicitly and goes without much mention. As we are introduced to different theoretical lenses, I assume that researchers (or me as a struggling one) tend to apply those lenses to their own life and see how effective, interpretive, or meaningful the lenses are to make sense or explain their life experience. I remember doing that when I was introduced to the research literature of world Englishes, non-native English speaking teachers (NNEST), teacher learning among others, and the theoretical framework of communities of practice to make sense of identity, and general (language) teacher identity research. For example, preparing for my dissertation research which was on professional identities of English as a second language (ESL) teacher candidates, I kept trying to re-remember my experience and reflecting on how I constructed my own professional identity during my teacher education program and afterwards. Later on, such reflection led me to become interested in language teacher educator identity since I was asking myself about language teacher educator knowledge base and identity development. I noticed that taking the 'risk' or venturing to implement a new teacher learning tool, CAN, in my linguistics and second language acquisition (SLA) classes involved an identity work as a teacher educator.

11.2   An Identity-Oriented Teacher Learning Activity: Critical Autoethnographic Narrative (CAN)

In my earlier work, I have described the potential use of CAN as a program-wide activity for language teacher candidates (Yazan, 2019a), its pilot implementation in one of my classes (Yazan, 2019b), and my agency (Yazan, 2018a) and identity negotiation via tensions (Yazan, 2022a) in this implementation. To prepare my reader for what is coming up in the remainder of this chapter, I would like to briefly summarize CAN and its use in teacher education. Mainly, what I did was to adapt and translate a qualitative research method of critical autoethnography (Boylorn & Orbe, 2014) into an instructional activity or action research project. My main goal was to support teacher candidates' engagement in explicit identity work by making sense of their experiences of learning, using, and teaching languages and by exploring the complex relationship between circulating ideologies and their identities. The ideal was to integrate it into my teacher education program as an ongoing reflective writing activity for teacher candidates to revise, add to, and learn from throughout their experiences in the initial teacher education program. However, the challenging logistics of that implementation led me to pilot it in my course in which I have relatively more "power" and "freedom" in making decisions. I had the opportunity to use CAN in my graduate classes in two different university-based teacher education programs in 2018, 2019, and 2021.

To describe the implementation of CAN, I had students complete their writing in four installments over the semester and share their final paper in an individual class presentation. In the first two installments, they storied all their experiences with languages by specifically recounting the significant incidents. In many cases, teacher candidates also included their family and community members' stories in their CAN. In the last two instalments, they selected and used a theoretical framework to analyze those incidents to explore what ideologies were dominant in their context, how they negotiated their identities, and how they navigated corresponding identity tensions. I scaffolded this writing process for teacher candidates through frequent feedback, class discussions, modelling analysis, and rubric co-construction. In initial weeks of the semester, we read articles on the relationship between professional identity construction, teacher-learning, and teaching practice and sample published autoethnographies (e.g., Canagarajah, 2012; Solano-Campos, 2014; Yazan, 2019c) and unpublished dissertations (e.g., Corah-Hopkins, 2015; Donnelly, 2015). I provided written feedback via MS word comment boxes on each installment and afterwards had one-on-one feedback sessions with teacher candidates after every installment to discuss how they are doing then and how they plan to proceed in their CAN. We had class discussions on potential theoretical frameworks they can use in their CAN such as second language socialization (e.g., Duff, 2012), translanguaging (e.g., García & Wei, 2014), critical multilingual awareness (e.g., Lindahl, 2020) and imagined communities and identities (e.g., Kanno & Norton, 2003). We also had data analysis workshops in two class meetings in which I modelled data analysis and we practiced the use of chosen theoretical frameworks.

11.3   A Theoretical Lens to Identity Work: Ethical Self-Formation

I have become interested in the theoretical framework of ethical self-formation thanks to the scholarship by Clarke (2009), Miller et al. (2017), and Reeves (2018). Clarke (2009) relies on Foucault's (1983) late work to theorize language teacher identity as ethical self-formation and exemplifies the use of that theorization with data. Recently, Miller et al. (2017) and Reeves (2018) have provided more detailed examples of analyzing teacher identity as ethical self-formation. Without subscribing to any moral code, this theorization of teacher identity foregrounds individual teachers' work on their self, "the care of the self" by the self (Clarke, 2009, p. 190) to further improve their self (Miller et al., 2017). Clarke calls this work as "identity work." Identity work, however, is not free from "the disciplinary effects of coercive power on the self," so self-formation can be viewed as "productive exercise of power" on teachers' ongoing identity (Miller et al., 2017). Borrowing Foucault's (1983) four axes of ethics, Clarke theorizes self-formation with four ethico-political axes of teacher identity: "substance of teacher identity, the authority sources of teacher identity, the self-practices of teacher identity, and the endpoint [telos] of teacher identity" (p. 190). All these axes are complexly and dynamically interrelated with each other. Teasing each axis out to analyze teacher identity work presents a fresh way to look at dimensions of identity without neglecting the complexity.

Substance of teacher identity refers to the bases or foundations from our self upon which we rely when constructing our teacher identity. What is it in our self that we draw from and upon to fashion our teacher identity? In other words, "what part of myself pertains to teaching and what forms of subjectivity constitute – or what forms do I use to constitute – my teaching self?" (Clarke, 2009, p. 190). These parts of our self and forms of subjectivity "will critically constrain and/or enable other possibilities" (p. 191) in the contours of our identity work. This axis highlights that our teacher identity does not emerge in isolation; it is in a constant interaction with our other identities. In Clarke's example, Neil views his teacher identity closely connected to his "character" which he does not believe is changeable or evolving, so he shuts down the possible directions his teacher identity can take and hence cannot address his feeling of "not a suitable person to teach" (p. 192).

The second axis, the authority sources of teacher identity, involves discourses to which we are exposed in our professional life and find important in evaluating what makes a "good" teacher. Miller et al. (2017) define them as "norms that serve as a framework by which teachers can weigh the merits of their identity work" (p. 97), and are intertwined with "the issues of power and politics" (Clarke, 2009, p. 191). Based on our past experience and other identities of ours, we act selectively in putting those norms together to form our framework or lens to approach teaching. Authority "sources might include particular learning theories, religious or ethical values, or political ideologies" (Reeves, 2018, p. 100). For example, Clarke discusses the authority of constructivist discourses of learning and how acknowledging this authority would require "particular forms of professional practice in the classroom in terms of environment, organization and activities" (p. 191).

The third axis, the self-practices of teacher identity, refers to "physical, mental, and even spiritual techniques" that we utilize to change "some aspect(s) of the self" (Miller et al., 2017, p. 98). This change might be emerging from the dialogue between our teacher identity and other identities and/or our responses to (i.e., countering or aligning with) authority sources. Miller et al. discusses Pavlenko's (2003) seminal work with teacher candidates to counter the dominant discourses of "nativeness" in defining themselves as language teachers and students as language learners and users. Reeves' (2018) example from Sarah's case is also interesting. Sarah adopted new teaching practices (e.g., scripted curriculum) aligning her identity with neoliberal definition of "good" teaching prescribed by her program and she thought these practices proved effective. However, then the authority sources of neoliberal ideologies had a conflict with her "caregiving teaching practices" (p. 104).

The fourth axis, the telos of teacher identity, is our "ultimate endpoint, goal or purpose as a teacher" constructed and reconstructed through the interaction between social discourses and our ongoing meaning-making in our professional life (Clarke, 2009, p. 191). Miller et al. (2017) also underscore the impact of "broader sociopolitical values and expectations" upon our telos (p. 100) and they expand the understanding of telos to include imagined teacher identity and our investment of time and energy to accomplish that imagination. Prone to changes, our telos of teacher identity is interplay with other axes of our self-formation. It could serve as a driving force for our self-practices, inform or be informed by what authority sources we adopt, and influence and be influenced by what parts of our self we choose to rest upon to fashion our teacher identity. In Reeves' (2018) study, Sarah renegotiates her telos through her interaction with the authority source of neoliberal curriculum adopted in her school program, and her revised telos involves "student academic achievement *in a caring environment*, not student academic achievement *at any cost*" (italics in original, p. 105).

In the remainder of this chapter, I will use the framework of ethical self-formation described above, to analyze my identity as a language teacher educator particularly during the use of critical autoethnographic narrative as an identity-oriented teacher learning tool since Spring 2018 semester. My chapter will be responding to calls for more studies into language teacher educators' practices (Peercy & Sharkey, 2020; Yuan & Lee, 2022), especially their identities given the diversity and complexity involved in serving as a teacher educator in the field of language education (Barkhuizen, 2021).

11.4   Zeroing in on My Identity as a Teacher Educator

11.4.1   Substance of Teacher Educator Identity

I need to admit that this component of my identity work has been the most challenging to analyze. I have gone back to all three studies which used this framework multiple times (Clarke, 2009; Miller et al., 2017; Reeves, 2018) to re-read the definition and examples as well as my synthesis above in this paper. Echoing Clarke's (2009) question, I kept asking what part of myself pertains to my identity as a teacher educator. My initial answer directed my attention to the ongoing interplay, exchange, and tension between my teacher educator identity and researcher identity that instigated the design of CAN. That is, as an important implication of my own and colleagues' research on teacher identity, I suggested that teacher identity should be integrated as an explicit goal in teacher education practices (Kanno & Stuart, 2011; Yazan, 2018b). At the same time, I reminded myself that my teacher education courses were not designed towards such an instructional goal. Four years after I started my first faculty job, I was able to assert agency to change one of my courses drastically to design CAN.

However, for some reason, this answer sounded too straightforward to me, so I kept pushing my reflection further and focused on two forms of subjectivity which pertain to the intersection of my self and researcher identity: border-crosser and story enthusiast. First, I view myself as a border-crosser who is in a constant dialogue about our self's complex relationship with others and surrounding discourses. Since I crossed the physical borders of nation-state and was situated within a new socio-cultural and sociopolitical context, I have been more conscious of that relationship. I can trace this consciousness back to the in-betweenness I felt back 'home' in Turkey between secular schooling and religious home, which might explain why I studied sectarian identity in Northern Ireland in my Master's thesis and ESOL teacher identity in my doctoral dissertation. Being positioned as an 'other' in the US, I started experiencing the impact of physical and ideological borders, which guided reflections on my relationship with others and the culture. Here is how I rest upon my border-crosser subjectivity to construct my identity as a teacher educator who ventured to use CAN in teacher education courses. I believe that teacher education practices, being a teacher candidate, and being a teacher educator are all influenced by ideological borders that patrol what we are allowed and supposed to act and be like and that are perpetuated by those in power (see Alsup, 2019; Rudolph et al., 2019; Sayer, 2012). In their professional identity work, teacher candidates are expected to cross the institutional borders between being a student and a teacher. Stepping into the realm of teaching, they are exposed to ideologies that will potentially lead to identity tensions. As teacher candidates write their CAN and analyze their situatedness within the context and the interplay between ideologies and their identities, they realize and problematize, to varying degrees, the impact of borders on the kind of language user, learner, and teacher they are and can be.

Second, I believe in the power of storytelling which we rely on to (re)organize and (re)construct knowledge and identities (see Barkhuizen, 2011; Johnson & Golombek, 2011). Growing up, I have listened to numerous stories which presented and rendered certain ideologically-laden identity positions as (un)available, (un)-desirable, and (im)possible (see Pavlenko & Blackledge, 2004). Stories are never just recounting events. Ideologies and identities are embedded into stories. That part of me has been prominent in my teacher educator identity. I value stories that teacher candidates bring into teacher education courses and I encourage teacher candidates to story their experiences and analyze those stories to better parse out their experiences and to see how they construct and enact their identities as learners, users, or teachers of languages in those experiences. This form of subjectivity was actively engaged in my design and implementation of CAN. In this assignment, I ask teacher candidates to narrate and analyze their stories with language in order to examine (a) the intricate ways in which ideologies attempt to define their identities, (b) the relationship between their professional learning, practice, and identity, and (c) the ways in which identity informs and is informed by our emotions, as well as professional agency and investment.

11.4.2   Authority Sources of Teacher Educator Identity

This component of my ethical self-formation involves a tension between standards-based language teacher education and critical language teacher education. When I used CAN in my teacher education classes in two universities, I was serving teacher candidates in a program housed in college of education. As those programs prepare teacher candidates for teacher certification in the state public schools, I needed to ensure that my course assignments should be tied to the state standards of teacher education. Therefore, preparing CAN and incorporating it into my linguistics and SLA courses, I felt pressure at two interrelated levels and corresponding tensions. On one level, I was concerned that CAN, as a new assignment to me and my students, might not easily fit into the 'traditional' ways of teaching linguistics and SLA which are defined by dominant discourses of language teacher education. That is, I knew there was a dominant way of teaching such courses, so my assignment, maybe little too unorthodox, might not be taken well by the students and they might choose not to tell their stories as much as I expected them. It differs a lot from most usual graduate course assignments, not only in terms of content but also in terms of implementation. I had never used it as a student; I had never observed a professor use it. I was going against the authority sources of 'mainstream' teacher education course design. On another level, weighing 70% of the total course grade, CAN does not promise to yield the data that directly demonstrate teacher candidates' 'growth' through the course. Especially when integrated in linguistics course, the nature of CAN needed to be explained so that it could count as legitimate evidence in reports prepared for state and national accreditation agencies. That is why I was also defying the standards-based teacher education evaluation practices.

On the other hand, the authority source that guided my practices as a language teacher educator was the conceptual and pedagogical orientation of critical language teacher education (Hawkins & Norton, 2009), also called as social justice teacher education in broader literature (see McDonald, 2005). This orientation mainly argues that language serves as "the tool through which representations and meanings are constructed and negotiated, and a primary means through which ideologies are transmitted" (Hawkins & Norton, 2009, p. 32). I view CAN as an activity that exemplifies critical orientation in teacher education. As teacher candidates work on their CAN, I expect them to better understand how individuals and communities are minoritized and marginalized due to their language practices and identities which could also be contextually associated with their culture, ethnicity, and race. Their analysis of critical incidents in their life could lead them to question, problematize, and even subvert ideologies that render this minoritization and marginalization 'normal' and 'invisible' in dominant discourses.

11.4.3 Self-Practices of Teacher Educator Identity

When I decided to use CAN in my linguistics course for the first time in Spring 2018, I was nervous about how it would be taken by the teacher candidates as an unorthodox assignment which they had not had any experience before. It was the same for me as an instructor. I had not used it in any course I had taught. I was cognizant that the integration of such a new pedagogical technique into my teaching was both cognitive and emotional investment for me, and I knew that this investment was part of my identity work. It would support my efforts to become a teacher educator whose practices are primarily based on teacher candidates' identity work. CAN as a self-practice would counter the authority sources which view teacher education as transmission of theories and acquisition of strategy tool kits. CAN would provide teacher candidates with discursive and experiential spaces to intentionally engage in teacher identity work.

This particular decision to invest in self-practices entailed a series of further sustained investment toward my imagined identity. To name a few, I needed to justify the assignment to students and make sure they trust me as an "autoethnography coach" (Yazan, 2022a) while they write their CAN without exactly gauging what kind of end product they would have. We read samples of autoethnography as a writing genre and discussed their features that teacher candidates can emulate in their CAN, but I felt students' hesitation about how this assignment should look like in its final version. In the first iteration, I had no former student work to share, and intentionally kept the expectations broad enough to give teacher candidates flexibility in their writing because CAN is such a personal writing practice. Additionally, I needed to modify the course content to open up some space for the extensive discussion of identity in language education and data collection workshops. Especially when selecting a theoretical framework to analyze their stories in CAN, teacher candidates needed support and guidance, which is why I brought in additional readings to discuss potential theoretical frameworks in class. Moreover, I provided each teacher candidate written feedback four times over the semester and I met with them individually to answer questions and give further feedback. In the first semester, I had not written an autoethnography myself which I deemed as a downside in the implementation of CAN, but I needed to learn how to give feedback on my students' CAN. I relied on bringing in my own experiences or critical incidents with languages and sharing my own tensions in the class to model analysis by making myself vulnerable and opening up for scrutiny. What I initially saw as a downside, later turned into an opportunity to practice "identity-as-pedagogy" orientation (Morgan, 2004) in my classes. Right after that semester, I wrote one myself to further contribute to my imagined teacher educator identity.

11.4.4 Telos of Teacher Educator Identity

My ultimate goal as a language teacher educator is to contribute to the provision of equitable educational services for language learners in the US schools and beyond. To that end, I aim to prepare all teachers to work with ethnically and linguistically minoritized and marginalized populations in that context. I want CAN to serve to that endpoint; contributing to the education of teachers with social justice orientation and advocacy. Criticality in CAN is informed by Pennycook's (2001) definition: "a constant questioning of the normative assumptions" in language education and addressing the intersectional questions of "gender, class, sexuality, race, ethnicity, culture, identity, politics, ideology, and discourse" (p. 10). As my investment towards that goal of criticality, CAN holds the methodological and instructional power or potential to help teachers engage in such criticality at differing degrees in their writing.

Additionally, I aim to prepare teacher candidates who can engage in identity work intentionally to practice care of their selves by themselves and to assert agency to direct the contours of their own identity work. Writing CAN, they can develop the autoethnographic thinking or reflexivity to constantly interrogate the relationship between self, others, and discourses. They can maintain and further develop this reflexivity in their professional life to use identity as a pedagogical frame or lens that (a) informs and is informed by their teaching practices, and (b) supports their awareness of the sociocultural and sociopolitical situatedness of their identities and practices. I would expect teachers with this pedagogical frame to better understand language learning in relation to learners' identities, agency, emotions, and investment more easily and translate that understanding into their pedagogical decisions and actions.

Lastly, my other goal is to be part of the grassroots endeavor to positioning teachers or practitioners in general as active agents of knowledge generation, rather than passive voices in research reports. Legutke (2016) observes how the discourse in published research of language teaching and teacher education has alienated teachers. I do not mean to further the ideologically laden divide between teachers and researchers, but the dominant discourses and practices still reify those two groups as separate from each other. Researchers tended to rely on teachers to collect data only. Teacher voices as active storytellers have been absent in the research discourse which theorizes language teaching for teachers. CAN writing positions teacher candidates as authors of their own stories, with agency. As they see similar stories being published in scholarly literature or having been accepted in Master's and Doctoral studies, teacher candidates could be more willing and confident to position themselves as theorizers of their own practice and constructors of their "personal practical knowledge" (Golombek, 1998).

11.5   Until I Retell My Story . . .

In this chapter, I present a self-analysis of my language teacher educator identity during the time I designed and implemented CAN as an identity-oriented teacher learning activity. The writing exercise here has been an intellectually stimulating activity which points to the intersection of my cognitive and emotional engagement with professional identity work. I think the fact that this chapter interrogated the sociocultural and sociopolitical situatedness of my identity and practices was the reason why I was initially "go[ing] against a resistance" (Anzaldúa, 1987, p. 67). Ending this chapter, I can better justify that resistance.

Applying ethical self-formation (Clarke, 2009) as a framework to my identity, I now have a stronger grasp of the connection between my research and practices of teacher education. Through this self-analysis, I made this connection further pronounced. And I find both my research and teacher education more meaningful to my 'self.' I admit that this chapter has been a challenging one to compose because it required me to make my private thoughts, emotions, and experiences public. However, we need more of such papers to further humanize the research process and researchers, and to disrupt the dichotomous relationship between the researcher and the researched as a goal that autoethnographers pursue (Hughes et al., 2012). We, researchers, are storytellers, by profession, but if we venture to risk opening up by telling and retelling our own stories, we can 'write' and 'envoice' our selves into 'text' (Canagarajah, 2013) that would resonate with the reader and have potential to transform self and others.

References

Alsup, J. (2019). *Millennial teacher identity discourses: Balancing self and other*. Routledge.

Anzaldúa, G. (1987). *Borderlands/La frontera: The new mestiza*. Aunt Lute Books.

Barkhuizen, G. (2011). Narrative knowledging in TESOL. *TESOL Quarterly, 45*, 391–414. https://doi.org/10.5054/tq.2011.261888

Barkhuizen, G. (2021). *Language teacher educator identity*. Cambridge University Press.

Boylorn, R. M., & Orbe, M. P. (Eds.). (2014). *Critical autoethnography: Intersecting cultural identities in everyday life*. Routledge.

Canagarajah, A. S. (2012). Teacher development in a global profession: An autoethnography. *TESOL Quarterly, 46*(2), 258–279. https://doi.org/10.1002/tesq.18

Canagarajah, S. (2013). *Translingual practice: Global Englishes and cosmopolitan relations*. Routledge.

Clarke, M. (2009). The ethico-politics of teacher identity. *Educational Philosophy and Theory, 41*(2), 185–200.

Corah-Hopkins, E. (2015). *The walled fortress: An autoethnography of an international student who became an ESL educator*. Unpublished doctoral dissertation. Wayne State University, Detroit, MI.

Donnelly, H. (2015). *Becoming an ESL teacher: An autoethnography*. Unpublished Master's thesis. Lakehead University, Thunder Bay, ON, Canada.

Duff, P. (2012). Second language socialization. In A. Duranti, E. Ochs, & B. Schieffelin (Eds.), *Handbook of language socialization* (pp. 564–586). Wiley-Blackwell.

Foucault, M. (1983). On the genealogy of ethics: An overview of work in progress. In H. Dreyfus & P. Rabinow (Eds.), *Michel Foucault: Beyond structuralism and hermeneutics* (pp. 208–264). University of Chicago Press.

García, O., & Wei, L. (2014). *Translanguaging: Language, bilingualism and education*. Palgrave Macmillan.

Golombek, P. R. (1998). A study of language teachers' personal practical knowledge. *TESOL Quarterly, 32*, 447–464. https://doi.org/10.2307/3588117

Hawkins, M., & Norton, B. (2009). Critical language teacher education. In A. Burns & J. Richards (Eds.), *Cambridge guide to second language teacher education* (pp. 30–39). Cambridge University Press.

Hughes, S., Pennington, J. L., & Makris, S. (2012). Translating autoethnography across the AERA standards: Toward understanding autoethnographic scholarship as empirical research. *Educational Researcher, 41*(6), 209–219.

Johnson, K. E., & Golombek, P. R. (2011). The transformative power of narrative in second language teacher education. *TESOL Quarterly, 45*(3), 486–509. https://doi.org/10.5054/tq.2011.256797

Kanno, Y., & Norton, B. (2003). Imagined communities and educational possibilities: Introduction. *Journal of Language, Identity, and Education, 2*(4), 241–249.

Kanno, Y., & Stuart, C. (2011). Learning to become a second language teacher: Identities-in-practice. *Modern Language Journal, 95*, 236–252. https://doi.org/10.1111/j.1540-4781.2011.01178.x

Legutke, M. (2016, March). *Teachers matter: Revisiting the territory and charting the future of foreign language teacher education*. Paper presented at the annual meeting of the American Association for Applied Linguistics, Orlando, FL, USA.

Lindahl, K. (2020). Connecting ideology and awareness: Critical multilingual awareness in CLIL contexts. *English Teaching & Learning, 44*(2), 211–228.

McDonald, M. A. (2005). The integration of social justice in teacher education: Dimensions of prospective teachers' opportunities to learn. *Journal of Teacher Education, 56*(5), 418–435.

Miller, E. R., Morgan, B., & Medina, A. L. (2017). Exploring language teacher identity work as ethical self-formation. *The Modern Language Journal, 101*(S1), 91–105.

Morgan, B. (2004). Teacher identity as pedagogy: Towards a field-internal conceptualization in bilingual and second language education. *International Journal of Bilingual Education and Bilingualism, 7*, 172–188. https://doi.org/10.1080/13670050408667807

Pavlenko, A. (2003). "I never knew I was a bilingual": Reimagining teacher identities in TESOL. *Journal of Language, Identity, and Education, 2*, 251–268.

Pavlenko, A., & Blackledge, A. (Eds.). (2004). *Negotiation of identities in multilingual contexts*. Multilingual Matters.

Peercy, M. M., & Sharkey, J. (2020). Missing a S-STEP? How self-study of teacher education practice can support the language teacher education knowledge base. *Language Teaching Research, 24*(1), 105–115. https://doi.org/10.1177/1362168818777526

Pennycook, A. (2001). *Critical applied linguistics: A critical introduction*. Routledge.

Reeves, J. (2018). Teacher identity work in neoliberal schooling spaces. *Teaching and Teacher Education, 72*, 98–106.

Rudolph, N., Yazan, B., & Rudolph, J. (2019). Negotiating 'ares,' 'cans' and 'shoulds' of being and becoming in ELT: Two teacher accounts from one Japanese university. *Asian Englishes, 21*(1), 22–37. https://doi.org/10.1080/13488678.2018.1471639

Sayer, P. (2012). *Ambiguities and tensions in English language teaching: Portraits of EFL teachers as legitimate speakers*. Routledge.

Solano-Campos, A. (2014). The making of an international educator: Transnationalism and nonnativeness in English teaching and learning. *TESOL Journal, 5*, 412–443. https://doi.org/10.1002/tesj.156

Yazan, B. (2018a). TESL teacher educators' professional self-development, identity, and agency. *TESL Canada Journal, 35*(2), 140–155. https://doi.org/10.18806/tesl.v35i2.12894

Yazan, B. (2018b). Being and becoming an ESOL teacher through coursework and internship: Three teacher candidates' identity negotiation. *Critical Inquiry in Language Studies, 15*(3), 205–227. https://doi.org/10.1080/15427587.2017.1408014

Yazan, B. (2019a). Towards identity-oriented teacher education: Critical autoethnographic narrative. *TESOL Journal, 10*(1), 1–15.

Yazan, B. (2019b). Identities and ideologies in a language teacher candidate's autoethnography: Making meaning of storied experience. *TESOL Journal, 10*(4), 1–21.

Yazan, B. (2019c). An autoethnography of a language teacher educator: Wrestling with ideologies and identity positions. *Teacher Education Quarterly, 46*(3), 34–56. https://www.jstor.org/stable/10.2307/26746049

Yazan, B. (2022a). Multivocal teacher educator identity: A self-study of a language teacher educator's use of critical autoethnography. In R. Yuan & I. Lee (Eds.), *Becoming and being a TESOL teacher educator: Research and practice* (pp. 246–265). Routledge.

Yazan, B. (2022b). Reflective practice as identity work: A teacher educator's reflections on identity tensions. In Z. Tajeddin & A. Watanabe (Eds.), *Teacher reflection policies, practices, and impacts: Studies in honor of Thomas S. C. Farrell*. Multilingual Matters.

Yuan, R., & Lee, I. (Eds.). (2022). *Becoming and being a TESOL teacher educator: Research and practice*. Routledge.

Chapter 12
Learning to Become an English Language Teacher: Examining Professional Identities of a Chinese ESL Teacher Candidate in the U.S.-Based Practicum

Feifei Fan and Ester J. de Jong

Abstract The purpose of this book chapter is to explore how a Chinese ESL teacher candidate, named Mei, constructed and negotiated her professional identities during an ESL-oriented teaching practicum in the southeastern United States. Drawing upon the exploratory lens of language teacher identity, this study adopted narrative inquiry methodology. Data sources included in-depth interviews, informal conversations, classroom observations, and journals. Retelling Mei's professional life journey, her story was constructed through analysis of narratives and narrative analysis. Findings revealed that through learning and teaching in different contexts, Mei shifted her language teacher identity from being around language proficiency focus as a non-native English-speaking teacher to being around professional knowledge focus as a competent English language teacher. In addition, being positioned by her mentor teacher and English language learners as an ESL professional, Mei constructed her legitimacy in English language teaching. The study calls for teacher educators to create mediational spaces for international teacher candidates to negotiate dominant ideologies and to provide them with rich opportunities for practicing teaching.

Keywords Language teacher identity · Teaching practicum · Language teacher education · Non-native English-speaking teachers · Identity negotiation

F. Fan (✉)
Mills High School, Millbrae, CA, USA
e-mail: feifeifan0530@gmail.com

E. J. de Jong
University of Colorado Denver, Denver, CO, USA
e-mail: Ester.dejong@ucdenver.edu

© The Author(s), under exclusive license to Springer Nature Switzerland AG 2022   165
K. Sadeghi, F. Ghaderi (eds.), *Theory and Practice in Second Language Teacher Identity*, Educational Linguistics 57, https://doi.org/10.1007/978-3-031-13161-5_12

12.1   Introduction

Numerous studies have questioned whether the practical experience or pedagogical knowledge developed in an English as a second language (ESL) context are appropriate for international TCs who likely will be teaching English as a foreign language (EFL) in non-English-dominant contexts after graduation (Ilieva et al., 2015; Lo, 2005; Stapleton & Shao, 2018; Yeh, 2011). Studies have also suggested that international TCs who are bilingual users of English lose confidence as teachers as their non-native English-speaking teacher (NNEST) identity is highlighted in English-dominant ESL contexts (Brutt-Griffler & Samimy, 1999; Fan & de Jong, 2019; Golombek & Jordan, 2005; Park, 2017; Pavlenko, 2003; Reis, 2015; Xuan, 2014).

Despite the continued enrollment of a large number of international teacher candidates (TCs) in U.S.-based TESOL teacher education programs, research on their experiences is limited. Using language teacher identity (LTI) as a lens, this chapter reports on a case study of a Chinese TC, Mei (pseudonym) who participated in a U.S.-based TESOL teacher program and who enrolled in a semester-long ESL practicum. Specifically, the study examined Mei's LTI negotiation and what factors influenced her LTI construction as she participated in the program and practicum. The chapter concludes with recommendations for teacher preparation.

12.2   Language Teacher Identity

To understand how international TCs construct and negotiate their professional identities during an U.S.-based practicum, this study uses LTI as an exploratory lens to unpack their experiences and perceptions of being prepared as English language teachers. LTI refers to "[language] teachers' dynamic self-conception and imagination of themselves as teachers, which shifts as they participate in varying communities, interact with other individuals, and position themselves (and are positioned by others) in social contexts" (Yazan, 2018a, p. 21). LTI has been found to play an important role in L2 teachers' pedagogical approaches and interactions with learners (Duff & Uchida, 1997; Kanno & Stuart, 2011; Martel, 2015; Martel & Wang, 2014; Menard-Warwick, 2008; Morgan, 2004) as well as in the process of L2 teachers' engagement in teacher preparation programs (Clarke, 2008; Gu & Benson, 2015; Park, 2017; Trent, 2011; Yazan, 2018b). LTI is thus central to the process of becoming and being a language teacher, which involves developing one's knowledge, beliefs, practices, and emotions into an identity (Kubanyiova, 2012).

Varghese et al. (2005) provide three lenses to understanding LTI, including identity-in-practice and identity-in-discourse, to holistically understand the identities of language teachers. Identity-in-practice is presented by the social group theories of LTI, while identity-in-discourse is expressed by the poststructuralist theories of LTI.

The identity-in-practice lens views LTI as action-oriented, which is operationalized through concrete tasks and practices taking place in institutional settings, such as teacher education programs and schools. For example, the two ESL TCs in Kanno and Stuart's (2011) study had rich opportunity to practice their basic instructional skills, including giving clear direction, defining a word, and answering elementary grammar questions. The daily instruction afforded the two TCs to practice their elementary teaching skills, shifting their feelings of incompetence to claiming themselves as a legitimate teacher.

The identity-in-discourse lens acknowledges that LTI is constructed, maintained, and negotiated through language and discourse, since "language (or discourse) is the tool through which representations and meanings are constructed and negotiated, and a primary means through which ideologies are transmitted" (Hawkins & Norton, 2009, p. 32). For language teachers, their linguistic identities are interrelated to their professional identities, in that their language competence is conflated with their knowledge of content or subject matter (Yazan & Rudolph, 2018). A number of studies have demonstrated how the native speaker discourse negatively impact the NNESTs' construction of their LTIs as legitimate teachers (Aneja, 2016; Park, 2012; Reis, 2015).

12.3 Methodology

In order to understand the Chinese ESL TC's professional identity construction and negotiation in a U.S.-based ESL-oriented teaching practicum, this study employs qualitative narrative inquiry as the methodological approach (Clandinin & Connelly, 2000; Creswell & Poth, 2018). Narrative inquiry empowers researchers to think through Chinese ESL TCs' unique experience of learning to teach from the past, present, and future while also understanding that this professional learning takes place through interacting with other people and social contexts (Clandinin & Rosiek, 2007).

12.3.1 Participant Selection

Convenient purposeful sampling (Patton, 2015) was used as a guideline to select the study participants. The two criteria for selecting participants included those (1) who enrolled in a U.S.-based master-level ESOL teacher preparation program at the College of Education and (2) who was in process of semester-long ESL-oriented practicum in the U.S.-based classroom. After getting the consent from the TCs in the program, three TCs eventually agreed to participate in the original study that was conducted during Fall of 2019 to Spring of 2020. For the purpose of this chapter, the focus is on one of the TCs Mei (pseudonym).

Born and raised in a provincial capital city in northern China, Mei grew up in a middle-class family with parents in the furniture business. She began to study English in the third grade at a public elementary school and she regarded this foreign language as an important subject among her other studies. During her secondary education, Mei continued to work diligently to learn English so she could achieve outstanding exam results. Due to the traditional EFL teaching in most developing cities in China at the beginning of twenty-first century, Mei learned English language within the exam-based educational environment in which students paid more attention to grammar, vocabulary, and reading and less to listening and speaking. Due to her high score of English in the college entrance exam, Mei was matriculated by the Business English Program at a Chinese ordinary university. Due to her love in English language, she had multiple teaching experiences tutoring middle school students English. One of Mei's aunts, who at the time was living in a college town in the Southeastern United States, invited her to visit her and the town in the fall of 2017. During her stay in this college town, Mei participated in the English Language Institute at a larger public university based on her curiosity around how American teachers teach English. Gradually, she enjoyed her life in this college town and wanted to pursue a career as an English language teacher. Admitted by a master's program in ESL teacher education at the same university, Mei began her teacher preparation journey in January 2018. In the fall of 2019, she enrolled in the practicum in the sheltered ESL classroom at a local public school which aimed to provide sixth- to eighth-grade English language learners (ELLs) with intensive English instruction.

12.3.2   Data Collection

In order to understand the participant's teacher preparation journey with a focus on her field experience, two semi-structured and open-ended narrative interviews were conducted before and after the practicum. With each interview lasting around 65 minutes, the pre-practicum interview aimed to gather information about the participant's personal history, her language teacher beliefs, and how she anticipated her roles and ESL practicum experiences in U.S.-based classroom. The post-practicum interview invited the participant to reflect on her field experience and look ahead to the future.

In addition to the interviews, two classroom observations with debriefing conversations on how the participant worked with the ELLs were conducted and field notes were taken. Moreover, documents including 30 practicum experience reflections and three more specific journal entries that specifically prompted her to think about topics related to LTIs were also collected and analyzed.

12.3.3 Data Analysis

For the initial phase of the analysis, the first author engaged in narrative coding (Clandinin & Connelly, 2000), highlighting and making notes of the transcribed data about "names of the characters that appeared, places where actions and events occurred, storylines that interweaved and interconnected, gaps or silences that become apparent, [emotions] and tensions that emerged" as possible codes (Clandinin, 2013, p. 131). Meaningful incidents and key feelings from the participant's narratives were identified. During the next phase, narrative analysis was used to gather events and happenings to produce explanatory stories (Polkinghorne, 1995). To ensure the trustworthiness of the study, data triangulation was conducted to compare and cross-check multiple sources of data. In addition, member checking took place through sending her the transcribed data and initial interpretations of data for her feedback. Moreover, the two authors acting as peer debriefers co-constructed the story to ensure the absence of misinterpretation of narrative data.

12.4 Stories from Mei

In laying out Mei's big story in a chronological order, four storylines emerged, which are explored in detail below. These story lines centered what it meant to learn English and becoming an English teacher, LTI construction as NNEST, the story of agency working with English language learners, and coming to terms with her NNEST identity.

12.4.1 Learning English as an Empowering Language

At the beginning of twenty-first century, secondary education in the majority of cities in China, including the place where Mei grew up, positioned exams at the center of teaching and learning. While Mei recalled her English learning experience at secondary schools during which she focused on memorization of grammar and vocabulary as well as drill-based practices, she voiced the importance of English to her not only as a foreign language that was valued in China, but also as an empowering language to demonstrate her value as a good student at schools. Due to her poor academic performance in math, Mei could not imagine her secondary school life without English. "If my English was as bad as my math exam results, I might be bullied by others," Mei recalled, "But I often got compliments from my English teacher, which made me think I have some values." In addition to the received compliments from teachers and increased respect from her classmates, Mei also noticed that she became "much more brave, confident and talkative," and would be able to "study and live in another country." Acutely aware that learning

English positively influenced her overall personality and allowed her to study overseas, Mei recognized that this language empowered her more than just as a student.

12.4.2   Wanting to Become an English Language Teacher

Despite her undergraduate major in business English, Mei voluntarily participated in English teaching at various rural schools during her college. Because of her interest in teaching English, she used her spare time to tutor exam-based English to middle school students in her hometown. Based on her teaching experiences, she proudly shared her gained "sense of achievement and satisfaction after teaching English". Through interaction with her students, Mei had a positive experience in which she understood the teaching profession could offer both students and teachers improvement. "Teaching is a two-way process of mutual interaction," she said, "When I teach the students, I learn with them. So being a teacher makes me always not only feel satisfied but also get improvement." Despite the end of her teaching job, her previous students continuously contacted Mei about their learning progress. She thought to herself, "I feel like I had credits too since I could inspire the students' interest in learning English." Therefore, Mei held a strong belief in English teaching that "teaching to fish is better than giving a fish".

Despite the fulfillment that emerged through her English teaching experiences, Mei recognized her unpreparedness as a professional English teacher and thus her need of formal teacher preparation in English language education. She recalled, "After realizing being an English teacher is suitable for me as a career, I decided to study in the TESOL program." As her aunt had been living in a college town located in the southeastern United States for about 20 years, Mei chose to stay in with her because there was a public university which housed a specialized program in TESOL in the College of Education. To further unpack her choice of investment in the U.S.-based TESOL teacher education, it derived from Mei's desires to "obtain a master's degree in TESOL from a high-ranked American university" and to "be more competitive on the job market and get higher salary" as soon as she got back to China.

12.4.3   Constructing Identity as a NNEST in TESOL Program

Within her 2-year TESOL teacher preparation, the first three semesters all consisted of university-based coursework. During her participation in the TESOL program, Mei interacted with a handful of American peers in classes. It was through these interactions that she ended up comparing herself with her American peers in terms of English language proficiency. "If we take a class with American peers, it is obvious that they are speaking up in class for most of time," Mei noted, "Because they neither need extra time to organize their language nor to think about whether it is accurately to say this or that to express their ideas." Comparing herself and other non-native English-speaking (NNES) peers with the native English-speaking teachers (NEST) in the TESOL program, Mei indicated that NNES TCs participated at the periphery of the program. Even more, she polarized NNESTs and NESTs in the TESOL program by using "we" and "they" discourse to refer to these two groups. Speaking of her past English teaching experiences in China, Mei pointed out, "I basically used Chinese to do instruction and didn't feel the incompetence. But now I realized my weakness." In contrast to her previous self-identification as a fulfilled English language teacher in China, Mei highlighted her identity as an NNEST and indicated the advantages of NESTs who spoke English fluently and addressed the inferiority of her oral English skill in the U.S. context.

During the time of this study, it was Mei's final semester in the TESOL program. According to the program design, Mei was enrolled in the ESL-oriented school-based practicum for a whole semester. Considering that she worked with middle school students previously, she chose to be placed in a sheltered ESL classroom at a local middle school. However, based on her deficit view towards her spoken English, Mei expressed the anxiety she felt with an upcoming practicum at an American middle school. "To be honest, I am worried about my English. I don't have much confidence to straightforwardly express what I want to say," she explained as being frowned. In response to her forthcoming field experience, Mei generated a series of negative emotions, including feelings of anxiety and fear, that stemmed from her linguistic concerns as a non-native English speaker.

12.4.4 Agency to Address the Needs of ELLs

Unlike her previous concerns and anxious feelings about participating in the practicum, the welcoming attitude of Mei's mentor teacher, Mrs. Cooper, and the students in the ESL classroom, made her feel relieved on the first day of the practicum. Her mentor teacher, being supportive, provided Mei with the shared classroom responsibilities and with abundant teaching opportunities. During her work with the ELLs in the practicum, Mei noticed that ELLs' first languages were not fully used during their ESL learning. Based on Mrs. Cooper's language policy in class, she valued the ELLs' first languages in the way that they were allowed to communicate with their peers in those languages. During the instruction, however, English became the only medium for the students to learn.

Recognizing the need of ELLs for linguistic support in learning, Mei decided to make changes during her teaching. One day as she taught a lesson on ten new words, Mei invited the ELLs who spoke Spanish, Arabic, Mandarin, and Portuguese to share the words of equivalent meaning in their home languages and encouraged them to take notes in both English and their first languages as they preferred. The students showed excitement as they heard various languages from their peers. A Portuguese boy who was a newcomer with limited English proficiency showed an obvious change, from zero participation previously to the active involvement in learning with a big smile on his face during Mei's instruction. To reflect on her paralingual support, Mei said,

> I love how students reacted when they saw their home languages. Putting myself into students' position, if I could see my language on the PowerPoint, I would feel so excited as well. In addition, providing their home languages is the most straightforward way to help them understand words and the content.

As she noticed the students' exciting reactions to the paralingual support, Mei strengthened her belief that the usage of the ELLs' first languages not only acknowledged their linguistic capital but also supported their understanding as funds of knowledge to bridge learning in a second language. In contrast to the English-only instruction that was dominated her mentor teacher's teaching and instructions, Mei acted her agency to address the needs of the ELLs and to provide them with paralingual support.

In addition to the linguistic support, Mei noticed that the ELLs were not offered with needs-relevant learning materials. "Teaching English as an additional language was different in the United States than that in China," Mei thought to herself. Unlike Mei's EFL learning experience at schools during which the students were offered systematic English textbooks prepared by the Department of Education and other supplementary learning materials prepared by the English teachers, Mrs. Cooper did not have any ESL curriculum guidance provided by the district level and Mei thought the materials used were repetitive and not sufficiently challenging. She gave an example about a Chinese ELL in the beginning-level class.

> We have a Chinese boy who just joined us this semester. Although he has difficulty in oral English, he knows pretty much English vocabulary words. His reading and writing ability are more advanced than other students in the beginner-level class, not to mention his knowledge in math. Normally in class, he could complete the tasks that my mentor assigned very quickly and then sits there having nothing to do. So, I felt it is necessary for the teacher to prepare various learning materials based on the students' individualized competence.

Pointing out the need for preparing differentiated materials for the ELLs at varying English proficiency levels in a same classroom, Mei argued that some newcomer ELLs who had beginning-level oral English proficiency might have higher literacy skills. As this recent arrival Chinese ELL's example illustrated, the materials that Mrs. Cooper provided could not match his needs. In response to the lack of effective learning materials, Mei exerted agency once again to provide the needs-relevant learning materials to the ELLs during her teaching practice in the practicum, including creating graphic organizers.

12.4.5 Acknowledging Her Competence as a NNEST

In response to Mei's teaching performance during the practicum, Mrs. Cooper spoke highly of her. "Your lesson was amazing. You commended the presence. You spoke with authority. You followed the transition. You were managing the technology. And this is your second language by the way," Mrs. Cooper made the comment one day after Mei finished a lesson. Mrs. Cooper's discourse indicated that Mei was assigned with the NNEST identity, but meanwhile with the confirmation on her competence as a capable English language teacher. Despite the different approaches of teaching ESL, Mrs. Cooper acknowledged Mei's professional knowledge in ESL education and regarded her as a member of the teacher team.

In addition to the assigned identity as a capable NNEST by her mentor teacher, Mei also constantly negotiated her identity as a NNEST during the practicum. Similar to her comparison between herself as a NNEST and American peers in the TESOL program, Mei continuously compared herself and American teachers during her practicum. She told a story in which an American substitute teacher showed up one day while her mentor teacher asked for a leave. "I was in charge of the students for most of time," said Mei with a big smile, "and when the students encountered some questions about their class work, they preferred asking me instead of the American teacher." As Mei implicitly pointed to the substitute teacher's linguistic identity as a native English speaker, it was obvious that she was still comparing herself with a NEST highlighting the NEST/NNEST dichotomy. However, the comparison with the American substitute teacher allowed Mei to recognize that she was acknowledged by the students. As a result, the students' validation of Mei transformed her self-identification as a competent English language teacher.

Besides being capable at identifying and addressing the need for ELLs, Mei used her professional knowledge to recognize the academic and social challenges of ELLs, to know them as individuals who came from different cultural backgrounds than herself, to value their cultural and linguistic capitals, and to take actions to support them. At the end of the practicum, when Mrs. Cooper spoke of Mei's engagement with the students, she insisted, "The kids loved her, some of them even really bonded with her. I think they could see that she was confident, competent, and hardworking." Mei's active engagement with the students gained the validation of the students as a competent NNEST. Her stories ended with a moment recalled by herself where she felt like an English teacher. She described,

> One morning Mrs. Cooper was not in the classroom. I entered the classroom, then wrote down the agenda on the board. Then I greeted students at the door. When bell rang, I gave out the worksheet to students to let them practice verbs. When they finished, I stood in front of the classroom, leading students to go over their answers and share their sentences. Many students raised hands and shouted "Me! Me!". At that moment, I felt I was part of the ESL class. I knew everyone's name. I knew which one I should call for because he/she did not answer questions frequently. I knew how to engage the students into the class activities. I am their "teacher" in the ESL classroom.

Through a series of actions described in this moment, Mei provided a snapshot of how she was capable of working with the ELLs involving formal instruction, active interaction, and familiarity to the students. Acknowledging her professional competence, Mei confidently asserted her constructed identity as a prepared English language teacher.

12.5   Discussion

The purpose of this study was to examine how an international TC constructed and negotiated her LTIs during an U.S.-based ESL-oriented practicum. Although case studies are highlight contextualized and therefore not generalizable, three findings emerged that provide insights into LTI construction for international TCs in ESL contexts.

First, LTI are dynamic and contextual. Mei shifted her perceptions of what it means to be an NNEST due to the different learning/teaching context. Starting her English teaching journey in China, Mei felt fulfilled about her teaching and interpreted her teaching competence from a professional knowledge perspective. As she transitioned to the United States and participated in the TESOL program, her status of being a NNEST was foregrounded in terms of oral English proficiency in comparison to the native English-speaking American peers. No longer viewing herself as a competent English language teacher vis-à-vis native English speakers, Mei accentuated her NNEST identity from a deficit lens, which was reinforced by the nativespeakerism ideology. Other research has similarly noted that when NNES transnational teachers tend to compare themselves with native speakers in terms of language proficiency and reinforce deficit views on NNEST (Fan & de Jong, 2019; Park, 2012; Reis, 2011). During her practicum, Mei did not stop comparing herself with her American mentor teacher but was able to acknowledge her expertise and reframe her NNEST status from a positive perspective. Through multiple opportunities working with ELLs, she was able to affirm her professional identity as a legitimate English language teacher in the U.S. context. Similar shifts were observed by Liao (2014) and Park (2012) who showed that the transnational teachers embraced their NNEST identity and understood that being a legitimate ESL teacher hinged on the professional competence to truly be able to help ELLs. This finding also further underscores the importance of the practicum as a mediating tool for the TCs to make sense of who they are as teachers (Farrelly, 2019; Gebhard, 2009; Oprandy, 2015).

A second finding is the importance of how TCs are positioned by members of the school community and how this contributed to Mei's professional identity. Both her mentor teacher and the students assigned Mei an identity as a qualified ESL professional. Mrs. Cooper acknowledged Mei's professional knowledge and competence and treated her as a professionally prepared ESL expert. She thus legitimized Mei's professionalism in the field of English language teaching. The students, as a crucial part of the school community, showed their trust and affirmation in Mei's capabilities through actions (e.g., active participation in Mei's teaching) and affections (e.g., love and bond). Such social and professional legitimation plays an important role in ESL/EFL TCs' LTI formation (Yazan & Peercy, 2018; Yuan, 2016). Studies by Park (2012) and Yuan and Lee (2015), on Chinese English language TCs illustrate that they reinforced their professional legitimacy after being positioned as valid English teachers by their mentor teachers. In contrast, the English language TCs in studies by Trent (2013), Yuan (2016) and Nguyen

(2017) were regarded by their mentor teachers as student teachers, assistants, and outsiders of school community, thus constraining them to develop their professional identity as a competent English language teacher.

Lastly, this study underscores the role of teacher agency in shifting Mei's professional identity. Teacher agency in this study refers to the capacity or willingness to act when individual teachers are assigned agentic positions (Kayi-Aydar, 2015). Teacher agency influences professional identity in the way that teachers "take up and perform new identities and . . . take concrete actions in pursuit of their goals" and "actively resist certain behaviors, practices, positionings" (Duff, 2012, p. 15). Contrary to studies where international ESL TCs chose to compromise when they experienced a contradiction between their preferred pedagogical approaches and the mentor teachers' teaching style of working with ELLs (Nguyen, 2017; Nguyen & Yang, 2018), Mei exerted agency to implement paralingual support and needs-relevant learning materials that she believed as useful to meet the needs of the ELLs. It did not mean that the power relationship between Mei and her mentor teacher did not exist. However, Mei's self-positioning as a helpful professional teacher positively influenced her to take actions and make changes.

12.6   Implications for Language Teacher Education

Considering Mei's stories within the broader literature of LTIs, three implications for teacher educators and TESOL teacher education programs can be proposed. Firstly, it is important to provide critical tools to negotiate dominant ideologies during the whole process of TESOL teacher education programs. Particularly it is crucial for TESOL programs to attend to the moments where international TCs have recently joined the English-dominant context, to help them mediate the dominant ideologies through unpacking their implicit beliefs, engaging in critical discussions, offering them empowered discourses such as multicompetent users (Cook, 1999). The usage of alternative discourses is not to deny the fact that international TCs speak English as a second or additional language, but to reframe their NNEST identity as a resource and empower them to be aware of their competence as a legitimate English teacher. In addition, teacher educators should be always aware of how international NNES TCs are positioned explicitly and implicitly in a program (Fan & de Jong, 2019).

Secondly, TESOL programs should be conscious of whether the program itself is essentialized nativeness in English (Leung, 2005; Yazan & Rudolph, 2018) or idealized western-based English language teaching (Kumaravadivelu, 2003). Studies have shown that international TCs feel struggling to assert their professional legitimacy despite the usefulness of counter-discourses (Golombek & Jordan, 2005; Xuan, 2014). If international NNESTs were provided with a space to demonstrate their professional knowledge or experiences from their perspectives during the university-based coursework, it might be easier for them to negotiate the symbolic capital and thus to acknowledge their bilingual identity and professional legitimacy.

Thirdly, the main story in this chapter demonstrates the crucial role of teaching practicum in constructing and negotiating international TCs' professional identities. In other words, field experience with real teaching opportunities serves as a mediational space for TCs to develop their professional identities (Park, 2012). In this sense, TESOL programs need to provide ample teaching opportunities to help fledging TCs build their sense of expertise.

References

Aneja, G. A. (2016). (Non)native speakered: Rethinking (non)nativeness and teacher identity in TESOL teacher education. *TESOL Quarterly, 50*(3), 572–596.

Brutt-Griffler, J., & Samimy, K. K. (1999). Revisiting the colonial in the postcolonial: Critical praxis for nonnative-English-speaking teachers in a TESOL program. *TESOL Quarterly, 33*, 413–431.

Clandinin, D. J. (2013). *Engaging in narrative inquiry*. Routledge.

Clandinin, D. J., & Connelly, F. M. (2000). *Narrative inquiry: Experience and story in qualitative research*. Jossey-Bass.

Clandinin, D. J., & Rosiek, J. (2007). Mapping a landscape of narrative inquiry: Borderland spaces and tensions. In D. J. Clandinin (Ed.), *Handbook of narrative inquiry: Mapping a methodology* (pp. 35–76). Sage.

Clarke, M. (2008). *Language teacher identities: Co-constructing discourse and community*. Multilingual Matters.

Cook, V. (1999). Going beyond the native speaker in language teaching. *TESOL Quarterly, 33*, 185–209.

Creswell, J. W., & Poth, C. N. (2018). *Qualitative inquiry research design: Choosing among five approaches* (4th ed.). Sage.

Duff, P. (2012). Identity, agency, and SLA. In A. Mackey & S. Gass (Eds.), *Handbook of second lanagueg acquisition* (pp. 410–426). Routledge.

Duff, P., & Uchida, Y. (1997). The negotiation of teachers' sociocultural identities and practices in postsecondary EFL classrooms. *TESOL Quarterly, 31*, 451–486.

Fan, F., & de Jong, E. J. (2019). Exploring professional identities of nonnative-English-speaking teachers in the United States: A narrative case study. *TESOL Journal, 10*(4). https://doi.org/10.1002/tesj.495

Farrelly, R. (2019). A TESOL practicum in the USA. In A. Cirocki, I. Madyarov, & L. Baecher (Eds.), *Current perspectives on the TESOL practicum: Cases from around the globe* (pp. 265–288). Springer.

Gebhard, J. G. (2009). The practicum. In A. Burns & J. C. Richards (Eds.), *The Cambridge guide to second language teacher education* (pp. 250–258). Cambridge University Press.

Golombek, P. R., & Jordan, S. R. (2005). Becoming 'lack lambs' not 'parrots': A poststructuralist orientation to intelligibility and identity. *TESOL Quarterly, 39*(3), 513–533.

Gu, M., & Benson, P. (2015). The formation of English teacher identities: A cross-cultural investigation. *Language Teaching Research, 19*(2), 187–206.

Hawkins, M., & Norton, B. (2009). Critical language teacher education. In A. Burns & J. Richards (Eds.), *Cambridge guide to second language teacher education* (pp. 30–39). Cambridge University Press.

Ilieva, R., Li, A., & Li, W. (2015). Negotiating TESOL discourses and EFL teaching contexts in China: Identities and practices of international graduates of a TESOL program. *Comparative and International Education, 44*(2), 1–16.

Kanno, Y., & Stuart, C. (2011). Learning to becoming a second language teacher: Identities-in-practice. *The Modern Language Journal, 95*(2), 236–252.

Kayi-Aydar, H. (2015). Teacher agency, positioning, and English language learners: Voices of pre-service classroom teachers. *Teaching and Teacher Education, 45*, 94–103.

Kubanyiova, M. (2012). *Teacher development in action: Understanding language teachers' conceptual change.* Palgrave Macmillan.

Kumaravadivelu, B. (2003). *Beyond methods: Macrostrategies for language teaching.* Yale University Press.

Leung, C. (2005). Convivial communication: Recontextualizing communicative competence. *International Journal of Applied Linguistics, 15*, 119–144.

Liao, P.-C. W. (2014). Identity negotiation and demonstration of agency in two non-native English speaking teachers in the United States. *NYS TESOL Journal, 1*(1), 27–38.

Lo, Y. G. (2005). Relevance of knowledge of second language acquisition. In N. Bartels (Ed.), *Applied linguistics and language teacher education* (pp. 135–158). Springer.

Martel, J. (2015). Learning to teach a foreign language: Identity negotiation and conceptualizations of pedagogical progress. *Foreign Language Annals, 48*(3), 394–412.

Martel, J., & Wang, A. (2014). Language teacher identity. In M. Bigelow & J. Ennser-Kananen (Eds.), *The Routledge handbook of educational linguistics* (pp. 289–300). Routledge.

Menard-Warwick, J. (2008). The cultural and intercultural identities of transnational English teachers: Two case studies from the Americas. *TESOL Quarterly, 42*(4), 617–640.

Morgan, B. (2004). Teacher identity as pedagogy: Towards a field-internal conceptualization in bilingual and second language education. *Bilingual Education and Bilingualism, 7*(2), 172–188.

Nguyen, M. H. (2017). Negotiating contradictions in developing teacher identity during the EAL practicum in Australia. *Asia-Pacific Journal of Teacher Education, 45*(4), 399–415.

Nguyen, H. T. M., & Yang, H. (2018). Learning to become a teacher in Australia: A study of pre-service teachers' identity development. *The Australian Educational Researcher, 45*(5), 625–645.

Oprandy, R. (2015). Refashioning the practicum by emphasizing attending and reflective skills. *The CATESOL Journal, 27*(2), 101–128.

Park, G. G. (2012). "I am never afraid of being recognized as an NNES": One teacher's journey in claiming and embracing her nonnative-speaker identity. *TESOL Quarterly, 46*(1), 127–151.

Park, G. G. (2017). *Narratives of east Asian women teachers of English: Where privilege meets marginalization.* Multilingual Matters.

Patton, M. Q. (2015). *Qualitative evaluation and research methods* (4th ed.). Sage.

Pavlenko, A. (2003). "I never knew I was a bilingual": Reimagining teacher identities in TESOL. *Journal of Language, Identity, and Education, 2*(4), 251–268.

Polkinghorne, D. E. (1995). Narrative configuration as qualitative analysis. In J. A. Hatch & R. Wisniewski (Eds.), *Life history and narrative* (pp. 5–25). Falmer Press.

Reis, D. S. (2011). Non-native English-speaking teachers (NNESTs) and professional legitimacy: A sociocultural theoretical perspective on identity transformation. *International Journal of the Sociology of Language, 208*(2011), 139–160.

Reis, D. S. (2015). Making sense of emotions in NNESTs' professional identities. In Y. L. Cheung, S. B. Said, & K. Park (Eds.), *Advances and current trends in language teacher identity research* (pp. 31–43). Routledge.

Stapleton, P., & Shao, Q. (2018). A worldwide survey of MATESOL programs in 2014: Patterns and perspectives. *Language Teaching Research, 22*(1), 10–28.

Trent, J. (2011). "Four years on, I'm ready to teach": Teacher education and the construction of teacher identities. *Teachers & Teaching, 17*(5), 529–543.

Varghese, M., Morgan, B., Johnston, B., & Johnson, K. (2005). Theorizing language teacher identity: Three perspectives and beyond. *Journal of Language, Identity, and Education, 4*(1), 21–44.

Xuan, P. T. T. (2014). Speaking out or keeping silent: International students' identity as legitimate speakers and teachers of English. *TESOL in Context, 24*(1), 7–27.

Yazan, B. (2018a). A conceptual framework to understand language teacher identities. *Journal of Second Language Teacher Education, 1*(1), 21–48.

Yazan, B. (2018b). Being and becoming an ESOL teacher through coursework and internship: Three teacher candidates' identity negotiation. *Critical Inquiry in Language Studies, 15*(3), 205–227.

Yazan, B., & Peercy, M. M. (2018). "Pedagogically speaking, I'm doing the right things": Three preservice ESOL teachers' identity formation. *Teacher Learning and Professional Development, 3*(1), 1–18.

Yazan, B., & Rudolph, N. (Eds.). (2018). *Criticality, teacher identity, and (in)equity in English language teaching: Issues and implications.* Springer.

Yeh, H. C. (2011). EFL teachers' challenges and dilemmas in transferring theories and practices cross-culturally. *Asia Pacific Education Review, 12*(1), 97–104.

Yuan, R. (2016). The dark side of mentoring on pre-service language teachers' identity formation. *Teaching and Teacher Education, 55*, 188–197.

Yuan, R., & Lee, I. (2015). The cognitive, social and emotional processes of teacher identity construction in a pre-service teacher education programme. *Research Papers in Education, 30*(4), 469–491.

Part III
Pandemic, Technology, and In-service L2 Teacher's Identity Development

Chapter 13
'Becoming More of a Fairy Godmother Type of Teacher': Teacher Identity Negotiation in a Time of Pandemic

Anne Burns

Abstract The first years of the worldwide Covid-19 pandemic have brought unanticipated and far-reaching change to the ways language teachers have had to conceptualise and implement their practices. Many teachers have been compelled to move rapidly from classroom to online teaching which has had a substantial impact not only on their sense of identity, but also their sense of confidence in their usual practices. In this chapter, I draw on the reflections of Australian teachers working with international students in the English Language Intensive Courses for Overseas Students (ELICOS) sector, several of whom I have worked with in these early pandemic years as a facilitator of action research, as part of their professional development. Together with their colleagues, they needed to rapidly adjust their professional expectations, roles and practices. The chapter draws on short narrative comments from these teachers and illustrates how they and their colleagues drew on new concepts and mindsets to negotiate their teacher identities and to discover how they could best work with their students in the change to online environments. The data show that social, cognitive and emotional factors were major influences on these negotiations of identity.

Keywords Language teacher identity · Action research · Professional development · Teacher agency · Educational change

13.1 Introduction

The Covid-19 pandemic years (2020–2022 so far) have shaken the foundations of language education and, in particular, the way many language teachers now have to interact with their students. The dramatic changes invoked in educational contexts have challenged teachers with questions such as: What is the nature of the context in which I now work? How do I continue to work with my students on such a context to engage them and sustain their learning? Who am I as a teacher and what is my new

A. Burns (✉)
Curtin University, Perth, WA, Australia

© The Author(s), under exclusive license to Springer Nature Switzerland AG 2022   181
K. Sadeghi, F. Ghaderi (eds.), *Theory and Practice in Second Language Teacher Identity*, Educational Linguistics 57, https://doi.org/10.1007/978-3-031-13161-5_13

persona and role? How do I recreate myself as a teacher when taken-for-granted practices and relationships must now be mediated through a medium where immediate social contact is removed? These questions go to fundamental issues of teacher identity and how teachers negotiate and renegotiate their identity.

13.2 Identity Theory

Over the last two decades, interest in second language teacher identity has grown exponentially. Finding its roots in research on learner identity (e.g., Norton's notion of investment: Darvin & Norton, 2016; Norton Peirce, 1995), the field of identity research has expanded to investigations of teacher identity and it has given rise to a burgeoning literature in this area. The notion of identity, as Barkhuizen (2016) notes, is a slippery one, not easily captured and defined. It has roots in multiple theoretical fields such as poststructuralism, socio-constructivism, social psychology, anthropology, discourse studies, communities of practice, and social identity theory (Barkhuizen, 2016; Varghese et al., 2005).

Despite this theoretical diversity, various key features are foregrounded. First, teacher identity formation is context-embedded, shaped within specific spheres of social and personal activity. It is constituted dynamically through social interaction with the individual's groups and communities. Second, identity is characterised, not by singularity, but multiplicity and mediated through the various communities in which an individual has membership, in the case of teachers, their broader professional fields, their institutions, and the participants within them, their colleagues and students. Nor can these professional identities be separated from others, such as cultural, ethnic, gendered, relational, or economic. Thus, rather than being fixed, one's identity is constantly in flux or under transformation, as different influences from these sources are experienced. Third, teacher identity is shaped by cognitions – the values, beliefs, philosophies, and knowledge an individual holds – mediated by the pervading discourses and interactions that impact on them.

Miller's (2009) perspective on identity summarises some of these features. She views identity as 'relational, negotiated, constructed, enacted, transforming, and transitional' (p. 174) and notes the central role of discourse in this conceptualisation of identity processes. In relation to this chapter, the notions of negotiated and transitional are particularly pertinent, as the pervading context of the global pandemic had a dramatic impact on the teachers highlighted in this account, requiring them to mediate and recreate taken-for-granted identities. As Edwards and Burns (2016) note, the negotiation of new or transitional identities is likely to be particularly prone to conflict or struggle. Under such conditions, triggered by unusual or unpredicted events, teachers must strive to renew their sense of being, or even construct different kinds of identities. For some, such situations may evoke a crisis of identity or a sense of extreme disequilibrium; for others, transitions in identity may be less confronting. The following accounts illustrate both these kinds of identity negotiation.

13.3   The Practical Context

The teachers with whom I worked are employed in various colleges and teaching centres across Australia where international students are taught in general or academic English classes, typically in preparation for entry into university and other forms of further study. Pre-Covid, this sector was considered to be a major Australian educational industry, coming third worldwide behind similar programs for international students studying in the USA or the UK. It performed as the fourth largest income earner for the country, with a revenue of 2.38 billion Australian dollars in 2019 (National ELICOS Market Report, 2020). As a result of government policies on restrictions to entry into Australia in early 2020, the number of international students enrolling in ELICOS courses in that year dropped by 47%. This situation was exacerbated in 2021 with a further drop of another 61% from the previous June. In total, enrolments dropped by 70% from 2019. Many of these losses were incurred from students returning home when Covid hit, deciding not to enrol, or moving to programs in countries other than Australia where accessing entry to courses was easier. A recent report commissioned by English Australia, the peak body representing the ELICOS industry, estimated that in 2020, 35% of staff lost their jobs and by the time of the writing of this chapter, 19% of ELICOS colleges had, for the present, stopped operating (National ELICOS Market Report, 2021).

Against this background of the impact of the pandemic, many ELICOS institutions rapidly moved to online teaching only. Thus, typically many international students who continued were studying offshore, while, like them, others who remained in Australia were unable to attend classes physically, and also needed to enrol online. This macro-environment, for an industry which had previously been well-established, created numerous professional shocks and challenges for teachers who remained. In the accounts that follow, my aim is to capture some of the major ways, socially, cognitively, and emotionally, in which the identities of these teachers were negotiated and reshaped.

13.4   The Impact of Covid-19 on ELICOS Teacher Identity

To gain insights into the impact of the pandemic on ELICOS teachers, I invited several with whom I worked in 2021, as well as teachers participating in an English Australia Special Interest Group (SIG) on action research to respond to the following questions: (1) What impact has the Covid-19 pandemic had on you as a teacher? (2) How has teaching online changed your sense of identity as a teacher? Teachers were asked to post their responses on the SIG Facebook site or, if they preferred, to email their views to me separately. There was no set format for the responses and teachers were at liberty to write as much or as little as they chose, or to add further to their comments later.

My main aim was to draw out what kinds of 'identity negotiation' (Edwards & Burns, 2016) teachers had navigated and were continuing to navigate as they accommodated to the new demands of teaching and learning. Conceiving of their responses as an 'identity negotiation' allowed for perceiving the complexities and dynamics of the mediation processes between institutional exigencies and personal and individual identity shifts. Of interest was the interconnections between the social, cognitive, and emotional dimensions of the teachers' perceptions. While these were often difficult to tease apart, it is possible to trace some major themes. Responses were received from 14 teachers and the insights identified below are drawn from these responses.

13.4.1   Identity Negotiation in the Social Domain

Teachers commented both on the larger social contexts of the sector and their institution, and on the social context of their own immediate online teaching environment.

The Sector and the Institution

Phillip,[1] who was also studying for a Master's and working as a trainer at the time, referred to the multiple identity transitions he had experienced, caused by the surrounding political and social conditions impacting on the sector:

> I have noticed the need to transition between different identities more often and much faster. For example, being in [a city where numerous lockdowns occurred] I have had to transition between face-to-face, hybrid and online teaching multiple times. Teaching from home means that I transition from teacher to parent as soon as I take my lunch break. Putting and taking off these different hats, teacher, parent, student, trainer or colleague... can be disorienting at times. If anyone has seen the Disney movie "Inside out", I think there are a number of new islands to my personality that didn't exist before.

He also highlighted the pressures caused by the external political and social environment against which teachers in this sector were now operating saying, 'I have lost a number of colleagues that were casually employed at our university, and unfortunately some areas associated with our pre-COVID teaching world appear to be gone forever!'

Transformations in the broader context had for some teachers brought about a sense of unreality and incredulity at the rapidity of the institutional changes demanded of them, and the assumptions that underpinned these demands. Vera's response conveys her sense of shock and dismay at the way in which she was forced to adopt a medium which confronted her preferred teaching mode. After commenting on her strong belief in the importance of direct classroom contact with her students, she laments:

---

[1] All names are pseudonyms and data are used with permission.

However, in March 2020, I did not have a choice. I had to start teaching online, quite literally, overnight. On Friday, we had training at work (come to think of it, it was the last time I was in our building; imagine all the rent we're paying for a building we're not using!) where IT staff handed out laptops and our coordinators introduced us to zoom. On Monday, I was teaching online.

Similarly, Rupert reported that:

the rapid transition to an exclusively online teaching platform for English for Academic Purposes (EAP) presented many challenges in 2020. [We] shifted from consideration of blended options complementing a traditional teaching model, to the investigation of a significantly changed set of online delivery methods.

Rupert's comment underpins the fact that, while new technological development and demands for more flexible ways of learning were, in any case, inevitably altering the ways ELICOS institutions were offering courses to their students, the pandemic created a 'disruptor' effect in the system (Larsen-Freeman & Cameron, 2008), catapulting teaching into a fully technological world.

For Andy, this change was leading him towards a realisation that a seismic and unpredictable shift had taken place; in particular, he was concerned about the impact on his students.

Students are still feeling the gulf between the physical learning space and the virtual classroom, and many are still struggling to accept that online delivery will remain for the foreseeable future.

In contrast, Simone appeared to take on the rapid changes more philosophically, seeing the inevitable moves to technology as an 'enhancement' and pondering that they:

... happen for a reason, and they serve their own purposes. Our job as teachers is to embrace those innovations and make them serve our students.

Echoing Rupert's point about broader movements that were already taking place in institutional modes of teaching, she believed the experience had enhanced her 'self-organisational skills necessary for the teacher/student survival in the digital continuum of multimodal literacies, multimedia content, and multiple affordances'. She commented that, as a result of this larger-scale contextual requirement, she had 'purposefully' set about adopting new virtual resources and organising her screen space into a different kind of classroom visual.

The Immediate Teaching Environment
In addition to the broader institutional social dimensions, teachers also commented on their sense of identity in their individual social context. While some teachers were still grappling with the loss of a familiar physical classroom, others felt comfortable in a virtual space.

Roz was one who believed her identity as a teacher was bound up with being in a classroom. As a result, she detected a large gap in her ability to relate to her students as she had done before:

> I miss the personal contact I manage to establish with my students in a face-to-face classroom. I still try to establish rapport but it is much harder. I feel I don't understand them as well as I usually do, and am therefore less effective in motivating them and adapting my teaching to their interests/learning style.

Roz clearly felt that her sense of self as a teacher had been undermined and was concerned that she had become less competent and effective in assisting her students. Her comments suggest a feeling of being lost or occupying an unsure state of transition. Similarly, Sally asserted she had 'been forced to change. The external environment has demanded this of me, making discomfort a familiar feel'. For these two teachers, the negotiation of new identities created a sense of disequilibrium.

Kristina offered a somewhat different perspective on her professional context, pointing to the contrast for her between the embodied nature of the classroom and the disembodied context of the screen. From her perspective it was important literally to be physically in the classroom context in a way that was impossible 'just being on the screen'. Her sense of a change in her identity was visceral, in that her students:

> ... can't see me race around the room, can't feel my energy. I just don't inhabit the same physical space as my students any more (sic), so this is quite altered. I like sharing the classroom with others, my students, but I'm a very tactile and sensory person (what's the adjective I need there – smiley face?).

In contrast to Kristina, Maria was direct in affirming her sense of a professional self that did not have to be physically located in a classroom:

> My identity as a teacher has not changed during online teaching in this time of pandemic. If you are an effective teacher in the classroom then it will be no different online.

She put this down to her philosophy that building a strong relationship was vital in any teaching situation. She asserted the importance of getting to 'know everyone and the dynamics of the different personalities in the cohort'. She believed that the online environment had even enabled some of her students to 'shine' in ways they would not have done in the physical classroom. She cited the example of a student who had become an online 'leader' who:

> shared her knowledge about Covid-testing sites, making vaccination appointments online, getting hold of translated fact sheets etc, her hidden skills were a surprise for everyone!

Taken together these comments compose a picture of teacher identities negotiating a complex, dynamic, and transitional social context, which had created considerable disequilibrium for some of these teachers. For most, it represented a discomforting change in dimensions of their identity. For one, it opened up new and exciting opportunities which she seemed ready to explore and even exploit. Whatever their stance, the disturbances in the social dynamic created by the pandemic were causing them to adapt their sense of being and belonging, as they sought to legitimise new kinds of social identities (Yuan & Lee, 2015).

13.4.2   Identity Negotiation in the Cognitive Domain

These types of perceptions related to teachers' concepts, beliefs or philosophies of pedagogy, including students' needs and learning. They also related to reconsideration of teacher-student roles and relationships. While the pedagogical approaches they reported adopting and their responses to student learning needs reflected the underpinning tenets they held as teachers, there was evidence of ways in which they now had to renegotiate them.

Pedagogical Concepts
Margaret reported that she was working hard to maintain her belief in a student-centred learning environment, where she preferred to operate as a 'facilitator'. Her approach was to utilise the 'breakout rooms' available on the online platform she used. However, at the same time, she noted that the online mode mitigated against her usual preference in that 'the lessons are naturally a bit more teacher-centred'. She also believed that, because the online medium had made students more nervous, 'that may add an extra layer of responsibility for the teacher too. I feel as though this puts me in more of a controller position than I'm comfortable with'. Andy too was committed to placing his students at the centre of his pedagogy. He stressed that even in a pandemic, he did not see teaching as 'confined to a desk, laptop, or office'. Rather, what motivated his pedagogy was 'strong relationships with students, even when face-to-face interaction is limited'. However, like Margaret, he had noticed an increase in students' dependence on the teacher 'to maintain connectedness to their learning, classroom, and peers'.

Maria did not feel that her approach to her pedagogy had changed substantially, except that online delivery was 'completely different'. She now had to do 'a lot more planning, creating, modifying, and presenting of content, which is extremely time-consuming'. In contrast, Sara felt that grappling with the technology and being removed from direct contact with her students had induced new perspectives in her teaching. She believed that she had 'upskilled'.

> Technological skills aside, I have understood I can give my teaching style an overhaul, learn more, be more open for successful delivery of online teaching.

She felt she had become more student-centred. As a result, she was attempting to learn how to balance a range of different activities to meet her students' needs and also to pay more attention to forms of classroom-based assessment and feedback that would help them to make progress.

While many of them were already reasonably competent and confident about the concept of technology as part of their pedagogy, almost all the teachers reported that they had needed to learn more about how to actually use the particular technologies of their institutions. For some, this had challenged their confidence as teachers considerably. Perhaps the most dramatic example was that of Vera, whose dismay at the sudden switch to online teaching was noted above. Vera reported that, while she was not averse to technology and could see its benefits, she had initially found the transition extremely challenging. She noted:

I firmly believe that my primary role is not to convey content to students but to inspire them, help them work out rules, strategies and approaches that work best for them. How could you do that online?

She recounted how she had initially resorted to using Powerpoints so that she could cover the required content. These had taken her considerable time to prepare but had also made her teaching feel 'rigid' and 'controlled', in complete antipathy to what she believed herself to be as a teacher:

> ... as soon as something didn't go to plan, I panicked and moved the lesson on to the next slide. I felt like a novice teacher who had prepared for hours but still failed to engage the masses.

She countered this insecurity by intensively researching after class how to improve her online teaching, signing up for training through her institution and other organisations, researching pressing issues on the internet ('How do I make sure students actually DO their work in breakout rooms?') and talking to colleagues:

> And, ever so slowly, I became more confident. I was excited about our new learning management system, Canvas, that allowed me to have discussions with my students – online! I was excited to find apps I could use with my students, so that lessons were not teacher-centred. Now, one year and four months later, I feel I have become a better teacher in many ways.

Vera shifted her sense of identity as an online teacher largely through her own agency. She reported that she had learned to 'relinquish control over every minute of the day' and that she was more confident to deal with problems as they arose. Her perceptions about what online learning could offer had enlarged to appreciate the way she could customise lessons to meet students' personal needs and encourage greater interaction and engagement, through activities such as self-recording. This comment indicates how she had renegotiated her perceptions of herself as an online teacher:

> Big win! I am actually worried what I'll do when we go back to the physical classroom. How will I deal with those students? How will I make time to allow everyone to talk?

Roles and Relationships

Another dimension of identity negotiation in the cognitive domain concerned teachers' sense of changed relationships with their students. While several of the comments above reveal the value teachers placed on good teacher-student relationships and the ability to create cooperative and positive classroom dynamics, it was clear that they believed that transitions were taking place. Some of these were to do with the level of 'pastoral care' (to use the term that the teachers utilised) that was now necessary.

Veronica used a colourful metaphor to express this change in students' needs and the new identity she felt it had created for her:

> I have found myself becoming more of a fairy godmother type of teacher. My students seem to need an enormous amount of encouragement, and sometimes they even need wishes granted (through extra lenient extensions) to help them get through. Life is so hard for me, but a million times harder for them.

Andy agreed with Veronica, pointing to what he saw as the 'unofficial pastoral care' he now had to offer. This had greatly expanded his teacher identity in unexpected directions:

> It's almost as if because I'm an Australian teacher, I am now required to disseminate information on a variety of topics, from vaccine knowledge, to when Australian borders will open, to why Australia has particular positions on certain foreign policy issues, to checking writing before an exam. Just my thoughts 🙂

Maria also referred to 'pastoral care', pointing to the fact that virtual learning could be more 'daunting for some and magnifies learner anxiety'. She was conscious that several of her students lacked any experience with online platforms, which had required heightened levels of personal attention and support from her. In addition, she was aware that for some there were external factors such as overcrowded houses, young children, distractions, feelings of isolation, lack of devices, and the cost of the internet that she needed to take into consideration. One challenge was that nearly half the students in her class did not have their own computer and had to use smart phone connections, which affected how she could work with them. She believed she had become much more conscious of her students' external learning situations and had tried to overcome these hurdles by developing her own online skills in order to help her students and accept 'any learning progress' they made.

Research on teacher cognition has burgeoned in the language teaching field over the last two decades (e.g., Borg, 2006; Burns et al., 2015). However, this research has not necessarily connected systematically to concepts of teacher identity (Varghese et al., 2005). Clearly, teacher cognitions, embedded and interconnected within the social contexts in which teachers work, mediate the way teachers negotiate new identities. The teachers' comments convey sites of cognitive struggle, stress, and pressure where demands for new kinds of self-identities were imposed on them. These struggles can create considerable tensions in teachers' concepts of who they are as teachers, their 'constructed' selves (Block, 2007), and who they have needed to become in circumstances of duress.

13.4.3 Identity Negotiation in the Emotional Domain

Recent literature on language education has placed increasing emphasis on the psychological and emotional dimensions of teaching (e.g., Gkonou et al., 2020; Mercer & Kostoulas, 2018). This research has gone beyond the concept of content knowledge and pedagogical skills to highlight the affective nature and emotional complexity of being in an educational context as a teacher. The diverse emotions that teachers experience in their teaching contexts shape and are shaped by their sense of who they are and what they aspire to achieve as teachers. Both positive and negative emotions are experienced in the negotiation of identity, particularly against a background of rapid transitions as in the case of these teachers.

Evidence of this dimension was already noticeable in the previous section, but here it is drawn out in greater detail to illuminate other emotional dimensions of the teachers' identity negotiation. Major themes were how one represented oneself as a teacher in an online classroom and how one's identity shifted within the online medium.

Representation as a Teacher

Margaret, who was known to be a highly experienced and confident teacher, expressed the requirement to materialise herself online almost as a kind of 'identity crisis':

> I think it has made me more self-conscious. Because I can see myself at all times and everything is also recorded, I think I'm a bit more nervous because I'm so "visible" and this is not the way I see myself as a teacher.

She went on to say that it was not the technology per se that made her uncomfortable, but rather the way the technology forced her to present herself as the teacher. Besides feeling that she was more of a 'controller' of students, as mentioned earlier, she also felt 'on display' and found that particular feature of the platform she was using to be 'exhausting'. She contrasted this experience with being in a face-to-face situation, such as a meeting with other people where 'you can tell if people are looking at you or not and you can relax at points, whereas in an [online] meeting you're always on'. Annie echoed this experience, adding that, 'I've also found that setting up to record the gallery view is a better experience rather than having me in full screen view'. She joked that:

> ... I've ended up buying a lipstick actually because of seeing myself so often on screen 😂 but guess what, it was all in a hurry and I don't know much about lipsticks so it's the same colour as my lips.

In her comment, Annie appeared to be mitigating the emotional stress of her demanding new circumstances, 'seeing myself so often on screen', through humour directed at herself.

Online Medium

Turning to how her identity had shifted because of the online medium, Vera noted 'It has made me humbler'. Although she believed she had always had a good rapport with her students, online teaching had made her 'more empathetic'. She now saw the technology as a 'fallible' rather than an authoritative medium for teaching, and had learned to respect her students' opinions when they told her that 'things did not work'. She no longer saw such comments from her students as their excuse to avoid completing tasks. This experience had led her to revise her view of her status as a teacher, commenting:

> I am ready to accept that I don't know everything, that students can help me as much as I can help them. I acknowledge their contributions, and I can see how this boosts their confidence and sense of self-worth.

She felt grateful for 'all the stories they have shared with me', an aspect of her practice she felt she had focused on much less in the physical classroom, and had started to 'share stories from my life as well'. Such experiences had built greater mutual trust, and Vera felt she had gained appreciation of the complexities of students' lives and could be 'more understanding when they don't perform as expected'. She concluded that 'being forced into online teaching has been a positive and rewarding experience for me as a teacher and as a human being'.

Sara expressed her realisation that 'learners (and their families) are going through scary times'. As a result, she felt she was more patient and understanding of her students' needs. She concluded that '[w]ithout a doubt, since 2020 the changes that have come with the pandemic have had a dramatic effect on the way I teach'.

While, little research has been done so far on the emotional effects of online teaching and learning related to its visual impacts, online commentary by cyberpsychologists such as Andrew Franklin (cited in Feder, 2020) provides some insights, which are also picked up in the teachers' comments.

Franklin suggests that, when online, participants are conscious of a critical 'imaginary audience' who may be fixating on their physical faults and limitations. In face-to-face interactions, speakers do not typically see themselves. Moreover, online interaction strips out the normal visual cues inherent in physical communication, such as gesture, body movements, and facial expression. Interactional moves that would be more obvious face-to-face cannot be easily interpreted, thus sometimes resulting in disjointed, overlapping or uneasy communication. A great deal of contextual physical information is also missing when the 'whole person' is absent, as people normally only see faces or the parts of a person that can readily be displayed on a small screen (see Sukhorukova, 2017). Franklin also cites a study (Sherman et al., 2013) which showed that close pairs of personal friends felt less bonded when communicating online. It seems that research on these issues in the field of language teaching is now urgent as it could prove fruitful in providing guidance for teachers on how to negotiate these new online identities.

13.5   Discussion

The data, collected to gain insights into teacher identity in this particular teaching sector, are limited by the small number of respondents and the open-ended and informal nature of the data collection. Nevertheless, they provide glimpses into the lived experiences of teachers in the ELICOS sector who continued to teach under unfamiliar conditions in different parts of the country.

While not all teachers mentioned it directly, in contrast to pre-Covid times, they now worked in a world of highly unpredictable employment and drastically reduced student enrolments, and had watched many of their colleagues lose their jobs, some in fact in the process of losing their own jobs. Several of the teachers' responses reflect their state of uncertainty and confusion about an unknown future, where familiar ways of working with their students might never return.

In most cases, the teachers' sense of who they had been as teachers had been shaken by dramatic and unpredictable changes in the sector and in the way that their colleges or centres had responded to these changes. As a result, for some their sense of who and how they were as teachers, as expressed through principles and practices they held dear, had been deeply disturbed and their identities as teachers were in a considerable state of flux. Others seemed to have clung ever more closely to what they felt were their established teacher identities and had used these cognitively and emotionally to weather the storms of the pandemic.

The comments also show that the teachers were discovering creative ways to negotiate new identities through their own agency (Kayi-Aydar et al., 2019). Several referred to the crisis of the pandemic and the move to online teaching as a catalyst to new learning, sometimes in the face of personal resistance to the fundamental premises of this enforced learning. They appeared to have explored the uses of technology, as well as its role in planning and content delivery, much more than they otherwise might. There was evidence too of deeper awareness and learning in relation to their own pedagogical beliefs and practices, as well as greatly enhanced relationships with and understanding of their students.

In the negotiation of their identities as teachers during this time of pandemic, these teachers were undergoing transformations socially, cognitively, and emotionally which involved a sense both of loss and opportunity and demonstrated a need for 'ambiguity tolerance'. The losses had been incurred through a crisis from which there was no turning back, but were gradually being replaced by a new view of the world where they operated, one where there was also scope for creativity. Most were still in the process of constructing this new world view with its continuing unpredictability and the nature of their roles and identities within it.

13.6   Conclusion

In this chapter I have used the responses of teachers working in the volatile international student sector in Australia to illuminate some of the impacts on these teachers of the first 2 years of the Covid-19 pandemic. In particular, the chapter aimed to draw out the identity negotiation required of these teachers as they adjusted to new professional expectations, particularly in relation to online teaching. What emerges from this discussion is that despite unprecedented changes in their educational circumstances caused by political, social and institutional ecological factors, teachers' sense of who they are as educators is ultimately focused on their students and the engagement of their students in effective learning.

In closing, it is possible to point briefly to some implications from this research for post-Covid practice, as well as to some directions for future research. Clearly, teaching institutions cannot continue to rely on traditional and prescribed notions of classroom and curriculum organisation and operation. Teachers and students need to be regularly consulted about their experiences of the Covid years and their voices and views must be taken seriously. Areas that are likely to be important for organisational change are curriculum, materials development and assessment practices. Teachers should be given professional opportunities to be intricately involved in such change, through working parties, learning circles and practitioner research, that help them act more autonomously and negotiate viable ways to change. Organisations will also need to focus on teacher and student emotional engagement and wellbeing. In the case of teachers, workloads have expanded enormously and ways of avoiding teacher burnout will need to be sought. Educational managers should be conscious of needing to explain workplace decisions to teachers and support them pedagogically and emotionally through evolving working conditions, including the use of technology. For students, organisations will need to find creative ways to ensure connectivity, support their access to knowledge and information, and seek to value the abilities and skills students already bring to learning.

To extend the kind of small-scale research reported in this chapter, it would be interesting to ask the teachers to revisit their experiences of online teaching at regular intervals to trace whether and how their views have changed and to identify new challenges that are further reshaping their identities. Case studies could also be conducted with a small number of individual teachers to gain deeper and more prolonged insights into the nature of their ongoing thinking and identity negotiation, socially, cognitively and emotionally. Alternatively, a quantitative approach could be taken with larger numbers of teachers in similar circumstances through a national or international survey, possibly through a professional body. Such an approach would provide a more global perspective on the nature of identity negotiation undertaken by teachers of international students.

Whatever the approach, what is very clear is that intriguing possibilities for new knowledge, topics, and research goals have been opened up through the unanticipated advent of Covid-19. It is very likely that the field of ELT will become all the richer and more creative because of it.

References

Barkhuizen, G. (2016). *Reflections on language teacher identity research*. Routledge.

Block, D. (2007). *Second language identities*. Continuum.

Borg, S. (2006). *Teacher cognition and language education: Research and practice*. Bloomsbury.

Burns, A., Freeman, D., & Edwards, E. (2015). Theorizing and studying the language-teaching-mind: Mapping research on language teacher cognition. *Modern Language Journal, 99*(3), 585–601.

Darvin, R., & Norton, B. (2016). Investment and language learning in the 21st century. *Langage et Societe, 157*(3), 19–38.

Edwards, E., & Burns, A. (2016). Language teacher-researcher identity negotiation: An ecological perspective. *TESOL Quarterly, 50*(3), 735–745.

Feder, S. (2020) A cyberpsychologist explains why you can't stop staring at yourself on Zoom calls (and everyone else is probably doing the same). *Insider*. https://www.insider.com/why-you-stare-at-yourself-zoom-calls-psychologist-2020-4.

Gkonou, C., Dewaele, J.-M., & King, J. (Eds.). (2020). *The emotional rollercoaster of language teaching*. Multilingual Matters.

Kayi-Aydar, H., Gao, X., Miller, E. R., Varghese, M., & Vitanova, G. (Eds.). (2019). *Theorizing and analyzing language teacher agency*. Multilingual Matters.

Larsen-Freeman, D., & Cameron, L. (2008). *Complex systems*. Oxford University Press.

Mercer, S., & Kostoulas, A. (Eds.). (2018). *Language teacher psychology*. Multilingual Matters.

Miller, J. (2009). Teacher identity. In A. Burns & J. C. Richards (Eds.), *Second language teacher education* (pp. 172–181). Cambridge University Press.

National ELICOS Market Report, 2019. (2020). *Executive summary*. English Australia.

National ELICOS Market Report, 2020. (2021). *Executive summary*. English Australia.

Norton Peirce, B. (1995). Social identity, investment, and language learning. *TESOL Quarterly, 29*(1), 9–31.

Sherman, L. E., Michikyan, M., & Greenfield, P. M. (2013). The effects of text, audio, video, and in-person communication on bonding between friends. *Cyberpsychology: Journal of Psychosocial Research on Cyberspace, 7*(2), 3. https://cyberpsychology.eu/article/view/4285/3330

Sukhorukova, L. (2017). Visual organization of a screen space in multimedia design. *Vestnik, 2*, 32–35.

Varghese, M., Morgan, B., Johnston, B., & Johnson, K. A. (2005). Theorizing language teacher identity: Three perspectives and beyond. *Journal of Language Identity and Education, 4*(1), 21–44.

Yuan, R., & Lee, I. (2015). The cognitive, social and emotional processes of teacher identity construction in a pre-service teacher education programme. *Research Papers in Education, 30*(4), 469–491.

Chapter 14
Novice Teachers' Technology Integration and Professional Identity Reframing in the Chinese as an Additional Language Classroom

Yang Frank Gong, Xuesong Andy Gao, and Chun Lai

Abstract This chapter reports on our inquiry into novice language teachers' technology integration and its interaction with their professional identities during the first 2 years of teaching. In the study, we collected data through longitudinal interviews with seven Chinese language teachers in Hong Kong's international schools. The analysis revealed that the participants went through a developmental trajectory of technology integration, moving towards using it for diversified instructional purposes and with a greater orientation towards student-centered learning over the years. The findings also suggested that the participants' increasing technology integration competence helped them to reframe their language teacher identity and expanded the range of professional identities that were available to them in Chinese language teaching. These findings offer fresh insights into the dynamic nature of technology integration and its contributions to language teachers' identity development at the beginning of their teaching career. To better support novice teachers' professional learning and development, educational stakeholders need to recognize their technology integration as a process of shifting self-identification.

Keywords Novice language teachers · Technology integration · Teacher identity · Chinese as an additional language · Teacher professional development

Y. F. Gong (✉) · X. A. Gao · C. Lai
University of Macau, Macau SAR, China

University of New South Wales, Sydney, NSW, Australia

University of Hong Kong, Hong Kong SAR, China
e-mail: frankgong@um.edu.mo

14.1   Introduction

The significance of technology integration in language education has been a popular topic of discussion among educators and researchers for over two decades (Gacs et al., 2020; Zhao, 2003). Changes brought by the use of information and communication technologies (ICT) in language education have greatly emphasized the importance of the teacher's role in integrating ICT in teaching, and in facilitating students to use digital resources.

However, teachers have also been criticized for not effectively infusing technologies into the curriculum or using technologies to improve their teaching (Gong & Lai, 2018; McNaughton & Billot, 2016; Rice, 2021). Relevant research has identified two kinds of barriers faced by teachers in integrating ICT in teaching (Hew & Brush, 2007; Liu et al., 2017): 1) first-order barriers refer to inadequate contextual/ external resources, such as limited equipment, time, and teacher training and support; and 2) second-order barriers concern personal/internal factors that hinder technology integration, including teachers' understanding of teacher-student roles, curricular emphasis, and assessment practices.

Positioning teachers as 'inherently anxious and/or resistant' in terms of technology integration in education (Rice, 2021, p. 524), researchers have proposed different linear models to examine their preparation for and development of technology in teaching, such as Gray's (1986) four-stage model (Initiation, Confusion, Application, and Integration), Puentedura's (2006) SAMR model (Substitution, Augmentation, Modification, and Redefinition), and Koehler and Mishra's (2009) TPACK model (Technological Pedagogical and Content Knowledge). While this increasing body of research endeavors to investigate teachers' professional development and relevant factors influencing their actual classroom practices related to technology integration, the current literature seems to lack a dynamic view and a recognition that improving teaching practices is a complex process requiring teachers to develop 'the whole way they understand themselves, their world, and the relationship between the two' (Kegan, 1994, p. 275).

Consequently, it is critical for researchers to understand teachers' effective use of technology in teaching from the viewpoint of teacher identity. However, scant attention has been paid to language teachers' development of technology integration and its interaction with their professional identity (Chronaki & Matos, 2014; Rice, 2021). Teacher identity is a pivotal construct that reflects teachers' views 'of "how to be", "how to act" and "how to understand" the work and their place in the society' (Sachs, 2005, p. 15), as well as being 'a pedagogical resource' (Morgan, 2004, p. 174) for instructional practices. Existing studies have mostly focused on mathematics and science teachers' identity regarding technology use in the classroom (e.g., Badia & Iglesias, 2019), but the voice of language teachers has been little heard. Moreover, although novice teachers experience a process of constant shifting and becoming at the beginning of their teaching career, there is a paucity of longitudinal studies specifically designed to examine technology integration among novice language teachers (Tondeur et al., 2017). Therefore, this study was conducted to investigate how a group of novice language teachers experienced the technology integration developmental process in their first two years of teaching Chinese as an additional language, and how their technology integration practices interacted with their professional identity.

14.2   Literature Review

14.2.1   Teacher Development in Technology Integration

Teachers' personal learning and professional development in terms of adopting technologies in the classroom is embedded within the broader developments and educational changes regarding technology integration over the past four decades. For example, a few contributions have paid attention to novice teachers' use of technology in teaching. Russell et al.'s (2003) survey of teachers in the USA identified six specific categories of instructional computer-based technology integration: (1) technology integration for teaching preparation, (2) technology integration for delivering instruction, (3) teacher directed student use of technology, (4) technology integration for special education and accommodation, (5) email use, and (6) technology integration for recording grades. The results indicated that novice teachers preferred to adopt technology for preparation, while more experienced teachers tended to use technology to deliver instruction or to engage students in learning activities. Similarly, Nguyen and Bower (2018) found that novice primary teachers rarely thought or employed pedagogical strategies of integrating ICT into classroom teaching.

A number of longitudinal studies have also examined novice teachers' technology integration over time. For instance, Clausen (2007) explored two novice elementary school teachers' use of instructional technologies in their first year of teaching, and reported that they exhibited different patterns of technology use although they encountered similar challenges in the early years of teaching. In particular, one participant used technology in her new career to motivate and engage students, while the other participant concentrated on classroom management and setting up routines and did not consider technology as an integrative part of instruction. Clausen (2007) attributed their different profiles of technology use to the instructional culture.

In another longitudinal study, Tondeur et al. (2017) found that novice teachers adopted a wide range of technological applications, mostly for structured instructional approaches, while few created opportunities for student-centered learning. In Singapore, Gao et al. (2011) identified that novice teachers had different profiles of technology integration: followers (occasional use to support teacher-centered instruction), doers (regular use to enhance teacher-centered instruction), and emerging teacher leaders (regular use to enhance student-centered learning). They further noted that learning to teach with ICT did not just require knowledge, skills, and changes to the teachers' attitudes and beliefs; it also involved 'negotiating and constructing personal meaning and developing a better understanding of technology integration from their own performances' (p. 221).

This suggests that teachers' technology integration practices not only enhance their technological and pedagogical competence, but also help them to establish their professional identity and engage them in the teaching community. This is indicative of the need to broaden our exanimations of teacher's technology integration by adopting a dynamic, identity-based perspective (Chronaki & Matos, 2014; Rice, 2021).

14.2.2   Technology Integration and Teacher Identity

Identity relates to 'our understanding of who we are and who we think other people are' in a specific context (Danielewicz, 2001, p. 10). Identity can be considered as the 'being' that informs 'doing', where being is one's way of viewing the context and oneself based on certain attitudes, beliefs and values, and doing is the way of living proceeding from this (Taylor, 1989; also see Barkhuizen, 2017). Consequently, language teacher identity can be conceptualized as the being and doing of the self-representation and stances of the language teacher's own and their professional community's values, ideologies, and imaginations (Gong et al., 2022; McNaughton & Billot, 2016). It can be contended that the widespread use of technologies in language education exemplifies profound changes, altering the educational environment as well as creating challenges and opportunities for language teachers' roles and practices. Consequently, it is necessary for researchers to pay attention to language teachers' professional identity in integrating technology in teaching.

Recent decades have seen increased research interest in teachers' relationships with technology integration in the classroom, and researchers have emphasized the dynamic and shifting nature of teachers' technology use through the perspective of identity. For instance, Badia and Iglesias (2019) found that teachers' different types of competence in technology use, including technological competence and pedagogical competence, contributed to different professional identities, namely as constructivist or instructivist teachers. Meanwhile, foregrounding the potential of 'meaning articulation/making' that took place in a university-based training course for technology integration in mathematics teaching, Chronaki and Matos (2014) reported that teachers' professional identity construction related directly to their pedagogical competence in technology use. At the same time, the teachers' technology integration for mathematical learning was primarily driven by student youth culture, which accorded with the nature of digital natives' computer use in their daily life.

In one of only a few studies on teachers' technology integration in language education, Stranger-Johannessen and Norton (2017) found that an English teacher (Monica) from a rural Ugandan school viewed the engagement of digital initiative as social and cultural capital, which consequently empowered her role of reading teacher and her future identity imaginations. In the same vein, Trent and Shroff (2013) also indicated that the identities of a group of Hong Kong pre-service English teachers were shaped by their engagement with an electronic teaching portfolio, such as a 'modern teacher' identity (p. 12). While most of the previous research on teachers' technology integration and their identity in the classroom teaching has been conducted in the context of science, mathematics, or English teaching, nevertheless this research provides some relevant insights, and has motivated us to undertake our own inquiry on Chinese as an additional language teachers' technology integration and its interaction with their identity during their first 2 years of teaching in Hong Kong. The study addresses the following two questions:

RQ1: What are the developing trajectories of novice language teachers' technology integration?

RQ2: How do novice language teachers' technology integration practices provide insight into their professional identity?

14.3 Methodology

14.3.1 Research Context and Participants

In the present study the target population comprised Chinese language teachers in international schools in Hong Kong. The Hong Kong Government defines international schools as educational institutions that 'follow a full non-local curriculum designed for the needs of particular cultural and linguistic groups and/or for students who do not sit for local examinations' (EDB, 2017).

The international schools in Hong Kong mostly aim to foster cognitive and skill development in students to equip them to use new and existing technologies. Therefore, teachers in international schools often need to keep track of technological innovations and implement them in the teaching process. In the majority of Hong Kong's international schools, Putonghua (also referred to as Mandarin outside the Chinese mainland) is timetabled either as an additional language or as a compulsory second language until secondary age (Davison & Lai, 2007).

Seven Chinese language teachers from five international schools participated voluntarily in this research. The only criterion for recruiting participants was that the sample should come from a wide variety of international schools with different organizational structures and student demographic profiles, and that they should have diverse backgrounds (e.g., gender, school level). This sampling method allowed the researchers to gain a comprehensive understanding of the research issues and to prioritize the participants' different views. Table 14.1 summarizes the seven participating teachers' profiles; their names are all pseudonyms.

Table 14.1 The study participants

Name	Age	Gender	School level	Education background	Computer use experience in university
Tao	29	Female	Secondary	Master's degree	Yes
Jing	25	Female	Primary	Master's degree	Yes
Hua	27	Female	Primary	Master's degree	Yes
Wei	28	Male	Primary	Master's degree	Yes
Gang	29	Male	Primary	Master's degree	Yes
Liang	28	Male	Secondary	Master's degree	Yes
Yong	30	Male	Primary	Master's degree	Yes

14.3.2 Data Collection

Concentrating on novice language teachers' developmental trajectory of technology integration in classrooms and its interaction with their professional identity, this research sought to elaborate on and interpret their experiential accounts in terms of their technology use, from the commencement of their work as in-service Chinese language teachers to the completion of their first two-year teaching cycle. Individual semi-structured interviews were conducted with the participants at the end of each of their first two induction years. The two-round interviews were framed around several general topics that allowed room for the participants to talk freely about their own experiences and views, and which enabled the interviewer to delve deeper into each participant's account (Mishler, 1986).

The following topics were addressed during the interviews: experiences of technology integration in the classroom, current school culture regarding technology use, ways of technology use, changes in their technology integration over time, projected teacher identity (e.g., roles in Chinese language teaching), and perceived influence of technology integration on their identity construction and reconstruction. The interview questions were first reviewed and assessed by one expert and one researcher interested in technology integration in language education and teacher identity. Then, the questions and the technique were pilot-tested with two Putonghua teachers not included in this study, their interpretations for each item were checked, suggestions on wording were elicited, and the interview questions were revised accordingly. Individual interviews were conducted with each participant in their native language, Putonghua, so that they could express themselves freely. Each interview lasted about 50 min.

14.3.3 Data Analysis

All the interviews were audio-taped and then transcribed verbatim in Chinese and double-checked for accuracy. To compare and analyze the data from the first and second interviews systematically, we adopted the constant comparative method

(Boeije, 2002) whereby newly collected data can be compared to previous data that were collected in the same study. The researchers first read through the interview transcripts five times to familiarize themselves with the data; valuable parts of the text that struck the researchers as interesting or important to the research were highlighted and coded. In-vivo coding was used in the open coding phase. Next, similar codes were aggregated into overarching categories, informed by both the literature and the data. For example, 'beneficial for students' analytical ability development' and 'students' attitudes of active participation and involvement are the most important' were categorized under the higher-order node 'technology integration focusing on student-centered learning', while 'up-to-date teacher', 'old-fashioned teacher', and 'facilitator' were clustered under 'teacher professional identity'. The initial coding of the overarching categories was also compared across the seven participants to find close or repeated responses and contrasting instances (Charmaz, 1990).

At the same time, patterns and interactions between the participants' technology integration practices and their professional identity in Chinese language teaching were explored by reexamining the data and repeatedly referring to relevant literature. For instance, the links between 'mixing online games' and 'Chinese learning together as a way of encouragement' and relevant professional identity codes such as 'encourager' and 'guide' were analyzed, and these nodes were arranged under another higher-order node, 'interaction between technology integration and teacher identity'. At last, the categories and the interrelations among them were combined to generate a storyline to reveal what had happened to the seven participating teachers' technology integration and their professional identity during the first two transition years.

14.4 Findings

Overall, the analysis of the data identified that the participants changed their strategies for technology integration in Chinese language teaching, in terms of both instruction and objectives, across their first 2 years. With increasing familiarity with teaching procedures and routines, students and classroom management, the novice teachers integrated technology more frequently in their classroom teaching. At the same time, they tended to concentrate more on student-centered learning as they gradually improved their technological competence and successfully addressed technological issues in terms of their language teaching.

The participants' accounts suggested that their technology integration practices played an important role in reframing their language teacher identity. On the one hand, the participants' classroom use of technology represented one critical feature of their professional identity as a 'modern language teacher'. On the other hand, the participants broadened their positionings as facilitators, guides, and motivators in Chinese language teaching as they engaged with technology integration, which reframed what it means to be an effective language teacher. It should also be noted that school culture played a significant part in the teachers' development trajectory during their first 2 years of teaching, mediating the interaction between their technology integration and professional identity development.

14.4.1 Changes in Technology Integration Over Time

The analysis suggested that all the participants (7/7) broadened the range of instructional purposes for which they used technologies, and changed from a focus on teacher-centered teaching to a greater focus on student-centered learning across their first two transition years. Table 14.2 summarizes the types of technologies that each participant used, their approaches to technology integration, and the instructional purposes of their technology use in classroom teaching. It shows that the types of technologies used increased over the 2 years. In their first year of teaching the participants usually reported utilizing a limited range of technologies such as PowerPoint (PPT) presentations, online learning games, and online audiovisual materials, while in the second year of teaching almost all the participants started to adopt a wider set of technologies including collaboration platforms and apps.

Not only was there an increase in the types of technology used, but also the instructional purposes of technology integration became more diversified and targeted at different educational tasks. In their first year of teaching the participants mostly used technologies for classroom management, drills and practices, and delivering instructional materials. The technologies were primarily used to facilitate or enrich in-class instruction. However, in the second year of teaching they reported using technologies to address diverse instructional purposes, such as assessment, differentiation, student demonstration of learning, and student participation in class. Almost all the participants integrated technologies not only for in-class instructional purposes but also in ways to facilitate student learning outside the classroom. In addition, some participating teachers (e.g., Jing, Liang, and Yong) further extended their instructional objectives from linguistic knowledge to communication competence in writing and speaking.

Moreover, the interview responses demonstrated that the participants experienced a shift in their focus regarding technology integration from teacher-centered instruction to student-centered learning. In the first year of teaching the participants mainly focused on adopting technology to diversify teaching content in order to engage and motivate students, but in the second year they started to focus more on providing a bespoke learning experience to support students' learning needs. For example, Tao described using technologies in her first year of teaching primarily to engage students in class participation:

> [1] I think technology use is simply to arouse my students' motivation. My work is mainly about how to make lessons more interesting and appealing.

Table 14.2 Types and purposes of technology integration

Name	Year 1	Year 2
Tao	Online information searching	Using different online resources to promote students' critical thinking
	Apps for school activities	
		Encouraging students to approach video platforms to broaden perspectives
	PPT	Social media for sharing out-of-class resources
		Video website for engaging and motivating students
Jing	Online games for group competitions	Interactive whiteboard for interactivity
		Apps for speaking assessment
	Using video for cultural information	Quizlet for differentiation and competition
	Online flashcards (Quizlet) for vocabulary learning	Sending links for additional resources to students and parents for out-of-class learning
	PPT	PPT for visual enhancement and video for attracting students' attention
Hua	Facilitating students to search information online	Using online games for vocabulary learning
	YouTube for students	PPT
		Google classroom
	Using learning games (Kahoot)	Using YouTube to motivate students
		Video editing software
Wei	PPT	Quizlet for reviewing learning content
		Using Seesaw to listen to Chinese stories
	Quizlet for checking students' vocabulary learning	YouTube for engaging and motivating students
	Collecting teaching materials online	Apps (Pinterest) for designing worksheets
Gang	PPT	Zoom for teaching and learning online
		Student video assignments
	Online flash games for vocabulary learning	Google class for assessing the quality of student assignments
Liang	Quizlet to teach new words	Social media for sharing out-of-class resources
	PPT to engage students	Google meet for teaching and learning online
		Google docs to check students' assignments
		Using projector to exhibit model essays
Yong	Using PPT to engage students	Using apps (Seesaw) to manage student assignments
	Quizlet for Chinese character learning	Quizlet for vocabulary use in real communications
	Word format tables for Chinese character writing assignments	Using online worksheet for Chinese character and Pinyin learning
		Google classroom

However, during her second year of teaching she recognized that technology integration was a very valuable way to improve students' independent learning ability and critical thinking:

> [2] Technologies can help students see ideas from different regions, different cultures, and different people through their own efforts. This is beneficial for their analytical ability development. Hence, the students can understand things in their lives more really and objectively.

Yong reported using the same technology with different orientations over the 2 years. While he used Quizlet in both first and second years of teaching, his methods and objectives varied. At the end of the first year he recalled using Quizlet to engage the whole class and facilitate students' Chinese character learning. At the end of the second year, however, he reported that his use of Quizlet was more about teaching vocabulary for daily use, like fruit names, and promoting students' communication competence. He summarized this change in his account:

> [3] My former teaching objectives mainly depended on my own perspective of learning a language, but now I think learning daily words can be more useful for students. I find this issue after teaching two years, so I improve myself to be student-oriented.

Jing's account also reflects a similar developmental trajectory in her Quizlet use across the 2 years, moving from a focus on engaging her students in class to facilitating students' individual needs to develop and improve learning strategies that suited them.

The analysis above reveals that the novice teachers did show a developmental trajectory in their technology integration in terms of instructional purposes and foci in Chinese language teaching: from serving a limited range of instructional functions towards supporting more diversified instructional purposes, and from a primary focus on self-functioning to a greater focus on promoting student learning ability. An excerpt from one participant, Jing, is highly representative: 'At the beginning, I was concerned mainly about how to complete my teaching tasks satisfactorily. Later, I started to focus on how to make it fun. Afterwards, my attention shifted to how to make it fun and effective.' As Wenger (1998) pointed out, 'identification takes place in the doing' (p. 193). Technology integration is not viewed merely as developing teachers' technological and pedagogical competence such as technical skills and instructional strategies; it is also fundamentally connected with their construction of identity and teaching styles in response to specific professional and social requirements/discourses that position them as language teachers in technologized educational settings (Rice, 2021).

14.4.2   Technology Integration and Teacher Identities

Technology Integration as a Critical Component of Language Teacher Identity
One of the themes that the participants reported in their interview accounts concerned the role they believed technology integration competence might have

played in the development and enhancement of their identities as Chinese language teachers. According to specific contributions to classroom teaching and learning, teachers need to develop at least two types of competence in technology use. The first is technological competence, which is related to handling and adopting ICT as well as basic and advanced ICT applications; the second is pedagogical competence, which is concerned with the skills that teachers use to appropriately implement digital resources in planning and implementing instructional practices. All the participants (7/7) unanimously defined themselves as 'high-skilled teacher' (Liang), 'up-to-date teacher' (Hua, Jing), 'open-minded teacher' (Liang, Tao, Gang), and 'modern teacher' (Liang), and they all claimed that these identities were closely related to their increasing technology integration competence in Chinese language teaching.

For instance, Tao suggested that the use of technologies not only shaped her self-positioning as an 'open-minded teacher', but also represented her professional learning and development in response to educational change:

[4] I think handling technologies must be helpful for teachers. I also believe the technological development will continually dramatically change the classroom in the future. . . . I am an open-mined teacher and like trying different technologies such as new websites or apps.

At the same time, the participants considered technology integration competence as a critical feature to differentiate themselves from other teachers who were positioned as 'old-fashioned' or 'conservative' in their accounts. During the interviews these identities were usually linked to teachers who 'have very limited competence in using technologies in teaching' (Liang), who 'need to be taught and helped by young colleagues regarding technology use' (Yong), and whose experience of technology integration was 'often very difficult and painful' (Tao). Some participants, such as Wei, even sought out opportunities and resources to improve his technology integration competence in order to avoid being seen as a 'low technology teacher' (Wei) by the peers in his own and other international schools.

Overall, for participants who highlighted their desired identities, both technological and pedagogical competence were generally considered as an important component that legitimized their identity as Chinese language teachers. The participants who assumed they had an advanced ability to integrate technologies into their Chinese language teaching were often more confident, and thus tended to define themselves as 'a technical helper towards other colleagues' (e.g., Tao, Yong, Gang, & Liang) within the professional community.

It should also be noted that almost half of the participants (3/7) did not perceive that technology integration competence was an integral aspect of teacher identity, although it was helpful to improve language teaching and learning quality. Liang talked about his understanding of technology use in his second year of teaching:

[5] The technology is clearly very important, but it is not the top thing. In my mind, the technology is always the 'icing on the cake' (in Chinese '錦上添花'). As a teacher, you cannot say you cannot teach without technologies. This is ridiculous.

Even though Liang usually played a leading role in promoting technology use in Chinese programs and in helping his colleagues to address different technical issues, nevertheless he seemed to regard pedagogical content knowledge, such as 'writing on the blackboard', as a more important pedagogical basis for Chinese language teachers.

Technology Integration Reframed Teacher Identities

Over 2 years of Chinese teaching, the participants not only described the positive changes that they believed occurred in their language teacher identity development through technology integration in the classroom, but also, since teachers' instructional practices and their identities are 'mutually constitutive' (Stranger-Johannessen & Norton, 2017, p. 51), their experiences of using technologies and enhancing their technology integration competence also reframed what it meant to be a language teacher. Gang's view reflected the statements made by the participants:

> [6] I feel like a 'shepherd dog' (in Chinese '牧羊犬') in my teaching. When they (students) become lost or take the wrong ways, I need to guide them to the right path. The use of technology can change me to be a better 'shepherd dog', because technologies make my guiding more effective and my teaching clearer.

In practice, as Gang integrated technologies into his Chinese teaching, technology integration competence seemed to assume the status of professional capital in the teaching community. His identity as a good teacher was enhanced, and his other professional roles were also validated by this capital. In the same vein, Tao assumed that 'technology use in the classroom enhances my teaching roles such as an encourager and a guide'. Indeed, as the participants became more active and innovative in their use of technologies in the classroom, technology integration empowered their Chinese language teaching and thus expanded the range of identities available to them.

Nevertheless, their school's culture of technology use in teaching also played a significant role in teacher professional development during the first 2 years of their teaching career, mediating the interaction between technology use and teacher identity. For instance, Hua worked in a school where 'using technologies in the classroom is not encouraged', and she adopted few technology-enhanced activities to enrich her teaching over the 2 years. Despite her desired identity as an up-to-date and student-centered teacher, her use of technology was highly content-driven. For Hua, technology integration competence was not valued professional capital, and hence there was no tangible connection with her language teacher identity.

14.5   Discussion

Overall, the findings presented above illustrate the participants' technology integration development, and how their technology integration interacted with their professional identities during their first 2 years of teaching Chinese as an additional language in Hong Kong. Beyond generally indicating the novice teachers' developmental trajectories in terms of their technology use, this research also found that technology integration competence enhanced their professional identity as Chinese language teachers, and expanded the range of professional identities available to them in their Chinese language teaching.

Regarding the participants' technology integration development, this study has revealed that their technology use during Chinese language teaching went through a developmental trajectory towards diversification and student-orientation. This developmental trend was shaped by their developing knowledge and skills in classroom organization, classroom management, and activity-based instruction, as well as their increasing competence in handling and using different technologies and employing them in their teaching practice in the classroom. This finding echoes the results of previous studies (e.g., Gao et al., 2011; Tondeur et al., 2017), which have consistently highlighted the importance of promoting teachers' pedagogical competence in integrating ICT into language education and supporting their practical strategies for learner-centered instruction in order to elevate their technology integration abilities.

At the same time, in line with previous studies by Clausen (2007) and Nguyen and Bower (2018), this research has indicated that novice teachers showed different profiles of technology integration and had different concerns at different stages in their professional development. In this regard, technology training for novice teachers should adopt a developmental perspective that aligns closely with their developing teaching competence. Specifically, the initial stage of technology training needs to concentrate on technology use that interferes less with classroom teaching, such as the use of technologies for varied and meaningful assignments and enriched out-of-class learning, as well as the introduction of technologies that facilitate classroom management. Novice teachers should also be encouraged to collaboratively address potential classroom management issues related to technology integration. As they familiarize themselves with students and classroom management, technology training should gradually shift towards helping them to improve their practical strategies and classroom management techniques for technology-enhanced learning-centered teaching (Gong et al., 2021b).

In terms of the interaction between technology integration and teacher identity, this research found that through their technology use over 2 years of teaching, the participants not only reinforced their identity as language teachers, but also increased their skills and broadened their views as language teachers, which contributed to the construction of other professional identities as 'modern', 'high-skilled' and 'up-to-date' teachers. Professional identity development is closely connected with daily practice and values that inform ways of being (Stranger-Johannessen & Norton, 2017). In this context, the experience of integrating technologies into Chinese language teaching represented one means to reframe their professional identities.

At the same time, the novice teachers' commitment to promoting their students' Chinese language proficiency and creating innovative learning experiences made their enhanced and enriched identities more tangible and meaningful. Hence, technology integration should be not regarded merely as development competence; it should also be examined in terms of the constantly shifting relationships between teachers and technologies (Rice, 2021). These relationships can play a critical role in shaping and regulating the weaving of certain professional positionings and instructional styles. In addition, the potential of technology integration can function as a tool to strength novice language teachers' identities and prepare them as emerging leaders for educational change, especially in the context of the COVID-19 pandemic, where teachers were suddenly required to transition to online teaching. This is also helpful for the novice teachers to consolidate and move forward in their careers.

14.6 Conclusion

The present study has examined a group of novice Chinese language teachers' technology integration during their first 2 years of teaching. Comparison and analysis of their first and second interview data suggested that the novice teachers went through a developmental trajectory in the frequency and nature of their technology integration. At the same time, they perceived that increasing their technology integration competence made a positive contribution to reframing their teacher identities.

It should be noted that this inquiry only involved a few Chinese language teachers in international school contexts in Hong Kong. Some of the research findings might have been affected by the educational backgrounds of the participants and their cultural and teaching settings. This makes it imperative for researchers to explore the issue of teacher technology integration and examine influencing cultural factors in different contexts. Although our longitudinal interview data was collected over 2 years and various strategic efforts were used to enhance the trustworthiness of the research findings, what was reported might be different from what was experienced in actual scenarios. With this in mind, a mixed-methods approach using both qualitative and quantitative perspectives could be used to identify the dynamics of technology integration development and its interaction with teacher identity in wider teacher populations (Gong et al., 2020, 2021a).

Despite these limitations, however, we believe that the findings of the present research demonstrate the significance of examining technology integration in the educational context of Chinese as an additional language. At the same time, this research also calls for more attention to the contributions of novice teachers' technology integration practices to their identity enhancement and enrichment, and may help policy makers to refine teacher education and development programs focusing on technology use in the language classroom.

References

Badia, A., & Iglesias, S. (2019). The science teacher identity and the use of technology in the classroom. *Journal of Science Education and Technology, 28*(5), 532–541. https://doi.org/10.1007/s10956-019-09784-w

Barkhuizen, G. (Ed.). (2017). *Reflections on language teacher identity research*. Routledge.

Boeije, H. (2002). A purposeful approach to the constant comparative method in the analysis of qualitative interviews. *Quality and Quantity, 36*(4), 391–409. https://doi.org/10.1023/A:1020909529486

Charmaz, K. (1990). 'Discovering' chronic illness: Using grounded theory. *Social Science & Medicine, 30*(11), 1161–1172. https://doi.org/10.1016/0277-9536(90)90256-R

Chronaki, A., & Matos, A. (2014). Technology use and mathematics teaching: Teacher change as discursive identity work. *Learning, Media and Technology, 39*(1), 107–125. https://doi.org/10.1080/17439884.2013.776076

Clausen, J. M. (2007). Beginning teachers' technology use: First-year teacher development and the institutional context's effect on new teachers' instructional technology use with students. *Journal of Research on Technology in Education, 39*(3), 245–261. https://doi.org/10.1080/15391523.2007.10782482

Danielewicz, J. (2001). *Teaching selves: Identity, pedagogy, and teacher education*. State University of New York Press.

Davison, C., & Lai, W. Y. A. (2007). Competing identities, common issues: Teaching (in) Putonghua. *Language Policy, 6*(1), 119–134. https://doi.org/10.1007/s10993-006-9038-z

EDB. (2017). *International Schools in Hong Kong*. https://edb.hkedcity.net/internationalschools/statistics_at_a_glance.php?lang=en

Gacs, A., Goertler, S., & Spasova, S. (2020). Planned online language education versus crisis-prompted online language teaching: Lessons for the future. *Foreign Language Annals, 53*(2), 380–392. https://doi.org/10.1111/flan.12460

Gao, P., Wong, A. F., Choy, D., & Wu, J. (2011). Beginning teachers' understanding performances of technology integration. *Asia Pacific Journal of Education, 31*(2), 211–223. https://doi.org/10.1080/02188791.2011.567003

Gong, Y., & Lai, C. (2018). Technology integration into the language classroom: Development trajectory of beginning teachers. *Frontiers of Education in China, 13*(1), 1–27. https://doi.org/10.1007/s11516-018-0001-5

Gong, Y., Gao, X., & Lyu, B. (2020). Teaching Chinese as a second or foreign language to non-Chinese learners in mainland China (2014–2018). *Language Teaching, 53*(1), 44–62. https://doi.org/10.1017/S0261444819000387

Gong, Y., Guo, Q., Li, M., Lai, C., & Wang, C. (2021a). Developing literacy or focusing on interaction: New Zealand students' strategic efforts related to Chinese language learning during study abroad in China. *System, 98*. https://doi.org/10.1016/j.system.2021.102462

Gong, Y., Fan, C. W., & Wang, C. (2021b). Teacher agency in adapting to online teaching during COVID-19: A case study on teachers of Chinese as an addtional language in Macau. *Journal of Technology and Chinese Language Teaching, 12*(1), 82–101. http://www.tclt.us/journal/2021v12n1/gongfanwang.pdf

Gong, Y., Lai, C., & Gao, X. (2022). Language teachers' identity in teaching intercultural communicative competence. *Language, Culture and Curriculum, 35*(2), 134–150. https://doi.org/10.1080/07908318.2021.1954938

Gray, R. A. (1986). A four-stage model for integration of microcomputers in teacher education. *Educational Technology, 26*(11), 28–32. http://www.jstor.org/stable/44424759

Hew, K. F., & Brush, T. (2007). Integrating technology into K-12 teaching and learning: Current knowledge gaps and recommendations for future research. *Educational Technology Research and Development, 55*(3), 223–252. https://doi.org/10.1007/s11423-006-9022-5

Kegan, R. (1994). *In over our heads: The mental demands of modern life*. Harvard University Press.

Koehler, M., & Mishra, P. (2009). What is technological pedagogical content knowledge (TPACK)? *Contemporary Issues in Technology and Teacher Education, 9*(1), 60–70. https://www.learntechlib.org/p/29544/

Liu, H., Lin, C. H., & Zhang, D. (2017). Pedagogical beliefs and attitudes toward information and communication technology: A survey of teachers of English as a foreign language in China. *Computer Assisted Language Learning, 30*(8), 745–765. https://doi.org/10.1080/09588221.2017.1347572

McNaughton, S. M., & Billot, J. (2016). Negotiating academic teacher identity shifts during higher education contextual change. *Teaching in Higher Education, 21*(6), 644–658. https://doi.org/10.1080/13562517.2016.1163669

Mishler, E. G. (1986). The analysis of interview-narratives. In T. P. Sarbin (Ed.), *Narrative psychology: The storied nature of human conduct* (pp. 233–255). Praeger Publishers/Greenwood Publishing Group.

Morgan, B. (2004). Teacher identity as pedagogy: Towards a field-internal conceptualisation in bilingual and second language education. *International Journal of Bilingual Education and Bilingualism, 7*(2–3), 172–188. https://doi.org/10.1080/13670050408667807

Nguyen, G. N., & Bower, M. (2018). Novice teacher technology-enhanced learning design practices: The case of the silent pedagogy. *British Journal of Educational Technology, 49*(6), 1027–1043. https://doi.org/10.1111/bjet.12681

Puentedura, R. (2006). *Transformation, technology, and education* [Blog post]. Retrieved from http://hippasus.com/resources/tte/

Rice, M. F. (2021). Reconceptualizing teacher professional learning about technology integration as intra-active entanglements. *Professional Development in Education, 47*(2–3), 524–537. https://doi.org/10.1080/19415257.2021.1891953

Russell, M., Bebell, D., O'Dwyer, L., & O'Connor, K. (2003). Examining teacher technology use: Implications for preservice and inservice teacher preparation. *Journal of Teacher Education, 54*(4), 297–310. https://doi.org/10.1177/0022487103255985

Sachs, J. (2005). Teacher education and the development of professional identity: Learning to be a teacher. In P. Denicolo & M. Kompf (Eds.), *Connecting policy and practice: Challenges for teaching and learning in schools and universities* (pp. 5–21). Routledge.

Stranger-Johannessen, E., & Norton, B. (2017). The African storybook and language teacher identity in digital times. *The Modern Language Journal, 101*(S1), 45–60. https://doi.org/10.1111/modl.12374

Taylor, C. (1989). *Sources of the self: The making of the modern identity*. Cambridge University Press.

Tondeur, J., Pareja Roblin, N., van Braak, J., Voogt, J., & Prestridge, S. (2017). Preparing beginning teachers for technology integration in education: Ready for take-off? *Technology, Pedagogy and Education, 26*(2), 157–177. https://doi.org/10.1080/1475939X.2016.1193556

Trent, J., & Shroff, R. H. (2013). Technology, identity, and community: The role of electronic teaching portfolios in becoming a teacher. *Technology, Pedagogy and Education, 22*(1), 3–20. https://doi.org/10.1080/1475939X.2012.720416

Wenger, E. (1998). *Communities of practice: Learning, meaning, and identity*. Cambridge University Press.

Zhao, Y. (2003). Recent developments in technology and language learning: A literature review and meta-analysis. *CALICO Journal, 21*, 7–27. http://www.jstor.org/stable/24149478

Chapter 15
Tasha's Story: An Account of Transnational Black American Language Teacher Identity

Andwatta L. Barnes and Donald Freeman

Abstract This chapter explores one Black American teacher's experiences of adjustment as an English-medium teacher in a public school in Abu Dhabi (UAE), and how her identities shaped those experiences. Arguing that the racial dimension is central to Black American identity, and that the teacher's racial/ethnic identities as a Black American woman are inextricably bound up their praxis, this study applies notions of personal, professional, and situated teacher identity, drawn from Day and Kington's (Pedagog Cult Soc 16:7–23, 2008) teacher identity framework, to examine how as a Black woman, Tasha, adapted to teaching and living in the UAE. Findings suggest that her identity as a Black woman from the United States, an experienced classroom teacher, a reading specialist, parent, and member of a transnational Black American community in Abu Dhabi all played significant roles in her transition.

Keywords Black identity · Teacher identity · Expatriate teaching · English-medium teaching

15.1 Introduction

Without exception, teaching in a new context, such as a new country and with new students, requires a process of adjustments and it offers opportunities for identity negotiation in response to that context (Pennington & Richards, 2016). Teachers who are believed to have a strong professional identity are characterized by these notions of 'adaptability' and 'flexibility' (Blackmore, 2014, p. 156). While there are studies that center the ways in which English language teachers have transitioned internationally (Nganga, 2014; Tran & Nguyen, 2015) issues of race, racialization, and racism, particularly within inquiry topics of English language teacher transnational identity, are still rare. This is the case especially when teachers' identities are

A. L. Barnes (✉) · D. Freeman
University of Michigan, Ann Arbor, MI, USA
e-mail: barneslu@umich.edu

at the intersection of racialized and native English speaking; that is, their life-long experiences in sociolinguistic environments were in English and their experiences in English teaching involve adapting across national contexts that have their own racial hierarchies.

Substantial research evidence shows that being perceived as a Western expatriate (from countries such as the United States, United Kingdom, Australia, etc.) greatly benefits professionals in countries such as the United Arab Emirates, where there is a practice of determining salaries by nationality with Western nationals receiving better opportunities than their non-Western counterparts, with the exclusion of national citizens (Millward, 2016). However, being perceived as a Westerner or a native speaker of English is often "a proxy of whiteness" (Kubota & Fujimoto, 2013, p. 197), while not all 'native speakers' are white. Further, the experiences and perceptions about race that racialized teachers of English possess may be quite unique and shape their experiences as English teachers in very unique ways. In this chapter, I explore the teacher identity of a Black woman teacher, Tasha, whose identity as an experienced schoolteacher, a reading specialist, parent, member of a transnational community, and as a Black woman from the United States plays a role in her transition to teaching in the United Arab Emirates.

Interlude One – Donald Freeman
This chapter centers on Barnes's on-going project documenting the experiences of Black American women teaching in English-medium classrooms in the United Arab Emirates. Her work is both reflexive and reciprocal in the fullest sense: As a Black American woman, she has taught in the UAE and those experiences inform the core of this work. Her work contributes in important ways to our thinking and under-standing of language teacher identity. I am an interloper in many senses – as a white, American male and not having taught in this context. I have worked with Barnes periodically on this project, at times in an academic role and as a colleague fascinated by its richness and complexity. Here I suggest some observations as short interludes in this chapter in the interstices of Barnes' account.

15.2   Review of Relevant Literature

Literature on teacher identity is extensive and often does not result in a singular definition; however, the concept is usually described as dynamic, unstable, and ongoing and involves the interactions between a teacher and a context (Beijaard et al., 2004). Further, examining teachers' identities can be a way to help us understand what it means to be a teacher across time, place, and space. To explore the identities of teachers who traverse the international teaching space, it is necessary to examine how teachers' multi-layered identities support or impede their ability to adapt to a vastly different professional context than what they were used to in their home countries. A framework of racialized transnational teacher identity was con-ceptualized drawing on Day and Kington's (2008) framework of teacher identity and

Rios and Longoria's (2021) framework of Black, Indigenous, Teachers of Color (BITOC) identity which posits that social-cultural and racial dimensions intersect with other key aspects of teachers' identities.

Day and Kington's (2008) teacher identity framework, with its *professional, personal*, and *situated contextual* dimensions, was used to ground this study in the traditional notions of teacher identity. Teachers' beliefs about how they should conduct themselves and what should be valued in education are central to *professional identity*. The professional dimension shifts due to external influences such as social trends, policy changes, and significant changes in workload, roles, and responsibilities. *Personal identity* speaks to teachers' lives outside of school and is linked to family and social roles. In this dimension, the process of development is active and can be influenced by a range of external experiences, such as life experiences (Flores & Day, 2006), and internal experiences, such as emotions and personal factors. Personal identity also involves the sense a teacher has of herself as an individual, including her self-image and self-awareness. It draws on a teacher's background or history and biography (Nganga, 2014). *Situated identity* is socially located. In this study, "local context" is used to refer to the aspect of identity formed or developed within a specific institution or geographic location. The personal and social dimensions cannot be considered without considering the influence and perceptions of others and the larger, or national, context within which these interactions are occurring. In this sense then, teacher identity is intimately related to the social, cultural, and political social environment of the local institution and the larger society (Duff & Uchida, 1997).

Racial and ethnic identities are also important in teacher identity, particularly across transnational contexts. Sahling and Carvalho (2021) argue that gender and race influence how the culture in which teachers have immersed themselves is both perceived and understood by them, since "culture influences people as much as they shape culture" (Mason, 2014, p. 236). While Black American teachers often identify as native speakers of English, their identities as American and "native" are often questioned or marginalized, as is their competence within the English teaching field (Cooper & Bryan, 2020), because they are not white. Black American experiences as they become teachers are shaped by a sense of community, multiculturalism, Black identity as well as the student populations of Black and Latinx children in the United States (Irvine, 2002) they feel that their programs have prepared them to teach. It is these notions of power, agency, and racialization that play a role in Black American identity formation and in the way teacher identity is situated. Black American women teachers, thus, are positioned as both vulnerable and valuable in any educational setting; this chapter reports on one teacher who exemplifies this complexity of identity in context.

Interlude Two – Donald Freeman

Barnes' work embodies the concept of intersectionality (Crenshaw, 1993) and makes it palpably real. Her framework is situated at the confluence of powerful ideas about race, gender, national identity, and language use. I am struck by how the literature on teacher identity in language teaching that I have and relied on, skirts or silences these ideas. In the views of teacher identity, I grew up with the concept of whiteness as the assumed default that usurped other worlds and experiences. Whiteness is more than a racial designation; it is any ideological stance that has functioned as what Ruth Frankenberg (1997) called the ""unmarked marker'... that has been handed down to many of us ... as the norm, as ... transparency, as a national/natural state of being" (pp. 15–16). The adjectives that Barnes has to use to define the focus of her work as the experiences of 'Black American' 'women' teachers underscore and illuminate these normative assumptions of whiteness about race, gender, and nationalism that undergird much of how we think about language teacher identity.

15.3 Research Question, Methodology, and Research Setting

To investigate the interplay among the personal, contextual, and racialized identities through the lived experiences of Black women teachers, this chapter explores the research question, *How does Tasha's identity as a Black American woman teacher shape her transition to teaching in the UAE context?* A qualitative interview approach (Creswell, 2014) was used to explore how Tasha (a pseudonym), an English-medium teacher (EMT), experienced teaching English to Emirati primary school children in Abu Dhabi. Analysis of detailed interviews about her past and present experiences offer insights into the ways her identity as a Black woman shaped how she adapted from teaching in the United States to teaching in the UAE.

15.3.1 Abu Dhabi Education Council's Public Schools

The choice of the Emirate of Abu Dhabi as the setting for this study is based on personal experience. For several years, I taught English at the UAE's flagship university in Abu Dhabi. Although free, state-provided schooling and tertiary education are offered to Emirati citizens and English is taught in all schools. Ten years ago when I was teaching, approximately 90% of Emirati university students were reported as not proficient enough in English to learn content in that language (Badri & Al Khaili, 2014; Chrystall, 2014). The Abu Dhabi Education Council, or ADEC, implemented a 'New School Model', or NSM, as a set of school reforms benchmarked to education systems from western countries that were highly respected in the UAE (Buckingham, 2017). ADEC's aims were to use the NSM to improve student learning experiences and to raise the academic outcomes of all Emirati students to become internationally competitive (Baker, 2017). To do so, professionally qualified teachers from predominantly white, English-speaking countries were recruited to provide child-centered approaches to instruction rather than the teacher-centered approach traditionally used in the country's schools (Baker, 2017). In the UAE, nationals comprise approximately 14% of the population (Dubai Online, 2021); and only 36% of teachers in state schools are nationals (Statistics Center of Abu Dhabi, 2017). Others are from across the world, including other Arab countries, South Asia, and English-speaking countries around the world.

'Tasha,' a Black American and native speaker of English, was one of many American teachers hired to teach English-as-the-medium-of-instruction, or EMI, in Abu Dhabi's state schools.[1] Her narrative reveals how social factors such as gender and culture shaped her personal experiences as well as her interactions with others and her emerging professional identity.

15.4 Tasha's Story

For Tasha, leaving to teach in the UAE after 20 years of teaching in the US, 14 of which were at one public school in an urban school system, had been a hard decision. As a child, Tasha grew up as part of a military family that relocated to Germany for a few years and her father had been stationed in the UAE during the Persian Gulf War. As an adult, before moving to the UAE, she had not traveled internationally and very little within the United States, and she had never travelled alone. Tasha grew up mostly in South Carolina, where she attended a small, Historically Black College or University (HBCU), became a licensed elementary school teacher, met and married her husband, and became a mother of three sons. In the early years of Tasha's career, she experienced defining moments of racial bias and challenges to her competence, although she produced positive results in student performance. Tasha loved the last U.S. school where she had taught for many years, even ensuring her own children attended the same school, but she also worked at multiple jobs while teaching. She was very active in extracurricular activities for her students and her sons, indicating that she was the "head band mom," because one of her sons played a musical instrument in the school band, and she supported his participation in the school's chorus. Outside of her work and familial obligations, she attended church regularly. Her youngest son, a young teen, had accompanied her to live in the UAE. Her husband remained in the United States to ensure that their eldest sons' schooling was not disrupted with a move overseas; he would join her once the middle son had graduated from high school and begun attending university.

---

[1] The case study in this chapter comes from my research with Black American women English-medium teachers in government schools in Abu Dhabi, conducted over the course of 6 weeks in 2018. Five women took part in the study; this chapter focuses only on one participant.

15.5   Findings

The analysis of the interview data revealed significant factors that helped Tasha, an experienced and committed teacher, navigate her transnational from general education teacher in the United States to English medium teacher in the United Arab Emirates. The themes that emerged span the professional, personal, and situated aspects of identity. While these themes were not the only ones identified, they were central in the shaping of Tasha's transnational teacher identity.

15.5.1   Professional Transitions

As an experienced teacher before arriving in the UAE, Tasha's identity as an English-medium teacher was being reconstructed through experiences that challenged her own educational ideals. Her professional identity had been shaped by her training, experience teaching in the U.S., and her successes as a reading teacher. For instance, Tasha described the surprise she felt when she first saw her classroom in the UAE based on her prior experiences as a teacher.

> I'm used to having resources. You know, butcher paper and construction paper. {Shoot! Sound} No chart paper, no pencils, no nothing! Not even a library for books! I'm talking about in my classroom. I'm used to having at least a thousand books in my classroom that are not textbooks, and that just broke me down. It literally tore my spirit apart that I couldn't even have a classroom library.

Tasha believed that in order to effectively teach young children, she needed to be able to cultivate a love of reading in her classroom, which required a large and varied classroom library. Tasha's reaction to seeing a bare classroom is tied to both her identity as an experienced reading teacher and to her childhood reading experiences.

Part of Tasha's identity is as an avid reader and reading teacher. She values literacy and children's early experiences with print texts. Getting children to love reading was important to her because as a child she had fallen in and out of love with reading.

> I remember that point in my life when I stopped loving to read. I used to be the nerd in the family and I was reading *The Hobbit* and things like that. And my sisters and brothers called me weird all the time. I just remembered at some point, a teacher missed something with me and they didn't instill that imagination portion and a love of reading. And I hated it after that. I didn't want another child to come across my class and to feel like that.

She explicitly described wanting to help Emirati students improve their literacy skills. Her prior experiences of teaching elementary school children and her own educational experiences shaped her identity as both a learner and teacher. Her beliefs about the importance of children's development and the habit of reading to achieve success in school transcended her context.

> I don't care if it's Arabic as long as they learn how to read. These kids gotta learn how to read. They gotta learn to pick up a book and just chill with it. That's just nonexistent here.

Tasha tried to cross the cultural barriers with her students in a variety of ways. She had no familiarity with Arabic prior to moving to the UAE, but she was willing to learn. In the UAE, English is a *lingua franca* for daily interactions; it is also Tasha's content and the medium of instruction. Therefore, tensions regarding learning a new language are unlike those in other settings in which English teachers are immersed in other languages. Even though teachers like Tasha are teaching through English, they are still exposed to Arabic in the classroom through the students. Taking on the challenge of learning Arabic, she is able to do more than simply survive in her daily interactions.

> I'm learning. My kids teach me a lot. They're like if they have to learn English, they want me to learn Arabic. Today, I learned *bint*. *Bint* is a girl. And they said, "Miss, *walid* is boy." They said more than one. They told me how to say multiple boys.

Tasha also had to adjust her instructional style because of the culturally influenced expectations of student behavior. She taught in a way that both communicated warmth and had a nonnegotiable demand for student effort and mutual respect and she tried to connect with her students by drawing on her successes with students in the United States.

> I really wanted to integrate their culture into the classroom. I was big on that with Hispanic kids back home. For their final project...I have Sudanese kids and Jordanian kids...They had to choose one cultural event, about their culture. They could bring anything they want to bring. You're talking about food for days!

However, in this new setting, Tasha described the children as 'in need of attention' and needing a firm hand. Her first weeks of teaching in each classroom she was assigned to were challenging in ways that she had been vaguely prepared for. She explained that there was a common practice of moving teachers around based on student behavior, whereby teachers with more experience and those who proved to have a firmer discipline style could be required to change classrooms with teachers who were less effective. Tasha felt compelled to compare her experiences with Emirati students' behavior to Black American children's, expressing her objections to stereotypes about Black American children's classroom behavior as problematic.

> It was rough. It was rough...There was actually no support in the classroom. Like I said, my kids were horrible. The worst kids I...No. No one should ever talk about Black [American] kids.

In light of her students' behavior, Tasha applied her unique and culturally specific teaching styles to this new context. She believed that with time, her efforts paid off in contributing to the students' academic success.

A critical part of adjusting to teaching in a new context involves navigating interactions with students' parents. Tasha's experience with parents in the United States had been a mix of successes and challenges. In the UAE, she felt inadequately prepared to handle difficult interactions with students' parents. At times, this was due to the language barrier, where the parents spoke little English and Tasha spoke practically no Arabic, and different cultural expectations regarding disciplining children.

> Last year, two of the parents decided to come up on the same day and they were blasting. I knew they were angry and they had the worst two kids in the whole school. And they were just [yelling sound].

Tasha was active in her school community in the U.S. and could easily navigate familiar interactions with students, their parents, school leaders, and fellow teachers. In the UAE, she was a competent educator who had to discover what the new context's limitations and freedoms were. When she was confronted by parents regarding a punishment she had given their sons for misbehaving in class, Tasha described the assistance she received in addressing the cultural communication barrier. Her Arabic-speaking teaching assistant (TA) showed a willingness to advocate for Tasha's effectiveness as a teacher.

> My TA walks in. She was standing there listening, and finally, she took her fist and did it like this [slams fist into hand]. [Ms. Tasha]. Like this. This is what your boys need. And she is hard and she does not play. You don't play in Tasha's class. After that conversation, that lady [the student's mother] looked at me and she said, [Tasha uses Arabic-accented English] "You need anything, you let me know…"

Upon reflecting about this exchange, she said:

> Even as wild as their kids are…they're still parents and they love their kids and they want the best for their kids. They just don't know how to do it. They haven't been in education that long. They just go about it the wrong way and their genuineness for their kids and their love, it's there. You know so you gotta, as a parent, you've gotta appreciate that.

Interlude Three – Donald Freeman

The flow of themes in Barnes' analysis seems to me to be in itself a view of Tasha's identity as she enters this teaching situation – coming to her new classroom and school, which offers a window into her role as an outsider-teacher and centering on her students and how they behave in this setting. It reminds us that a classroom is not just a place and students are not just the people who inhabit it. In Tasha's observations, we see that classroom and students literally make each other happen in time and space. Likewise, she sees her teaching not simply as something she does, but as a fusion of who and of what. She sees her students through the lens of her instruction and what they can learn to do – to love reading. Who Tasha is as Black American woman and teacher centers these understandings. While these processes are not unique, they can often go unremarked, or they are attributed to dimensions of who the teacher is that diverge from unstated norms.

15.5.2   Personal Transitions

The interactions and experiences in the personal life of Tasha are intimately linked to the performance of her professional self. Outside of school, Tasha negotiated roles as mother, teacher homeschooling her son, long-distance wife, and active community member in a Black American UAE family. Although Tasha felt supported by her family and friends, and she was confident that her decision to take a job teaching in the UAE was the right one, she described an incident in the airport that revealed the onset of loneliness due to realizing she would be away from family.

> I was bawling, crying. The security guard had to stop me. She was giving me a hug. She was praying over me. I had never left my family, ever, ever. I had never left my kids behind and it was just a major breakdown. It was insane how bad I was crying. She [another Black woman ADEK teacher] saw me and was like, "Come on let's go."

She created support systems to make her transition to the UAE manageable and, upon seeing another Black woman educator preparing to fly to the UAE, she found comfort.

Tasha's personal identity as a Black woman in the presence of students who expressed anti-Black sentiments in her classroom put her in a precarious position. She believed that racial issues arose in the classroom, particularly those that seemed anti-Black, required her to intervene.

> You know, one of my kids called one of the other kids 'black'. I said, 'What? What do you mean black?' 'He black, Miss.' 'What're you trying to say?' He said, 'You know, Black!' He didn't really understand. He was being rude, but didn't know how to be rude with it. So, I said, what are you? He said, 'Black!' You know, most Emiratis don't call themselves black.

Tasha explained that this was the way she would have handled the situation had her students been American. She also described seeing familiarity and Blackness reflected in Emiratis as well. These encounters were not merely about national or ethnic differences to her.

> I went to one of the cultural days at one of the other schools and I sat down next to a woman. She was making these amazing crepes and she was amazed that I was sitting with her. She just kept cooking and she'd talk to me [in Arabic]. And I'm just nodding and smiling and I'm like look at this beautiful woman. I'm looking at her hands and this woman has worked in her lifetime. She's the real Emirati. She's the original one. I was just amazed. She was like my grand mom.

In having an opportunity to connect with the local community, where Bedouin traditions can still be found, she saw herself, and her family, reflected in the faces of an older Emirati generation.

In the ways in which she interacted with her students and their families, Tasha saw her own efforts as central to students' success. She worked towards developing culturally informed relationships with students by exchanging language lessons and working with their parents by working with her teaching assistant to ensure her students behaved responsibly. At the same time, she held herself, her colleagues, and their institutions accountable for students' academic progress.

Interlude Four – Donald Freeman

It makes sense that Tasha's experiences of being Black and racialized in these situations and interactions in the UAE feature in this broad category of personal identity. If the themes in her professional identity organize intersectional experiences, these personal themes foreground an intercentric one in which her Blackness anchors her life at school and in her community in the UAE. Solórzano and Yosso (2002) write that intercentricity is ". . . the premise that race and racism are endemic, permanent, and in the words of Margaret Russell (1992), 'a central rather than marginal factor in defining and explaining individual experiences...'" (p. 25). Barnes' analysis here shows dimensions of Tasha's intercentric experience, some of which are corrosive while others are affirming. Recognizing this commingling in her experience is an important aspect of the complex view that Barnes' work offers us.

15.5.3 Contextual Transitions

Being seen as 'American' is an aspect of living in the UAE reflected when Tasha shares her perspectives on race and racialization. She described how she navigated and adapted to this sociocultural and historical context as she talked about how well-qualified, professional, Black residents from other countries are positioned in the UAE.

> I think because we're American, they [residents in the UAE] respect us a lot more because they know we're educated. If we're over here, we're highly educated. They treat us better than the Filipinos and Africans. You know, most of the Africans are very educated, you know, more so than us, their degrees are just from the wrong place. It's sad. You feel sorry for them, they don't pay them as much, but at the same time, we don't get treated as well as the Emirati.

Blackness also figured prominently in her broader transition to the UAE, offering what Nganga (2014) calls 'transitional resources', a source of support as a Black international teacher transitioning to the new context. She immediately formed relationships with other Black American educators who proved to be key resources in helping those new to ADEC to adapt to the local ethics, values, and priorities of the school system. Having an extensive network of Black educators familiar with working in Abu Dhabi's government schools was key in her transition. Her participation in a community with other Black Americans was essential to her adjustment. She began forming networks with other new Black American ADEK teachers just prior to arriving in the UAE. Groups on social media became important means to manage her apprehension about leaving the United States to live on her own and abroad for the first time. This new community of educators – school leaders and teachers, whom she explicitly refers to as 'family' – offered an extensive support system without the professional hierarchies that she experienced in education in the United States.

> When you come over here, you get to build the family you didn't have at home. I'm not talking about the blood family, but everybody has the same goal here. Even the principals. I have a lot of principal friends, VP [vice principal] friends, teacher friends and it's not like, oh, you're just a teacher, I'm not talking to you...for the most part, we're struggling together.

In addition to forming a network of fellow Black educators, Tasha joined the teachers in her large apartment complex in a variety of activities and shared community-like responsibilities that deepened their bond and made their experiences in the UAE feel to them like 'home'.

> We eat dinner almost every night together. It's always at somebody's house or a couple of people cooking or whatever because it's just after...[pause] being with those little people...First of all, you need some adult time. Talk to people, but you've just gotta let it go.

Forming this family-like network was important. While she was open to building new kinds of relationships with her Arabic- and English-speaking colleagues, Tasha seemed to derive real joy from having regular opportunities to connect and build relationships with other Black Americans.

Interlude Five – Donald Freeman
As I read Barnes' analysis of how social context interacts with and shapes Tasha's experiences in the UAE, I am struck by how the classic themes of cross-cultural adjustment seem to poke through. But they are different here: They are refracted by the racialization of Tasha's personal and professional selves. When cross-cultural adjustment is focused on as a process, often the centricity of race is obscured intentionally or not. Barnes' analysis makes clear that this obfuscation is more likely a product of how people's experiences are being conceived and therefore researched. It is not that people bring their defined identities to this process of cross-cultural entry but rather that the process is a function of who the people are. In other words, Tasha's coming to the UAE to teach, what transpires for her, in working, in finding her community are aspects of her unfolding self as a Black American woman. Were I to live through these events and interactions, while there could be some parallels, much would be different; it would be my process of adjustment. The person and the process are inseparable. To borrow from Yeats', the poet's, line, "How can we know the dancer from the dance", how can we know the person from their lived experience?

15.6   Discussion and Concluding Thoughts

Tasha's adjustment to life in the UAE was facilitated through a combination of the personal, professional, contextual, and racial dimensions of her identity. Her identity was being negotiated in relation to her life and learning experiences with co-workers, students, her teaching environment, and her community of Black educators outside of school. Tasha drew on a range of these identity resources to navigate the transition to teaching and living in the UAE. She faced challenges and successes in the classroom while building networks to adapt to life in the UAE. The experiences shaped her identity even as the meanings she constructed from those experiences continued to evolve, and, like other teachers in international contexts, those personal experiences interacted with the social, cultural, and institutional environments in which they work.

When Tasha spoke about herself as an educator, there was an underlying theme of self-awareness and self-efficacy. She talked in race-neutral terms about being unprepared to begin teaching in this new setting in which no orientation was provided; of what 'good' instruction and sufficient materials in literacy and, setting up classroom were; and of the curriculum with its challenges of English-language accessibility and 'unrealistic' aims. In general, these themes are common across research on international teachers' experiences with adapting to a new context. Her identity as an English-medium teacher in the UAE was influenced by her commitment to her profession, her competence as a literacy educator, and her orientation to her local community. She began her journey confident that her professional background and skills as a mainstream classroom teacher in the United States would help her to be successful teaching in the UAE. She was confident that her successes in developing children's literacy skills and her comfort in handling their classroom behavior with a fair firm approach would show that she was the 'right teacher for the job'. However, she realized that English-medium teaching in Abu Dhabi differed from what she had been used to in the United States. Even though Tasha adapted her established approaches to language instruction using observations of the local context and she was not a trained ESL teacher. She showed signs that she was actively developing her cultural competence by integrating her students' culture into her practice — engaging in a language exchange, encouraging Arabic reading, and local food projects.

Part of Tasha's transition in the UAE came from recognizing ways the larger societal context was reflected in the local school context and her position within it. She talked about having privilege in the UAE as an educated professional, who was also American, which she contrasted with being Black and deemed 'unskilled labor' as a cleaner or domestic worker and from continental Africa. The racialization of other people who present as Black or African affected her own reflections of who she was as a Black woman. Her observations about her students' and the local community's elders reflected an awareness of the diasporic nature of Blackness and how she was linked to Emiratis through it. Jenkins (2019) would consider these observations as a form of collective racial solidarity that shows that "local and global struggles are connected amongst Black peoples" (Flynn, 2017, p. 262).

For Black teachers, cultural identity is a central part of who they are. It is important to acknowledge that to serve the needs of their students that their identity as "teacher" is not all that matters. Black teachers embody multiple layers of identity including their professional, practice-centered, and culture-neutral teacher identity (Rios & Longoria, 2021). In Tasha's case, her teacher identity is largely informed by cultural values in concert with professional practice. In the UAE, her teacher identity uniquely layered across other social identities. Research shows that teachers may experience tensions within and between their various identities, but these tensions between personal and situated identities are heightened by race. Additionally, when there is a shared racial identity but there is a difference in social status, as in this case between Black women from the United States and those from continental Africa in the UAE, "blackness takes a back seat and individuals highlight their differences by performing other facets of identity as primary (i.e., class, nationality, and regionality)" (Jenkins, 2019, p. 811).

Tasha's professional-personal network of Black American expatriates became her home community and gave her a sense of family and was integral to her navigation of a culturally unfamiliar setting. Howard-Hamilton (2003) argues that it is helpful to consider when Black women can connect with others who can support and validate their experiences. Mosely (2018) contends this sense of "community in the struggle" can help to decrease feelings of isolation among racialized expatriates in general.

In closing, I argue that Black American women English-medium teachers' experiences in this context reflect not only Day and Kington's (2008) notion of professional, personal, and situated aspects of their teacher identity, but also imprints of a complex, interrelated mix of life experiences which involve cultural and racial identities. The analysis offered builds on established concepts of teacher identity and extends these ideas with layers of racialization. I use the term *transnational Black American language teacher identity* to suggest that Black women teachers, who are usually bidialectal and often teach children of marginalized backgrounds in the United States, are specifically positioned to work effectively in multilingual, transnational contexts. Tasha's transition in the UAE was not uncommon. It illustrates the need to support practices that recognize teachers' unique histories and previous experiences (Peeler & Jane, 2005). It is important from the standpoints of both research and administrative practice to understand how Black American English-medium teachers negotiate their identities while teaching in the UAE in order to better support their classroom instruction as they learn unfamiliar work traditions.

References

Badri, M., & Al Khaili, M. (2014). Migration of P-12 education from its current state to one of high quality – The aspirations of Abu Dhabi. *Journal of Policy Futures in Education, 12*(2), 200–220.

Baker, F. (2017). National pride and the new school model: English language education in Abu Dhabi, UAE. In R. Kirkpatrick (Ed.), *English language education policy in the Middle East and North Africa* (pp. 279–300). Springer International Publishing.

Beijaard, D., Meijer, P. C., & Verloop, N. (2004). Reconsidering research on teachers' professional identity. *Teaching and Teacher Education, 20*(2), 107–128. https://doi.org/10.1016/j.tate.2003.07.001

Blackmore, J. (2014). Portable personhood: Travelling teachers, changing workscapes and professional identities in international labour markets. In R. Arber, J. Blackmore, & A. Vongalis-Macrow (Eds.), *Mobile teachers, teacher identity, and international schooling* (pp. 141–161). Sense.

Buckingham, L. (2017). Introduction. In L. Buckingham (Ed.), *Language, identity and education on the Arabian Peninsula: Bilingual policies in a multilingual context* (Vol. 1, pp. 1–9). Multilingual Matters.

Chrystall, S. (2014). The westernization of Arab pedagogies: Abu Dhabi attempts to move towards a knowledge economy. *Policy Futures in Education, 12*(8), 1101–1110.

Cooper, A. C., & Bryan, K. C. (2020). Reading, writing, and race: Sharing the narratives of Black TESOL professionals. In B. Yazan & K. Lindahl (Eds.), *Language teacher identity in TESOL: Teacher education and practice as identity work* (Vol. 1, pp. 125–142). Routledge.

Crenshaw, K. (1993). Mapping the margins: Intersectionality, identity politics, and the violence against women of color. *Stanford Law Review, 43*, 1241–1299.

Creswell, J. W. (2014). *Research design: Qualitative, quantitative, and mixed methods approaches* (4th ed.). SAGE Publications.

Day, C., & Kington, A. (2008). Identity, well-being and effectiveness: The emotional contexts of teaching. *Pedagogy, Culture & Society, 16*(1), 7–23. https://doi.org/10.1080/14681360701877743

Dubai Online. (2021). *UAE population and demographics.* Retrieved November 01, 2021, from https://www.dubai-online.com/essential/uae-population-and-demographics/

Duff, P. A., & Uchida, Y. (1997). The negotiation of teachers' sociocultural identities and practices in postsecondary EFL classrooms. *TESOL Quarterly, 31*(3), 451. https://doi.org/10.2307/3587834

Flores, M. A., & Day, C. (2006). Contexts which shape and reshape new teachers' identities: A multi-perspective study. *Teaching and Teacher Education, 22*(2), 219–232. https://doi.org/10.1016/j.tate.2005.09.002

Flynn, K. (2017). Reconfiguring black internationalism: English as foreign language teachers of African descent in South Korea. *Journal of African Diaspora Archaeology and Heritage, 6*(3), 262–283. https://doi.org/10.1080/21619441.2017.1385960

Frankenberg, R. (1997). Introduction: Local whiteness, locating whiteness. In R. Frankenberg (Ed.), *Displacing whiteness: Essays in social and cultural criticism* (pp. 1–34). Duke University Press.

Howard-Hamilton, M. F. (2003). Theoretical frameworks for African American women. *New Directions for Student Services, 2003*(104), 19–27.

Irvine, J. J. (2002). African American teachers' culturally specific pedagogy: The collective stories. In J. J. Irvine (Ed.), *In search of wholeness: African American teachers and their culturally specific classroom practices* (pp. 139–146). Palgrave.

Jenkins, N. D. (2019). Contested identities: African diaspora and identity-making in a hair braiding salon. *Journal of Contemporary Ethnography, 48*(6), 806–835. https://doi.org/10.1177/0891241619829210

Kubota, R., & Fujimoto, D. (2013). Racialized native speakers: Voices of Japanese American English language professionals. In S. A. Houghton & D. J. Rivers (Eds.), *Native-speakerism in Japan: Intergroup dynamics in foreign language education* (Vol. 151, pp. 196–206). Multilingual Matters.

Mason, M. (2014). Comparing cultures. In M. Bray, B. Adamson, & M. Mason (Eds.), *Comparative education research: Approaches and methods* (pp. 221–257). Comparative Education Research Centre.

Millward, A. (2016). *A critical overview of racialization in the United Arab Emirates.* (Working Paper). Centre for Ethnicity and Racism Studies (CERS). file:///C:/Users/AB/Documents/dissertation/UAE/Millward,%202016,%20Racialisation-in-the-United-Arab-Emirates.pdf

Mosely, M. (2018). The Black teacher project: How racial affinity professional development sustains Black teachers. *The Urban Review, 50*(2), 267–283. https://doi.org/10.1007/s11256-018-0450-4

Nganga, C. W. (2014). Teacher identities in transition. In C. M. Wilson & S. Douglass Horsford (Eds.), *Advancing equity and achievement in America's diverse schools: Inclusive theories, policies, and practices* (pp. 123–139). Taylor & Francis Group.

Peeler, E., & Jane, B. (2005). Mentoring: Immigrant teachers bridging professional practices. *Teaching Education, 16*(4), 325–336.

Pennington, M. C., & Richards, J. C. (2016). Teacher identity in language teaching: Integrating personal, contextual, and professional factors. *RELC Journal, 47*(1), 5–23. https://doi.org/10.1177/0033688216631219

Rios, F., & Longoria, A. (2021). *Creating a home in schools: Sustaining identities for Black, Indigenous, and Teachers of Color.* Teachers College Press. http://proxy.lib.umich.edu/login?url=http://search.ebscohost.com/login.aspx?direct=true&db=nlebk&AN=2734235&site=ehost-live&scope=site

Sahling, J., & De Carvalho, R. (2021). Understanding teacher identity as an international teacher: An autoethnographic approach to (developing) reflective practice. *Journal of Research in International Education, 20*(1), 33–49. https://doi.org/10.1177/14752409211005380

Solórzano, D. G., & Yosso, T. J. (2002). Critical race methodology: Counter-storytelling as an analytical framework for education research. *Qualitative Inquiry, 8*(1), 23–44. https://doi.org/10.1177/107780040200800103

Statistics Center of Abu Dhabi. (2017). *Statistical Yearbook of Abu Dhabi 2017.* Retrieved July 6, 2020 from https://www.scad.ae/Release%20Documents/Statistical%20Yearbook%20-%20Population%20-%20EN.pdf.

Tran, L. T., & Nguyen, N. T. (2015). Re-imagining teachers' identity and professionalism under the condition of international education. *Teachers and Teaching, 21*(8), 958–973. https://doi.org/10.1080/13540602.2015.1005866

Chapter 16
Revisiting Past Selves: Race, Gender and the Dynamic Nature of Language Teacher Identity

Luke Lawrence and Yuzuko Nagashima

Abstract Language teacher identities (LTIs) can be seen to be in a state of constant flux and development as teachers engage with students, institutions, and wider society. Even seemingly static and essentialised categories such as race and gender undergo a series of iterations as teachers evolve their identities, and the world around them changes. In this longitudinal study, the authors act as researcher-participants to revisit data collected through a duoethnographic process 5 years ago and employ a form of reflective narrative in order to evaluate how our respective teacher identities have changed over the last 5 years. Our findings indicate that through a process of gaining experience, concentrated academic study, aging, demographic shifts in the working environment, and a major realignment of global and societal values, that our identities underwent significant changes. By examining snapshots of individual teacher identities 5 years apart, we hope to show the value of revisiting past data in order to uncover how our past teacher selves relate to our present and future teacher identities.

Keywords Teacher identity · Duoethnography · Reflective narratives · Gender · Race

16.1 Introduction

In his comprehensive, composite definition of Language Teacher Identity (LTI), Barkhuizen (2017) states that "LTIs change, short-term and over time – discursively in social interaction with teacher educators, learners, teachers, administrators, and the wider community" (p. 4). In this chapter, we investigate the dynamic nature of

L. Lawrence (✉)
Toyo University, Tokyo, Japan

Y. Nagashima
Yokohama City University, Yokohama, Japan

teacher identity as something that is in a perpetual state of evolution and change, placing a focus on gender and race.

One of the difficulties of capturing LTIs through empirical research is that identities are not static. The poststructuralist approach to identity that this chapter embraces sees identities as fluid, shifting, and multi-dimensional based on context and social processes (Norton, 2013). In this understanding of social interactions, identity is understood "in terms of *who people are to each other*, and how different kinds of identities are produced in spoken interaction and written texts" (Benwell & Stokoe, 2006, p. 6; italics original). This approach, while recognizing the fluid nature of identity, can be seen to focus on an "in the moment" understanding of identity production.

For the purpose of this chapter, Bucholtz and Hall's (2005) three-level model of identity serves as a useful reference point. This model encompasses: "(a) macro-level demographic categories; (b) local, ethnographically specific cultural positions; and (c) temporary and interactionally specific stances and participant roles" (p. 592). The macro-level demographic categories that we focus on are those of race and gender; and the local context is that of a higher education institution in Japan. The key part of this model is the recognition of roles that participants play and the fact that these are temporary and interactionally specific.

In this chapter we revisit data collected through the duoethnographic method 5 years ago (see Lawrence & Nagashima, 2020) and use reflective narratives in the form of vignettes to appraise how our identities as language teachers have developed since that time. By focusing on race and gender, we hope to highlight the importance of these categories to LTIs, and also to examine the manner in which identities change over time.

16.2   Teacher Identity, Gender, and Age

Teacher identity in relation to gender has been widely documented in English Language Teaching (ELT) (e.g. Norton, 2013; Pavlenko et al., 2001) partially because ELT has been viewed as historically gendered predominantly as a female profession. However, in the context of east Asia, where this study is based, it is rather disproportionately occupied by Western men (Kobayashi, 2014), whose masculinity and male identity are treated as invisible and unmarked (Appleby, 2014). In this regard, when examining gender identity in relation to language learning and teaching, other social categories such as race, ethnicity, sexuality, and age need to be taken into account since one's identity is considered to be constituted with intersecting and multitudinous dimensions (Nagatomo, 2014).

Through the spread of globalization and the results of transnationalism, it is often indicated the ELT industry has been heavily sexualised and romanticised (e.g. Appleby, 2014; Takahashi, 2012). Especially in the context of Japanese ELT, research has documented the way foreign English teachers and English language learning materials have been heteronormatively sexualised and racialised but targeted differently based on the gender and race of the teachers and learners. Particularly, Piller and Takahashi (2010) postulate how White, male, native-English speaker teachers are "eroticized as sensitive Prince Charmings in marketing aimed at Japanese women" (p. 548) whereas white female teachers tend to be hypersexualised targeted toward Japanese men. Even in university-level English classrooms, such highly sexually-charged attitudes and behavior toward Western, male, sometimes much older teachers, have been reported to be rampant among female college students (Appleby, 2014). It has been suggested that these female students may see their Western, male teachers as "safe" targets to flirt with since they are academic teachers in higher education (Nagatomo, 2016).

Finally, ageism is another form of oppression that has been underexplored especially in ELT (Mason & Chik, 2020). Considering age as socially constructed, recent research has suggested that age should also be seen vis-a-vis other social dimensions, particularly gender. Gendered ageism, referred to as "double jeopardy", situates older women in a more socially and culturally vulnerable position within the intersecting power relations of age and gender (Krekula et al., 2018). However, Krekula et al. (2018) propose a more critical lens to conceptualise gendered ageism as "doing" and as a power dynamic, which signifies that ageism "is situationally and interactionally accomplished rather than a natural category" (p. 37). This enables us to critically scrutinise and question the conventional and normative view on gendered ageism since it adversely affects only aging women as victims. They posit that ageism needs to be examined as to how it could impact not only older women but young individuals and men in different ages in conjunction with multiple forms of marginalization.

16.3   Teacher Identity, Native-Speakerism, and Race

In her recent *ELT Journal* anniversary article, Kubota (2021) calls for teachers in ELT to engage in an antiracist approach and pedagogy that should "question power and ideologies that reproduce the system of domination and subordination and enact antiracism with critical reflexivity on power dynamics, one's own privilege, and potential pitfalls in enactment" (p. 241). In the ELT field, the main push for social justice has been concerned with the native-speaker movement and securing rights for non-native speaker teachers. The effect of this has often been the erasure of the stark differences that exist within communities of so-called native-speaker and non-native speakers.

In Japan, the native-speakerism debate is nuanced and complex. Holliday (2006) conceptualised native-speakerism as discrimination in the ELT field against those perceived as being non-native speakers of English, and an ideology that positions Western institutions and pedagogical practices as superior. This definition was expanded on by Houghton and Rivers (2013) to include discrimination against either native-speaker or non-native speaker teachers based on their linguistic status. This redefinition of native-speakerism was enacted against the backdrop of the Japanese context, where a glass ceiling is said to exist for non-Japanese language teachers (Houghton & Rivers, 2013). Although, raising some important points, this expansion of the concept has been criticised for focusing on discrimination faced by individual teachers and failing to take into account the wider political ideology that upholds the native-speakerism paradigm (Lowe, 2020).

It also fails to account for discrimination and marginalisation based on non-linguistic aspects of identity and acts to essentialise native-speaker and non-native speaker as monolithic opposites. Far from being a purely linguistic issue, perceptions of the idealised native speaker teacher as being white, from an Inner Circle country, and in the case of Japan, male (Appleby, 2014) remain steadfast. Thus, even within the privileged domain of native-speaker English teachers, there is a clear hierarchy that marginalises black teachers (Rivers & Ross, 2013), and in the context of Japan, female teachers also (Nagatomo, 2016).

16.4   Methodology

In this chapter we draw on two distinct methods of data, with data sets being collected 5 years apart. The first data set in each theme is comprised of duoethnographic dialogue between ourselves as researcher/participants (collected in 2016 for a separate project, but unused at the time), and the second data set in each example utilises a form of narrative reflection produced through revisiting the duoethnographic dialogue, presented as short vignettes and collected in 2021. Although our individual positionalities emerge naturally out of the data below, in brief, Luke is a white, male, so-called native-speaker English teacher, and Yuzuko is a Japanese female, so-called non-native speaker English teacher. There is an approximate 10-year age gap between us and at the time when the first set of data was collected, Luke was in his late-thirties and Yuzuko in her late-twenties. We both teach at the university level in Japan.

16.5   Duoethnography

Duoethnography is a still-emerging research methodology that involves two or more researcher-participants engaging in dialogic discussion in order to situate their own lived experiences as a research site within which to explore an agreed upon topic (Norris & Sawyer, 2012; Sawyer & Norris, 2013).

A series of non-prescriptive tenets underpin the theoretical base of a duoethnographic approach. These include, but are not limited to: a poststructuralist worldview that embraces multiple and dynamic aspects of identities, the disruption of grand narratives, and a commitment to social justice (Sawyer & Norris, 2013).

The poststructuralist approach makes duoethnography especially suited to identity research and has been used to this effect in the ELT field (e.g. Nagashima & Lawrence, 2020; Nagashima & Hunter, 2020). By focusing on and juxtaposing individual experiences, "duoethnographers may provide idiosyncratic counternarratives which disrupt dominant discourses" (Lawrence & Lowe, 2020, p. 12). Finally, duoethnography's adherence to promoting social justice aligns with the broad aim of critical applied linguistics, which this chapter places itself under the umbrella of.

Dialogic data is created by two researchers engaging in a series of conversations (either verbal or written) on a given topic. These conversations are recorded and transcribed in the usual manner concordant with qualitative research. The verbatim transcriptions are then reconstructed into coherent, accessible dialogues. This reconstruction adds an extra level of validity, acting as another stage of data analysis and a form of member checking.

16.6 Reflective Narratives

In the past few decades, reflective practice has become a prominent element of teacher education and professional development in ELT with a variety of frameworks available to reflective practitioners (Mann & Walsh, 2017). This is partially derived from the paradigm shift in teacher cognition research that now teachers are seen not as mere transmitters of knowledge to their students, but rather as producers of knowledge within complex social contexts through their personal, lived experiences (Johnson & Golombek, 2002).

Additionally, more research reveals that teacher identities and their knowledge and belief in pedagogy are intricately connected and influencing each other, and teacher identities can be placed as the central component of their pedagogy in practice (Kanno & Stuart, 2011). In this sense, inquiring into teacher identities in relation to their teaching belief and practice can be a useful method to further advance their professional identities and their praxis. Moreover, through recounting personal stories about their lived experiences with others, teachers build knowledge and understanding of the world and themselves, which can lead to transforming professional identities (Tsui, 2007). Drawing on Johnson and Golombek's (2002) definition of teachers' narrative inquiry as "systematic exploration that is conducted by teachers and for teachers through their own stories and language" (p. 6), this current study attempts to show that personal narratives in reflective practice (in this study termed as "reflective narratives") can be utilised as an insightful tool to develop and transform teachers' knowledge, beliefs, and identities in ELT. In this study, we apply this method to reflect on our own data of 5 years ago in order to take stock and chart our changing identities as language teachers.

16.7 Findings

As we revisited our data set from 5 years ago, three salient examples emerged from the data, which we present below as examples: minoritised status in the workplace, racial privilege, and student-teacher interaction.

16.7.1 Example 1: Minoritised Status in the Workplace

The following interaction is extracted from our discussion on gender and how it could affect not only our teaching practice in the classroom but also the workplace power dynamics. The English language program that we belonged to at the time of the original data collection was predominantly white, male, middle-aged, native-English speakers from the Inner Circle.

Duoethnography 2016 Excerpt

Luke: So, this university is basically all men. There are only two female teachers, and you're one of them. How do you feel about working in a mostly male office?

Yuzuko: Um well, I get along with them here, but I do have a problem with the fact that there are not many female teachers.

Luke: That's understandable. I remember in that faculty meeting when some of the male teachers were making suggestive comments about how they would be happy to teach the nursing course. It's a pretty blokey atmosphere.

Yuzuko: I think the problem is that they are not aware of what they are doing and what it means.

Luke: Right, but they are only not aware because it's such a male-dominant environment. If there were more women present they might be more careful.

Yuzuko: Yeah, very small things like that really bother me sometimes, but I feel I'm not really in the place to bring that up.

Luke: Why not?

Yuzuko: Because I know what they would say, you know, c'mon, it's nothing, it's not a big deal. And I also don't want to make a big deal out of it, especially if I'm the only one who'd be affected by it.

Luke: They would probably claim that it's just banter, as we say in England.

Yuzuko: So yeah, I sometimes feel out of place. I don't know how it's related, but I feel the same way about my language status. I feel like I never deserve to offer my opinions in meetings because I'm not a native English speaker.

Luke: Oh really? How so?

Yuzuko: Yeah, I feel like I'm not qualified. Even if there were something that I wanted to say, I'd just wait for someone else to say it or just stay silent. I feel intimidated because I'd be worried about other teachers and you know, they are mostly native English speaker teachers with extensive teaching experiences, although they are mostly nice and friendly people. So, I guess I could also say the same thing, if there were more non-native English speaker teachers here, I may feel less hesitant to speak up during meetings as well.

Reflective Vignette 2021 – Yuzuko

I was surprised to revisit the original dialogue to find out how powerless I had felt 5 years ago. In retrospect, I feel that I had been deeply ingrained with the native-speakerist myth which made me feel that I was by default an inferior teacher than others because of my non-native English speaker status. Now I am probably one of the most vocal teachers in meetings and daily interactions at work. I am also willing to play more leadership roles to take charge of other, still mainly white, male, native English speaker teachers in our daily teaching tasks. With more teaching experience, it makes sense that I have now gained more confidence as a teacher and feel more comfortable in the workplace. However, I doubt it is just time and experience that I have gained as a teacher that brought about such drastic changes. I feel I am more recognised and trusted by the director to assign me tasks that require a certain degree of expertise that non-native English teachers would not have been asked before. I have also been helping advertise the language program for media coverage. I had always felt that there would never be a place for someone who looks like me as a Japanese woman to represent an English language program in Japan as a teacher, so that made me feel validated. Another thing that I noticed while talking with Luke is that it does make a difference that now we have more female teachers than before and they are all vocal, trustworthy, and competent teachers that other (male) teachers do trust and rely on. It makes me feel legitimised and proud when female teachers take more leadership and decision-making roles because their expertise in praxis is valued and appreciated in a still male-dominated workplace.

Analysis

The original excerpt suggests that Yuzuko was struggling with the double jeopardy of her gender and language status as an (inexperienced) female and non-native English speaker in the workplace. Although Yuzuko speculated her experience of being minoritised as a woman and being a Japanese, non-native English speaker may be separate issues, they can be seen as interconnected with each other. While Yuzuko admitted its overall friendly working environment, her disclosure that she felt incongruous and silenced did not seem to be as visible to those who did not share the same minority status in the program, which can be revealed from Luke's seeming surprise in his response, "Oh really". In addition, her perceived invisibility was exacerbated by the native-speaker myth that Yuzuko had internalised that native

English speakers are inherently better teachers and thus a more valuable asset to the program.

However, the reflective narrative shows that gradual, yet drastic changes have been brought about in her teacher identity. With more teaching knowledge and experiences, she seems to have gained a greater degree of confidence and comfort in articulating herself at work. Reciprocally, she indicates that she has gained more trust from others including her supervisor and in turn, her job quality has also shifted, which makes Yuzuko feel more visible and validated regardless of her prescribed language status as a non-native English speaker. Moreover, the increase in the number of female teachers in the program seems to help her feel more comfortable and prouder, which motivates her to engage more actively in building her career further. This is exemplified with Yuzuko demonstrating more leadership roles along with other female teachers in the workplace. This example illustrates the way in which teacher identity is developed socially and discursively in relation to others in interaction, beyond the extent of individual conscious efforts and consequential experiences and knowledge. It also illuminates that systemic oppression is often-times intertwined with multiple forms of marginalization, including gender, language status, and possibly others such as age, race, and nationality in a local context.

16.7.2   Example 2: Racial Privilege

In this second example, we examine Luke's underdeveloped understanding of racial privilege (as well as gender) as a white man, as he conflates discrimination against "native speaker" teachers in Japan with globalised forms of systemic oppression. From the original data set, we join the conversation as Luke is questioning why there is not more protest from "native speaker" teachers experiencing discrimination in Japan:

Duoethnography 2016 Excerpt

Luke:	There is not really any proper push to change the system from anyone, from native speakers, from anywhere. Why not? Where's the hashtag "native speaker lives matter"? I don't know... I don't understand why it's accepted on all sides.
Yuzuko:	(long pause). I'm not really sure we are talking about the same thing.
Luke:	I think we are. My idea is that we know that there's a problem and there's a glass ceiling and there's not equality for native speaker teachers, but people don't try to do anything about it.
Yuzuko:	Many Japanese people probably don't really agree with that about (white) native speaker teachers.
Luke:	OK, but why aren't the native speakers trying to do something about it? Where are the protests and the movements?
Yuzuko:	I don't know.

Luke:	Also, do you think there are some parallels between like the kind of microaggressions that women face and the kind of microaggressions that foreigners or native speaker teachers face on a daily basis? (long pause, no answer). It seems to me they're very similar. (long pause, no answer). Not really big things, but you know, little comments here, little comments there. Do you think there are parallels between the two experiences?
Yuzuko:	Hm, yeah, I am not sure. Can you give me any examples?
Luke:	Just the idea that you can't do something because you are a woman. I think people have the same idea that 'you can't do this because you're a foreigner'.
Yuzuko:	(skeptically) Hmm maybe... I mean, the microaggressions against women come from systemic oppression, so...

Reflective Vignette 2021 – Luke

Listening back to the discussion now, I feel quite ashamed to hear my naivety and arrogance. Far from the simplistic understanding of the "native speaker" as a single monolithic entity, I am now aware of the oppression and discrimination perpetrated against English teachers that do not fit into the idealized image of the, white, male with a prestige accent from an inner circle country.

Five years ago, I was heavily influenced by the alternative definition of native-speakerism that was propagated by Houghton and Rivers. Since then, I have come to understand that this rendering of native-speakerism fails to attend to the systemic discrimination facing "non-native speakers", whilst at the same time failing to distinguish between differences in "native speaker" teachers.

In the last 5 years, through study at the Doctorate level (prompted by this project), I have dedicated myself to reading deeply on issues of race and gender as they relate to native-speakerism and the ELT field. Also, like most people, I have also been affected by the global conversation on systemic racism that has emerged in the wake of the murder of George Floyd. In addition, through participating in a number of research projects with my regular co-author (Yuzuko) I have come to a new understanding of the nature of racial and gender privilege and the complexity of the native-speakerism debate. Through this research and my classroom pedagogy, I have attempted to use this privilege to expose inequalities and explore the experiences of marginalised members of the ELT community.

Analysis

It seems clear that at the time of the first data collection, Luke positioned himself as a "native speaker" English teacher that was part of an oppressed minority in the context of Japanese society. By suggesting that there should be a #nativespeakerlivesmatter movement and directly comparing the experiences of native speakers in Japan to the global oppression of women, he positioned the "native speaker" as a monolithic entity. This erased the racial hierarchies that exist within the category of "native speaker" and failed to recognise his privilege as a white, male, native speaker English teacher. In addition, his insistence on the parallels between the treatment of "native speakers" in Japan and the global discrimination against women ignored the systemic nature of patriarchal female oppression.

In his reflective vignette, Luke acknowledges these past failings and repositions his identity as not simply a "native speaker" English teacher, but as a white, male, "native speaker" English teacher. By acknowledging the privileged status that his race and gender allow in a global hierarchy that places the white, male, inner circle teacher as the idealised language teacher, Luke shifts the parameters and possibilities of his language teacher identity. These possibilities extend to a feeling of responsibility to utilise this privilege for the purposes of social justice in the ELT field. This is an outcome that would not have been possible without a fundamental repositioning of his own identity position and participant role (Bucholtz & Hall, 2005) as a language teacher and researcher.

16.7.3   Example 3: Student-Teacher Interaction

In this final example, we discuss student-teacher classroom dynamics and the somewhat taboo topic of flirtatious interactions by students towards their teachers. In this short extract, aspects of race, gender, age and native-speaker status are all touched upon.

Duoethnography 2016 Excerpt

Luke: Do you think that a lot of students flirt with their teachers, and is that just part of the dynamics of a language classroom?

Yuzuko: Um, I'm not sure but I think some students do... flirtation... that's a hard word to define but um, sometimes it feels like it's expected to be kind of part of our job.

Luke: Right, it does seem to be part of being a teacher, and I don't know how I feel about it.

Yuzuko: Yeah, it kind of makes me feel uncomfortable, but I guess it doesn't bother me as much as I get older because it can't be real, you know, it's obvious that they can't be anything serious because now I am getting much older than my students.

Luke: Yeah, I think as I get older there is less of a sexualised or romantic element to it, which is good for me, but I think there is still a residual amount there. From the students, I mean, not from my side, of course! I think it still exists, even though I'm more than double their age. I don't know how I feel about it. I mean, when it comes to eikaiwa*, it's seen as accepted practice, but even at the university level, I think it's there, too.

	Maybe it's in all forms of language teaching, I don't know. Do you get asked by your students if you have a boyfriend, or if you are married?

Yuzuko: Sure, like "What's your type?"

Luke: Yeah. "Do you like Japanese girls?" I often get asked that.

Yuzuko: Really?

Luke: Sure. Even by female students... especially by female students. Maybe students seem to think it is somehow more acceptable to be more friendly and personal towards foreign teachers.

Yuzuko: That's a good point, I've never thought of that before. I wonder if this is ever gonna change, you know, as we get older?

Luke: Right, I guess it will. Although, it might be less so for white, foreign men like me. That seems to be the usual way.

Yuzuko: Yeah, I do find myself wondering about that sometimes cuz students generally seem to enjoy my class and my teaching now, but it makes me wonder, is this just because I'm young?

Luke: It's terrible to say, but I think it's probably part of it.

Yuzuko: So, does that mean students will like me less as I get older?

Luke: Maybe. I suppose it's different for men, though. I'm nearly 10 years older than you and it doesn't seem to have changed too much for me in the last 10 years.

Yuzuko: I don't know, maybe it's just part of the English education system.

Luke: But should it be? I suppose it's because the whole identity of the teacher goes into the classroom isn't it?

*commercial English conversation schools prevalent in Japan.

Reflective Vignette 2021
Yuzuko

It is quite a striking difference that the way students interact with me in the classroom has drastically changed over the 5 years. I feel that most students now see me just as a teacher and respect where the boundaries are set. Barely any students would attempt to ask me flirtatious, personal, oftentimes heteronormative questions or comments, particularly from male students. Now that I think about it, this may be related to the fact that I now foreground my Japanese or bilingual/bicultural self a lot more instead of the American persona that I used to think was important to present as an English teacher. I wonder if this is connected to the stronger sense of authority that I am able to manage in the classroom now. I still feel the same way that these possibly flirtatious interactions would make me feel uncomfortable and somewhat disrespected, especially if it were initiated by male students. You could probably say this is an example of the gendered aspect of ageism that it affects women differently and unequally than men, and I seem to no longer be their sexualised and romanticised object because of my aging process. But I would have to say this change helps me feel less tense and anxious in the classroom and has helped me build a stronger sense of professionalism as a language teacher in the classroom. I think I am pretty lucky that the students' lack of interest or curiosity about my personal life does not seem to influence how they see me as a teacher. They still interact with me actively and seem to genuinely enjoy my classes regardless of their gender. Maybe you can call it a positive aspect of gendered ageism in this case, but I wonder if it stays the same as I continue to age.

Luke

In contrast to Yuzuko, I don't feel like much has changed in the 5 years since we had this conversation. Despite the fact that I am now in my mid-forties and probably very close to the age of my students' parents, I still get similar questions from my students about my relationship status, age and other things. Since 2016, I have become very active in terms of academic research and I think that this aspect of my teacher identity is more prominent in the classroom. For example, when I introduce myself at the beginning of the year, I used to focus on personal aspects such as hobbies, interests and length of time in Japan. This has been replaced by an introduction that focuses on my teaching philosophy and research interests, with a brief mention of interests at the end. I don't know if this is a subconscious attempt to present a more professional "university teacher" persona to my students, but if so, it appears to be only partially successful. Although we used the ambiguous and slightly suggestive word "flirting" in our original discussion, I'm not sure if that is the correct word for this kind of behaviour as I experience it now (and also then, maybe), but I can't think of a better word either. As I get further and further from the age of my students, and possibly also as the researcher side of my teacher identity grows, I definitely feel more uncomfortable with and less tolerant of these kinds of interactions.

Analysis
This theme touched on a complex intersection of a number of identity aspects. In the initial conversation, both Yuzuko and Luke revealed that they do feel that there is a certain amount of student-led flirtatious interactions that may be seen as part of the dynamics of all language classrooms. With Luke as a white, male, native-speaker teacher, he speculated that students may feel more emboldened to interact with him playfully and in a personal manner. For Yuzuko, it was her relative youth that allowed students to feel able to ask personal questions. Added to this was the fact that in 2016, she was still fresh from being in the United States for an extended period and her American persona was stronger than it is now, making her a pseudo native-speaker in the eyes of the students. These similarities of 5 years ago were completely changed in the 2021 vignettes. For Luke, although he is now 5 years older and has attempted to present a more professional teacher persona to his students, by emphasising his academic research, he feels that little has changed. However, for Yuzuko, despite the fact that she is still 4 years younger than Luke was 5 years ago, she reports that she no longer receives personal questions from students and that they see her simply as a teacher. This points to a gendered, native-speakerist, ageist aspect to teacher identity construction that sexualises young female teachers and fetishises white, male teachers regardless of age or professional standing. This highlights global systems of gender and age discrimination that devalue female teachers over a certain age and favours white, male, native speaker teachers. However, in this instance, being freed of

potentially uncomfortable situations is seen by Yuzuko as a positive aspect of gendered ageism in the classroom context. Similarly, this privilege extended to white, male teachers in the Japanese context is seen by Luke as something that he is struggling to change as he attempts to reposition his teacher identity to accommodate a more professional teacher/researcher role.

16.8 Conclusion

As the data shows, LTIs are constantly changing and evolving over time, through social interaction, and can be agentive or structured. By revisiting and reflecting on data that represented a previous incarnation of our teacher identities we were able to track these changes even with seemingly fixed aspects of identity such as race and gender.

Drawing on Bucholtz and Hall (2005), we can understand that the changes in our teacher identities that we observed in reflective narratives also occurred in the three-level model of identity. First, the macro-level demographic categories, the social contexts and processes that we were surrounded by changed over time in that societal conventions and norms seem to become more critical regarding sociopolitical issues including gender and race on a global scale. For example, Luke opens up that his more critical understanding of his own positioning in relation to power and privileges based on his race and gender has been impacted by the global conversation surrounding race and privilege that has occurred in recent years. For Yuzuko, the drastic changes that she experienced in the gender dynamics in the workplace is in part due to the increase in the number of female teachers in the language program, which can be seen as an active response to a global call for gender equality and equity.

In terms of our local, ethnographically specific cultural positions, the fetishization of the white, male English teacher that appears to be still strong in Japan has served as a barrier to any meaningful change in Luke's teacher/student interactions, despite the passage of time. In contrast to this, Yuzuko's repositioning as an older, experienced, female teacher, with less attachment to a pseudo-American persona has allowed her identity to shift in a more positive, professional direction.

Finally, the temporary stances and roles that determined our LTI positions can be seen most clearly in Luke's ontological shift in his understandings of race and privilege as it pertains to language teacher identity. It can also be seen in Yuzuko's increased confidence in taking on leadership and decision-making roles in the department and the positive impact on her identity of an increase in the number of female colleagues.

By viewing teacher identities as fluid, dynamic, and in constant flux in relation to macro, meso and micro levels of interaction, we can come to new understandings of language teacher identity. Taking a longitudinal approach by exploring different aspects of our identities 5 years apart we were able to take stock of not only personal and professional changes in our LTIs, but also wider social, cultural, and political shifts that contributed to these changes.

References

Appleby, R. (2014). *Men and masculinities in global English language teaching*. Palgrave Macmillan.

Barkhuizen, G. (2017). Language teacher identity research: An introduction. In G. Barkhuizen (Ed.), *Reflections on language teacher identity research* (pp. 1–11). Routledge.

Benwell, B., & Stokoe, E. (2006). *Discourse and identity*. Edinburgh University Press.

Bucholtz, M., & Hall, K. (2005). Identity and interaction: A sociocultural linguistic approach. *Discourse Studies, 7*(4–5), 585–614. https://doi.org/10.1177/1461445605054407

Holliday, A. (2006). Native-speakerism. *ELT Journal, 60*(4), 385–387. https://doi.org/10.1093/elt/ccl030

Houghton, S. A., & Rivers, D. J. (2013). Introduction: Redefining native-speakerism. In S. A. Houghton & D. J. Rivers (Eds.), *Native-speakerism in Japan: Intergroup dynamics in foreign language education* (pp. 1–14). Multilingual Matters.

Johnson, K. E., & Golombek, P. R. (2002). *Teachers' narrative inquiry as professional development*. Cambridge University Press.

Kanno, Y., & Stuart, C. (2011). Learning to become a second language teacher: Identities-in-practice. *The Modern Language Journal, 95*(2), 236–252. https://doi.org/10.1111/j.1540-4781.2011.01178.x

Kobayashi, Y. (2014). Gender gap in the EFL classroom in East Asia. *Applied Linguistics, 35*(2), 219–223. https://doi.org/10.1093/applin/amu008

Krekula, C., Nikander, P., & Wilinska, M. (2018). Multiple marginalizations based on age: Gendered ageism and beyond. In L. Ayalon & C. Tesch-Romer (Eds.), *Contemporary perspectives on ageism* (pp. 33–50). Springer.

Kubota, R. (2021). Critical antiracist pedagogy in ELT. *ELT Journal, 75*(3), 237–246. https://doi.org/10.1093/elt/ccab015

Lawrence, L., & Lowe, R. J. (2020). An introduction to duoethnography. In R. J. Lowe & L. Lawrence (Eds.), *Duoethnography in English language teaching: Research, reflection and classroom application* (pp. 1–26). Multilingual Matters.

Lawrence, L., & Nagashima, Y. (2020). The intersectionality of gender, sexuality, race, and native-speakerness: Investigating teacher identity through duoethnography. *Journal of Language, Identity & Education, 19*(1), 42–55. https://doi.org/10.1080/15348458.2019.1672173

Lowe, R. J. (2020). *Uncovering ideology in English language teaching: Identifying the 'native speaker' frame*. Springer.

Mann, S., & Walsh, S. (2017). *Reflective practice in English language teaching: Research-based principles and practices*. Routledge.

Mason, S. L., & Chik, A. (2020). Age, gender and language teacher identity: Narratives from higher education. *Sexuality & Culture, 24*, 1028–1045. https://doi.org/10.1007/s12119-020-09749-x

Nagashima, Y., & Hunter, C. (2020). Critical ELT in Japan: A duoethnographic exploration of origins, identities, obstacles and concerns. In R. J. Lowe & L. Lawrence (Eds.), *Duoethnography in English language teaching: Research, reflection and classroom application* (pp. 50–70). Multilingual Matters.

Nagashima, Y., & Lawrence, L. (2020). *To translanguage or not to translanguage: Ideology, practice, and intersectional identities*. Applied Linguistics Review. Advance online publication. https://doi.org/10.1515/applirev-2019-0040.

Nagatomo, D. H. (2014). In the ivory tower and out of the loop: Racialized and gendered identities of university EFL teachers in Japan. In Y. L. Cheung, S. B. Said, & K. Park (Eds.), *Advances and current trends in language teacher identity research* (pp. 102–115). Routledge.

Nagatomo, D. H. (2016). *Identity, gender, and teaching English in Japan*. Multilingual Matters.

Norris, J., & Sawyer, R. D. (2012). Towards a dialogic methodology. In J. Norris, R. D. Sawyer, & D. E. Lund (Eds.), *Duoethnography: Dialogic methods for social, health and educational research* (pp. 9–40). Left Coast Press Inc.

Norton, B. (2013). *Identity and language learning: Extending the conversation* (2nd ed.). Multilingual Matters.

Pavlenko, A., Blackledge, A., Piller, I., & Teutsch-Dwyer, M. (Eds.). (2001). *Multilingualism, second language learning, and gender.* Mouton de Gruyter.

Piller, I., & Takahashi, L. (2010). At the intersection of gender, language, and transnationalism. In N. Coupland (Ed.), *The handbook of language and globalization* (pp. 540–554). Wiley-Blackwell.

Rivers, D. J., & Ross, A. S. (2013). Idealized English teachers: The implicit influence of race in Japan. *Journal of Language, Identity & Education, 12*(5), 321–339. https://doi.org/10.1080/15348458.2013.835575

Sawyer, R. D., & Norris, J. (2013). *Duoethnography: Understanding qualitative research.* Oxford University Press.

Takahashi, K. (2012). *Language learning, gender and desire: Japanese women on the move.* Multilingual Matters.

Tsui, A. B. M. (2007). Complexities of identity formation: A narrative inquiry of an EFL teacher. *TESOL Quarterly, 41*(4), 657–680.

Chapter 17
Exploring Modern Language Teachers' Professional Identity Through Visual Self-Representations of Professional Lifelong Journeys

Matilde Gallardo Barbarroja

Abstract Research into language teacher identity often refers to individuals' self-position as teachers, their affiliations to different aspects of their work and their attachments to communities of practice. To these, it is important to add the role of personal agency in shaping teachers' lives and in making decisions about their own professional learning. This study aims to contribute to the existing body of research on language teachers' identity. It explores the multidimensional idiosyncrasy of language teachers in the UK and their sense of agency in responding to and acting upon the transnational, fragmented, social and pedagogical landscapes they navigate. Within the narrative frameworks present in twenty one graphic self-representations of teachers' professional journeys in which cognitive activity is mediated by semiotic tools, this study applies Narrative Inquiry and Keyword Theory in the analysis of socially prominent words (e.g. teaching, anxiety, learning) and critical incidents to investigate and draw up territories of interest in the development of teachers' professional identities. The results show that language teachers' professional journeys are marked by academic achievement as well as by transnational experiences associated with academic and professional progression. The desire for learning opportunities and a *passion* for language teaching often feature as a key aspect in shaping individuals' motivation for becoming teachers.

Keywords Language teacher identity · Agency · Narrative inquiry · Graphic representations

M. Gallardo Barbarroja (✉)
King's College London, London, UK
e-mail: matilde.gallardo@kcl.ac.uk

K. Sadeghi, F. Ghaderi (eds.), *Theory and Practice in Second Language Teacher Identity*, Educational Linguistics 57, https://doi.org/10.1007/978-3-031-13161-5_17

17.1 Introduction

In a complex world defined by transnational and translingual aspects of globalization, national identity labels often assigned to teachers of languages are difficult to justify. Block (2015) drew attention to language teacher identity in relation to how individuals self-position themselves and are positioned by others as teachers; how they identify with different aspects of their work and how they develop attachments to communities of practice. Additionally, post-structuralist socio-cultural theorists in Second Language Acquisition (SLA) (e.g. Akkerman & Meijer, 2011; Baxter, 2016; Giddens, 2004; Norton, 2013; Pavlenko & Lantolf, 2000) have argued that language teacher identity is dynamic and conditioned by the socio-cultural and historical contexts of their lived-experiences, validating the idea that teachers represent the embodiment of "hybrid, multiple and dynamic identities" (Gallardo, 2019, p. 19), which are conditioned by the geographical and cross-cultural spaces they dwell in. This line of thought, sustained by educators and language researchers (e.g. Kalaja et al., 2016; Tsui, 2011; Vähäsantanen, 2015; Varghese et al., 2016; White, 2018) positions language teachers as pivotal participants in the process of identity construction. It also assumes teachers' flexibility to adapt to multiple sociocultural, and institutional factors and advocates the role of agency in shaping teachers' identities in their professional contexts, and in making choices about their own professional growth and learning (Pillen et al., 2013).

Furthermore, the international dimension of language teaching and learning in many parts of the world is a reality which has led researchers to break away from the traditional view of language and culture pedagogy as part of a closed national universe and to approach it as a complex and dynamic subject characterised by transnational flows of people and ideas (Risager, 2007). Language teachers, as part of the global migratory social economy, personify the concept of *transnationalism*, understood as motion in space and time across national borders (Rothberg, 2014) and play a key role in influencing social, educational and cultural attitudes (Gallardo, 2019). The contribution they make and the skills they bring to the social and educational fabric of society is particularly worth studying in the current climate of uncertainty world-wide and in particular in the UK as a result of Brexit.

This study aims to offer insights into the multidimensionality of UK-based transnational language teachers' professional identity and their sense of agency in responding to and acting upon the geographical and cultural spaces they navigate; as well as to the dispersed, social and pedagogical landscapes they inhabit. The focus is to explore the development of language teachers' professional identities across the narrative frameworks of graphic self-representations of lifelong journeys in which the social and cognitive activity is mediated by semiotic tools. In this context, this study seeks to answer the following questions:

1. How do transnational language teachers in the UK imagine and portray their professional journeys?

   – what aspects (critical incidents) are significant to them?
   – which are the common characteristics that define their professional journeys?

2. What do these graphic narratives tell us about teachers as agents in their professional journeys?

Key aspects to consider in connection to the above questions include (a) the inhabited geographically determined spaces as embedded in teachers' lived experiences and the feelings/emotions connected with them; (b) the idea of temporality associated to their transfer between cultures and languages and (c) teachers' understanding of their own subjectivity (who they are) and alterity (who the others are).

17.2   Context of the Research

The discipline of modern languages has been a topic of debate in the UK education system for more than two decades. The present decline in the number of young people studying languages in schools and universities, the shifting trends in education, the inconsistency of official language policies and the expansion of English as an international language are some of the reasons given in official reports and commissioned reviews (Collen, 2020; Polisca et al., 2019). In addition, the recent UK historical departure from the European Union has had a negative impact on attitudes to language learning and brought new challenges to schools which lack the capacity to deliver high quality language teaching (Collen, 2020) and to modern foreign language departments in the higher and tertiary education sectors resulting in closures, casualization and job losses, as well as in low professional recognition for the language teaching community at institutional level (Polisca et al., 2019).

This investigation draws from the Diasporic Identities and Politics of Language (DIPL) strand of the Language Acts and Worldmaking research project,[1] which investigated modern language teachers in the UK, their perceptions and beliefs of professional identity, with a view to change attitudes about modern language education. In the context of the larger scale inquiry, the present study builds up on previous research published by the author in 2019. This follow up study represents an original contribution in that it offers an insight into language teachers' self-constructed professional identity through a corpus of graphic representations which connect their personal and professional stories.

---

[1]Language Acts and Worldmaking, LAWM, is part of the Arts and Humanities Research Council's Open World Research initiative, https://languageacts.org/

17.2.1 Participants

Teachers involved in the DIPL project who agreed to participate in this study shared the following profile:

- Gender: 95% female.
- Currently working in higher education: language centres and modern languages departments, but with considerable cross-sector teaching experience, including private, primary and secondary education, as well as adult and further education.
- Languages: French, Spanish, German, Italian, Arabic, Portuguese, English.
- Highest level of education attained: Master (61%) and Doctorate (39%)

In addition, participants shared the following characteristics:

- Being competent language users in two or more languages.
- Having specialist knowledge in linguistics, literature and having received pedagogical training.
- Having transnational and cross-cultural itineraries: lived and worked/studied in different countries.
- Being *cosmopolitan*, based on the surface of contact: they inhabit and work in cities, which act as translation zones.

17.3 Methodology

This investigation, grounded in sociocultural theory, follows the principles of Person-Centred Ethnography (Hollan, 1997) that focus on how the person's subjective experiences shape and are also shaped by social and cultural processes, and Cross-Cultural Ethnography (Brislin, 1976; Wutich & Brewis, 2019), a novel approach in modern language studies that examines patterns in sociocultural phenomena through emic-etic perspectives, both important in life history research (Brislin, 1976; Olive, 2014). While the *emic* perspective is relevant for understanding behaviours in a particular culture group on the basis of what individuals consider meaningful and important, an *etic* stance is beneficial in that it enables the researcher to make comparisons across differing cultures and populations and to develop cross-cultural arguments and ideas.

17.3.1 Narrative Inquiry Through Graphic Representations and Keywords

According to Barkhuizen & Wette "narratives are texts which tell stories of lived experience" (2008, p. 374), but as individuals tell their stories in the context of their situation and their culture, narratives also become the central point to understand "the social construction of each person's subjectivity" (Goodson, 2013, p.30) as they re-interpret their lived histories through language and their own culture. As narratives and case studies have revealed some aspects of beliefs not reported through other approaches (Kalaja et al., 2016), examining transnational language teachers' autobiographical narratives, personal stories of cross-cultural and linguistic encounters and their evolutionary journeys through time and space gives visibility to teachers as learners and as practitioners, and by extent to the professional community they are part of.

This study explores the narrative frameworks of twenty one graphic depictions of professional journeys, in which the social and cognitive activity is mediated by semiotic tools. The visual representations trace language teachers' life histories from a starting point and include critical events, encounters and incidents they consider significant in their trajectories. These autobiographical visual narratives are investigated using a Narrative Inquiry methodological approach (Barkhuizen et al., 2014; Clandinin, 2016; De Fina & Georgakopoulou, 2015; Nunan & Choi, 2010) which facilitates the exploration of "spatial and temporal scenarios that go beyond the here and now" (De Costa & Norton, 2017, p. 6) and allows for the interpretation of the semiotic elements and accompanying keywords. The temporal dimension and the spatial settings in which the stories are located are significant aspects to investigate, but the teachers themselves and their lived experiences hold a central position, as it is only through the relationship between those dimensions and the participants that their stories can be understood by the individual and by the researcher (Barkhuizen & Wette, 2008). In the context of this investigation, the term *narrative* refers to the combination of drawings, images and words used by participants to reflect and look back on their lived histories and tell their stories. This formula provides the qualitative rich data that reveals the complexities and the nature of what is being studied. It also offers versatility and spontaneity allowing participants to be creative and imaginative when opening into their internal world, whilst acknowledging that the graphic representations are a product created exclusively in response to an external request and that the researcher's interpretation may be influenced by her own experiences and views.

The validity of drawings in psychological empirical research is not exempt from controversy (Leibowitz, 1999). Still, in the field of psychotherapy and art therapy, drawings are studied, among other purposes, "as a means through which an individual communicates his interior world" (Quaglia, 2011, abstract). This investigation echoes that idea and agrees that transnational language teachers, when drawing, embark on a cognitive imaginative process of representation to create/re-create their professional selves through the narrative of visual metaphors. From a Jungian perspective, a word or an image is symbolic when it conveys something more than its immediate meaning and connects with the unconscious (Suzuki & Childs, 2015). As teachers' conscious thoughts, memories and emotions are unfolded within the unconscious when drawing, the symbols and visual metaphors that highlight critical events of their professional journeys become key elements in the process of identity construction. To explore and interpret teachers' constructed identity through their lived experiences, as implicit in their consciousness and visualised through draw-ings, this study follows Furth's (2002) Practical Systematic Analysis, widely used in psychotherapy, as a tool to guide the researcher in the interpretation of the implicit unconscious messages in the visual narratives.

However, this interpretation would not be complete without a study of the keywords accompanying the graphic compositions. A keyword is defined as "a word or concept that is very important in a particular context" one that provides "a solution or explanation" or one that is "of particular importance or significance." (Oxford dictionary, 2001). Keywords not only facilitate the accurate understanding of the message, they also provide additional information needed to locate the narrative inside its social and cultural context (Goodson, 2013). This study follows William's Keyword Theory (1975) which considers keywords as cues to understand, but also to apprehend, specific meanings at a particular time. Being a quantitative technique, it focuses on the centrality and significance of words and concepts: the more central a word or concept in a text, the more frequently it will be used and its recurrence in a given narrative.

Although the author agrees with the idea that meanings are made and changed over time as a result of diverse social groups' usages (Williams, 1975), the focus here is on the social and the cultural rather than the historical aspect of the vocabulary. This approach narrows down the scope by focusing on (a) the choice/selection of central terms made by language teachers in connection to critical incidents or specific landmarks in their professional history; and (b) the usage of those terms by this particular group and how that supports the meaning and significance of the drawings and images they are associated with. The outcomes of this analysis will shed light on the central vocabulary and associated debates that shape language teachers' professional identity in the UK.

17.4 Data Collection and Analysis

Language teachers participating in the DIPL project were encouraged to create a graphic illustration of their professional journey during the course of a workshop held in January 2017. As this research is set up in time, participants were asked to look back retrospectively, to reflect on past and present actions and to consider critical incidents which marked changes in their professional careers. Our intention was to elicit teachers' self-narrated professional journeys from the naturalistic discourse of drawings and pictorial representations highlighting the actions, encoun-ters and critical incidents (Farrell, 2013), which determined their constructed identity as practitioners. No specific guidelines or templates were used and each individual approached the task according to her/his own imagination and creative skills. Although the idea might have been off-putting for some, interested teachers did not object and approached the task enthusiastically.

With no formal set up, visual representations tend coincide considerably in format and outlook. Data was collected from twenty one graphic narratives in which images/drawings and written text share the narrative space. Each image emerges from self-perception and develops into a series of connected critical incidents selected by the participants. Teachers' visual representations, except one, were hand-drawn on an A4 paper and consisted of diagrams and mind-maps with symbolic elements including some projective representations of themselves. The exception was a Word document sent electronically on the day, which includes photographic images, as well as written text. Stickers were used to highlight the importance of events and, in most cases, brief sentences, words mostly, accompanied and supported the composition and played an essential role in the elucidation of the images. Teachers were free to use the language they wanted to explain and accompany their visual representations and although some used a mixed approach (e.g. Spanish, Italian, other, plus English), the majority opted for English, in line with the lingua franca used in the workshop. Ethical aspects were adhered to, following the British Educational Research Association, BERA, guidelines. Images were scanned and stored securely in the workshop organisers' internal drive. Teachers were reassured about confidentiality and gave their consent to use their graphic compositions for the purpose of this research.

On the basis of the two elements that made up the narratives, the pictorial and the linguistic, the qualitative analysis of the data required a dual approach which would enable the researcher to formulate key general aspects influencing teachers' professional journeys. As already mentioned, the analysis of drawings followed Jungian principles used in analytical psychology and more specifically Furth's guidelines for the interpretation of drawings, on the understanding that "drawings reveal information about the individual who executes them" (Furth, 2002, p. xiii). However, Leibowitz's Impressionistic Analysis critical theoretical view has also been considered. The Impressionistic Analysis is not intended to be an exhaustive method (Leibowitz, 1999), but it pays attention to the emotions and feelings an image projects as evoked through the symbolic nature of its representation. Although the drawings, specially those with projective techniques, are individual work and subjective creations the analysis does not focus on personality traits, but in noticing patterns and highlighted landmarks in personal trajectories and by extent, in eliciting the commonalities and pointing out significant divergences, when occurring, as well as metaphors and symbols used by participants to represent their stories. We agree with Furth in that "The idea is not to decipher with accuracy what is within the picture. . .as much as it is to ask concise questions as to what the picture may be communicating" (2002, p. 13). Hence, the analysis is concerned with the subject(s), the examiner, the picture and the context. Table 17.1 below shows the key aspects that guided our analysis:

Furth admits that "an open mind is vital to the productive interpretation of a drawing" (2002, p. 16). Therefore, although the researcher's familiarisation with the professional context could provide useful contextual knowledge and information, it was important to avoid influencing the interpretation and analysis of data with preconceived ideas.

Table 17.1 Key aspects in the interpretation of drawings

Key aspects in the interpretation of drawings based on Furth's principles
1. Initial impression of a drawing/image: feelings, not interpretations.
2. Objective analysis of each drawing/image.
3. Looking at focal points systematically
4. Looking for emotions, feelings, thoughts and affects and how are they represented through symbols and words.
5. Establishing how accompanying text or words support the symbolic representations and the conveyed message.
6. Synthesizing what has been learned from individual components and assemble this information into a whole.

17.5 Interpretation and Analysis of Findings

The scrutiny of data gave the following findings as shown in Table 17.2 below. The analysis of these findings requires an interpretation based on the interconnectedness of these elements, as explained in the following sub-sections.

17.5.1 The Metaphor of the Journey

The concept of the *journey* is used as a metaphor to represent teachers' professional trajectories. Teachers made use of linear (horizontal and/or vertical, ascendant or descendent), circular, wave shaped designs or a metaphorical image (e.g. a rocket) when illustrating the chronology of their professional journeys: where they started and where they were at the point of this exercise. This arrangement enabled them to recreate and re-visit episodes of the past in which dates and locations are linked to relevant events and experiences (e.g. teaching positions, academic achievements, other) having reflected upon and extending them into the present. By inserting these 'memory images' (Bergson, 1992) into temporal motions they present themselves simultaneously at what Scarino defines as "two time scales: in the time of the narrative and at the time of the telling" (2013, p. x). Teachers' graphic narratives show episodes and events connected in time as they are assembled and joined in particular ways (e.g. arrows, lines, diagrams, etc.). Temporality and spatiality, therefore, provide the structure for these narratives of mobility in order to make them meaningful for narrators and their audience.

UK-based language teachers' professional journeys often start in their country of origin (e.g. Spain, Italy, France, other) where they studied for a relevant degree in language studies and a teacher training qualification and continue with further

Table 17.2 Main themes in language teachers' graphic representations

THEMES	DESCRIPTION
Locations	Europe (UK, Spain, Italy, Germany, Ireland, France, Scotland, Greece, Poland, Norway, Belgium). Canada, USA, Ecuador, Argentina. Kuwait, China, Japan. Australia. Egypt, Tunisia.
Qualifications	Degree (e.g. Philology), MA (e.g. Applied Linguistics, translation), PhD, TESOL/ ELT, PGCE/ Teacher training, Montessori training. Some teachers (10) did not specify.
Teaching and related experience	Either in different stages and/or in combination: Higher Education (including distance education and/or Language Centres), Further and Adult Education, Secondary and Primary Education (public and private), teaching assistant, editorial work, private teaching, examiner. Arts College.
Languages taught and related activity	Italian, Spanish, EAP/EFL/ESOL, French, German, Arabic, Catalan. Linguistics. Teacher training, academic manager.
Research	7 out of 21 teachers: book, research related to PhD, research projects (e.g. Francophone Africa). Future objective.
Critical incidents	*Performing Languages* project, Mandarin language course, book publication, moving to the UK, teaching women migrants, teaching positions, teaching at university, becoming a reflective teacher trainer, first salary, finding love and marriage, Paris.
Emotions and feelings	Excitement, passion (frequent), adaptation, anxiety (frequent), nostalgia, uncertainty (frequent)

studies or/and teaching positions in Europe, USA, North African, Latin American and Asian countries before reaching a position in the UK (see Table 17.2). Locations are packed with meaning associated to achievement and satisfaction and positive experiences, as captured in the images displayed in these sub-sections.

The geographical range in these narratives of mobility illustrates the internationalization that characterises these professionals. The notion of 'trans', however, not only emphasises movement in space across national borders, but, as Assmann clearly explains, "...it also stands for 'translations', the cultural work of reconfiguring established national themes, references, representations, images and concepts" (2014, p. 547). The perception is, therefore, that language teachers are carriers and transmitters of ideas and intercultural attitudes, but also learners and interpreters of new ideas themselves, which they take to their students and to society. However, as the unequivocal impact of free human mobility across social and national spaces has been affected by recent worldwide scenarios and more specifically in the case of the UK by recently enforced barriers to people's freedom of movement,[2] the lives and expectations for the future of many transnational language teachers in the UK have inevitably changed. This time of incertitude in terms of job stability and personal wellbeing raises negative feelings which will be explored in Sect. 17.5.3.

17.5.2   Professional Development and Teaching Career

Modern language teachers' transnational lives are often associated with better job options, but also with the desire for learning opportunities and professional growth. The graphic narratives show a strong commitment to professional development and a desire for learning, an aspect linked to motivation (Han & Yin, 2016), which may encourage teachers to support progressive education. Professional journeys are marked by academic achievement (e.g. post-graduate qualifications, learning a new language) (see Table 17.2), which demonstrates that lifelong learning is an important aspect in language education and language teacher professional identity. Similarly, academic development goes hand-in-hand with professional progression as teachers take opportunities for learning when they work outside their home country and many fulfil their academic ambition (e.g. MA, Doctorate) when abroad, as illustrated in the following Image 17.1.

Teaching journeys have taken the majority of the participants through the broad educational spectrum in the UK and/or abroad (see Table 17.2). Narratives show evidence that although teachers might be highly qualified to teach a second language (e.g. EFL), in most cases they are employed to teach their first language, as the essentialist native-speaker perspective (Song, 2018) still prevails in many educational settings. In a broad sense, language teaching in higher education implies

Image 17.1 A teacher's illustration of her academic development and professional progression (Source: The Open University, UK)

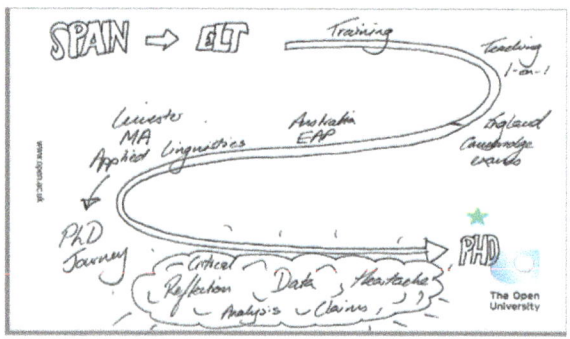

_____

[2] We refer to the new regulations on border control between the UK and the EU after Brexit, which affect EU citizens' rights to live and work in the UK.

Image 17.2 A teacher's illustration of her progression to a managerial position (Source: The Open University, UK)

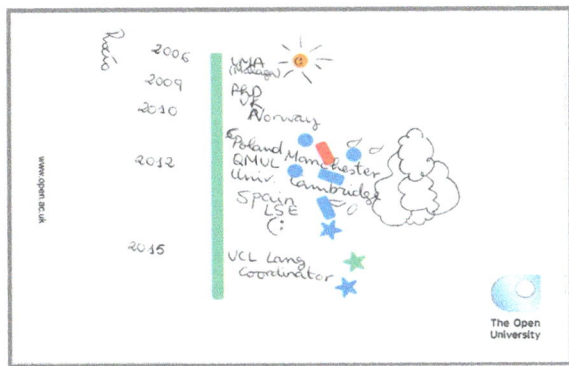

teaching a language for communication and/or specific purposes as part of a department of languages or, in many cases, in a Language Centre (Polisca et al., 2019). However, the reality of the fractured environment in which language teachers operate in the UK makes the nature of the work consistently precarious. Teachers have to juggle several part-time positions across organisations and levels (Gallardo, 2019; Gkonou & Miller, 2021) and, unlike colleagues working in other disciplines, they may be subject to contracts in which research does not feature as a requirement. However, although only a few acknowledge to be research active (see Table 17.2), research is a clear objective for the future, an aspiration, and many teachers seek opportunities to get involved in research projects and/or embark on higher postgraduate qualifications (e.g. Doctorate studies) as a source of motivation and professional development. On the other hand, the reality of career progression for most teachers is marked by gaining a managerial position which may require them to apply empirical knowledge as trainers in the professional development of other teachers, as observed below (Image 17.2).

17.5.3 Emotions and Feelings

SLA research on emotions has acknowledged their importance in shaping "teacher identities, classroom practice, and teacher professionalization" (Gkonou & Miller, 2021, p. 135). Emotions as part of teachers' identity construction have been studied through the lens of reflective activity in autobiographical accounts (Pavlenko, 2007). This is particularly pertinent in the case of transnational language teachers since the accounts of their professional lived-stories are emotionally loaded with feelings and thoughts connected to their cross-cultural, linguistic and pedagogical experiences.

Emotions and feelings are represented through a combination of drawn symbols and shapes (e.g. star shapes, smileys, question marks, bubbles or clouds), colourful small stickers (blue, red, green) and keywords (placed inside/outside the shapes), and are connected to critical events, locations and the future. Self-representations are also included in some cases in the form of doll-like drawings or images, usually

Image 17.3 A teacher's view of her position in her professional environment (Source: The Open University, UK)

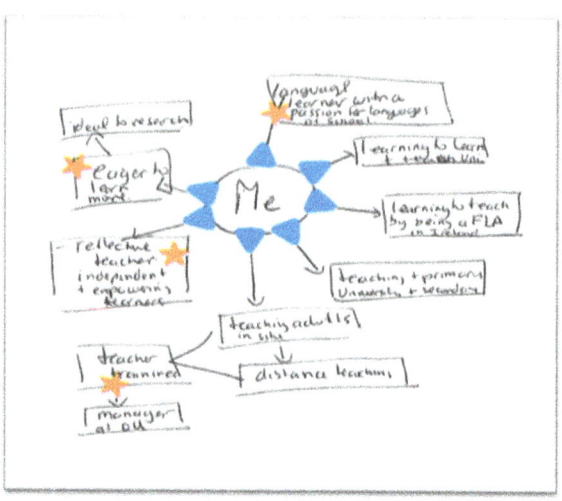

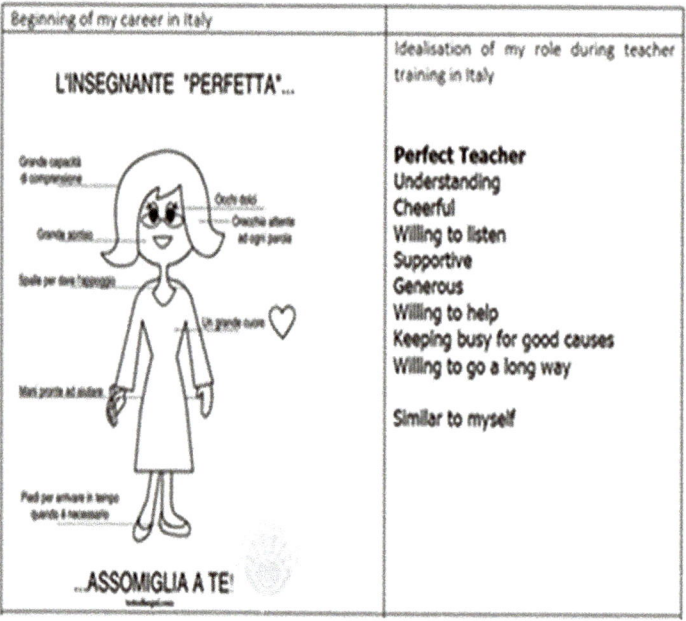

Image 17.4 A teacher's idealisation of the language teacher role (Source: The Open University, UK)

placed in a prominent place and/or in a bigger size. These *projective pictures of the self* (Leibowitz, 1999) draw attention to how teachers view themselves at the centre of their constructed identity and their position within the professional environment. This may include an idealisation of the language teacher role, as illustrated in the following examples (Images 17.3 and 17.4).

Image 17.5 A teacher's illustration showing uncertainty for the future (Source: The Open University, UK)

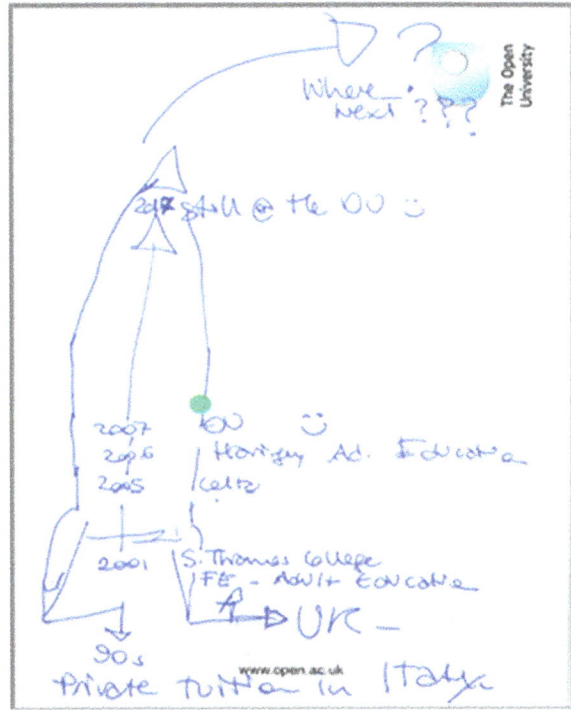

Graphic narratives display teachers' positive and negative emotions and feelings. Positive emotions, those that enable teachers "to reap emotional rewards" (Gkonou & Miller, 2021, p. 135) refer to past experiences, "significant outcomes that are already completed and known" (Ickes & Cheng, 2011, 6). On the other hand, negative emotions emerge associated to the future (e.g. job insecurity).

Passion, frequently linked to the first teaching job, is associated with teachers' interest in teaching and consequently with the motivation that drives their professionalization and teaching career. Feelings connected with working and living in other countries vary from that of *excitement* associated to intercultural encounters, to those of *adaptation* and *challenges* involved in the process of acculturation and adjustment to new cultural, pedagogical and professional settings. Connectivity, belonging but also alienation, are expressed in feelings of *nostalgia* and *anxiety* to manage the "existential strangeness" (Coffey, 2013, p. 266) innate to individuals' relationship with familiar/unfamiliar cultural and linguistic spaces. This contradictory set of emotions characteristic of the so-called 'third space metaphor' (Bhabha, 1994) has been understood by others as an intrinsic aspect of the "symbolic nature of the multilingual subject" (Kramsch, 2009, p. 200). As teachers' careers develop in sometimes precarious and unstable social and educational environments, the feeling of *uncertainty* becomes noticeable in their thoughts about their future, as illustrated by the following representation (Image 17.5).

Emotions, therefore, not only involve personal or psychological aspects, but also social and educational experiences linked to the socio-cultural and institutional environments in which language teachers construct their professional identity. The analysis of these graphic autobiographical narratives reports distinct emotions and feelings occurring in connection with past events, but also in relation to future-directed thoughts about professional identity.

17.5.4   Critical Incidents

Critical incidents are valuable in this investigation, not only because they refer to "significant turning points" (Tripp, 2012, p. 24) in teachers' professional journeys, but also because they facilitate reflection on practice (Babaii et al., 2021; Farrell, 2008) which makes them a valuable instrument in teachers' autobiographical accounts as they ease the task of enacting their identity in a timely way: the moment they narrated and the moment they remembered.

As presented in these graphic narratives, critical incidents relate to individuals' meaningful experiences that happened in given times and places, raised positive feelings and perceptions of themselves and consecutively influenced their professional journeys (e.g. new teaching position, marriage, first salary, book publication, participation in scholarly projects, etc.). These personal events turned into critical instances as teachers were faced with important decisions which affected their professional lives in the medium/long-term. The significance of these events is marked in the narratives with a range of symbols and techniques (e.g. different colour/format, lines/arrows), which are part of the linearity in time and space of the graphic representations and are emphasised by keywords. In addition, critical events are strongly connected with emotions and characterise the spatial and temporal stories represented in these narratives. As illustrated in the above images, they may appear connected to specific places and times, but their significance has a continuous effect on developing professional identities.

17.5.5   Keywords

Keywords are crucial to the interpretation of meanings and ideas in teachers' graphic narrative compositions. Their location in the narrative space relates to their functionality, either as part of the drawings and images or inserted in the accompanying brief written texts. This analysis focuses on the nature and the frequency of keywords and their associated concepts, as those aspects determine their significance to describe and interpret emotions and feelings as well as to elicit ideologies and thoughts. To facilitate the analysis, keywords have been grouped into semantic fields and explained according to their contextual functionality, as indicated in Table 17.3:

Table 17.3 Semantic fields and keywords

TEACHING	LEARNING	LANGUAGE	RESEARCH	EMOTIONS	SETTINGS
•Languages	•Learner	•Language education	•Project	•Passion,	•Policies
•Teacher	•Acquisition	•Language in education	•PhD	•Excitement	•Fees (student)
•Skills	•Empowering	•Metalanguage	•Reflection	•Anxiety	•University
•Communicative	•Independent	•Modern languages	•Analysis	•Uncertainty	•Schools
•Reflective	•individual/collaborative		•Critical	•Eagerness	•Informal/formal
•International	•Immersion		•Ideal		•Distance
•Cultural aspects	•Minorities				
•Innovation					
•Training/education					
•Career path					
•Manager					
•Future					
•Challenges					

The field of 'Teaching', unsurprisingly attracts the largest number of keywords. A brief look at Fig. 1 reveals the multifaceted aspects that teaching represents for language teachers: a compound of skills, languages, methodological approaches, cultural elements and learning opportunities, as well as concerns about the future of the profession. The diversity and the range of teaching practices that characterise language teachers' careers, as explained in Sect. 17.5.2, are reinforced by keywords in the field of 'Settings' such as, *informal/formal, distance, schools, university*. In addition, 'Emotions' keywords further assist the meaning of teachers' understanding of teaching and their stake in it (e.g. *passion for teaching*). For example, the word *anxiety* (*ansiedad* in Spanish) in Image 17.6 evidences the challenges faced by the teacher in relation to her/his teaching job at a particular time and location:

The field of 'Learning' includes compelling keywords such as *empowering* and *independent* which show teachers' strong beliefs in education as a changing force in society. Other words (e.g. *acquisition, immersion, collaborative*) as well as those in 'Language' suggest familiarisation with concepts and ideas in SLA theory. Keywords in these two fields, therefore, refer to teachers as practitioners with pedagogical knowledge and expertise. Keywords in the field of 'Research', confirm the strong interest in pursuing research, as represented by the word *ideal*, while showing that teachers are not necessarily alien to this activity. *Project*, a frequent keyword in many graphic narratives, shows teachers' active involvement with collective scholarly and research activities institutionally organised and/or externally funded (e.g. Performing Languages project, Flexible Learning project), which are also critical landmarks in their professional journey.

In summary, the analysis of these graphic narratives provides us with insights into language teachers' lived histories and professional trajectories, while also answering the question of what aspects of their professional journeys are significant in the process of identity construction. Although this interpretation may suggest the idea of

Image 17.6 A teacher's illustration of the emotional challenges in his teaching job

a collective body with a shared set of values and ideologies, it also reinforces the role of personal agency in shaping teachers' lives, as illustrated by their subjective investment in conscious choices within their professional environments, and the transformative effect of these choices on individuals' practices and professional identities. As teachers make decisions about their professional learning and their motivation to become language teachers, they become agents in constructing their identity as members of the profession. Graphic narratives help us to understand how teachers have become what they are, what motivates them and what matters to them. Similarly, engaging with the process of drawing their lived-histories as a reflective exercise is also part of an identity-building operation.

17.6   Conclusions

This study has explored language teachers' professional identity construction through autobiographical accounts of their professional journeys in which life-changing conscious choices and decisions led them to pursue professional advancement. Through the conceptual lens of visual self-representations (graphic and textual compositions), participants narrated their professional trajectories as well as their approaches to pedagogic situations and issues. These narrated identities, shaped by individuals' histories, language(s) and culture(s), form the configurations that influence their judgments and give them, as explained by Werbińska "... individual agentive powers … when confronted with critical events and tensions or forced to make decisions" (2017, p. 45).

A better understanding of language teaching undoubtedly needs insightful knowledge about language teachers. The analysis of the visual representations show that the nature of the language teaching profession in the UK, as represented by the sample in this study, is defined by transnationalism and by a strong interest in personal and professional growth, as well as by economic causes and learning opportunities. As part of the migratory phenomenon that characterises the global economy, language teachers navigate between communities, academic posts and organisations not only transferring knowledge and skills, but good practice and educational models to the benefit of learners and educational establishments. By bringing two or more domains together, teachers make a useful contribution to building the social fabric. The cross-cultural experiences and practices that distinguish the language teaching community offer crucial tools for addressing global issues which affect people of all cultures in present times (e.g. lived-experiences of migration, intercultural communication and diversity, among others).

References

Akkerman, S. F., & Meijer, P. C. (2011). A dialogical approach to conceptualizing teacher identity. *Teaching and Teacher Education, 27*, 308–319.

Assmann, A. (2014). Transnational memories. *European Review, 22*(4), 546–556.

Babaii, E., Molana, K., & Nazari, M. (2021). Contributions of assessment-related critical incidents to language teacher identity development. *Innovation in Language Learning and Teaching, 15*(5), 442–457. https://doi.org/10.1080/17501229.2020.1824234

Barkhuizen, G., & Wette, R. (2008). Narrative frames for investigating the experiences of language teachers. *System, 36*(3), 372–387. https://www.researchgate.net/publication/250733489

Barkhuizen, G., Benson, P., & Chik, A. (2014). *Narrative inquiry in language teaching and learning research*. Routledge.

Baxter, J. (2016). Positioning language and identity: Poststructuralist perspectives. In S. Preece (Ed.), *The Routledge handbook of language and identity* (pp. 34–50). Routledge.

Bergson, H. (1992). *The creative mind: An introduction to metaphysics*. Citadel Press.

Bhabha, H. K. (1994). *The location of culture*. Routledge.

Block, D. (2015). Becoming a language teacher: Constrains and negotiations in the emergence of new identities. *Bellaterra Journal of Teaching and Learning language and literature, 8*(3), 9–26.

Brislin, R. W. (1976). Comparative research methodology: Cross-cultural studies. *International Journal of Psychology, 11*(3), 215–229. https://doi.org/10.1080/00207597608247359

Clandinin, J. (2016). *Engaging in narrative inquiry*. Routledge.

Coffey, S. (2013). Strangerhood and intercultural subjectivity. *Language and Intercultural Communication, 13*(3), 266–282. https://doi.org/10.1080/14708477.2013.804532

Collen, I. (2020). *Language Trends 2020. Language teaching in primary and secondary schools in England*. Survey report. https://www.britishcouncil.org/sites/default/files/language_trends_2020_0.pdf

De Costa, P. I., & Norton, B. (2017). Introduction: Identity, transdisciplinarity and the good language teacher. *The Modern Language Journal, 101*(S1), 3–14. https://doi.org/10.1111/modl.123680026-7902/17/3-14

De Fina, A. & Georgakopoulou, A. (Eds.). (2015). *The handbook of narrative analysis*. Wiley Blackwell.

Farrell, T. S. C. (2008). Critical incidents in ELT initial teacher training. *ELT Journal, 62*(1), 3–10. https://doi.org/10.1093/elt/ccm072

Farrell, T. S. C. (2013). *Reflective practice in ESL teacher development groups*. Palgrave Macmillan.

Furth, G. M. (2002). *The secret world of drawings: A Jungian approach to healing through art*. Inner City Books.

Gallardo, M. (2019). Transcultural voices: Exploring notions of identity in transnational language teachers' personal narratives. In M. Gallardo (Ed.), *Negotiating identity in modern foreign language teaching* (pp. 17–43). Palgrave Macmillan.

Giddens, A. (2004). *Modernity and self-identity*. Blackwell Publishing.

Gkonou, C., & Miller, E. R. (2021). An exploration of language teacher reflection, emotion labor, and emotional capital. *TESOL Quarterly, 55*(1), 134–155. https://doi.org/10.1002/tesq.580

Goodson, I. F. (2013). *Developing narrative theory: Life histories and personal representation*. Routledge.

Han, J., & Yin, H. (2016). Teacher motivation: Definition, research development and implications for teachers. In M. Boylan, (Reviewing Ed.). *Cogent Education, 3*(1). https://doi.org/10.1080/2331186X.2016.1217819

Hollan, D. (1997). The relevance of person-centered ethnography to cross-cultural psychiatry. *Transcultural Psychiatry, 34*(2), 219–234. https://doi.org/10.1177/136346159703400203

Ickes, W., & Cheng, W. (2011). How do thoughts differ from feelings? Putting the differences into words. *Language and Cognitive Processes, 26*(1), 1–23. https://doi.org/10.1080/01690961003603046

Kalaja, P., Barcelos, A. M., Aro, M., & Ruohotie-Lyhty, M. (Eds.). (2016). *Beliefs, agency and Identity in Foreign language learning and teaching*. Palgrave Macmillan.

Kramsch, C. (2009). *The multilingual subject*. Oxford University Press.

Leibowitz, M. (1999). *Interpreting projective drawings: A self-psychological approach*. Routledge. https://doi.org/10.4324/9780203777992

Norton, B. (2013). *Identity and language learning: Extending the conversation*. Multilingual Matters.

Nunan, D., & Choi, J. (Eds.). (2010). *Language and culture. Reflective narratives and the emergence of identity*. Routledge.

Olive, J. L. (2014). Reflecting on the tensions between emic and etic perspectives in life history research: Lessons learned. *Forum: Qualitative Social Research, 15*(2) Article 6. http://nbn-resolving.de/urn:nbn:de:0114-fqs140268

Oxford English Dictionary. (n.d.). Keywords. In Oxford English Dictionary 2001. Retrieved 2021, June 10 from https://www.oed.com/.

Pavlenko, A. (2007). Autobiographical narratives as data in applied linguistics. *Applied Linguistics, 28*(2), 163–188.

Pavlenko, A., & Lantolf, J. A. (2000). Second language learning as participation in the reconstruction of the selves. In J. A. Lantolf (Ed.), *Sociocultural theory and second language learning* (pp. 155–177). Oxford University Press.

Pillen, M., Beijaard, D., & den Brok, P. (2013). Tensions in beginning teachers' professional identity development, accompanying feelings and coping strategies. *European Journal of Teacher Education, 36*(3), 240–260. https://doi.org/10.1080/02619768.2012.696192

Polisca, E., Wright, V., Álvarez, I., & Montoro, C. (2019). *Language provision in UK MFL departments 2019 survey (report 2)*. University Council of Modern Languages (UCML). https://university-council-modern-languages.org/wp-content/uploads/2021/04/LanguageProvisionMFLsSurvey2019.pdf

Quaglia, R. (2011). The use of drawing in psychotherapy. *International Journal of Developmental and Educational Psychology: INFAD, Revista de Psicología, 1*(1), 465–472.

Risager, K. (2007). *Language and culture pedagogy: From a national to a transnational paradigm*. Multilingual Matters.

Rothberg, M. (2014). Locating transnational memory. *European Review, 22*(4), 652–656.

Scarino, A. (2013). Foreword. In L. Harbon & R. Moloney (Eds.), *Language teachers' narratives of practice* (pp. viii–xiii). Cambridge Scholars Publishing.

Song, J. (2018). Critical approaches to emotions of non-native English speaking teachers. *Chinese Journal of Applied Linguistics, 41*(4), 453–467. https://doi.org/10.1515/cjal-2018-0033

Suzuki, S., & Childs, M. R. (2015). Drawings reveal the beliefs of Japanese university students. In C. Gkonou et al. (Eds.), *New directions in learning psychology* (pp. 159–183). Springer International Publishing. http://ebookcentral.proquest.com/lib/kcl/detail.action?docID=4179464

Tripp, D. (2012). *Critical incidents in teaching: Developing professional judgement*. Routledge.

Tsui, A. B. M. (2011). Teacher education and teacher development. In E. Hinkel (Ed.), *Handbook of research in second language teaching and learning* (pp. 21–40). Routledge.

Vähäsantanen, K. (2015). Professional agency in the stream of change: Understanding educational change and teachers' professional identities. *Teaching and Teacher Education, 47*. https://doi.org/10.1016/j.tate.2014.11.006

Varghese, M. M., Motha, S., Trent, J., Park, G., & Reeves, J. (Eds.). (2016). Language teacher identity in (multi)lingual settings. *TESOL Quarterly, 50*(3), 545–571.

Werbińska, D. (2017). *The formation of language teacher professional identity. A Phenomenographic-narrative study*. Akademia Pomorska w Słupsk.

White, C. (2018). Language teacher agency. In S. Mercer & A. Kostoulas (Eds.), *Language teacher psychology* (pp. 196–210). Multilingual Matters.

Williams, R. (1975). *Keywords: A vocabulary of culture and society*. Fontana.

Wutich, A., & Brewis, A. (2019). Data collection in cross-cultural ethnographic research. *Field Methods, 31*(2), 181–189. https://doi.org/10.1177/1525822X19837397

Chapter 18
The Interplay of Ecological Influences in Language Teacher Identity and Agency Negotiation

Anna Sanczyk-Cruz and Elizabeth R. Miller

Abstract The purpose of this narrative study is to explore the identity and agency negotiations of three adult ESL instructors who teach at a two-year community college in the southeastern United States. Drawing on an ecological view of teacher identity (Edwards & Burns, *TESOL Quarterly 50*:735–745, 2016) and teacher agency (Priestley et al. *Teacher agency: An ecological approach.* Bloomsbury, 2015), we explore teacher participants' accounts of their cultural backgrounds, life histories, teaching experiences, and institutional contexts. The narrative analysis revealed that the participants constructed differing identities that changed over time. We found that they all actively sought out new experiences and desired to learn about different cultures and traditions, including those of their students. We trace several ecological influences that contributed to the development of their teacher identities by examining participants' accounts of their complex teaching journeys. In analyzing how teachers worked to address the diverse linguistic and cultural needs of their adult ESL students, while still contending with numerous institutional and personal constraints, the chapter provides insights into important ecological influences on the development of language teacher identity and their differing capacities to exercise agency in their role as language teacher.

Keywords Agency · Ecological perspective · Critical reflection · Narrative inquiry · Identity

A. Sanczyk-Cruz (✉)
University of Bialystok, Białystok, Poland
e-mail: a.sanczyk@uwb.edu.pl

E. R. Miller
University of North Carolina at Charlotte, Charlotte, NC, USA

© The Author(s), under exclusive license to Springer Nature Switzerland AG 2022   263
K. Sadeghi, F. Ghaderi (eds.), *Theory and Practice in Second Language Teacher Identity*, Educational Linguistics 57, https://doi.org/10.1007/978-3-031-13161-5_18

18.1   Introduction

Numerous studies have pointed to the importance of teachers engaging in critical reflection regarding the cultural, social, political, and economic influences on their classrooms, schools, and communities. They have shown that it can lead to transformation in teachers' practices and relationships with their linguistically and culturally diverse students (Flessner et al., 2012; Kumaravadivelu, 2012; Pantić & Florian, 2015). Critical reflection can inspire teachers to strive to better understand students' needs, build inclusive schools, strengthen classroom communities, and become agents of change in their local contexts (Flessner et al., 2012). Given these findings, this study intentionally engaged teachers in self-reflection of their own identities, experiences, dispositions, and institutional environments, particularly in relation to their teaching and relationship building with culturally and linguistically diverse students. In this study, critical reflection is understood to facilitate teacher identity and agency negotiation.

This study highlights aspects of each teacher's educational setting, social relationships, and personal and professional experiences that allow us to better understand how their contexts shape their sense of agency and changing identities. In incorporating an ecological approach to agency, we regard teacher agency as achieved and exercised across a range of settings and as shaped by individuals' past experiences (Priestley et al., 2012) with a focus on how it is constructed "within the ecological conditions through which it is exercised and enacted" (White, 2018: 200). In supporting our theoretical understanding of agency, this narrative inquiry explores how participants' past and present contexts and future aspirations influence their understandings of their teacher agency along with their identities (Edwards & Burns, 2016) in relation to their teaching practice. The research question for this study is as follows: How have the ESL teachers' various contexts and experiences shaped their identity and agency in teaching culturally and linguistically diverse learners?

18.2   Literature Review

Research has shown that teacher identity work is achieved, at least in part, through how teachers describe themselves as they construct narratives of their personal and professional experiences (Barkhuizen, 2017). It also demonstrates that teacher identity is negotiated throughout their careers, continually influenced by teachers' personal, educational, professional, and political experiences (Buchanan, 2015; Edwards & Burns, 2016; Kumaravadivelu, 2012; Varghese et al., 2005). Such identity formation is likewise impacted by power structures, as noted by Kumaravadivelu (2012) and Ollerhead and Burns (2016), who describe many of the institutional and political constraints teachers have to contend with during their teaching careers.

In conceptualizing teacher identity as dynamic, experiential, and as fundamental to teacher practice and teacher development, we understand that teachers' capacity to exercise agency is inextricably influenced by and influences their identity work. As Barkhuizen (2017: 4) wrote, language teacher identities include "being and doing." We thus draw on Priestley et al.'s (2015) ecological approach to agency. They understand teacher agency as temporal, relational, dynamic, contingent upon one's experiences and environment, and as "doing" something. Tao and Gao (2021) note that an ecological perspective emphasizes how one's professional agency develops in terms of one's current contexts but also one's life history. This temporal dimension, emphasized in the triad of iterational (past), projective (future imaginings) and the practical-evaluative (present) elements of agency, as first proposed by Emirbayer and Mische (1998), has been applied to teacher experiences by Priestley et al. (2012, 2015). This approach helps us understand teacher agency as a "situated achievement" (Priestley et al., 2015: 29) that is influenced by teachers' past experiences, their current situations, and their aspirations for the future (Kayi-Aydar, 2019). We thus align with Barkhuizen's (2017: 4) understanding of teacher identity—and we would add teacher agency to this definition—as "both inside the teacher and outside in the social, material and technological world." Identity and agency develop and are exercised at the interface of individuals interacting in, responding to, and sometimes transforming their professional contexts.

Current research examining language teacher identity as well as agency, and which adopts an ecological perspective to teacher agency by analyzing the triad of iterational, projective and practical-evaluative elements, is still relatively scarce. Vitanova's (2018) case study research of three pre-service language teachers is an exception. In arguing for the intersection of identity and agency, Vitanova focused on how language teachers' iterative experiences and practical-evaluative situations helped shape their identities and their capacities to exercise agency in taking up social justice initiatives. We believe more research focusing on this intersection of language teacher identity and agency through using the triad of agency elements is still needed, particularly with in-service experienced language teachers, in order to gain a more wholistic understanding of the key constructs of teacher identity and agency.

18.3 Methodology

One of the aims of this narrative research project was to provide a safe space for three adult ESL instructors to share their personal and professional stories in an effort to better understand their identity and agency negotiation. This study focused on narratives in the form of biographical case studies (Barkhuizen et al., 2014). In following this approach to narrative inquiry, we elicited information from the teacher participants using multiple data collection procedures and then created narratives using their verbatim comments along with researcher-created syntheses of teachers' comments and research field notes.

Table 18.1 Language Teachers' Demographic Information

Pseudonym	Gender	Race	Teaching experience	Credentials	Classes taught
Agnes	Female	White	5 years	M.A.T.[a] in TESOL	High intermediate, adult ESL
Mary	Female	White	10 years	M.A.T. in TESOL	Intermediate, adult ESL
Sebastian	Male	White	25 years	M.A.T. in TESOL	High intermediate, adult ESL

[a]Master of Arts in Teaching Degree

18.3.1 Participants

The language teacher participants all worked at a community college (an institution providing two-year degrees and vocational training) in the southeastern United States. This institution serves English Language Learners (ELLs) representing more than 150 countries and is one of the largest community colleges in the state. It offers a variety of classes for ELLs who want to enhance their language and academic skills. Table 18.1 provides demographic information on the three focal language teachers, who are identified by pseudonyms.

18.3.2 Data Collection and Analysis

To address the research question, data were collected from face-to-face semi-structured interviews, journal entries, and classroom observations. Interviews provided insight into teachers' aspirations for the future, their past and current lived experiences, and the meanings they created from those experiences. Each participant was interviewed three times for approximately 1 h each time. During the interviews, the teacher participants were asked open-ended questions that encouraged them to share stories about their experiences, significant events, environments, and relationships. Each participant also engaged in critical reflective journaling and completed ten journal entries in response to researcher-developed prompts that encouraged the teachers to critically reflect on their teaching practices. Drawing on Freire (1970), we invited participants to engage in critical reflection to encourage them to develop deeper awareness of the interconnections among their various experiences, contexts, relationships, and teaching practices. Each teacher's classroom was observed twice. The purpose of these observations was to learn about the setting, the activities that took place in that setting, interactions between the instructor and students, and verbal and nonverbal communications which were recorded in hand-written field notes.

Informed by Polkinghorne (1995), we created narratives out of participants' stories by drawing on their words produced in their interviews and journal entries, and from the field notes based on the classroom observations. The researcher-created narratives provided below are based on the connections we found across the participants' accounts of their teaching experiences and as corroborated in classroom observations.

18.4   Identity and Agency Negotiation in Teacher Narratives

Teacher narratives reveal and perform identity work as they are vehicles for linking together and making relevant "the important interpersonal and social relationships one has formed, and [for providing] a sense of one's values, beliefs, and worldviews in the storyteller's own words" (Atkinson, 2007: 234). Their construction of stories articulated a sense of self and was itself a form of identity work because the production of such narrative accounts "helps individuals to make sense of and come to terms with their life and adjust to changes in their lives" (Biesta, 2008: 20). In analyzing and recreating the focal teachers' narratives into the accounts presented below, we also paid careful attention to the interplay of the iterational, the projective, and the practical-evaluative dimensions of teacher agency. The iterational aspects of agency include the skills, knowledge, beliefs, and values that played a crucial role in teachers' past personal and professional experiences. The projective dimension comprises their individual hopes, motivations, aspirations, and goals. The practical-evaluative dimension of agency refers to how they described exercising agency in the present (Priestley et al., 2015).

18.4.1   Agnes

18.4.1.1   A Language Explorer

Agnes was in her late 20s and had been teaching for over 5 years at the time the study was conducted. She grew up in a small town in New York and attended schools that were not diverse at all. Even so, from a young age, she has been passionate about learning languages and learning about other cultures. For example, Agnes commented as follows:

> My favorite subject in school was Spanish because I loved learning about different cultures, so I decided to major in Spanish in college. I was drawn to the students from other countries and began to spend time with people from many different countries including Mexico, Republic of Georgia, Armenia, Russia, and Colombia. I loved getting different perspectives of the world.

Thus, she sought opportunities to learn about fellow students' home countries and listened to their various perspectives. However, she did not stop at that. She wanted to explore the Spanish language and culture in more depth and decided to enroll in the study abroad program in college.

> My most influential experience with other cultures and diversity began when I studied
> abroad in Spain in my sophomore year of college. Living in Spain gave me the opportunity
> to experience diversity in a way I never had before. I had to be open to learning not only a
> new language, but a different way of life.

She reminisced that one of the most impactful experiences during her study abroad term was seeing children's and parents' enthusiasm when she taught them English. She also met her husband in Spain, and witnessed the challenges he experienced in learning English and American culture when they both arrived in the United States. Her own rewarding language immersion experience, coupled with her husband's challenging transition experience, prompted her to enroll in a Master of Arts in Teaching (M.A.T.) program with a concentration in teaching English as a Second Language.

18.4.1.2   An Immigrant Advocate

Living and studying in Spain and seeing her husband struggle to learn English and work on his citizenship paperwork transformed Agnes into an advocate for her students and someone who intentionally pursues opportunities to connect with the Spanish speaking community in her hometown. While taking graduate classes and teaching at a high school for 3 years, she volunteered in the community as an adult ESL teacher helping Latino students learn the English language and cultural practices of their new communities.

> I worked a lot with the Hispanic/Latino students. I made many phone calls home for other
> teachers, as well as translate for parent conferences. This showed me the struggle these
> students have both socially and academically because of the language barrier.

After graduating, she took on another position in the local community college and had been teaching adult ESL for over a year at the time of this study. She described this teaching experience as fulfilling and exceptional and explained that her teaching philosophy focuses on building a learning community that provides a safe space for exploration, dialogue, and mutual appreciation.

> My main belief about teaching is to first have that relationship with the students and really
> connect, and then they learn better. And I believe it is also about teaching to what they need
> to learn, their interests and what will help them succeed in their career or community,
> whatever they're doing.

She concentrates on providing students with materials and activities that meet their needs and relate to their backgrounds and interests. Agnes explores their cultures through asking them a lot of questions, adapting instruction to reflect their backgrounds, and offering additional resources, such as community event brochures, job fair pamphlets, and emails about activities that bring them closer to the community in which they live. She strives to help students explore opportunities to not only improve their linguistic skills but also to thrive in their new communities. Her passion lies in creating change in her students' lives and making them more comfortable in their new communities.

18.4.1.3 An Empowering Educator

Agnes deeply connects with her students and makes sure her teaching addresses their needs. She "listens to them and adjusts [her] instruction accordingly". She noted that her own personal experiences empowered her to be a compassionate and understanding teacher, who puts students' needs first. Going through the immigration and green card process with her husband and working with immigrant families in public schools and the community gave her a clearer understanding of her students' deeply challenging situations. She added, "Seeing how some Americans treat immigrants who do not speak English perfectly opened my eyes to the prejudice and discrimination many immigrants face". She has dedicated her career to helping immigrants thrive in new communities. That is why she makes sure to create a welcoming, transformative learning community in her classroom and brings additional resources to the classroom, promotes events in the community, and engages students in sharing perspectives, experiences, and challenges. She works hard to "make students feel safe and validated". However, sometimes she feels isolated in her classroom and feels pressured by standardized testing and funding requirements.

> The difficulties I have faced is trying to balance the expectations of the institution (testing) with the diverse needs of my students. The school wants to focus on test scores because that is how we get funding for the program. This can negatively affect the classroom environment sometimes, and I try to encourage them not to focus on their test scores.

Since Agnes works part-time, rarely does she have opportunities to collaborate with other faculty, be part of professional development efforts, and seek out support from the administration. She hopes for "more collaboration among the faculty and administration in the department". At the end of the research project, she shared great news. She had been successfully admitted to a PhD program at a local university. She expressed her hope to continue her advocacy efforts by preparing future language teachers to understand and address the needs of ELLs.

To summarize, Agnes is a persistent explorer who has exhibited resilience and perseverance. Her past encounters of discrimination that she witnessed her husband and her students experiencing, the current institutional constraints she faces when teaching at the community college, and her future goals of finishing a doctoral degree developed her identity and sense of agency. She has negotiated her identity throughout her personal and professional life: she was a language explorer, then became an immigrant advocate, and transitioned to becoming an empowering educator who treats her ELLs as her priority. She has exhibited a strong sense of agency in supporting her ELLs by showing compassion, modifying her teaching content and strategies, exploring their needs, and building genuine relationships with them.

18.4.2 Mary

18.4.2.1 A Social Justice Activist

Mary is in her fifties and has been teaching for over 10 years. She identifies as a Jewish American. She said, "Because I have experienced anti-Semitism and marginalization first-hand, I have dedicated my career to helping minority and immigrant students feel welcome and meaningful in their communities". She received an M.A.T. degree in TESOL at a university where she had the opportunity to learn from professors whom she described as knowledgeable and passionate, and who nurtured her social justice aspirations by giving her space to raise concerns about language and power struggles as well as cultural and societal issues. After her graduation, she started her work with adult ELLs in a refugee program that hosted classes in off-campus locations, such as at churches and libraries. That literacy program provided a venue for her social justice efforts. She was involved in curriculum development, engaged in community events, created lessons, and provided resources that would help refugee students integrate into their new communities. She focused on helping students explore new language and cultural practices, so they could feel more welcomed in their new communities.

> I build in a lot of inquiry, sharing, and cultural inclusion throughout the class. Students can feel comfortable sharing their views, culture, and traditions with others. I also have a set of ground rules at the beginning of each course to set a tone of respect and inclusion in the group. My classroom is a community.

After a few years, due to a student-enrollment drop in the refugee program, she transitioned to teaching on-campus classes at the community college. Mary described her new teaching experience as very different from her work with refugees. She noted that there is less community involvement and a stronger focus on academic skills. Therefore, she intentionally brings in additional resources, such as books, brochures, handouts, audio recordings, and videos and works to create a safe environment for discussing cultural differences and social issues in her classes. Her work towards social justice takes a different form in the ESL classroom. She needs to focus on teaching communicative skills but still tries to infuse "topics that relate to students' backgrounds, needs, and the complex issues they experience in their communities". She asks students a lot of questions about their cultures, invites them to bring home food into the classroom, supplements materials that relate to their backgrounds, and promotes examination of their own views, challenges, and inequalities.

18.4.2.2 A Disheartened Educator

At the same time, Mary commented on the scarcity of resources and professional development for teachers. To overcome it, she described how she works to "stay current on research, seek out professional development opportunities and stay focused on the goal of student achievement". She is also concerned that "some instructors do not understand where the students come from, their traditions, and what they need". She commented that it is often difficult to be responsive to what students need, and that it is very challenging to do while working on campus because "the contact hours with students have shrunk. Funding too has shrunk, and student growth has shrunk". More recently, she began teaching higher level classes, but explained, "it is a different environment since the students are not connected to the community as much". Thus, she makes the effort to promote events happening in the community in her classroom, so students can feel more connected to their surrounding communities. She approaches each student individually and reflects on his or her uniqueness.

> Teachers focus on meeting standards and objectives, but teaching ELLs requires a secondary focus on the individuals and group dynamics. The environment in the class must be conducive to learning and students need to feel safe, challenged, and connected. Through the process of reflection, I unpack the elements to see what needs are being met in the most productive manner. Sometimes there are gaps, and it becomes a learning moment for future classes.

At the end of this research project, during a follow-up meeting, Mary shared that she had resigned from the position as an adult ESL teacher, explaining that she had fought for her immigrant students too long and decided she needed to make a change.

In conclusion, Mary's experiences demonstrate a language teacher's varied capacity to exercise agency. She negotiated her identity as a social justice advocate by exploring different strategies to help students feel welcomed in their new communities. Her efforts point to a strong sense of agency in advocating for ELLs, impacted by her own personal beliefs of inclusion and equity, and influenced by her past experiences contending with anti-Semitism and her interest in social justice while a university student. However, dealing with increasing professional insecurities and recognizing that her personal values often run counter to the current language teaching practices advocated by her institution have affected her sense of agency. As a result, her relentless support for her students took a different form. Due to such a discouraging teaching context and her goals of supporting students, Mary quit her teaching job and moved to other community projects that she hopes can help immigrants thrive in the community, pointing to how these future goals have shaped her actions in negotiating her identity as a social justice activist.

18.4.3 Sebastian

18.4.3.1 A Lifelong Learner

Sebastian is a third generation American with European roots. He earned an M.A.T. degree in TESOL and pursued an academic career. He described some of his formative interests:

> I have had an interest in geography and different cultures from childhood, and my life has been in large part an exploration of this and of language. It was only natural that I feel comfortable in an environment that gives me exposure to both. Being an English language teacher in an ESL program provides this daily.

Sebastian taught English in different schools in Asia and Middle East. During that traveling period of his life, he collected an array of experiences where his traditional norms and values were challenged as the Asian and Middle Eastern cultures were so different from what he had known. Sebastian decided to come back to the United States and has been teaching adult ESL for over 15 years at the community college.

Sebastian described his teaching philosophy as focused on language acquisition and mainly on communicative skills. He believes that if "students' cultures and identities are valued, then there is a higher chance of language acquisition". Therefore, language and culture are strongly interconnected in his view. He provides opportunities for students to share their experiences, expertise, and knowledge to advance their language abilities. He frequently creates his own teaching materials, adjusts his instruction based on students' needs, and provides explorative experiences for students to learn practical English, such as by organizing field trips, inviting guest speakers to the class, and showing short films. His aim is to sustain a genuine, communicative learning environment in his classroom where students can explore multiple resources.

18.4.3.2   A Cautious and Creative Teacher

In his reflective journal, Sebastian shared that he also promotes learning about the local community by offering opportunities to explore the city. He has taken students to "tour museums, libraries, and watch documentaries at [a local] movie theatre". He encourages learning about each other through inviting students to share knowledge about diverse cuisines and traditions.

> Rarely have I found textbooks to be so well-constructed that there is not a need for me to add or subtract. I was faced with a challenge that I readily welcomed. From the beginning of my teaching career, I have often and consistently created my own materials.

These additional materials include showing documentaries that represent life in different countries in his classes, bringing pictures that depict various ethnicities and cultures, and incorporating readings that illustrate different social norms. He reflected that he does not shy away from teaching any given topic "unless it is a subject that would lend itself to highlighting some students' life experiences in a negative way". Some of the issues he does not bring up in discussions are immigration, politics, abortion, and religion. He believes these are "highly sensitive issues and potentially too personal". He noted that when he has introduced some of these topics, it was only to "push students to read challenging material and to engage in critical thinking but not to address social justice issues". He wants to create a safe, welcoming, nurturing, respectful, and interesting learning environment, where each student feels comfortable in improving their communication skills and cultural knowledge, and thus avoids topics that may cause conflict or embarrassment.

He also reported that "for the most part, the main challenge I face is the time constraint brought on by teaching schedule". He is also aware of testing pressures in the program and recognizes that students' level gains are tied to funding. Thus, he actively "incorporates multiple choice exercises that require critical thinking skills" and discussions based on resolving problems when students work in groups on reading activities. Using such exercises helps students, Sebastian believes, by "advancing in their language ability and taking a step toward their goals".

To sum up, a collection of life events has shaped Sebastian's identity of a life-long learner. He has always been fond of traveling and learning about languages and cultures. That rich repertoire of past experiences has impacted Sebastian's strong sense of agency in his current context which leads him to support his students through building on their interests and adapting teaching materials accordingly, but also by consciously avoiding sensitive topics, so his students feel comfortable in his classroom. He became a creative but also cautious teacher who aspires to support student success even though he faces institutional challenges that often constrain his actions. Sebastian agreed that the reflective processes during this research helped him better understand his classroom practices and improve them, and that he is looking forward to engaging in culturally responsive teaching more consistently in the future.

18.5   Discussion

The above narratives show that the participants' life stories demonstrate a range of identities that they have negotiated throughout their lives. They illustrate that teacher identity is not fixed and that teachers' multiple identities continually shift throughout their life course (Buchanan, 2015; Varghese et al., 2005). For example, Agnes's explorer identity was developed during her educational journey of studying abroad and building international friendships and relationships. Her language teacher identity shifted to becoming an ELL advocate in the local community after seeing her husband, who is from Spain, struggle in learning English, finding a job, and getting his citizenship after arrival to the United States. These hardships empowered her to get an M.A.T. degree in TESOL, become an adult ESL teacher, and pursue a Ph.D. degree. Mary's cultural and religious background also impacted her identity formation. She is of Jewish heritage, traveled to many countries, and learned Spanish. These diverse cultural experiences empowered her to become an adult ESL instructor and a social justice advocate. Her own experience with anti-Semitism helped her relate to some of the discrimination that immigrants often experience in the U.S. and led her to become an active social justice worker who fights for students' rights and works to help them become part of their local communities. Sebastian's lifelong learner identity is visible in his continuous quest to learn about different countries and languages. He is invested in learning about students' unique backgrounds, needs, and interests. These findings add to the recent research studies showing that teacher identity is constantly negotiated through their personal experiences, interactions, values, and aspirations, and that personal and professional identities are intertwined (Buchanan, 2015; Bukor, 2015). The three language teachers in this study drew on their past experiences of traveling, diverse friendships and relationships, and their cultural heritage when teaching. It is evident that all the participants enjoyed bringing information about community events into the classrooms and taking students out into the community through organizing fieldtrips. Thus, we can see that past and current varied personal experiences have deeply influenced the participants' teaching practices.

The narratives also show that these three participants work to learn about students' unique cultural and linguistic backgrounds and their individual goals and to use that information to strengthen their teaching. However, even though all teachers make sure that their students feel comfortable and validated in their classrooms, they did not all make the same choices in their classrooms. Agnes and Mary actively exercise their agency in their efforts to work for social change. They treat their classrooms as venues for giving students' a voice to share their unique stories, raise concerns, and exchange cultural values and perspectives. Sebastian, however, is cautious and intentionally avoids discussing sensitive topics that pertain to religion, immigration, or politics because he does not want students to feel uneasy. These findings demonstrate that participants make agentive choices in their classrooms that they believe are in the best interest of their students. However, they exercise agency differently in enacting culturally responsive teaching practices when faced with institutional constraints and challenges, such as testing pressures, feelings of isolation, and lack of resources. The teachers' quest to learn about and meet students' needs in the classroom is also visible in their efforts to promote community integration, such as by taking students on field trips. These findings show that language teachers' agency is affected by the interplay of past and present personal and professional experiences, current power structures, institutional resources, and institutional environments, as well as their hopes and future goals (Priestley et al., 2015).

As far as the iterational dimension of agency is concerned, this study provided evidence of the influence of teachers' life histories, beliefs, and values on their agency. Participants' past experiences such as extensive traveling and language learning backgrounds and their beliefs and values connected to creating and sustaining inclusive communities influenced their advocacy efforts, and thus, they became resilient in supporting their ELLs. As far as the practical-evaluative dimension of agency is concerned, the participants' pressuring institutional environments constrained their sense of agency in their current teaching contexts. However, in the face of such constraints participants still showed commitment to meeting their culturally and linguistically diverse students' needs and motivated them to transform their classrooms into welcoming and culturally responsive spaces. Their aspirations for the future, the projective element of agency, led one teacher to stop teaching ESL and seek another outlet to work for the benefit of these students, and a second one enrolled in a Ph.D. program to expand her support efforts, while the third one remained committed to teaching ELLs and to improving his practices. Thus, this research shows the interplay of these various elements for language teachers as they exercise agency (Priestley et al., 2015), which is further impacted by teachers' changing identities.

The findings of this study provide insight into how reflecting on professional identities, experiences, practices, as well as one's social, political, and economic environments can nurture teacher agency, and "help teachers recognize that inclusive practices are not isolated from the structural and cultural contexts of their workplace that might encourage or impede such practices" (Pantić & Florian, 2015: 345). Since the participants of this study have had numerous opportunities to explore other cultures, countries, and values, they have become supportive and intentional teachers who exercise agency in teaching culturally and linguistically diverse learners and working to meet their needs. The data analysis showed that participants took risks in going to foreign places and learning new languages, showed commitment to building diverse relationships, and were inquisitive teachers. These ecological factors influenced their strong sense of agency in supporting their ELL students while also contributing to their changing teaching identities.

18.6 Conclusion

The findings of this study validate that there is a symbiotic relationship between teacher identity and agency as teacher identity plays a crucial role in teachers' agentive moves. The teacher narratives in our study indicate that language teachers exercise agency in their personal and professional spheres. In their classrooms, teachers exercise agency in deliberately evaluating, choosing, and modifying materials and teaching approaches with the goal of addressing students' needs. However, it is crucial to remember that identity and agency are not static and can change in different circumstances and conditions. This study adds to the growing body of research that explores how ecological factors shape teachers' sense of agency. It confirms that teachers' capacity to exercise agency is shaped by multiple experiences, contexts, beliefs, and hopes intertwined with their reflections on their past, present, and future selves. This research study thus provides empirical support demonstrating the multiple factors that relate to the iterative, practical-evaluative, and projective dimensions of teacher agency (Priestley et al., 2015), with emphasis given to language teachers who work with culturally and linguistically diverse students.

References

Atkinson, R. (2007). The life story interview as a bridge in narrative inquiry. In D. J. Clandinin (Ed.), *Handbook of narrative inquiry* (pp. 224–245). Sage Publications.

Barkhuizen, G. (2017). *Reflections on language teacher identity research*. Routledge.

Barkhuizen, G., Benson, P., & Chik, A. (2014). *Narrative inquiry in language teaching and learning research*. Routledge.

Biesta, G. (2008). Learning lives: Learning, identity and agency in the life-course. In *Full research report, ESRC end of award report, RES-139-25-0111*. ESRC.

Buchanan, R. (2015). Teacher identity and agency in an era of accountability. *Teachers and Teaching, 21*(6), 700–719. https://doi.org/10.1080/13540602.2015.1044329

Bukor, E. (2015). Exploring teacher identity from a holistic perspective: Reconstructing and reconnecting personal and professional selves. *Teachers and Teaching, 21*(3), 305–327. https://doi.org/10.1080/13540602.2014.953818

Edwards, E., & Burns, A. (2016). Language teacher–researcher identity negotiation: An ecological perspective. *TESOL Quarterly, 50*(3), 735–745. https://doi.org/10.1002/tesq.313

Emirbayer, M., & Mische, A. (1998). What is agency? *American Journal of Sociology, 103*(4), 962–1023. https://doi.org/10.1086/231294

Flessner, R., Grant, M., Horwitz, J., & Patrizio, K. (2012). *Agency through teacher education. Reflection, community, and learning.* Rowman and Littlefield Publishers.

Freire, P. (1970). *Pedagogy of the oppressed.* Continuum.

Kayi-Aydar, H. (2019). Language teacher agency: Major theoretical considerations, conceptualizations and methodological choices. In H. Kayi-Aydar, X. Gao, E. R. Miller, M. Varghese, & G. Vitanova (Eds.), *Theorizing and analyzing language teacher agency* (pp. 10–22). Multilingual Matters.

Kumaravadivelu, B. (2012). *Language teacher education for a global society: A modular model for knowing, analyzing, recognizing, doing, and seeing.* Routledge.

Ollerhead, S., & Burns, B. (2016). Creativity as resistance: Implications for language teaching and teacher education. In R. H. Jones & J. C. Richards (Eds.), *Creativity in language teaching: Perspectives from research and practice* (pp. 227–240). Routledge.

Pantić, N., & Florian, L. (2015). Developing teachers as agents of inclusion and social justice. *Education Inquiry, 6*(3), 333–351. https://doi.org/10.3402/edui.v6.27311

Polkinghorne, D. E. (1995). Narrative configuration in qualitative analysis. *Qualitative Studies in Education, 8*, 5–23. https://doi.org/10.1080/0951839950080103

Priestley, M., Edwards, R., Priestley, A., & Miller, K. (2012). Teacher agency in curriculum making: Agents of change and spaces for maneuver. *Curriculum Inquiry, 42*(2), 191–214. https://doi.org/10.1111/j.1467-873X.2012.00588.x

Priestley, M., Biesta, G. J. J., & Robinson, S. (2015). *Teacher agency: An ecological approach.* Bloomsbury.

Tao, J., & Gao, X. (2021). *Language teacher agency.* Cambridge University Press.

Varghese, A., Morgan, B., Johnson, B., & Johnson, K. A. (2005). Theorizing language teacher identity: Three perspectives and beyond. *Journal of Language, Identity & Education, 4*(1), 21–44. https://doi.org/10.1207/s15327701jlie0401_2

Vitanova, G. (2018). "Just treat me as a teacher!" mapping language teacher agency through gender, race, and professional discourses. *System, 79*, 28–37. https://doi.org/10.1016/j.system.2018.05.013

White, C. (2018). Language teacher agency. In S. Mercer & A. Kostoulas (Eds.), *Language teacher psychology* (pp. 196–210). Multilingual Matters.

Chapter 19
Understanding Positional Identities of ESL Teachers in Response to Identity Conflicts Through an Analysis of Emotions and Agency

Kate Shea, Shi Li, and Hayriye Kayi-Aydar

Abstract This study examines how ESL instructors position themselves through agentic actions and emotions in situations that involve identity conflicts in the work environment. Through a written interview, participants responded to 10 real-life scenarios adapted from scholarly literature in which an ESL/EFL teacher experienced an identity conflict. The teacher-participants were asked (a) what emotion (s) they would experience in such situations and (b) how they would act in the situations described in the survey. Based on the emotions and identities identified in the responses, a follow-up focus group interview was conducted with selected participants to further understand the nuances of emotionality, agency, and identity work. The thematic analysis through qualitative coding indicates that (a) the privileged identities of the teacher-participants created uncertainty in understanding and identifying with marginalized identities, (b) teachers reported agentic action by seeking administrative support instead of dealing with the identity conflict directly, and (c) collective agency played a crucial role in teachers' professional identity construction. These findings shed further light on the interconnectedness of teacher identity, emotions, and agency and offer implications for language teachers, administrators, and teacher educators.

Keywords Teacher emotions · Teacher identity · Teacher agency · Identity conflict

19.1 Introduction

Language teacher identity construction is an ongoing process that is reflected through actions and emotions. During classroom teaching and interactions, teachers may experience a wide array of emotions, which influence and are also influenced by numerous contextual factors (Benesch, 2017; Hayik & Weiner-Levy, 2019; Song,

K. Shea · S. Li · H. Kayi-Aydar (✉)
University of Arizona, Tucson, AZ, USA
e-mail: hkaydar@arizona.edu

© The Author(s), under exclusive license to Springer Nature Switzerland AG 2022 277
K. Sadeghi, F. Ghaderi (eds.), *Theory and Practice in Second Language Teacher Identity*, Educational Linguistics 57, https://doi.org/10.1007/978-3-031-13161-5_19

2016). As Wolff and De Costa (2017) argue, emotions extend "beyond the self to include cultural and social forces" and are "bound with identities" (p. 79). Examining the role of emotions in teaching thus offers insights about teachers' identities, classroom decisions, and agentic actions, which ultimately sheds light on the intricacies of classroom teaching and learning.

In this study, we focus on the complex interplay between language teacher identity, agency, and emotions by utilizing a scenario-based written interview and semi-structured focus group interviews. By particularly focusing on contexts that include a conflict as well as a variety of identities, mostly marginalized (see Appendix 1), we aim to understand what emotions our participants express, what agentic actions they might take, and what positional identities they construct as they respond to the presented scenarios. The strategies, emotions, and potential actions reported by the teacher-participants in this study offer useful insights and implications for TESOL professionals in similar contexts.

19.1.1   Theoretical Concepts

This study is built on the interrelationship of theoretical concepts of emotions, agency, and identity. We draw upon the poststructural work by Zembylas (2011) in defining, understanding, and analyzing teacher emotions in relation to teacher identity and agency. In his poststructural theorization of emotions in the context of teaching, Zembylas (2011) argues that

> emotions are not private or universal and are not impulses that simply happen to passive sufferers (the Aristotelian view). Instead, emotions are constituted through language and refer to wider social life. (p. 34)

Emotions are embedded in power relations, ideologies, as well as moral and cultural values. According to Zembylas (2011), emotions are *interactive* and *performative* as the words used to describe emotions "are themselves practices performed to serve specific purposes in the process of negotiating reality" (p. 33). Emotions also have the power to (trans)form individuals, social interactions, and power relations and are thus *transformative* in nature. Emotions therefore provide an appropriate lens to understand teacher agency and identity as emotional experiences of teachers influence their thinking, risk-taking, planning, and acting, and ultimately their becoming certain kinds of teachers (Reio Jr., 2005).

Similar to emotions, teacher identities and agency are also context-dependent, socially-constructed, power-driven, and situation-specific (Varghese et al., 2005). In this chapter, we understand teacher agency as an intentional *author*ity to make decisions, act, and reflect on the actions taken, which is shaped by power relations, identity, and contextual circumstances (Davies, 2000; Kayi-Aydar, 2019; Tao & Gao, 2017). Individuals can "move within and between discourses" to "counteract, modify, refuse, or go beyond" those discourses (Davies, 2000, p. 2), ultimately shaping and being shaped by the subject positions available to them. In this poststructural conceptualization of agency, self is portrayed as "an agentive act of investment in, or identification with, already available subject positions" (Gray & Morton, 2018, p. 10). These positions are constructed momentarily as individuals locate themselves and others in interactions and narrated events (Davies & Harré, 1999), and an accumulation of those positions over time and across settings form certain identities for individuals, which are called *positional identities* (Kayi-Aydar, 2018).

19.2 Literature Review

Emotions, identity, and agency have received strong attention in the second/foreign language teacher education literature. While most of the studies have concentrated on each separately, others have examined them in pairs, such as emotions and agency (e.g., Benesch, 2018), teacher identity and agency (e.g., Wernicke, 2018), or emotions and identity (e.g., Reio Jr., 2005). Emotionality as it impacts research in second/foreign language teacher agency has been documented in situations where emotions experienced by the teachers have clashed with workplace policies. These studies have concentrated on English instructors' felt emotions on issues such as plagiarism (e.g., Benesch, 2018), teachers' perception of teaching-as-caring and the everyday emotional labor of classroom management (e.g., Miller & Gkonou, 2018), attendance (e.g., Benesch, 2017), and student advocacy and social justice (e.g., Maddamsetti, 2021). Taken together, these studies reiterate that emotions are an inherent feature of any language classroom and experienced in all aspects of language teaching with contextual factors varying from macro-level socio-political or cultural factors to micro-level classroom management choices and encounters.

Studies have also shed light on the relationship between second/foreign language identity and agency (e.g., Edwards, 2019; Kayi-Aydar, 2015; Wernicke, 2018), most often indicating how agentic actions play a significant role as language teachers attempt to sustain and project an ideal or a desired professional self. Tao and Gao (2017), for example, found out that, during curriculum reform at a Chinese university, English for Specific Purposes (ESP) teachers' agentic choices were mediated by their identity commitment; in other words, the kinds of teachers that they desired to become. In their analysis of critical classroom incidents experienced by four Korean English language teachers, Hiver and Whitehead (2018) similarly observed that teachers exercised agency in classroom practice through "deliberately enacting their individual values, beliefs, and goals" (p. 8). They concluded that "agency was, therefore, tightly connected to the ways in which individual teachers constructed a sense of meaning and purpose for their professional role, and how they deliberately called on the autobiographical reasoning that contributed to their identity" (p. 9).

Another line of research has focused on second/foreign language teacher emotions and identity (e.g., Song, 2016; Wolff & De Costa, 2017). An emphasis in this area of literature is on teacher reflection. Song (2016), for example, showed in a study on South Korean teachers of EFL that teachers are able to recognize their emotions, identify the sources, and understand their own practice. Such reflections in the Song study ultimately brought a change in teacher-participants' professional identities as the teachers experienced a shift in their emotions from a closed to open vulnerability. In a similar study, Maddamsetti (2021) illustrated how one elementary school ESL teacher's reflections on her emotions in different times and spaces were integral to her agency and identity. The contextual raciolinguistic ideologies as well as the professional relationships with her peers and other scholar-activists affected this teacher's emotions and accordingly her construction of her identities of advocacy. Both studies and others (e.g., Hayik & Weiner-Levy, 2019) highlight the importance of identifying and analyzing emotions experienced by language teachers and offering support to teachers so that they can form competent professional identities.

While these studies have advanced the scholarly knowledge about each of the three concepts, very few studies have examined the interrelationships among them. We argue that teacher identity, emotions, and agency are inseparable and interdependent, and a comprehensive understanding of who language teachers are demands an investigation of these interrelated concepts. We aim to understand what kinds of positional identities ESL teachers construct by analyzing their self-reported agentive (in)actions and emotions. Building on the studies reviewed above, we ask: What positional identities emerge in ESL teachers' reported actions and emotions in contexts that involve a conflict?

19.3 Methods

This qualitative study used different data sources. By collecting data from participants with different perspectives and experiences and from a follow-up focus group interview with a subset of the same participants, we were able to establish triangulation and ensure the trustworthiness of our study (Merriam, 2009).

19.3.1 Participants and Context

We invited individuals who were current (at the time of the study) or past students in an M.A. or Ph.D. language teacher education program (with a TESOL focus) in a Southwestern University in the U.S. ESL teachers working in adult/college ESL programs in the local context were also invited to participate. We recruited participants through: (a) current and alumni listservs of a local MA TESOL and Ph.D. program, (b) state-wide English instructor professional communities, (c) local non-profits offering English instruction, and (d) social media posts in affiliated Facebook groups. Seven participants completed written responses, and among them, four volunteered to participate in a focus group interview. At the time of the

Table 19.1 Demographic data of participants

Written interview participants:				Focus group interview participants:			
Gender	Age	Years of experience	Race/ ethnicity	Gender	Age	Years of experience	Race/ ethnicity
7 female	Range: 29–74 Average: 45.6	Range: 1.5–20 Average: 8.8	White, Caucasian	4 female	Range: 29–48 Average: 36.25	Range: 5–16 Average: 9	White, Caucasian

study, all the participants were teaching ESL in different settings (e.g., college intensive English programs, community ESL, and/or online). Table 19.1 includes participants' demographic data.

19.3.2 Data Collection

We designed and conducted the study in two phases. In the first phase, the participants provided demographic information by completing a background questionnaire, and they also responded, in writing, to a series of scenarios (see Appendix 2 for a sample) via Qualtrics XM online survey (Qualtrics, 2020). The survey, in the form of a written interview, presented participants with 10 research-based scenarios (see Appendix 1) that described some identity crises/conflicts experienced by ESL teachers. In creating the scenarios, we did only minimal changes to the language of the articles we used in order to reflect the cases and research findings accurately. For most scenarios, upon reading each story, participants were asked two questions: (1) How would you feel if you were the individual described in the scenario? (2) What action would you take if you were the individual? For two scenarios, participants were asked to respond as a colleague of the character. The identity conflict aspect of the study was not made explicitly clear to participants, and the scenarios presented in the written interview were introduced as emotions experienced in everyday teaching scenarios. In this way, the research may be seen as complementary but still different from other scenario-based interview studies (e.g., Miller & Gkonou, 2018) where labels of common emotions were initially shared with participants to facilitate responses.

The participants who volunteered for a semi-structured focus group interview also participated in the second phase of data collection. The follow-up interview was held via Zoom, was audio recorded for transcription, and totaled 64 minutes. Participants were reminded that they had the option to keep their camera off and update their Zoom username to a pseudonym to ensure as much privacy as desired. All participants' names noted in the findings are pseudonyms that were either self-selected in the focus group interview or assigned by our research team. The interview was semi-structured and aimed to elicit participants' thoughts about the emotions and actions provided in their responses in the first phase. Based on their own professional experience, the teachers were also invited to discuss the scenarios in which they could relate more strongly, or reversely, those scenarios with which they found it difficult to relate.

19.3.3   Data Analysis

The data were elicited using the background questionnaire, scenario-based written interview, and focus group interview. We analyzed the data collected from the written interview and the follow-up focus group interview inductively. In the first stage, we exported the responses to the two questions (how they would feel and act) in the written interview from Qualtrics into two separate files and analyzed them through open-coding to generate categories and themes. Each response was first examined by one researcher and reviewed by another to ensure consistency. When coding the participants' answers about their feelings in response to the events described in the scenarios, we looked for emotion words like *sad*, *frustrated*, or *angry*, and also which specific part of the scenario aroused those emotions (e.g., feeling sad about losing the job *vs.* feeling sad for the students). We highlighted the words and listed them after each scenario or at the margin of the page. We then grouped similar emotions to yield categories. In regards to the responses about how the teachers would act when facing the situations in the scenarios, we first marked all the expressions about actions (e.g., *I would try to make workshops for the students.*) and listed them to let clusters of codes emerge. We regrouped the emerging categories so that we could see the common themes. This first stage was a data-driven, inductive process. In the second stage, the focus group interview transcript was first auto-generated by Zoom and proofread by two of us (the first two authors). We focused on positioning by identifying how the teachers assigned positions to themselves and others. Once we completed the coding process, we conducted a final cross-scenario analysis in which we revisited our categories and themes across different scenarios and data sources and refined them whenever necessary. This recursive process eventually led to three main themes, which we shall discuss in the following section, centering around the interrelationship between ESL teachers' emotions, actions, and the development of their positional identities in a context of conflict.

19.4   Findings

Using qualitative data, this study aimed to understand what kinds of positional identities were constructed in response to identity conflicts by a group of ESL teachers in the same geographical region but in different teaching settings. In order to understand this, we analyzed (in)actions and emotions reported by our participants.

In the following sections, we elaborate on the emotions and accompanying actions reported by the teachers as we discuss the positional identities of the participants and address our research question. An inductive and recursive analysis of the data is presented here in the grouped thematic findings of (a) positional dissonance due to privilege and experience(s), (b) the invisible positional identities in cultural relationships, and (c) the construction of positional identity as an agent through collective agency and support.

19.4.1 Positional Dissonance Due to Privilege and Experience(s)

We asked participants to describe their emotions and actions in response to a number of real-life scenarios, several of which prompted resistance from participants. The relatively privileged identities of the participants, in contrast to many of the individuals depicted in the scenarios, were the most commonly cited reason for positional dissonance, although teaching context, age, and professional experience were also noted factors. In the written interview, participants explained they would struggle to provide an answer given their different life experiences. Rochelle, for example, noted in the written interview that she had a "really hard time responding" to a particular scenario as "[she has not] experienced discrimination in this way before." In the focus group, all four participants explicitly acknowledged privilege as a factor in struggling to position themselves as the scenarios' main characters. While they positioned themselves as empathetic to the character, they seemed to be troubled in knowing what actions to take or what emotions to feel, as seen in Rochelle's remarks below:

> It was a little difficult for me to respond to the questions like, "If you were this person, how would you feel? And what would you do?", especially the "how you feel" part because uh, some of the people were non-native English speakers, non-white, and I am a native English speaker and I am white and so to say "Oh, I would feel this way" felt uncomfortable to me, because I... I can't put myself in their shoes and say "this is how I would feel" without considering that, that disconnect between their experience and my experience. (Rochelle, focus group interview)

Ashley also shared similar reflections:

> I have not had a similar experience, which I definitely understand is a very privileged thing to be able to say. Even though I'm third generation to this country, I still consider myself very proud of where my family came from. And for somebody to be in a place where they are, like proud of that, but then also embarrassed enough to have to lie to accommodate other people, I just, I couldn't imagine feeling that, I mean I could but, I haven't had to. (Ashley, focus group interview)

In contrast to the empathy or sadness often described in response to instances of marginalized identities, feelings of frustration were most often shared in the two scenarios in which participants were asked to respond as a mentor of the white American instructor presented in the scenario. In the focus group interview, one participant justified their frustration due to their shared privileged positional identity saying:

> I feel like I can criticize her because I'm a white American woman and so is this Emily. Why didn't she try to learn a little bit of the language or take a weekend TEFL course? So, I didn't feel quite as bad for her as I did for some of the other people in the other situation so I thought, well, if that were me I would have prepared. (Beth, focus group interview)

As seen in Beth's comment above and throughout our data, the participants could position themselves as an agent by offering strategies, describing the actions that they would take, and acknowledging their emotions explicitly when they could make linguistic, ethnic, racial, or gendered connections. In one scenario, Puja, an immigrant, non-native English-speaking instructor in the U.S. felt uncomfortable with her students' advanced knowledge about U.S. culture and idioms as she was simultaneously learning the content herself. Rather than mirror the feelings of discomfort, inadequacy, or fear, that Puja described feeling in the teaching context, participants described contrasting emotions from a Western-centric view of classroom management that typically positions the classroom teacher as a co-learner and collaborator in the classroom (e.g., Dennen, 2011):

> excited to learn from my students. (Laura, written interview)

> excited about an opportunity to model lifelong learning. (Kelly, written interview)

The participants recast Puja's anxiety-inducing identity experience more positively by describing an alternate pedagogical approach:

> I often try to take a co-teaching or co-learning approach, so this seems like a good opportunity for shared exploration into American culture. I think I would frame activities like this as a collaborative self-discovery process. (Kat, written interview)

> I would absolutely demonstrate that the language learning process is ongoing by exemplifying learning behaviors to my students. This might mean saying "I don't know what that idiom means, let's look it up!" or "I haven't watched it! I'll put it on my list!" This positions me as a co-learner with students rather than an expert. I may be a bit further along the path than my students, but we can still go down unexplored paths together! (Rochelle, written interview)

By these comments, participants provided more agentic actions and positive emotional responses than were described in the scenario with almost no attention to the identity conflict Puja experienced due to her ethnic and linguistic background. These reflections further indicate the teacher-participants' struggle in moving beyond their own identities and contexts to make sense of identity conflicts experienced by others.

19.4.2 Occupying Invisible Positional Identities: Cultural Relationships

Highlighting the importance of relationships in assuming a positional identity, participants' responses frequently reflected a desire to know more details so as to contextualize their response, offering statements such as:

This would depend a bit on my relationship to Neal, and my perception of his openness to conversation. (Kate, written interview)

When asked explicitly how the participants handled their emotional responses in different scenarios, agency again surfaced as a determining factor:

I try to take it on myself and see where I can change, where do I have agency? Not even where I can do better, where do I have agency to change things? (Rochelle, focus group interview)

I think like Rochelle said when I'm in a situation where I don't have agency, that's really hard for me to deal with and that's the kind of thing that I would sit in and stew in and have a hard time finding my way out of. (Kelly, focus group interview)

Rochelle and Kelly's statements highlight how agency, or the lack of, impacts their ability to process emotions. Our written interviews and focus group findings also reflect the emotional labor (Hochschild, 1983) in teaching contexts when there was a lack of agency and suppressed emotions due to the context or relationship described. In the focus group interview, we asked participants to elaborate on how professional and personal relationships in different cultural contexts informed their actions and emotions. Kelly shared the following:

I didn't really have anybody to talk about it with. I think I just kind of had to figure out how I was going to keep myself okay so I accommodated to some degree like I would pull my bangs back, so that when I wore my veil it would only be my face, and we're full veil. I also helped run a girls mentoring center and I had gotten close with these girls. The idea was to help them stay in school, and I was helping this girl write her speech for the end of the year ceremony and I touched her hand while she was writing and she yanked her hand back like, you know, this non-Muslim had touched her and she was very alarmed by that. And that was super hurtful. Super hurtful. (Kelly, focus group interview)

Later in the interview Kelly acknowledged that she did not make those emotions known to the student in her anecdote and also kept her feelings to herself and took no action in other similar incidents. As seen in her anecdote, the relationships Kelly had with her students, shaped by the cultural context, played a role in the emotional labor Kelly experienced. She chose not to exercise agency by hiding her emotions. Such withdrawal seemed to position her as a more integrated community member at the expense of more positive emotions in her professional role as a teacher. In another related example, Beth described choosing inaction in the face of sexual discrimination in the workplace and later feeling regret at how it was handled.

Beth: Then, in a completely different situation where a colleague and I were with a boss and a visitor onto the campus. My colleague and I were both women and my boss was a man, and afterward we checked in with each other to say "did you feel like as women we were told to shut up and let the man handle it?" And she's like "yeah, yeah it was", and we never confronted him about it. We just didn't feel comfortable doing that. He was her boss. And certainly, we were working in ESL; there's no money, so it's not like we were going to get a promotion anyway so there's no danger to us, of not getting the promotion or, you know, not getting the reward because there was no reward. Now if that had been different maybe we could have said something, but that would have been a situation where it would have been a different kind of conflict that we were not comfortable with.

Researcher 3: So, I think a lot of the time it's really all about 'what is at stake'? Right? It's very contextual in a sense?

> Beth: Or do I want to ruin this relationship? There's no monetary risk or reward here, but now I've got a pretty good working relationship with that person. Do I want to go there and ruin it over this, when solving it isn't going to really do anything for me except maybe, you know, I don't know. He's - maybe I could have changed his mind but I didn't have a lot of hope in that situation. So, yeah, but looking back it's one of those things that you regret later you're like "well come on we should have - We should have stood up for ourselves there," but hopefully we will have another chance to. (Beth, focus group interview)

Kelly chose inaction to maintain her position and relationship in her community as someone above an emotional response, but then still feels the emotional sting of her student's actions. Beth also chose inaction when she weighed the merits of action versus inaction in pointing out workplace discrimination later causing her to feel regret that she had not "stood up for herself." In these examples, participants' agency, identities, and emotions were all interconnected and shaped by their relationships with others in their local cultural contexts. Their action or inaction was determined by the positions they wanted to assume in relation to colleagues or community members and were dependent on their current relationship and power differences.

19.4.3   Becoming an Agentic Self: Seeking Collective Agency and Emotional Support

While privileged identities and relationships guided the adopted positional identities in situations with an identity conflict, the roles of supervisors, work administration, and colleagues in constructing agentic selves were discussed at length by participants. The support by administrators was reported to be significant in inspiring instructors' positive emotional response while engaged in work:

> Well in my current job I feel very trusted. I feel like my bosses know that I do good work. They trust me to be creative. They trust me to solve these problems and I feel really empowered and that has just snowballed into growing a lot as a professional. (Kelly, focus group interview)

> I'm part-time adjunct to two different universities. And it's not that I'm treated badly at one and completely positively at the other, but there is one where I feel so much more empowered and trusted. The other one where it's like, "well I'd better do what they say because they're not really open to anything else." And it... I mean, it makes such a huge difference, right? That you feel you can experiment, try something a little different. (Beth, focus group interview)

When asked what they would do in the face of conflicts, the teachers repeatedly showed a strong orientation to initiate conversations with school administrators and the supervisors: "I would talk to the supervisory level" (Maggie, written interview), or "definitely bring this to someone higher up than myself" (Ashley, written interview). However, when the working environment seemed illiberal or difficult to obtain backing from, teachers were more inclined to play a passive role rather than to take any actions at all: "If you are in a situation where you fear being fired, then you're not going to say anything" (Beth, focus group interview). These comments point out the importance of administrative support, or lack thereof, in constructing and empowering agentic teacher selves, as agency and identity are both shaped by power relationships and are thus context-dependent (Tao & Gao, 2017; Varghese et al., 2005).

Participants did not always position themselves as passive colleagues in their relations with supervisors. In response to various scenarios where there was an apparent lack of administrative support, participants not only took a proactive stance when confronting the school administration, but they also turned to colleagues and professional communities to seek peer support:

> I might reach out to my local TESOL or other professional groups to see if anyone else had had success challenging these policies. I would then pull together a group of colleagues with the goal of educating admin, school board, and staff about language varieties, and advocating for changes to the policies. (Kelly, written interview)

Alongside their call for assistance from coworkers and the community in the absence of work administration, participants also provided examples and comments on collegial companionship and peer support from professional communities as vital resources to help them work through difficult emotions. As most participants noted, when charged with negative feelings, their first reaction was to "seek validation" (Rochelle and Beth, focus group interview) from colleagues through "complaining and venting" (Rochelle, Kelly, and Beth, focus group interview). The data also implied the importance of a collegial bond for healthy emotional well-being. Additionally, in half of the scenarios, respondents stated their intention to solicit collective and communal support as the coping mechanism for conflict situations. By joining small groups of school faculty, larger professional bodies (e.g., the local TESOL chapter or the union), or virtual communities (like an online teachers group), teachers shared their experiences and thoughts, built solidarity among like-minded peers, and acted through the exercise of collective agency, as one participant said, "As professionals, we need to help each other." (Laura, written interview).

19.5 Discussion and Implications

In this study, we examined the construction of positional teacher identities, through an analysis of teacher emotions and actions, in contexts that involved an identity conflict. In selecting scenarios that represented a variety of researched L2 teacher experiences, the participants were presented with both similar and dissimilar experiences to respond to and asked to imagine their ensuing actions. The focus group interview allowed for additional clarification and triangulation on findings from the written interviews to better understand the interconnectedness of teacher identity, agency, and emotions.

Unlike in previous studies (e.g., Mueller & O'Connor, 2007) in which teachers avoided or resisted critically exploring their own identities, our participants were aware of the privileged identity positions, in particular due to their race (white) and language background (English native speaker). Furthermore, in most scenarios, they could also effectively identify different forms of -isms (e.g., racism, sexism, etc.) in relation to the identity conflict. However, the privileged identities of our participants prevented them from putting themselves into the shoes of those with minoritized or marginalized identities. The teachers showed uncertainty in terms of the emotions they would feel or the actions they would take in such situations. Furthermore, similar to other studies that reported how unequal power relations between teachers and their supervisors shaped teachers' agency (e.g., Fones, 2019), our study indicated that the relationships involving unequal power relations in the work environment played a significant role in teachers' professional identity construction. Our findings further illustrate that the teachers often sought support from administration or peers in dealing with an identity conflict, a finding also reported in various studies (e.g., Maddamsetti, 2021).

Based on the findings, we offer several recommendations for teachers, administrators, and teacher educators. The marginalized and minoritized teacher identities have been widely documented in the TESOL teacher education scholarly literature, which should be integrated into TESOL teacher education curricula. Given the struggles our participants reported due to their privileged identities, it is important that language teacher educators offer opportunities in their classrooms for teachers to share their identity-oriented experiences. This allows students with less privileged identities to share their perspectives. Sharing stories and reflecting on them collectively as a group will allow teachers to learn from life experiences that differ from their own and develop strategies to overcome difficult emotions and identity conflicts. As reported by our participants, administrators play a crucial role in situations that involve identity related tensions. Individuals in administrative positions that work directly or closely with teachers can help build safe spaces where teachers can share their experiences, seek support, and learn to negotiate conflict. Such opportunities promote collective agency that is necessary for empowered professional identities. In the context of second/foreign language teaching, studies on the interrelationships among teacher emotions, agency, and identities have mostly focused on situations where emotions experienced by teachers are negatively impacted by contextual forces surrounding their teaching practice (see Kayi-Aydar et al., 2019 for a collection of studies). However, it is important to note that emotions, both positive and negative, are guiding forces in change and growth, and in furthering research on emotionality in the teaching context, we advocate for awareness of its impact on teachers' lives in support of their practice, institutional support, and professional development.

A limitation of this study was the similar background and demographics of the recruited participants. While recruitment was intended to be broad but localized, all of the participants identified as white women. While this is a reflection of the U.S. teaching professoriate more broadly (Hancock, 2017), this lack of diversity in both the larger educator population and our sampling is challenging to researchers of teacher agency, teacher identity, and teacher emotions, as these interconnected elements also exist within larger societal constructs where intersecting identities are crucial considerations and add to the complexity and understandings we can draw from research.

19.6 Conclusion

This study sheds further light on the interconnectedness of language teacher identities, emotions, and agency. An analysis of teacher emotions and agency offers a nuanced understanding of professional identities of teachers. Through critical reflections and collectively sharing personal and professional experiences, language teachers can also learn more about themselves and make sense of the privileged or subordinated identities in their work environments. This study supports the common finding in the literature that teacher identities, emotions, and agency are all contextually shaped. We can understand language teachers' struggles, values, emotions, beliefs, practices, and ultimately their identities by focusing on and understanding their contexts and relationships, for which we need systematic collection and analysis of stories, experiences, and practices of English language teachers from diverse geographical, cultural, and social settings.

Appendices

Appendix 1: Identities Reflected in the Scenario Prompts

Literature from which sample narrative/identity conflict was drawn:	Identities Discussed:				
	Gender	Racial	Linguistic	Cultural	Professional
Reeves, J. (2009). (K-12, U.-S. Language Arts instructor, white, male, novice teacher)			✓		✓
Liu, Y., & Xu, Y. (2011). (Univ., China, EFL, Chinese, female, novice teacher)				✓	✓
Mumford, M. J., & Rubadeau, K. (2020). (Univ., South Korea, ESL, expat instructor, male)		✓	✓	✓	✓
Simon-Maeda, A. (2004). (Univ., Japan, EFL, Korean immigrant instructor, female)	✓	✓		✓	✓
Motha, S. (2006). (K-12, U.S., TESOL, white, female)		✓	✓		
Song, J. (2020). (K-12, U.S., ESL, white, female, novice teacher)					✓
Kocabaş-Gedik, P. & Hart, D. O. (2021). (Univ., Turkey, ESL, expat instructor, white, female, novice teacher)				✓	
Aneja, G. A. (2016). (K-12, U.S., TESOL, expat instructor from India, female)		✓	✓		

(continued)

Literature from which sample narrative/identity conflict was drawn:	Identities Discussed:				
	Gender	Racial	Linguistic	Cultural	Professional
Maddamsetti, J. (2021). (K-12, U.S., ESL, Hispanic, female)		✓	✓	✓	
Wolff, D., & De Costa, P. (2017). (Advance learners, U.S., ESL, NNEST from Bangladesh, female)		✓	✓	✓	

Appendix 2: Sample Scenario from Written Interview Prompts

The following sample excerpt was adapted from research conducted by: Reeves, J. (2009). Teacher investment in learner identity. *Teaching and Teacher Education,* 25(1), 34–41.

Neal was in his mid-20s who had worked with a few ELLs in his English language arts classes. He had taught approximately 12 ELLs in his 4 years of teaching. Neal, like the great majority of his teaching colleagues at Eaglepoint High School (a pseudonym), was White and a native speaker of English. Neal perceived his colleagues to position ELLs as different from other students and in need of special care, which, in Neal's view, only served to disadvantage ELLs. Neal's primary positioning of ELLs was "just like any [other] kid" (Neal, interview, October 24, 2001, p. 5). The learning of English was no different, or at least not significantly different, for ELLs than it was for English proficient students. While Neal did note that ELLs had a linguistic difference in that they were not yet proficient in English, this difference held little saliency for him. The elimination of the linguistic difference, in Neal's view, was important for life beyond schools, and the way to eliminate ELLs' linguistic difference was to ignore it. "[I]n society it's not like you're going to wear a badge that says 'English is not my first language. Be Patient.' You know? Everybody can't...and so, I mean, and that's how I always try to apply it to society (Neal, interview, October 24, 2001, p. 7)."

Q1. If you were an ESL teacher in Neal's school, how would you feel about Neal's remarks about ELLs and his classroom practice?

Q2. If you were an ESL teacher in Neal's school, what would you do?

References

Benesch, S. (2017). *Emotions and English language teaching: Exploring teachers' emotion labor.* Routledge.

Benesch, S. (2018). Emotions as agency: Feeling rules, emotion labor, and English language teachers' decision-making. *System, 79,* 60–69. https://doi.org/10.1016/j.system.2018.03.015

Davies, B. (2000). *A body of writing, 1990–1999*. Rowman & Littlefield.

Davies, B., & Harré, R. (1999). Positioning and personhood. In R. Harré & L. van Langenhove (Eds.), *Positioning theory* (pp. 32–52). Wiley-Blackwell.

Dennen, V. (2011). Facilitator presence and identity in online discourse: Use of positioning theory as an analytic framework. *Instructional Science, 39*(4), 527–541. https://doi.org/10.1007/s11251-010-9139-0

Edwards, E. (2019). English language teachers' agency and identity mediation through action research: A Vygotskian sociocultural analysis. In *Theorizing and analyzing language teacher agency* (pp. 141–159). Multilingual Matters.

Fones, A. (2019). Examining high school English language learner teacher agency: Opportunities and constraints. In *Theorizing and analyzing language teacher agency* (pp. 24–43). Multilingual Matters.

Gray, J., & Morton, T. (2018). *Social interaction and English language teacher identity*. EUP.

Hancock, S. (2017). *White women's work: Examining the intersectionality of teaching, identity, and race*. Information Age Publishing.

Hayik, R., & Weiner-Levy, N. (2019). Prospective Arab teachers' emotions as mirrors to their identities and culture. *Teaching and Teacher Education, 85*, 36–44.

Hiver, P., & Whitehead, G. E. K. (2018). Sites of struggle: Classroom practice and the complex dynamic entanglement of language teacher agency and identity. *System*. https://doi.org/10.1016/j.system.2018.04.015

Hochschild. (1983). *The Managed heart: Commercialization of human feeling*. University of California Press.

Kayi-Aydar, H. (2015). Multiple identities, negotiations, and agency across time and space: A narrative inquiry of a foreign language teacher candidate. *Critical Inquiry in Language Studies, 12*(2), 137–160.

Kayi-Aydar, H. (2018). *Positioning theory in applied linguistics*. Palgrave Macmillan.

Kayi-Aydar, H. (2019). Language teacher agency: Major theoretical considerations, conceptualizations and methodological choices. In H. Kayi-Aydar, X. (Andy) Gao, E. R. Miller, M. Varghese, & G. Vitanova (Eds.), *Theorizing and analyzing language teacher agency* (pp. 10–22). Multilingual Matters. https://doi.org/10.21832/9781788923927-004

Kayi-Aydar, H., Gao, X., Miller, E. R., Varghese, M., & Vitanova, G. (2019). Theorizing and analyzing language teacher agency. *Multilingual Matters*. https://doi.org/10.21832/9781788923927-004

Maddamsetti, J. (2021). Exploring an elementary ESL teacher's emotions and advocacy identity. *International Multilingual Research Journal, 15*(3), 235–252. https://doi.org/10.1080/19313152.2021.1883792

Merriam, S. B. (2009). *Qualitative research: A guide to design and implementation*. Jossey-Bass.

Miller, E. R., & Gkonou, C. (2018). Language teacher agency, emotion labor and emotional rewards in tertiary-level English language programs. *System, 79*, 49–59. https://doi.org/10.1016/j.system.2018.03.002

Mueller, J., & O'Connor, C. (2007). Telling and retelling about self and "others": How pre-service teachers (re) interpret privilege and disadvantage in one college classroom. *Teaching and Teacher Education, 23*(6), 840–856. https://doi.org/10.1016/j.tate.2006.01.011

Qualtrics. (2020). *Qualtrics XM*. (Version September 2021) [software]. https://www.qualtrics.com

Reio, T. G., Jr. (2005). Emotions as a lens to explore teacher identity and change: A commentary. *Teaching and Teacher Education, 21*(8), 985–993. https://doi.org/10.1016/j.tate.2005.06.008

Song, J. (2016). Emotions and language teacher identity: Conflicts, vulnerability, and transformation. *TESOL Quarterly, 50*(3), 631–654. https://doi.org/10.1002/tesq.312

Tao, J., & Gao, X. (2017). Teacher agency and identity commitment in curricular reform. *Teaching and Teacher Education, 63*, 346–355. https://doi.org/10.1016/j.tate.2017.01.010

Varghese, M., Morgan, B., Johnston, B., & Johnson, K. A. (2005). Theorizing language teacher identity: Three perspectives and beyond. *Journal of language, Identity, and Education, 4*(1), 21–44. https://doi.org/10.1207/s15327701jlie0401_2

Wernicke, M. (2018). Plurilingualism as agentive resource in L2 teacher identity. *System, 79*, 91–102. https://doi.org/10.1016/j.system.2018.07.005

Wolff, D., & De Costa, P. I. (2017). Expanding the language teacher identity landscape: An investigation of the emotions and strategies of a NNEST: Expanding the language teacher identity landscape. *The Modern Language Journal, 101*(S1), 76–90. https://doi.org/10.1111/modl.12370

Zembylas, M. (2011). Teaching and teacher emotions: A post-structural perspective. In C. Day & J. C. K. Lee (Eds.), *New understandings of teacher's work: Professional learning and development in schools and higher education* (pp. 31–43). Springer.

Chapter 20
The Development of EFL Teachers' Identity Through Forming Visions

Karim Sadeghi (ID), **Teymour Rahmati, and Farah Ghaderi** (ID)

Abstract English as a Second/Foreign Language (L2) teacher identity has recently attracted researchers worldwide and a number of new concepts have been identified as influential in L2 teachers' identity formation. The present study examined one of those concepts, namely vision, and such relevant issues as vision trajectories as well as strategies that enhance the ability to form a vision. To that end, data were collected through semi-structured interviews, a research-informed vision enhancement strategies inventory, and a vision timeline diagram. Open and selective coding analysis of the data revealed that Iranian in-service L2 teachers' visions of their future ideal selves lacked some of the essential conditions of a full-fledged vision. Moreover, low income, lack of necessary tools, restricted teacher autonomy, and heterogeneity in students' proficiency levels were the main challenges impeding the development of a vivid vision among the participants. Regarding vision trajectories, the study found that some L2 teachers initially formed clear visions of their future ideal selves, but their visions lost specificity in the face of practical realities. The participants believed that raising awareness, organizing regular in-service training courses, and improving working conditions could enhance L2 teachers' capacity to form visions.

Keywords Language teacher identity · Language teacher vision · Possible selves · Ideal self · Language teacher's voice · Vision-enhancing strategy

20.1 Introduction

The relationship between self and society is complex, multifaceted and undeniable. On the one hand, specific properties of an individual's identity are formed under the influence of social and cultural milieu. A particular society, on the other hand, is an

K. Sadeghi · F. Ghaderi
Urmia University, Urmia, Iran
e-mail: k.sadeghi@urmia.ac.ir

T. Rahmati (✉)
English Department, School of Medicine, Guilan University of Medical Sciences, Rasht, Iran
e-mail: trahmati@gums.ac.ir

aggregate of individuals who interact within that society. Indeed, the development of identity is informed and constrained by social and cultural expectations (Way & Rogers, 2015) and macro-level sociocultural features are derived from micro-level individual identities. A grave concern, however, is how personal ideals and fears, on the one hand, and social expectations, on the other, interact in the process of identity formation. To address this very concern, Markus and Nurius (1986) proposed possible selves model according to which an individual's possible identity is a combination of the ideal-self one would like to develop, the ought-to-self one is expected to develop based on social norms and expectations, and the feared-self one is afraid of developing in case the ideals do not materialize and/or the expectations are not met. An umbrella term combining all these three possible selves is the concept of vision. The present chapter investigates the role of vision in the development of language teachers' motivational identity.

Language teacher identity research has recently witnessed a surge of interest (Pennington & Richards, 2016; Trent, 2016; Yuan & Mak, 2018) due to the significant role attributed to the concept of self in educational and psychological theories. One of the most relevant developments has been the introduction of the construct of language teacher vision (Dörnyei & Kubanyiova, 2014; Kubanyiova, 2014). Vision is defined as 'the mental representation of the sensory experience of a future goal state' (Muir & Dörnyei, 2013, p. 357). The words *representation* and *sensory* in this definition imply the involvement of all senses in the formation of a mental image of a future state. Thus, the sensory component of a vision distinguishes it from the abstract concept of goal and, accordingly, an L2 teacher vision can be conceptualized as a self-image of the ideal L2 teacher one would like to develop in the future.

The significance of the study of language teacher vision lies in its potential to generate and sustain motivation. Dörnyei and Kubanyiova (2014, p. 4), for instance, suggest that vision is understood 'to be one of the highest-order motivational forces'. Nevertheless, L2 teacher vision has only been recently proposed and the exact manner in which it influences configurations of language teacher identity requires ample evidence from a wide variety of contexts. As such, the present study contributes to the relevant body of literature by investigating L2 teacher vision among Iranian L2 teachers. The main objective is to address such significant issues as the characteristics of the vision developed by Iranian L2 teachers, the vision trajectories (developmental changes) they experience during their professional career, the challenges they contend with in forming their visions, and their voice in designing strategies that enhance the ability to form a vision.

20.2   Theoretical Framework

Drawing upon Dörnyei's (2005) L2 Learner's Motivational Self System, Kubanyiova (2009) developed a parallel *Language Teachers' Possible Selves* model, which composed of the *Ideal Language Teacher Self* or an L2 teacher's image of oneself as the ideal teacher they would like to become, *Ought-to Language Teacher Self* representing the L2 teacher's images of who they should become, and *Feared Language Teacher Self* referring to the image the L2 teacher might become if they do not achieve their ideal or ought-to self-image (Kubanyiova, 2014). Later, in their co-authored volume, Dörnyei and Kubanyiova (2014) introduced the concept of *vision* as the common core of both language learners' and teachers' possible selves frameworks.

An important point, however, is that a number of conditions, known as the fully-functioning conditions of vision, have to be met for the motivational capacity of vision to materialize. The *availability* and *clarity* conditions posit that a person must have a future self-image which is sufficiently detailed. The *difference* condition demands a gap between the ideal future self and the current self while the *plausibility* and *certainty* conditions require, respectively, that the vision be realistic and possible to reach though not 'comfortably certain' (Dörnyei & Kubanyiova, 2014, p. 13) to achieve automatically. The *congruence* condition specifies that the ideal self-image should be in harmony with the ought-to-self expected by significant others. The *roadmap* condition necessitates the development of an action plan to achieve the future self-image. As there are always a number of contenders that may distract one's attention from their future self-image, the *activation* condition demands the regular activation of vision in one's working self-concept. Finally, *feared-self* condition requires the availability of a feared possible self which depicts 'the negative consequences of failing to achieve the desired end state' (Dörnyei & Kubanyiova, 2014, p. 14). Without these conditions being met a vision may remain passive forever.

20.3 Empirical Background

Since its inception, L2 teacher vision has been able to attract some researchers. Hiver (2013), for instance, demonstrated that possible language teacher selves played a central role in the motivation and professional development of seven Korean L2 teachers. Gao and Xu (2014) reported that being an L2 teacher was not part of the personal vision of eight out of ten Chinese English teachers. Participation in a teacher education program, however, helped seven teachers to associate L2 teaching with their ideal selves although tensions between the ideal self and contextual reality made two teachers leave the profession. In an attempt to develop a visionary framework, Chan (2013) reported that vision motivated behavior, prevented negative consequences, provided cognitive rehearsal, and created excitement among three aspiring L2 teachers from China, Iran, and Taiwan who were doing a doctoral program at a British university. Regarding changes in L2 teachers' vision, Kumazawa (2013) indicated that the four Japanese L2 teacher participants of his study possessed a vivid vision at the pre-service stage, particularly in terms of teaching English communicatively. During the in-service stage, however, extra workload and contextual realities suppressed the power of ideal self and only after exercising agency could they regain their vision although one teacher quit the profession.

Among the relevant studies in the Iranian context, Zarrinabadi and Tavakoli (2017) found that the two participants of their study possessed clear visions of their future L2 selves prior to starting teaching English at a private English institute, but they lost their vision and motivation upon actually entering L2 teaching profession. In another mixed-methods study, Rahmati et al. (2019) found a positive relationship (r = .59) between vision and motivation among Iranian in-service L2 teachers working at state high schools. Moreover, the study revealed that in order to motivate behavior, vision must meet a number of conditions. Thus, the researchers suggested examining the nature of vision as well as L2 teachers' vision trajectories as major agendas for future explorations of the issue. Regarding vision trajectories, Sadeghi and Rahmati (2021) reported that one of their cases forgot about his vision at about the third decade of his professional experience as a result of the mismatch between his ideal self-image and practical realities.

Hence, the most prominent issues regarding L2 teacher vision research include an examination of the ability to form a vision, challenges in forming a vision, vision trajectories, the nature of the formed vision in terms of meeting the essential conditions, vision enhancement strategies, the impact of teacher education programs on L2 teacher vision, and the dynamic interplay of vision and contextual factors. The studies above have pioneered in examining these issues in their own specific contexts and teach us at least two lessons. First, the potential of vision in facilitating L2 teachers' professional growth and identity formation is affected by contextual factors. Next, a number of strategies seem to enhance L2 teachers' ability to form visions of their future selves.

The present study contributes to the growing body of literature by investigating the nature of Iranian L2 teachers' visions and the changes, or trajectories, they experience in their vision during their professional career. This hopefully provides us with new insights into L2 teachers' visions drawn from a different context. Additionally, the study attends to Iranian L2 teachers' voice in those strategies which may enhance vision. Taking account of L2 teachers' voice in this respect has thus far been a neglected area. Thus, the current study is guided by the following research questions:

1. What are the challenges (if any) to the formation of vision among Iranian public sector in-service L2 teachers?
2. What changes do Iranian public sector in-service L2 teachers experience in their vision during their professional career?
3. What are the strategies Iranian public sector in-service L2 teachers believe to be effective in enhancing their vision formation ability?

20.4   Methodology

20.4.1   Context and Participants

The present research was set in the Iranian state sector language education context in which all decisions regarding materials, teaching methods, and assessment procedures are made centrally by the Ministry of Education (Papi & Abdollahzadeh, 2012). Iranian public sector English teachers are generally divided into two groups; those who enter Teacher Education (Farhangian) University immediately after high school and study for four years to become teachers (after gaining a qualified teacher status) and those who graduate from mainstream universities and pass the state-run teacher recruitment exams. The latter group has to attend teacher training courses at Farhangian University for a year prior to actually entering the teaching profession. Iranian L2 teachers work for 24 hours per week, except those with more than 20 years of experience whose weekly teaching hours is reduced to 20 hours. The most recent development in the Iranian public sector language education was a change of previously grammar-translation oriented textbooks and teaching methods into a communicative one, which aims at working on all four language skills and sub-skills.

Fifteen Iranian public school in-service L2 teachers drawn through convenience sampling took part in the current study. Table 20.1 presents the participants' profiles.

20.4.2   Instruments

The data for the purposes of the current study were collected through semi-structured interviews, a research-informed inventory of strategies that enhance the capacity to form visions, and a vision timeline diagram. The interview protocol, which was expert viewed by two researchers familiar with the concept of L2 teacher vision, consisted of a demographic information section and a main section. The demographic section was aimed at collecting L2 teachers' background information while the main interview section collected information on the participants' future L2 teacher vision and perspective on how to enhance the ability to form a vision. Examples of the interview questions (translated from Farsi) included, *'Do you have a vision of your future ideal L2 teacher self? Are you aware of the kind of L2 teacher the society expects you to become? How is your current self different from your ideal self? What do you think are the most effective strategies in enhancing L2 teachers' vision formation ability?'*

Additionally, the participants were provided with an inventory of strategies that enhance the ability to form visions. The strategies incorporated on the inventory were informed by previous research. These strategies included raising L2 teachers' awareness of the motivational force of vision (Dörnyei, 2009), perseverance, creating a supportive environment, and encouraging teachers to fill the gap between their

Table 20.1 Participants' demographics

| Gender (%) | | M/A (years) | Degree (%) | | Major (%) | | | Teaching level (%) | | MTE (years) | MWTH |
male	Female		B.A.	M.A.	TEFL	EL	L	J	H		
66.67	33.33	42.33	53.33	46.67	46.67	20	33.33	33.33	46.67	23.06	21.73

Notes: *M/A* mean age, *B.A.* Bachelor of Arts, *M.A.* Master of Arts, *TEFL* Teaching English as a Foreign Language, *EL* English Literature, *L* Linguistics, *J* Junior High School, *H* High School, *MTE* Mean Teaching Experience, *MWTH* Mean Weekly Teaching Hours current and ideal selves (Kubanyiova, 2012), and providing models of visionary L2 teachers (Kubanyiova, 2014). The participants were asked to rank these strategies based on their views on how effective they were in enhancing vision formation ability.

To gain a graphic representation of their vision trajectories, the participants were provided with a template of a vision timeline diagram in which the horizontal line denoted teaching experience in years while the vertical line represented the levels of clarity of vision. Microsoft Office Word 2016 Gridlines option was used to divide the vertical line into 3 equal levels of low, mid, and high and the horizontal line into six 5-year intervals (see Fig. 20.2). The use of intervals was meant to assist teachers in producing a reasonably accurate recall of the developments in their vision throughout their career. Although timelines were previously used as data collection instruments by Song and Kim (2016), the application of a timeline template with an area divided into equal cells was an innovation introduced by the present researchers.

20.4.3   Data Collection and Analysis

Prior to the interview session, the L2 teachers were invited to take part in a study on their future visions. Moreover, the participants' rights to voluntary participation, anonymity, and confidential treatment of their data were clearly explained. Upon granting consent, further arrangements regarding interview time and venue were made. The interviews were conducted in Farsi (the first language of the teachers) to ensure comprehension and provide teachers with the opportunity to express themselves freely. The interviews were conducted by one of the researchers and audio-recorded using a smartphone. The shortest and longest interviews lasted 15':36 and 24':50", respectively (18':06" on average).

Next, the participants were asked to rank the five most frequently mentioned vision enhancing strategies proposed by previous researchers from 1 (the most effective) to 5 (the least effective) in terms of how effective they were in improving vision formation ability. Finally, the L2 teachers were invited to draw a timeline of their vision. To that end, they were provided with the template of a vision timeline diagram, were allowed to take it home, and do the task at their own pace. The interviewer collected the timelines as soon as being informed about their completion by the participants.

To analyze the data, the audio-recorded interviews were transcribed verbatim and imported to MAXQDA Analytics Pro version 12.3. The initial open coding analysis of the data resulted in the emergence of some remarks such as *'I think my vision of my future self is realistic'* and *'I always imagine myself speaking in English in my classes'*. In the selective coding phase, the relevant interview extracts were categorized under fully-functioning conditions of vision, challenges to the formation of a vision, and vision-enhancing strategies. For instance, *'low wages'* and *'limited teacher autonomy'* were categorized under the working conditions of vision formation challenges while *'creativity'* and *'self-confidence'* were coded under teacher-related vision enhancing strategies.

The individual vision timelines were also carried over onto a collective diagram to represent a full image of the participants' vision trajectories. This was done using Microsoft Office Word 2016 Insert Shapes (Scribble) option assisted by the original division of the area of vision timeline diagram into equal cells.

The participants' rankings of research-informed vision enhancement strategies were, in turn, analyzed using two procedures. First, the strategies were organized from 1 to 5 according to the highest frequency of ranks (1–5) attracted by each strategy. Next, to account for all of the different ranks (1, 2, etc.) assigned to a particular strategy, scores of 5, 4, 3, 2, and 1 were allocated to ranks of 1–5, respectively. Thus, the total score for each strategy was the sum of the frequency of different ranks assigned to each strategy multiplied by their relevant allocated scores. Then, the strategies were organized based on their total scores. The two procedures produced the same results.

20.5 Findings

20.5.1 Vision Formation Challenges

Data analysis showed that only 4, out of 15, participants possessed visions of their future L2 teacher selves and were able to describe their visions. Interviewee 07, for instance, stated,

Extract 1: Since the very first day I started teaching, I have imagined myself being remembered as the best teacher by my students.

Two L2 teachers borrowed their visions from their previous English teachers as their models. Interviewee 15 mentioned,

Extract 2: I even wished to have a car exactly like my English teacher's car.

Four more L2 teachers confirmed that they had a vision although they did not provide a clear description of their visions. In answering the interviewer's request to describe their vision, interviewee 13 described a dream, rather than a future vision.

Extract 3: At nights, I dreamed of the words I had taught during the day.

Two of the participants had forgotten about their visions of their future L2 teacher selves in the face of contextual constraints, as shown in extract 4 by interviewee 10.

Extract 4: I had a vision of my future self when I was a university student. Later, however, when I began teaching I found that there was a big difference between my imagination and classroom realities.

The remaining three participants had never formed visions of their future L2 teacher selves. A representative statement here was made by interviewee 01 in extract 5.

Extract 5: I did not form any image of my future ideal L2 teacher self, and being an English teacher was not my first priority though I did not have any problem with becoming a teacher.

A number of challenges prevented the participants from developing a fully-functioning vision. Some of these challenges were rooted in the characteristics of the visions developed by the L2 teachers while others stemmed from contextual factors. Regarding challenges related to the features of vision, the findings revealed that only the *difference*, *plausibility*, and *certainty* conditions were met by most participants. They believed their current selves were different from their future selves.

Extract 6: My future self is different from my present self in some details. I love teaching and I do my best while teaching, but I wish I could speak English with greater confidence (interviewee 03).

Furthermore, most L2 teachers' visions were realistic and possible to achieve but not without hard work and commitment (interviewee 02, extract 7).

Extract 7: I think my future vision is a realistic one and I can achieve that vision if I really want and try hard.

The rest of the fully-functioning conditions of vision, however, remained unmet. In terms of *clarity* condition, for instance, interviewee 11, who possessed a vision but was not able to describe it, mentioned,

Extract 8: I had a vision, but it wasn't so vivid that I could see it in my mind's eye.

Concerning *congruence* condition, interviewee 14, who borrowed his vision from a previous teacher, pointed out,

Extract 9: People expect me to be up-to-date in terms of using technology, for example, but I am not that good at making use of technology.

With respect to the *roadmap* condition, most participants were not able to specify their plans to achieve their visions. A representative remark on the *roadmap* condition was expressed by interviewee 13, who reflected,

Extract 10: I do not have any carefully designed plan. I just know that high proficiency in English can be helpful, but I usually do not have time to improve my linguistic proficiency.

The *activation* and *feared-self* conditions were missing in the visions of all participants except interviewee 02 who said,

Extract 11: I always have my vision in my mind and I am afraid of becoming an L2 teacher who constantly fails to answer learners' questions.

Concerning contextual factors, the identified themes were organized into three categories. First, there were factors relating to working conditions, including low wages, lack of facilities, restricted teacher autonomy, and limited effective in-service training. Low wages, for instance, made the participants turn to private teaching and the ensuing extra workload deprived them of the time needed to improve their professional knowledge. As a piece of evidence, interviewee 15 pinpointed,

Extract 12: I think my working hours at private sector are very long and this is because teachers do not earn enough. Long hours of teaching take my time and I can neither study nor do my duties as a teacher.

With regard to lack of facilities, interviewee 01 reflected,

Extract 13: I do not have access to the necessary audio-visual equipment and the Internet at most schools. Moreover, every school should have a specific room for English classes where I can put posters on the wall, which is not the case, unfortunately.

Regarding restricted teacher autonomy, interviewee 14 observed,

Extract 14: Teachers are not allowed to introduce books and materials that are useful in enhancing students' language proficiency.

Interviewee 14 complained about limited opportunities for professional development.

Extract 15: In-service training courses, which were regularly held in the past and were really helpful, are not run that regularly anymore.

Next, there were such student factors as low proficiency (particularly in rural schools), heterogeneous classes, and lack of success in learning English on the part of the learners. In a representative remark interviewee 12 expressed,

Extract 16: Students are not homogeneous in terms of linguistic ability, and teachers have to translate the whole book into Farsi.

Finally, non-teaching responsibilities, such as taking care of a family, functioned as vision contenders among the present participants. Interviewee 05, for instance, stated,

Extract 17: I am a mother and a housewife in addition to being a teacher.

The code matrix in Fig. 20.1 presents the summary of these findings.

20.5.2   Vision Trajectories

Among the four L2 teachers, who possessed a detailed vision, interviewee 02 marked her timeline as having three phases of highly clear initial vision, which later became less vivid due to lack of motivation. Admission to a master's degree, however, helped her re-form her vision. Entrance to a higher education program also assisted interviewee 07 to refine his vision of future ideal L2 teacher self. Interviewees 03 and

Code System	Int.01	Int.02	Int.03	Int.04	Int.05	Int.06	Int.07	Int.08	Int.09	Int.10	Int.11	Int.12	Int.13	Int.14	Int.15	SUM
available		■	■			■		■								4
borrowed vision														■	■	2
available-unclear					■					■	■	■				4
forgotten vision								■		■						2
non-available	■			■	■											3
clear		■	■			■		■								4
differences		■	■			■		■	■	■	■	■	■			10
plausible		■	■			■	■	■	■	■	■	■	■	■		12
not certain/needs effort		■	■			■	■	■	■	■	■	■	■	■		11
congruence		■				■	■							■		5
roadmap						■										1
activation		■														1
feared-self		■														1
∨ working conditions																0
low wages	■									■			■	■	■	6
tools	■					■				■		■				4
lack of teacher autonomy					■	■	■						■			4
lack of regular in-service training				■									■			2
∨ student factors																0
heterogeneous classes						■						■	■			3
low proficiency		■						■								2
lack of success							■									1
non-teaching responsibilities				■	■											2

Fig. 20.1 Characteristics of L2 teachers' vision and vision formation challenges

09, on the other hand, lost specifications of their visions as a result of lack of effective teacher training.

Interviewee 14 lost the clarity of his borrowed vision due to low income and lack of regular in-service training while interviewee 15 retained the clear vision borrowed from a previous teacher. Interviewees 08 and 10 were about to retire, but they had forgotten their visions almost early in their career because of restricted teacher autonomy and low income, respectively. Among the four L2 teachers with unclear visions, interviewee 06's vision improved as he developed an interest in L2 teaching, interviewee 11's vision became even less clear since he was dissatisfied with teaching income, and interviewees 12 and 13 did not return their vision timeline diagrams. The other three participants without a vision were not asked to provide any vision timeline.

The participants' vision timelines are collectively presented in Fig. 20.2, in which different line styles are used to differentiate overlapping vision timelines.

20.5.3 Vision Enhancement Strategies

The analysis of the interview data regarding L2 teachers' voice in adopting strategies that boost the ability to form visions revealed that the L2 participants of the current research identified a number of *teacher-related characteristics* and *improvements in working conditions* as essential in this respect. Interest in L2 teaching profession was the most commonly reported teacher-related factor in heightening the ability to develop a fully-functioning vision. Interviewee 06, for instance, believed,

Extract 18: If teachers are interested in their job, they can form a vision. Without interest, however, one may never form a future vision.

As another teacher-related aspect, interviewee 05 assumed adaptability to change as a pre-requisite to developing a vision and stated,

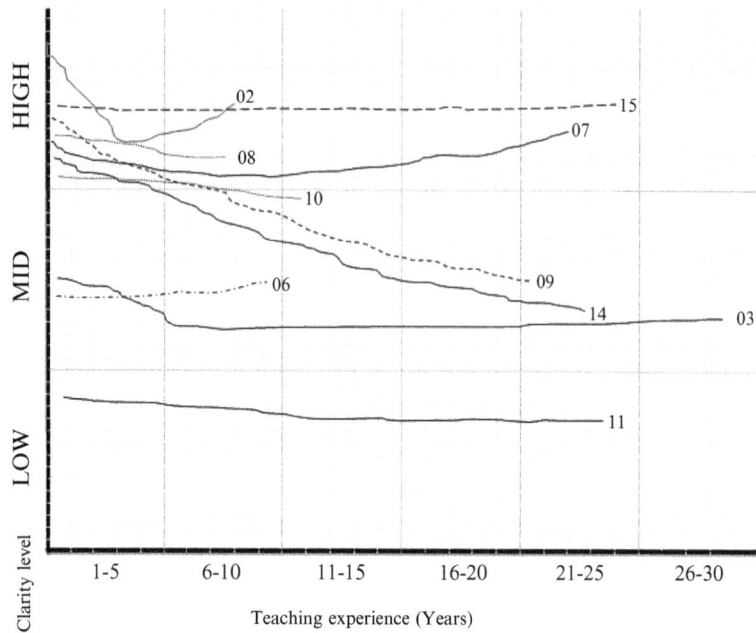

Fig. 20.2 L2 teachers' timelines of their vision trajectories

Extract 19: L2 teachers should be able to adapt themselves to new conditions and
changes in teaching materials and leave their old methods while trying some
new ones.

To interviewees 08 and 11, teachers' *'creativity in teaching'* and *'patience with low
proficiency level learners'*, respectively, served as key vision enhancement strategies. Interviewees 11 and 03 suggested, respectively, that *'L2 teachers improve their
own linguistic proficiency and professional skills'* and *'boost their self-confidence by
focusing on their strengths'* to empower themselves with the ability to form fully-
functioning visions of their future selves.

Furthermore, the participants believed that improvements in working conditions
could enhance their vision formation capacity. In particular, L2 teachers desired
'regular and effective in-service training' (interviewee 15) in which *'L2 teachers'
awareness about the power of vision in developing effective teaching practices'*
(interviewee 12) is raised. L2 teachers also believed *'attending to teachers' such
problems as housing and living expenses by increasing remuneration'* (interviewee
07) could eliminate stress and positively impact their interest in adopting a vision of
their future selves. Other effective strategies from L2 teachers' perspective were
'providing schools with adequate audio-visual and educational technologies' (interviewee 01), *'observing educational equality through offering equal opportunities
for learning to rural and urban students'* (interviewee 12), and *'designing books at
the right proficiency level for learners'* (interviewee 04).

Finally, the analysis of the participants' rankings of vision enhancement strategies proposed by previous researchers demonstrated that *raising awareness on the motivational force of vision* was L2 teachers' most preferred strategy. *Providing L2 teachers with models of successful teachers* followed next and *giving hope to teachers that people are not born as expert teachers but become great teachers through perseverance and practice* ranked the third important vision-enhancing strategy. The final two strategies were *creating a supportive environment to help teachers achieve their visions of the ideal L2 teacher self* and *encouraging L2 teachers to eliminate the gap between their current and their ideal selves.*

20.6 Discussion

The findings of the present study on L2 teachers' vision and vision formation capacity reveal that most Iranian in-service L2 teachers working in public sector do not develop a fully-functioning vision of their future ideal selves. This is mainly due to contextual factors such as the conditions of the workplace, student characteristics, and everyday life responsibilities. L2 teachers doubt the efficacy of a future vision in a working environment where most schools are not equipped with the necessary audio-visual technology, teachers have limited autonomy, and effective in-service training is not provided regularly. Moreover, low remuneration, which forces L2 teachers to resort to private teaching, and such non-teaching responsibilities as taking care of a family serve as vision contenders impeding the development of a vivid and activated ideal L2 teacher vision. The examination of vision timelines also demonstrates that most L2 teachers initially possess a clear vision of their future selves, but later their visions lose some specifications in the face of practical realities. Furthermore, the strategies proposed by the L2 teachers to enhance vision formation capacity reflect the importance of teacher agency and improvements in working environment. This lends support to those strategies proposed by the previous literature (Kubanyiova, 2012) in which L2 teachers' perseverance and practice are assumed to be valuable strategies. Nevertheless, there are a number of other issues, such as improving teachers' living conditions and providing students from different geographical areas with equal learning opportunities, about which macro-level decision makers have to take due measures.

The present findings are in line with the results of most relevant literature. Concerning the role of working conditions, for instance, Nguyen (2017) found that low pay negatively influenced Vietnamese L2 teachers' efficacy and professional identities. Externally imposed curricula, the state of being undertrained in discipline-specific areas, and economic conditions were also reported by Dörnyei and Ushioda (2011) as factors eroding L2 teacher efficacy, vision, and motivation. L2 teachers' desire for regular effective teacher training courses with a focus on the power of vision in directing behavior is another noteworthy finding already confirmed by Gao and Xu (2014) and Kumazawa (2013).

Moreover, the present findings are relevant to some recent theoretical strands in L2 teaching. First, the study lends support to Activity Theory in which the significant role of tools, rules (teacher autonomy and income), community (students' proficiency level), and division of labor (extra workload) in forming and achieving a vision of one's ideal L2 teacher self has been reiterated (Rahmati & Sadeghi, 2021). Next, Muir and Dörnyei (2013) and Henry et al. (2015) have introduced Directed Motivational Currents (DMCs) as a recent development in the study of motivation. Vision-orientedness is one of the main components of DMCs model and how DMCs influence visionary L2 teachers is a promising area of study within language teacher identity research. Finally, the findings provide supporting evidence for the role of positive psychology (MacIntyre et al., 2016) which identifies positive emotions, positive traits and positive institutions as essential factors in enhancing L2 teachers' well-being, efficacy, and professional development. Positive emotions such as interest in L2 profession, positive traits like adaptability, creativity, patience, and self-confidence as well as calls for positive institutions with improved working conditions are all reflected in L2 teachers' proposed vision-enhancing strategies here in this study.

Despite such limitations as the number of participants and lack of access to real time thought processes behind L2 teachers' recall of their vision trajectories, the study has some implications. It shows that exploiting the power of vision for the emotional and professional well-being of L2 teachers requires concerted effort and systematic measures by all stakeholders including teachers, administrators, and policymakers. Most importantly, the findings call for a reconsideration of the content of L2 teacher education programs to include personal aspects along with professional and procedural know-how. Further investigations are needed to integrate relevant research findings, theoretical propositions, L2 teachers' voice, and practical considerations into a fully operational framework to materialize the power of vision in language teacher education. Hopefully, such an integrated framework will provide constructive insights into and a better understanding of the vision phenomenon in L2 teaching.

20.7   Conclusion

The findings of the study revealed that a number of interrelated factors, including teacher traits, institutional specifications, and living conditions were in operation in the formation and functioning of an L2 teacher's identity.

The study suggests that an approach in which the attainment of a future identity hinges upon meeting a number of conditions per se may not be conducive to harnessing the power of vision. Arguably, and in tandem with current theoretical avenues, exploiting the full capacity of vision in (re)shaping identity and directing behavior requires improvements in L2 teachers' professional knowledge, practical skills, living conditions, and general educational institutions. It should be noted, however, that the findings of the present study are highly context-specific and similar studies in a variety of contexts can contribute to a better representation of the role of vision in the formation of identity.

References

Chan, L. (2013). Facets of imagery in academic and professional achievements: A study of three doctoral students. *Studies in Second Language Learning and Teaching, 3*(3), 397–418. https://doi.org/10.14746/ssllt.2013.3.3.5

Dörnyei, Z. (2005). *The psychology of the language learner: Individual differences in second language acquisition*. Erlbaum.

Dörnyei, Z. (2009). The L2 motivational self-system. In Z. Dörnyei & E. Ushioda (Eds.), *Motivation, language identity and the L2 self* (pp. 9–42). Multilingual Matters.

Dörnyei, Z., & Kubanyiova, M. (2014). *Motivating learners, motivating teachers: Building vision in the language classroom*. Cambridge University Press.

Dörnyei, Z., & Ushioda, E. (2011). *Teaching and researching motivation* (2nd ed.). Longman.

Gao, X., & Xu, H. (2014). The dilemma of being English language teachers: Interpreting teachers' motivation to teach, and professional commitment in China's hinterland regions. *Language Teaching Research, 18*(2), 152–168. https://doi.org/10.1177/1362168813505938

Henry, A., Davydenko, S., & Dörnyei, Z. (2015). The anatomy of directed motivational currents: Exploring intense and enduring periods of L2 motivation. *The Modern Language Journal, 99*(2), 329–345. https://doi.org/10.1111/modl.12214

Hiver, P. (2013). The interplay of possible language teacher selves in professional development choices. *Language Teaching Research, 17*(2), 210–227. https://doi.org/10.1177/1362168813475944

Kubanyiova, M. (2009). Possible selves in language teacher development. In Z. Dörnyei & E. Ushioda (Eds.), *Motivation, language identity and the L2 self* (pp. 314–332). Multilingual Matters.

Kubanyiova, M. (2012). *Teacher development in action: Understanding language teachers' conceptual change*. Palgrave Macmillan.

Kubanyiova, M. (2014). Motivating language teachers: Inspiring vision. In D. Lasagabaster, A. Doiz, & J. M. Sierra (Eds.), *Motivation and foreign language learning: From theory to practice* (pp. 71–89). John Benjamins Publishing Company.

Kumazawa, M. (2013). Gaps too large: Four novice EFL teachers' self-concept and motivation. *Teaching and Teacher Education, 33*, 45–55. https://doi.org/10.1016/j.tate.2013.02.005

MacIntyre, P., Gregersen, T., & Mercer, S. (Eds.). (2016). *Positive psychology in SLA*. Multilingual Matters.

Markus, H., & Nurius, P. (1986). Possible selves. *American Psychologist, 41*(9), 954–969. https://doi.org/10.1037/0003-066X.41.9.954

Muir, C., & Dörnyei, Z. (2013). Directed motivational currents: Using vision to create effective motivational pathways. *Studies in Second Language Learning and Teaching, 3*(3), 357–375. https://doi.org/10.14746/ssllt.2013.3.3.3

Nguyen, C. D. (2017). Beyond the school setting: Language teachers and tensions of everyday life. *Teachers and Teaching, 23*(7), 766–780. https://doi.org/10.1080/13540602.2016.1276054

Papi, M., & Abdollahzadeh, E. (2012). Teacher motivational practices, student motivation, and possible L2 selves: An examination in the Iranian EFL context. *Language Learning, 62*(2), 571–594. https://doi.org/10.1111/j.1467-9922.2011.00632.x

Pennington, M. C., & Richards, J. C. (2016). Teacher identity in language teaching: Integrating personal, contextual, and professional factors. *RELC Journal, 47*(1), 5–23. https://doi.org/10.1177/0033688216631219

Rahmati, T., & Sadeghi, K. (2021). English as a foreign language teachers' motivation: An activity theory perspective. *The Qualitative Report, 26*(4), 1084–1105. https://doi.org/10.46743/2160-3715/2021.4472

Rahmati, T., Sadeghi, K., & Ghaderi, F. (2019). English language teachers' vision and motivation: Possible selves and activity theory perspectives. *RELC Journal, 50*(3), 457–474. https://doi.org/10.1177/0033688218777321

Sadeghi, K., & Rahmati, T. (2021). English as a foreign language teacher motivation: Dynamic interplay of vision, context, and agency. In Z. Tajeddin & B. Mahmoodi-Bakhtiari (Eds.), *Research on second language teachers* (pp. 153–180). Allameh Tabataba'i University Press.

Song, B., & Kim, T.-Y. (2016). Teacher (de)motivation from an activity theory perspective: Cases of two experienced EFL teachers in South Korea. *System, 57*, 134–145. https://doi.org/10.1016/j.system.2016.02.006

Trent, J. (2016). The identity construction of experiences of early career English language teachers in Hong Kong: Great expectations and practical realities. *Research Papers in Education, 31*(3), 316–336. https://doi.org/10.1080/02671522.2015.1037336

Way, N., & Rogers, O. (2015). [T]hey say black men won't make it, but I know I'm gonna make it: Ethnic and racial identity development in the context of cultural stereo-types. In K. McLean & M. Syed (Eds.), *The Oxford handbook of identity development* (pp. 269–285). Oxford University Press.

Yuan, R., & Mak, P. (2018). Reflective learning and identity construction in practice, discourse, and activity: Experiences of pre-service language teachers in Hong Kong. *Teaching and Teacher Education, 74*, 205–214. https://doi.org/10.1016/j.tate.2018.05.009

Zarrinabadi, N., & Tavakoli, M. (2017). Exploring motivational surges among Iranian EFL teacher trainees: Directed motivational currents in focus. *TESOL Quarterly, 51*(1), 155–166. https://doi.org/10.1002/tesq.332

Afterword: Second Language Teacher Identity and More

Peter I. De Costa

As I write this afterword just a few days before Christmas 2021, the world is being hit by the fifth wave of the COVID-19 pandemic as yet another new variant – Omicron – is spreading quickly across countries. At this point, no one knows when the coronavirus will be contained. But if there is one thing that is certain, it is the pandemic's impact on teachers across the globe, which has been debilitating. Teachers, often overlooked as essential workers in this health crisis, are increasingly feeling the weight of the pandemic. Over the past two years, many have shuttled back and forth between teaching online and in-person instruction. Desperate to make up for valuable classroom instruction time, many language teaching professionals have also been highly creative in (re)designing their pedagogy to keep their students engaged. But such remarkable teaching efforts have also come at a price because teachers have reported encountering burnt out, thus making calls to add teacher wellbeing to the applied linguistics research agenda (Mercer & Gregersen, 2020; see also Burns, Chap. 13, this volume) both timely and significant.

Equally timely and significant is this edited book on theory and practice in second language teacher identity because the volume is an apt reminder that teacher identity is inextricably linked to teacher agency (e.g., Reeves, Chap. 6, this volume), teacher emotion (e.g., Ng & Yin, Chap. 5, this volume) and teacher ideology (e.g., Fan & de Jong, Chap. 12, this volume). In other words, it is increasingly difficult to tease apart these constructs, thus making it vitally important for us to examine them in conjunction with each other (De Costa et al., 2018; Wolff & De Costa, 2017). At the same time, however, we also need to problematize what kinds of teacher identities are ratified and what types are denigrated. Given the aforementioned pandemic, teachers who are constructed as 'resilient' are seen in a more positive light, while teachers who express their frustration are viewed negatively. Here again, we see how emotional inflections (e.g., resilience vs. frustration) are inevitably connected to teacher identities and perceptions of the 'good' language teacher (De Costa & Norton, 2017). Put differently, the positioning of L2 teachers and their own identity

P. I. De Costa
Michigan State University, East Lansing, MI, USA

© The Author(s), under exclusive license to Springer Nature Switzerland AG 2022 309
K. Sadeghi, F. Ghaderi (eds.), *Theory and Practice in Second Language Teacher Identity*, Educational Linguistics 57, https://doi.org/10.1007/978-3-031-13161-5

construction need to be examined against a larger neoliberally-inflected educational landscape as governments (e.g., Hayes, Chap. 3, this volume) attempt to recast their educational systems in order to prepare their youth for a globalized world. In this globalized and networked world, teachers are expected to assume English-speaking global identities. But these identities are further particularized in that teacher identities are often indexed to 'standard' English or certain varieties of English. That teacher identity construction is thus deeply ideological in nature is further amplified when examining the identity development processes negotiated by non-native English speaking teachers or NNESTs (e.g., Fan & de Jong, Chap. 12, this volume).

Indeed, dialectical tensions (e.g., Thompson, Chap. 4, this volume) abound and novice teachers, in particular, find themselves having to wrestle with not only developing awareness of subject pedagogy but also acculturating themselves to their new workplace. As a consequence, L2 teacher education today needs to do more than just equip teachers with the ability to teach the core skills of reading, writing, listening, speaking and grammar. Rather, and as we have seen in this volume, the ability to help students and the teachers themselves develop an intercultural stance (e.g., Harbon, Chap. 7, this volume; Ping Yang, Chap. 9, this volume) and competence to integrate technology effectively to their pedagogical repertoire (Gong et al., Chap. 14. this volume) are equally important. In other words, L2 teacher education needs to make professional identity development a core component of its curriculum, one that enables teacher agency so that teachers can advocate for themselves and their charges.

Moving forward, we see that L2 teacher identity research has undoubtedly established itself as a fixture within applied linguistics. Reviews of the field (e.g., Ng & Yin, Chap. 5, this volume; Sadeghi & Bahari, Chap. 2, this volume) bear strong testament to the fact that there is vibrant interest in L2 teacher identity work. Related to my earlier point about how L2 teacher identity needs to be investigated in relation to teacher emotion and teacher agency, I was delighted to see how the contributors to this volume (e.g., Barnes & Freeman, Chap. 15, this volume; Lawrence & Nagashima, Chap. 16, this volume) built on Kimberlé Crenshaw's (Crenshaw, 1993) pathbreaking work on intersectionality and identity politics. After all, it is not uncommon to find teachers having to confront social inequities *inter alia* racial and gendered prejudice in both school and society. In view of the multitude of challenges that teachers have to manage, it is crucial, as Sadeghi and Bahari remind us in the opening chapter of this book, that we take into account the various sociocultural factors that could impact teacher identity development. One highly effective way to do this is to take an ecological approach (Peña-Pincheira & De Costa, 2021; Sanczyk-Cruz & Miller, Chap. 18, this volume) to examine L2 teacher identity. At the same time, however, this approach also needs to be mated with a temporal dimension. In other words, we need to examine how teacher identity is shaped by past experiences (e.g., Barnes & Freeman, Chap. 15, this volume; Lawrence & Nagashima, Chap. 16, this volume) as well as plans for the future (e.g., Pitkänen-Huhta et al., Chap. 10, this volume; Reeves, Chap. 6, this volume; Sadeghi et al., Chap. 20, this volume) as teachers start envisioning and investing in their professional identity development.

On a methodological note, L2 teacher identity work has demonstrated that it can flexibly partner various (and often a combination of) data collection approaches. For example, in this volume, we observe how the contributing authors effectively adopt autoethnography (e.g., Yazan, Chap. 11, this volume), Conversation Analysis (e.g., Li Li, Chap. 8, this volume), and visual representations (e.g., Barbaroja, Chap. 17, this vloume) to mediate their queries. In the spirit of methodological diversity, I anticipate that future teacher identity researchers will continue to innovate and expand their methodological toolkit. It is my wish, however, that the identities of teachers of languages other than English will be investigated more in the future (a notable exception in this volume is the chapter by Gong et al. who examined the identities of teachers of Chinese as an additional language). The identities of teachers who teach Indigenous languages, heritage languages and other minoritized languages also warrant further investigation because for too long, much of applied linguistics research has focused on university foreign language students. Equally compelling and needed would be research on how teachers develop their professional identities when working with less privileged student populations such as immigrant and refugee language learners. Indeed, how we teach, as noted at the outset of this afterword, is rapidly changing as many of us have been forced to migrate to online platforms in the pandemic era. But the proverbial genie is now out of the bottle. To a large extent, we have to concede that online teaching will only grow in time to come. Thus, and correspondingly, we'll need to develop new methodological tools to complement our investigations of teacher identity construction.

In closing, and given the centrality of L2 identity work in applied linguistics today, I foresee that more work on this important topic will be conducted in the coming years. This volume will constitute a valuable part of this ongoing and expanding intellectual endeavor, an endeavor which I hope will also make teacher reflexivity its cornerstone. After all, while necessary, it is not enough that teachers reflect on their pedagogical practices and relate these practices to theories within teacher education. Equally important is their need to be reflexive (Peercy et al., 2019) about their own instruction because they have to take into account how power differentials operate across the different layers of the complex ecologies in which they are embedded. I think we are well primed for the next phase of L2 teacher identity research. And I am excited to see how it will unfold.

References

Crenshaw, K. (1993). Mapping the margins: Intersectionality, identity politics, and the violence against women of color. *Stanford Law Review, 43*, 1241–1299.

De Costa, P. I., & Norton, B. (2017). Identity, transdisciplinarity, and the good language teacher. *Modern Language Journal, 101-S*, 3–14.

De Costa, P. I., Rawal, H., & Li, W. (2018). Broadening the second language teacher agenda: International perspectives on teacher emotions. *Chinese Journal of Applied Linguistics, 41*(4), 401–409.

Mercer, S., & Gregersen, T. (2020). *Teacher wellbeing*. Oxford University Press.

Peercy, M. M., Sharkey, J., Baecher, L., Motha, S., & Varghese, M. (2019). Exploring TESOL teacher educators as learners and reflective scholars: A shared narrative inquiry. *TESOL Journal, 10*(4), 1–16.

Peña-Pincheira, R., & De Costa, P. I. (2021). Language teacher agency for educational justice-oriented work: An ecological model. *TESOL Journal, 12*(2), 1–13.

Wolff, D., & De Costa, P. I. (2017). Expanding the language teacher identity landscape: An investigation of the emotions and strategies of a NNEST. *Modern Language Journal, 101-S*, 76–90.

Milton Keynes UK
Ingram Content Group UK Ltd.
UKHW021824220923
429226UK00001B/4